THE REPUBLIC OF INDONESIA

The Republic of
INDONESIA

by

DOROTHY WOODMAN

LONDON
THE CRESSET PRESS
MCMLV

First published in 1955
by The Cresset Press Ltd., 11 Fitzroy Square, London, W.1

Printed in Great Britain by
Western Printing Services Ltd., Bristol

CONTENTS

v

CONTENTS

PREFACE

DURING the Second World War I became deeply interested in the struggle of the people of Indonesia for independence both from the Japanese and from the Dutch. In 1951 I visited the country and was able, as the result of Indonesian courtesy, to see for myself how the problems of this new Republic were being tackled and the impact of independence not only on Java, where Dutch administration had everywhere been effective for three centuries, but also on Sumatra, Sulawesi, Kalimantan and Bali. I believe that many misconceptions about the Republic, as well as about Dutch rule, arise from too great a concentration on Djakarta, the administrative centre of a vast area, covering more than three thousand islands, each group with its own culture or cultures.

I am greatly indebted to many Indonesians, who, in their own country and in England, have helped me to look at Indonesia through their own eyes. Some of them were officials, but the greater number of them were men and women I met in Indonesia, often casually, and usually unknown by name.

I have also had the advantage of consulting many Dutch experts who have been invariably helpful. Some of them have welcomed my efforts to describe the past and the present of Indonesia from a non-colonial point of view.

To Tony Roberts I owe a special debt of gratitude. While serving as a member of the Staff of the Committee of Good Offices of the United Nations he gained an intimate knowledge of Indonesia and a sympathetic understanding of the young Republic. He has placed both freely at my disposal; ours has indeed been a happy and generous co-operation. Neither he nor, of course, any of my Indonesian and Dutch friends are in any way responsible for the views I have expressed or the mistakes that I have no doubt made.

To Mrs. Betty Paddon I owe much thanks for her co-operation in research and for the preparation of the Index.

I want to thank the Staffs of the following Libraries who have never failed to give me their generous help in research: The Royal Institute of International Affairs; The London Library; The Library of the Royal Empire Society; The Library of Malaya House, and, in 1951, the Libraries of the National Museum in Djakarta and the Raffles Museum in Singapore.

There are three authors with whom I am not always in agreement but from whose outstanding contributions to the study of Indonesia I have frequently benefited: Dr. Bernard H. M. Vlekke, the author of *Nusantara*; Mr. J. S. Furnivall, the author of *Netherlands India*; and Professor George Kahin, the author of *Nationalism and Revolution in Indonesia*. And lastly, I must thank Mrs. Winawer and Miss Mary Borman for their co-operation in typing the manuscript.

D.W.

A NOTE ON INDONESIAN PLACE NAMES AND CURRENCY

First of all, the name itself, 'Indonesia'. In a collection of Dr. Hatta's articles and speeches, entitled *Verspreide Geschriften* (ed. C. P. G. Van der Peet, Djakarta, 1952, p. 344), it is stated that a certain G. W. Earl was the first to describe the inhabitants of Indonesia as 'Indu-nesians'. But the British ethnologist, G. R. Logan, in 1850, was the first to call the Netherlands East Indies 'the Indonesian Archipelago'. In 1884, the German, Bastian, published a work entitled *Indonesien oder die Inseln des Malayischen Archipels*. The term 'Indonesia' was first used in a political context by Perhimpoenan Indonesia, in 1922. In 1928, when Suprato wrote a national anthem for the nationalist movement, he called it 'Indonesia Raya'. When the Japanese occupied the country in 1942, and the Indonesian language was encouraged, Indonesia became the accepted name. In 1945, when the Republic was proclaimed, it was its official name. Finally, the Netherlands Constitution of 1948 replaced the words 'Netherlands Indies' by the word 'Indonesie'.

Secondly, the word 'Kalimantan' which is used throughout the book to describe the island more widely known as 'Borneo'. Like the word 'Borneo', which it pre-dates, it is probably related to a type of mango, after its shape. But it might also be derived from the name of one of the oldest stocks inhabiting the island and known as the 'Klemantans'. There is, as yet, no conclusive ruling on this matter. In 1942, when the Japanese forbade the use of Dutch words, the name Kalimantan was used to describe that part of the island of Borneo under Dutch rule. When the Republic was proclaimed in 1945, Kalimantan became the official Indonesian name.

Thirdly, the word 'Sulawesi' which is used throughout the book to describe the island known in Dutch times as 'Celebes'. The word 'Celebes' is of foreign origin. It was most probably the mispronunciation by the earliest Westerners, the Portuguese, of the words Seli Besi, an iron kris carried by the people. When they first misunderstood the Portuguese questions as to the name of the country, they used the words 'Seli Besi', and this was easily changed into 'Celebes'. In 1942, the Japanese used the earlier name Sulawesi and in 1945 this was also the name officially used by the Republic.

In the case of both place names and the names of people, the letter 'u' is used to express the sound 'u' (as in flute) where the Dutch used 'oe'. This is in keeping with official Indonesian practice as laid down in what is known as the Suwandi decree. Suwandi was Minister of Education at the time and the decree of March 19th, 1947, No. 264/Bhg. A. lays down the regulations for pronunciation in all official documents and for common use.

Since the transfer of sovereignty in December 1949, the Rupiah has been the standard Indonesian currency. From then until February 4th, 1952, there were 10.64 Rupiahs to the pound sterling. On that date its value was changed to 31.92 to the pound sterling.

PART ONE

In Time and Space

CHAPTER I

THE COUNTRY OF STEPPING-STONES

FRINGED along the Equator, the 3,000 islands of Indonesia stretch from the southernmost tip of the Philippines to the northernmost tip of Australia. They are the next-door neighbours of Malaya in the west and of Australian New Guinea in the east. Travellers by air to Australia from Japan or from China, from Europe or from India, halt for a few hours in the capital city, Djakarta. Travellers by sea from the Indian and the Pacific Ocean coast alongside Sumatra, the most western island, and, having passed through the Straits of Singapore, Kalimantan (Borneo), the largest island, lies away to the east. Men coming from the west first stumbled on these islands in their search for a way round the world. To all but the Dutch they remained only stepping-stones. From the seventeenth century until Japanese troops invaded them in 1942, Dutchmen regarded these 3,000 islands as their 'tropical Holland'; they were the Netherlands East Indies. They became stepping-stones again in 1945 when Australian and American troops used them as bases in their island-hopping campaign from New Guinea to Japan.

The islands that became familiar can be counted on the fingers of one hand: Java, Sumatra, Bali, Kalimantan (Borneo), and Sulawesi (Celebes). Peoples of different islands were largely unknown to one another. 'I know all the rivers and towns of Europe,' a young Indonesian said to me. 'I can recite the Dutch kings and queens from memory. But I know so little about my own countrymen in Sulawesi or Kalimantan and I have never been to Bali.'

Indonesians, to whom the Dutch transferred the sovereignty of these islands (with the exception of West Irian) in December 1949, are faced, like their predecessors, by these inescapable facts of geography. The largest island group in the world is now theirs to administer; 3,000 islands strung along the Equator for 3,000 miles, the distance between the Mountains of Killarney and the Caspian Sea; Java and Madura, as large as England and Wales; Sumatra, a little larger than Italy; Bali, the size of Northern Ireland; Kalimantan, slightly smaller than France, and Sulawesi, nearly as large as Roumania. Around and about these larger islands there is a wide variety of others, all sizes and shapes; small atolls built by millions of coral polyps; island volcanoes; islands of undisturbed green jungle; islands where no foreigner has wandered and unknown to most Indonesians; islands that hug the coast of thickly-populated Java; a string of islands appearing like a row of distant steamers along the coast of Sumatra; hundreds of islands in the Moluccas famous for the spices and cloves and pepper which first attracted visitors from the Western world; islands that are rich in tin; islands thickly covered with rubber trees; islands rich in oil. Throughout these islands and islets the sun always shines; there is no winter, no spring, no autumn, only a wet season and a dry. Peoples, separated by narrow seas, have different languages, customs, and widely different cultural levels.

The first visitors to these islands were Chinese, who, it is surmised, were sent over by the Han Emperor, Wang Mang, to find a rhinoceros for his Imperial Zoological Garden. They probably acquired one in Sumatra, though 'better evidence' of Chinese visitors, a Dutch historian suggests, 'may be found in the fact that numerous specimens of Chinese ceramics of the Han period have been found in southern Sumatra, western Java and eastern Borneo'.[1] Far more important culturally was the arrival of the Hindus from South India. They came in the second century A.D. and then at different times and in varying numbers for the next 700 years, settling down along the coast of Sumatra, Java, and sometimes in Kalimantan (Borneo) and Sulawesi (Celebes), introducing their religions—Buddhism and Hinduism—and enriching the indigenous culture. Chinese traders followed and formed coastal settlements which exist to this day. Then came Muslim traders from South India, who traded their merchandise and made converts to Islam with

4

equal fervour. The Portuguese who followed in the early sixteenth century were much less successful, and although they
were the first Europeans to appreciate the riches of Indonesia,
they failed to consolidate their power. The British followed, and
then the Dutch.

Let us go back in our imagination to the winter months of
the year 1579 when we might have heard the sound of Drake's
drum as the *Golden Hind* sailed through the Indonesian waters
until it came in sight of

> 'foure high piked Ilands; their names, Tirenate, Tidore,
> Matchan, Batchan, all of them very fruitfull and yeelding
> abundance of cloves, whereof wee furnished ourselues of as
> much as we desired at a very cheape rate'.[2]

Sir Francis Drake, then on his voyage round the world, anchored
in Ternate where the Sultan Batur received him, joining his
canoe to the *Golden Hind* and sharing the 'musicall paradise' of
'trumpets and other instruments of musick both of still and loud
noise'.[3]

After making a commercial treaty with the Sultan, Sir Francis
Drake and his companions sailed round and round in the beautiful Gulf of Gorontalo, before they could continue their south-
wards journey. The *Golden Hind* was entangled in hundreds of
islands—the Moluccas—and ran on to a reef of live coral. Taking
shelter on an island which was uninhabited, they watched

> 'an infinite swarme of fierie-seeming-wormes flying in the aire
> whose bodies (no bigger than an ordinary flie) did make a
> shew and giue such light as if every twigge on every tree had
> been a lighted candle, or as if that place had beene the starry
> sphere'.[4]

Passing the southern coast of Sulawesi (Celebes) they cast
anchor in Timor and greatly admired the people 'of handsome
body and comely stature, of civill demeanour, very just in dealing, and courteous to strangers'.[5] On they went, coasting along
the Lesser Sunda Islands—Flores, Sumba, Sumbawa, Lombok,
and Bali—until they set anchor on the coast of Java, a few miles
below the city of Djogjakarta. 'Few were the dayes', Sir Francis

records,[6] 'that one or more of these Kings did misse to visit us' bringing food, hens, goats, coconuts, and bananas.

'One day amongst the rest, viz March 21 [1580] Raia Donan coming aboard us, in requitall of our musick, which was made to him, presented our Generall with his country musick, which though it were of a very strange kind, yet the sound was pleasant and delightfull . . .'[7]

The 'musick' referred to was the gamelan and the performance the first that was ever given to an English audience.

Sailing west-south-west from Djogjakarta towards the Cape of Good Hope, the *Golden Hind* left Indonesian waters. To Sir Francis Drake, as to his predecessors, the 3,000 islands were but stepping-stones on his journey from the Pacific Ocean to the shores of the Atlantic.

Within a few years, British traders who followed in the wake of the *Golden Hind* fought battles with Portuguese and Dutch rivals for the control of spices, cloves, and pepper. Dutchmen won the competition and settled down to develop a monopoly for their countrymen, whilst British traders and empire-builders concentrated their attention on India. For the Dutch these Islands became outposts of empire on the day in 1602 when the Dutch East India Company was formed.

The first trading posts were in the islands of the Moluccas. Their monopoly unchallenged abroad, and their methods uncriticized at home, Dutch traders built their Asian Empire free from embarrassing restrictions. Sultan was encouraged to fight Sultan. Slaves could be trafficked from island to island with immunity. Rice supplies could be cut off and people die of hunger. Crops could be destroyed or compulsorily produced whichever method was the more profitable.

Finding that the quickest and biggest profits could be made in the central island of Java, the Dutch East India Company chose this area on which to concentrate their trade and their administration. Here, on this island the size of England and Wales, stretching 600 miles from west to east with a breadth varying from 56 to 136 miles, they found communications were easier than in other islands. Their centre became the town of

6

Batavia which Jan Pieterszoon Coen founded in 1602. Tough and ruthless as he appears in Rembrandt's famous painting, he built it on the site of an earlier Javanese town called Djajakerta (shortened by the Dutch to Jakatra) and called it Batavia after the 'Batavi', a Germanic tribe in the Low Countries.

Dutch historians have not hidden the behaviour or the affairs of the Dutch East India Company; many of them have frankly described traders who studied only their own financial interests; who found compliant Sultans equally eager to make profits and equally indifferent to the cost in lives of their own countrymen. In 1796 affairs had reached such scandalous proportions of corruption that the Dutch Government appointed a Committee to take charge of the administration of the Company. The result was that its Charter was never again renewed, and the State took over all possessions and all its debts.

> 'And thus,' a Dutch historian writes, 'for the sum of 134,000,000 guilders, the total amount of the debts, it acquired the whole colonial empire with all its resources—definitely a profitable deal.'[8]

Let us go back again in our imagination this time to February 1795, to a house in Kew where British and Indonesian history were suddenly interwoven. Prince William of Orange, Chief Director of the Dutch East India Company, had escaped from Amsterdam a month earlier when Napoleon's troops were marching on the city. The Dutch Government which then took over affairs made an alliance with Napoleon. Holland as a result became involved in the French war with Britain. Prince William, from the safety of his home in London, sent a document known as the 'Circular Note of Kew' to all Governors and Commanders of the Dutch Empire telling them to admit British troops and to hand over their administration to British officials. When normal conditions prevailed in Holland, he added, the colonies would be returned to their legal owner—the Dutch.

In the midst of a confusing situation which then arose in Indonesia, there emerged a young Englishman who was to play a decisive role in its history. Across the Straits of Malacca, Thomas Stamford Raffles, with the full confidence of Lord

7

Minto, then Governor-General of India, believed that Java was a point from which the French might attack British possessions. He made preparations to prevent it; he sent emissaries to Bali and to the Sultans of East Java to win them over to the British side. This would ensure food supplies and even troops from those areas if and when the French attacked. His intelligence reports to Lord Minto were extraordinarily well-informed about conditions throughout the islands, but above all about Java. He believed that the ties with Holland were broken for ever, and that these rich islands should be permanently part of the British Empire.

> 'All my views,' he told his cousin, Dr. Raffles, 'all my plans and all my mind were devoted to create such an interest regarding Java as should lead to its annexation to our Eastern empire.'[9]

Lord Minto's views were the same; when he announced the capture of Java to his Government in London, he described it as having been

> 'added to the dominion of the British crown, and converted from a seat of hostile machinations and commercial competition, into an augmentation of British power and prosperity'.[10]

For five years—from 1811 to 1816—Thomas Raffles was Lieutenant-Governor of the island of Java and its dependencies. He ruled with much intelligence and he acquired a genuine and scholarly interest in the lives and the culture of the people. But his rule was short-lived. A British-Dutch Convention signed in 1814 stipulated that Dutch colonial possessions, as they existed in 1803, should be returned, and a treaty which was signed in 1824 laid down for more than a century the British and Dutch spheres of influence; Holland settled down to develop Indonesia just as Britain secured a virtual monopoly in the development of India.

But the return to Dutch rule in Indonesia was a signal for resistance in every one of the five large islands. Central Java became a battlefield. A war which started as a protest against the insistence of Dutch troops on building a road through a

Sultan's territory in Djogjakarta in 1825, lasted for five years. Sumatra was particularly difficult to pacify. In Central Sumatra, a rebellion led by fanatical Muslim Padris gained such support in the villages that Dutch expeditions did not succeed in establishing their authority until 1837. In East Sumatra, Sultans of Palembang, with the support of guerrillas in the surrounding uplands, continued to resist Dutch pressure and defeat one expedition after another until 1903. In North Sumatra, the tough, independent Achinese defeated a long succession of Dutch expeditions, until a long-drawn-out war ended in 1912. In Kalimantan (Borneo) a similar policy of pacification was adopted. In West Kalimantan, Dutch authority was only established in 1855. In southern parts of the island, resistance was not finally broken until 1905 when Dutch police banished from their homes the local Rajahs who were unwilling to submit to their rule. The island of Sulawesi (Celebes) presents the same picture. In the Toradja lands of the central uplands, a military expedition of two and a half battalions finally ended resistance in 1905. In the south, where feudal lords asserted their independence, Dutch troops only occupied the country, district by district, in 1911. Rebellions, the most famous of which was the Pattimura in 1817, took place in the Molucca islands. The Balinese, extremely individualistic and brave, presented the would-be Dutch rulers with a difficult problem. A war in North Bali ended only in 1849 when the local Rajahs agreed to acknowledge Dutch authority, whilst the Dutch agreed not to occupy the island, and to refrain from interference in its internal affairs. Subsequently, by playing off one Rajah against another, by sending expeditions when local rebellions occurred and by placing their officials in strategic positions, the Dutch were able to establish themselves in North Bali by the end of the century. The conquest of South Bali began in 1900, and it was only in 1906, after extraordinarily brave resistance by the Balinese, that the Dutch were able to occupy the whole island. Their army stayed on till 1914.

Throughout Indonesia there are living legends of men and women who resisted Dutch occupation. In Borneo, people still remember chiefs who refused to submit to the Dutch in 1905 and were taken off as prisoners. In Atjeh, people will tell you

B*

9

about the war which ended only in 1908 when their Muslim priests were hunted into the mountains and captured. In South Bali, relatives of the Agung of Klungkung, the last of the independent Rajahs, will describe how he was killed after heroically resisting Dutch troops in 1911. Many Balinese remember watching the last troops leave the island in 1914 when Bali was considered 'pacified'. Dutch historians usually describe these men and women as 'rebels'; to Indonesians they are heroes. Wander into the poorest home, or the most distant village, into any public building and you will find photographs of these local heroes side by side with that of President Sukarno under whose leadership Dutch rule finally ended.

The spirit of resistance to foreign rule is alive in every nation. Its embodiment in nationalist movements is the most important factor in the twentieth-century history of Asia. In Indonesia, Japanese occupation for three and a half years had the effect of increasing opportunities for Indonesians to fill posts only open in Dutch times to Dutchmen, and the Republic of Indonesia was proclaimed on August 17th, 1945. Two days later, the country was divided into eight provinces: West Java, Middle Java, East Java, Sumatra, Kalimantan (Borneo), Sulawesi (Celebes), Maluku (the Moluccas), and Sunda-Ketjil (Lesser Sunda Islands). President Sukarno appointed a local governor for each province. The Central Indonesian National Committee, now acting as the Government, instructed one of its own members from these provinces to set up provincial Committees; they were usually men and women known and trusted for their work in the nationalist struggle. Indonesians had taken over their own country.

Dutchmen, assisted in their return by British troops under the command of S.E.A.C., did not accept this fact; they were not far-sighted enough to understand that nationalist leaders whom they had imprisoned ten or twenty years earlier were now the acknowledged leaders of the country; practically every member of the first Cabinet had spent years in prison camps or in exile. Twice, in 1947 and again in 1948, Dutchmen tried to regain these rich lands on which one in every six of the people of Holland depended for their living. Finally, after the United

Nations had intervened, at the request of its Indian and Australian members, the Dutch Government transferred sovereignty to the people of Indonesia on December 28th, 1949.

Indonesian rulers face many of the problems which faced their Dutch predecessors; difficulties of administration in a country so scattered among so many islands, with a diversity of peoples, languages, customs, cultural levels. To Dutch rulers, as to all builders of empires, this diversity was a welcome guarantee of disunity; not one people, they argued, but many; not a nation but groups of men and women divided by sea as they were by language and custom, held together by the disciplined management of Dutch officials at the centre and by the Dutch Navy which protected them from one another as well as from the greedy intentions of would-be traders.

To Dutch rulers, the needs of Dutchmen inevitably had priority; the demands of shareholders in Holland were bound to press more heavily than the less clamant, less organized, and less formulated requests of the rubber-tapper, the rice-cultivator, workers on rubber, coffee, tea, and cinchona plantations, drillers of oil, and tin-miners. Vast stretches of jungle could be left virgin on one island—Sumatra is a good example—whilst across a narrow strip of water, the land is tilled up to the very edge of the volcano's crater. It was important, but not urgent, to the Dutch that of 78 million people, 52 million lived on the small island of Java, whilst in the much larger islands of Sumatra, Kalimantan (Borneo), and Sulawesi (Celebes) the population was respectively 12 millions, 3 millions, and 5 millions. The needs of the foreigner, not of Indonesians, dictated every form of development; the pattern is familiar throughout the colonial countries of Asia. Railways, built to serve the needs of foreign traders, do not exist outside Java, with the exception of those that handle the plantation traffic in Sumatra. Inter-island transport, primarily concerned with the needs of foreign trade and a limited tourist industry, played little part in bringing together the island peoples. In the field of production, the type of crop and its distribution had to fit into the Dutch pattern; the incentive was the richest yield in the shortest period; Dutch economy was the main beneficiary from a colony which

11

was a producer of such highly profitable raw materials as rubber and oil. It did not matter to Dutchmen that few Indonesians had any technical knowledge, that the majority of workers used the same methods and the same tools that were the custom when the islands were first occupied. The fact that less than ten in every hundred Indonesians were literate was not important in the general plans of Dutch rule, any more than similar figures caused embarrassment in India and in Indo-China to the colonial powers which ruled them. All the highest posts and the majority of those which required specialized training could be filled by men and women from Holland, who did their work efficiently and conscientiously.

But the requirements of Dutch economy reduced to a minimum the factors which are essential for the growth of a nation; a common language, a similar cultural level, a national consciousness arising from personal contacts and common interests —all were largely absent in the Netherlands East Indies. One desire was common; the desire to be free from foreign rule. This was the driving force of nationalism, the ideal for which men and women gave their lives, or spent many years in the malarial swamps where political workers were exiled; it inspired people from every island, aristocrat and rice-cultivator, intellectual and illiterate. Nationalism transformed the Netherlands East Indies into the Republic of Indonesia.

That diversity of culture and language, of customs and people which was used by the colonial power to prevent unity and a common nationhood is regarded by Republican leaders as lending colour to unity, adding liveliness to nationhood. Indeed, this is the theme written on their national insignia: 'Bhinneka Tunggal Ika', meaning 'Unity in Diversity', symbolic of the affiliation of islands and peoples all over Indonesia into one great Union. Nevertheless, though the victory of Nationalism released the creative energies which are indispensable in helping a new nation to achieve maturity, it did not automatically give birth to a consolidated nation. This is a far greater task than that of administering a colony.

The Republican Government must give priority to the people's needs. They are clearly formulated by politically conscious men and women in organizations which have their support to a lesser or greater degree in every island; men and women in Lombok and Halmahera begin to ask why their children have less doctors, less teachers than the children of Java; young men in Borneo, with schemes to drain swamps where enough rice could be grown to make up for the country's total rice deficit, ask for their share in technical assistance—in dredgers, pumps, and bulldozers; people living in remote islands ask for better communications; women's organizations everywhere demand better health services, better working conditions for women; young men as well as young women more technically minded than their parents, demand technical training, more machinery, more amenities of life; workers on the large plantations of Java and Sumatra ask for better housing conditions; from villages in Bali and from small fishing communities in the Moluccas the demand comes for more schools for the children and for literacy classes for their parents. Indeed, there is not and there cannot be any limit to the improvements which a newly liberated people believe to be implicit in their liberation. Added to which a new demand is growing louder and louder —that these 78 million people should have an opportunity to elect their Government, for there has not yet been a general election.[11]

Those who rule the Republic today, and they are mainly young men and women without any previous experience of administration, have a dual task to perform. Simultaneously, they have to run the highly complex financial and commercial system taken over from one of the most experienced and efficient trading nations in the world, and raise the standards of education, social welfare, and economic development of a widely scattered people. Inevitably this means a concentration of power at the centre, and herein lies one of the most complex problems; how to centralize and to encourage incentive at the same time, if the dead hand of colonial rule is not to be followed by paralysis of a top-heavy administration in Java. Yet it is by encouraging and responding to the creative energies in Celebes and Borneo, Sumatra, Bali, and a thousand other places that the growth of a balanced nation depends; it is on the development of their

13

resources that the Republic must rely if they are to satisfy demands in every field of life.

The Indonesian nation is now taking shape. The name 'Indonesia' itself is only eighty years old. To follow the story of Indonesia involves drawing a sketch of Java's crowded history, and then studying the island groups—Sumatra, Kalimantan (Borneo), Sulawesi (Celebes), and Bali, each with its own individual background. How far has the Republic moved towards the achievement of the aim described on their national insignia: Bhinneka Tunggal Ika—Unity in Diversity?

This was the question I set out to answer in a visit which took me through all these islands in 1951, when the Republic had had power for only a year.

NOTES

[1] *Nusantara*, by Bernard H. M. Vlekke, Harvard University Press, 1943, p. 12.

[2] *The World Encompassed by Sir Francis Drake*, compiled by Francis Fletcher, p. 137. Published 1628, and reprinted by the Hakluyt Society, 1854.

[3] Ibid., p. 141.

[4] Ibid., p. 149.

[5] Ibid., p. 158.

[6] Ibid., p. 160.

[7] Ibid., p. 161.

[8] *Nusantara*, by Bernard H. M. Vlekke, p. 223.

[9] *Memoir of Sir Thomas Raffles*, by Lady Raffles, p. 90. John Murray, 1830.

[10] Ibid., p. 96.

[11] In April 1955, it was announced that elections for Parliament and the Constituent Assembly would be held on September 29th and December 15th, 1955, respectively.

CHAPTER II

JAVA, THE CENTRE

O N Sundays, the midday meal in the Hotel des Indes (Djakarta) was a ritualistic performance. Residents were mainly Dutchmen, tall, prosperous, blond and tanned; the women neat and rather large, often bored as European women are in the tropics. Here, in a Dutch-owned hotel, they felt at home, Tuans to the swarms of small Indonesian boys waiting for their orders. The ritual started when the head waiter appeared carrying a large deep bowl of hot, dry, white rice. Behind him a long procession of waiters carried dishes precisely and gracefully with the rhythm of a ballet sequence; vegetable curry, fried bananas, chicken (fried, boiled, and disguised in half a dozen ways), fried duck, fish in a variety of dishes, eggs, liver, pancakes, finely chopped onion, coconut, a bewilderment of sauces and finally, krupuk made of crispy shrimps like over-sized pieces of pink toast.

Sunday dinner is called 'rijst-tafel'; it is a Dutch invention, though the cooks are Indonesian, and the produce is all home-grown. To most Indonesians the Dutchman's 'rijst-tafel' would be a gargantuan feast: to Dutchmen 'rijst-tafel' is a standard meal with an extra splendid one on Sundays. In Dutch times, waiters wore a headdress called a 'kain kepala', a square piece of Batik folded into a chirpily picturesque turban. When the Republic was proclaimed they went on strike for several days for the right to wear their black velvet hats, the symbol of independence, which President Sukarno invariably wears, combining a political idea with an intuitive sense of the photogenic.

The Hotel des Indes, silent and correct as a fortress, the symbol of conquest, was naturally selected by the Japanese as their headquarters. High-ranking British officials followed at the end of the war, when British troops took back the Dutch; they were succeeded by the United Nations Good Offices Committee, the

United Nations Commission on Indonesia, members of International Organizations and diplomatic missions from every part of the world; journalists flock here, living in rooms with verandas joining those of the world's V.I.P.s; business men forgather here from all corners of the earth. Here in this retreat, visitors see Indonesia through Dutch eyes; they read Dutch newspapers neatly arranged in the reading room; and Dutch Agency messages pinned on the notice board.

The flaming orange and purple bougainvillaea trees with their flowers riotously intertwined seem like interlopers in these sedate surroundings. Beyond, a street runs down both sides of a canal for two miles from Weltevreden ('well content') to the oldest part of the city, built by Jan Pieterszoon Coen. It clatters with the sound of overcrowded trams and cars driven with reckless impatience. Dutchmen still refer to this street as Molenvliet (mill stream); Indonesians have renamed it Gadjah Mada, a name that now appears in many places in Java.

Gadjah Mada is one of the great figures of Indonesian history; he is symbolic of the Republic. Historians already attribute to Gadjah Mada an eminent role in the story of their country, and describe the period in which he lived as the 'Golden Age' of their history. His leonine head is already prominent among monuments to their national heroes, and the new university in Djogjakarta is named after him. Gadjah Mada, whose name is said to mean 'an elephant, powerful, impassioned, but without wisdom unswayed by passion', was born round about the year 1300 in a Javanese village. He rose to the rank of Commander of the Palace Guards of the then King Djajanagara, whose murder he arranged and then himself killed the assassin. He was subsequently given the highest post in the land—that of Patih, for which our nearest equivalent is Prime Minister, and he skilfully remained in office until he died in 1364. More powerful than the kings he served, a courageous and ambitious soldier, he pledged himself before the Court to unite all Indonesian territory within the Madjapahit Kingdom. Apart from an uprising in Bali, he met with little resistance; Sunda, then Sumatra and Malaya, parts of the Philippines and Cambodia came under his rule; trade and cultural relations increased with India, Burma,

16

and China. He more than fulfilled his promises. According to the Javanese poet, Prapantja, Gadjah Mada had foresight and logic, the ability to inspire confidence, trueness of heart in the service of his people and his sovereign, the gift of rhetoric, gentleness and subtlety, determination and diligence, joy of living, patience and reasonableness, unselfishness, compassion, steadfastness, asceticism, conscientiousness, relentlessness in crushing enemies of those he served. In cultural, economic, and political matters Gadjah Mada also distinguished himself. He ordered the priests, for they were the only men who were literate, to make inventories of all the temples and to keep up-to-date the national archives. His fleet visited outlying islands, collecting tribute and spices, already a profitable trade. He was responsible for the first codification of Javanese laws and customs and he drew up a list of rules on which the country was to be administered.

When he died a normal death in 1364, four Ministers were appointed to do his work. But the Madjapahit Empire itself lasted only until 1478; it collapsed for internal reasons, Court intrigues and rivalry amongst the women, and because foreign ideas and foreign trade had already begun to penetrate the islands. After its fall, these 3,000 islands of Indonesia were never again united under a single rule until President Sukarno proclaimed the Republic on August 17th, 1945. Thus the name of Gadjah Mada has a special significance to Indonesians whilst the days of Madjapahit are described in Indonesian schools with national pride like the Elizabethan Age in this country or the Tang Dynasty in China.

The Hindu-Indonesian period came to an end in 1478, with the fall of the Madjapahit Empire. The island was divided in those days, as it is today, into West, Central, and East Java. Kingdoms rose and fell; Sultans behaved like feudal lords and families intrigued against one another; heads fell easily; beautiful women created havoc in Court circles and the Courts were the scene of extravagant ceremonies. Peasants tilled the land and they provided the armies. Their poverty and their backwardness were in great contrast with the splendour of the Courts and the elegant culture of the Javanese aristocracy.

The Western world and the Chinese Empire now began to make their impact on Indonesian history, above all, on that of Java. From the West came the introduction of Islam. By the time the Madjapahit Kingdom had lost its power, Islamic doctrines had already penetrated the north-east coast of Sumatra, and, following the shipping routes, Islamic traders from Southern India had spread their religion along the coastal areas of East Java. When it is remembered how important a role Islam has played in Indonesia, it seems strange that this transition from Hinduism to Islam is so little documented. Indeed, Indonesian historiography is more slender on this than on any other period since the last days of the Madjapahit Kingdom. One point seems certain; when the Portuguese traders followed those from Southern India, they failed to consolidate their economic power and were unable to impose their own religion. They made the mistake of mixed objectives; they were building up their trading account in pepper and spices and trying to fight Islam simultaneously. The Sultans were not averse to a good bargain in a shipload of pepper, but like all new converts they met a hostile religion with aggressive behaviour.

Meanwhile, in 1596 the first Dutch traders appeared on Java's west coast. Within a short time they secured a treaty with the Sultan of Banten. Records of the period describe the friendliness of traders—Javanese, Chinese and Indians from Gujerat. The Sultan of Banten swore 'to maintain this friendship and alliance and to order all our subjects to do the same'. Dutch aims were commercial; the Dutch East India Company was purely a trading concern. Local Sultans, absolute rulers over their own kingdoms, inevitably began to anticipate a share in the riches of their soil. Sultan after Sultan made agreements which seemed to offer considerable financial advantage. Where there was resistance to Dutch advances it was local and personal. The Sultans quarrelled with one another. The Dutch found Mataram against Banten and Balambangan against Mataram. The result was a long succession of localized wars, intrigues, and diplomatic manoeuvres for nearly two hundred years.

Had there been any centralized authority in Java, or had the Sultans been prepared to co-operate with one another, the

Dutch East India Company would have found it much more difficult to resist their demands and gain control. When this period of their history is described by Republican historians, there are certain names that are placed on the roll of honour of Indonesian nationalism; Sultan Agung Hanjokrokusumo who, in 1629, led the battle against the Dutch in Jakatra (as Djakarta was then called), and Trunodjojo, Prince of Madura, who organized a revolt in 1674 which lasted for six years. Trunodjojo, supported by exiles from Makassar, launched his attack on the Dutch East India Company at a weak moment when Holland was involved in war against Britain and France. He accused the Company of being motivated only by the lust for gold, and he declared himself ready to fight for his land, his people and his religion. Resistance was only overcome when Dutch forces, assisted by rival Sultans, stormed Trunodjojo's palace and killed him and his family. Surapati is another national hero. A runaway slave from Bali, he won the support of other slaves as well as of the local people in the area south of Djakarta, and later of the Susuhunan. At the time of his death in 1706, when the Dutch troops surrounded him in Pasuruan, he was in control of a considerable area of East Java. On his death-bed, his four sons swore an oath never to acknowledge the Dutch East India Company.

But there was still resistance in East Java. The leader of the rising in 1712 was the Susuhunan's friend, the Adipati of Surabaya. When the Dutch instructed him to kill the Adipati, the Susuhunan was in a quandary; he couldn't afford to insult the Dutch, and on the other hand he was repelled by the idea of killing a friend. His solution was to write a letter to the Adipati telling him of the Dutch request. At the end of one month, the old Adipati, having decided to give up his life rather than risk trouble for his friend, dressed himself in white robes, and walked to the Susuhunan's Court. The guards plunged their weapons into his body, and gave the corpse to his brother. He and his followers were so much moved that they at once began to organize their revenge. The result was a civil war which the Dutch were unable to put down until 1717.

The next threat to the Company came from Chinese who

until now had been given every encouragement to settle in Batavia and elsewhere, acting as middlemen, as money-lenders, and running markets and bazaars. Their industry was such that within a few years of their entry as more or less penniless immigrants, they made small fortunes. The Company began to regard them as competitors and finally cut down immigration figures and deported many Chinese from their small shops in the interior of Java to Banda, or Ceylon, or South Africa. When the rumour spread that a boatload of Chinese would be thrown overboard on their way to Ceylon, their compatriots, already suffering from the persecutions of the Company, raised the standard of rebellion. Javanese, who saw in this resistance to the Company a way of ridding themselves of its ruthless control, joined forces with the Chinese, and even the Susuhunan himself gave them his support. The Dutch crushed the rebellion in 1740 by a terrible massacre of 10,000 Chinese which Dutch historians describe as the 'Batavian Fury'. Javanese resistance was only temporarily broken; the Susuhunan's brother, joined by forces from Madura and East Java, fought a war with the Dutch which began in 1745 and lasted until 1757. It cost the Company over four million florins, the countryside was laid waste, and thousands were killed on both sides. Before the end of the war the Susuhunan was compelled on his deathbed to sign a deed by which he agreed 'to abdicate for himself and his heirs, the sovereignty of the country, conferring the same on the Dutch East India Company, and leaving it to them to dispose of it, in future, to any person they might think competent to govern it for the benefit of the Company and of Java'. On the basis of this deed, the Company subsequently granted in fee the administration of those provinces where Javanese were still in control. The brother of the deceased Susuhunan continued guerrilla warfare for some years. But he too finally gave way and signed a treaty of reconciliation with the Dutch, dividing the empire of Mataram into two parts; one state, Surakarta, was given a ruler with the title Susuhunan Pakubuwana, the other, Djogjakarta, was given the title Sultan Hamengkubuwono. Today, nearly two centuries afterwards, these two titles remain.

But resistance now came from Balinese guerrillas in East Java. When they were defeated in 1774, the Dutch East India Company settled down to consolidate its power over the whole of the island. What had begun as a purely trading company had developed into a Government. The Governor-General was appointed by the Government in The Hague, but below him rulers were ranked according to the status they held in the Company. Their job was to obtain revenue; their main sources were the contributions levied on all the Javanese Regents in payment for the positions they held as Dutch vassals, and profits from goods which the Regents were forced to supply at the Company's price. The system was known as 'Forced Deliveries and Contingencies'. The Company could dictate the crops, as well as where they could be grown, irrespective of the results on the countryside. From 1770 to 1780 the Company's average yearly sales exceeded twenty million florins; the shares in 1781 were 215% above their original value. But these were unreal figures hiding the rottenness of the Company which was only discovered when books were examined for the first time revealing embezzlements and corruption to such an extent that officers of the Company were taxed on their illicit gains. In 1796 the Company gave over the administration to a Committee appointed by the Government. The Charter was not renewed. Finally, the State took over all possessions and all debts.

The spectacular scandals of the Dutch East India Company coincided with events in Europe which led to the Netherlands East Indies becoming part of the British Empire. During the British interregnum, Sir Thomas Raffles also made Java the centre of his policy. He imposed a new pattern of colonial government which led to many changes, some of which the Dutch retained in their administration when, with great reluctance, he handed it back to them. He made a new village system based on the free election of Headmen by the inhabitants of the village; he made a new system of land tenure, based on his belief that the State was the sole proprietor of land; he substituted a land rent for the Dutch system of feudal imports and levies, by this means depriving the Sultans of their political and financial interests and substituting a disinterested civil administration.

When Raffles left Batavia in 1816, he found the decks of the boat *Ganges*, on which he sailed to England, filled with fruit, flowers, poultry, and anything people thought might add to his comfort on the voyage. On the way home he had an interview with Napoleon. His reception an English Captain describes as

'not only not dignified or graceful, but absolutely vulgar and authoritative'. Napoleon, he says, 'appeared to be acquainted with the value and importance of the Island, but put some strange questions to Mr. Raffles, such as how the King of Java conducted himself. On Mr. Raffles explaining, he seemed most attentive, and then asked whether the spice plantations at Amboyna were doing well, and whether the Spice Islands were also to be restored to the Dutch.'[1]

At home in England, Raffles was entirely absorbed in the three thousand islands he had left behind with such reluctance. Although he was a sick man, he was determined to make his countrymen

'sensible of the loss sustained by the relinquishment of so flourishing a colony to a foreign and a rival power'.[2]

Between October 1816 and May 1817, he wrote his monumental *History of Java*. Lady Raffles writes that

'a few sheets were rapidly written off every morning for the printer, and corrected at night on his return from his dinner engagements'.[3]

It was an extraordinary achievement, reflecting the passionate interest Raffles had acquired in the country. He was a brilliant linguist and his comparative vocabulary of Malayu, Javanese, Madurese, Bali, and Lampung languages with their English translations all classified under thirty-two headings was the first skeleton dictionary to be composed. He described in detail the Court life and the life of the peasants; their customs and dress, their occupations and their arts; he described the various types of wayang; he described classical and contemporary Javanese literature and poetry and translated the most famous of Javanese epic poems, the 'Brata Yudha'. He described scientifically and at great length the flora and fauna, the geology and the natural resources of the islands. Raffles' *History of Java* was unparalleled in colonial literature, and it is most unlikely that any Governor, before or since, had a more intelligent, friendly, scholarly, or genuine interest in the people he was called on to govern. He also revived the Batavian Society of Science and Art, and laid the foundations of an immense amount of study which Dutch scholars and scientists subsequently devoted to Java. He opened up a new vista not only to the Javanese themselves, but to their Dutch rulers.

Whatever were his failures—and some of them arose from the shortness of his rule—it is now generally recognized that Raffles introduced a liberal spirit into the administration of Java by accepting the right of the people to govern themselves, by recognizing the roots and the growth of Javanese culture, and by making the people's welfare rather than the profits from their soil and labour the criterion of colonial government.

The return to Dutch rule was met with a good deal of resistance. The clock began to turn back towards the days of the Dutch East India Company; the Sultans regained some of their lost power and their rights over the people. The foundation of the Nederlandsche Handelmaatschappij (N.H.M.) to secure a monopoly for Dutch traders put an end to the free peasant cultivation which was the basis of Raffles' economy. A conservative Dutch historian, de Klerck, writes that this policy

'not only nipped in the bud the beginnings of an organised native agricultural industry, but which may also be considered as one of the principal causes of the revolt in Central Java, by which the land was stricken for nearly five years and Dutch authority threatened with ruin'.[4]

Around the city of Djogjakarta, the cultivation of coffee had introduced considerable prosperity; under the Raffles regime land had been let out on leases and earlier restrictions removed. When his successor, Van Capellen, ended them he aroused a great deal of hostility. When Dutch officials were put in as

supervisors and when Chinese were given leases of land, and the
toll-gates leased to them at ever-increasing prices, the atmosphere was ripe for revolt. People became poorer and poorer
whilst the Sultans lived in increasing luxury; Klerck records
that 'adultery and debauchery prevailed at both the courts,
religious duties were neglected, extortion and abuse of power
knew no limits'.[5]

It is against this background that Diponegoro emerges as a
hero second only to Gadjah Mada in the history of Java. Indeed,
his photograph is often found next to that of President Sukarno
in the houses of Javanese peasants as well as in public buildings.
His wife too has her claims to fame. In 1954, when a girls'
dormitory was opened in the Gadjah Mada University, the
Minister of Education, Mohamad Yamin, called it Ratnaning-
sih—the name of Diponegoro's wife. Painters, writers, and poets
have already immortalized him as one who first saw the bright
light of nationalism. He was an unusual man. The fact that a
Court intrigue pushed him out of the line of succession, so that
he was a Prince and never a Sultan, is used by some Dutch
writers to explain his behaviour. But contemporary evidence
suggests that this was not so; he was an ascetic who lived as a
hermit in protest against the corruption and immorality of the
Courts; he was a mystic—and mysticism still plays a not insignificant role in the life of Djogjakarta—who had visions and
dreamed dreams that he was preordained to end the overlord-
ship of Dutch rulers and the corruption of the Sultanates. He
hated violence and he was not naturally a man of action. He
read the Koran night and day, and Arabic books containing Islamic laws as written by Imam Sh'aafi, poems of the Persian
writer Imam Casali, old Javanese literature, and the histories of
Persia and Arabia as well as that of his own country. 'One lives
to praise Allah' was his conception of life, and this young mystic
—he was born in 1785—was building a mosque when an event
occurred which changed him from a man of dreams to the leader
of a rebellion. In 1825, he saw Dutchmen putting up poles across
his lands without asking his permission. They were marking out
a roadway which would pass straight through the graveyard of

Diponegoro's ancestors. Several times the peasants who regarded him as their champion took down the poles, and when they were replaced by stockades those too they removed. Finally, in a skirmish between the people and the Dutch who persisted in what seemed an outrage, a Dutch officer was killed. A platoon of Dutch cavalry soon appeared, ransacked and burnt Diponegoro's house. Seated on a black horse with white feet, as contemporary records describe, he saw not the red flames, but a yellow light which was the symbol of the new Sultanate he was called on to build on the ashes of the old. A war which was to last five years had begun.

Diponegoro had the support of the people in Djogjakarta where he was well known, and, as the war went on, many other Princes rallied to his cause. This is how the war was described on the basis of eye-witness reports in November 1825:

'Upon the whole we are inclined to consider that the present is not only the most formidable and general insurrection against the European authority in Java which has ever taken place, but even the most widespread combination against European domination which the annals of India have hitherto afforded. The hopes of the Netherlands Government, it is clear to us, must rest solely upon the probable quarrels and disunion of the natives amongst themselves and not upon an European force, however numerous and well disciplined, for what could they do against five millions of people resolved upon resistance and tolerably united, fighting for their independence among the woods—marshes—mountains and defiles of a country containing an area of 40,000 squares miles.'[6]

The war, which spread over a large part of Central Java, was fought with guerrilla tactics; people armed with pikes left their villages, and returned to plant their rice in the rainy season. The Dutch brought in troops from the other islands, and at the end of 1827, reinforcements came from Europe. This Expeditionary Division was composed of 3,000 infantry, troopers, and artillerymen. They were encamped at Djogjakarta, and in the fields near Magelang where Raffles had had the great Borobodur rebuilt. The turning-point came in the war a year later when Diponegoro's armies suffered a heavy setback near Magelang, and lost many lives. His right-hand adviser, Kjahi Maja, left him, and in 1829 several of his most important commanders gave up the struggle. He himself lost a great deal of prestige when he married the daughter of his guru (religious teacher) against her father's wishes. It was a serious fall from grace for a leader with his background. As one after the other of the Princes deserted, and people became tired and exhausted, Diponegoro was reduced to live as an outlaw with the price of 50,000 guilders on his head, dead or alive. Finally, in January 1830, when only two young men and two horses remained with him, he contacted the Dutch headquarters in Magelang. Insisting that this was not a surrender but a meeting to discuss terms, he refused to see anyone other than the Dutch Commander himself, General de Kock. Then came the period of Puasa, the Muslim Lent. When the fast was over, the two men met. Magelang was crowded with people whose curiosity was naturally aroused. Diponegoro arrived on horseback and was received by Dutch officers in the Resident's house. He stated his terms to the Dutch General: an independent state under the Sultan's leadership and a society formed on the basis of Islam. Those terms were much too high, the General told him, and offered to give him the title of Pangeran. Diponegoro replied that this was already his title, given to him by his father. Whereupon the General ordered his officers to arrest this presumptuous Javanese nobleman. The arrest was hidden from the crowds of Diponegoro's friends, because General de Kock accompanied him to the northern part of Magelang, and there made him a prisoner. He was exiled to a prison in Makassar. He wrote poetry describing his loneliness and his desire that Allah would forgive him for his sins, and help his wife and children who had devoutly followed Islam. In January 1855, at the age of seventy, he died.

With the death of Diponegoro, Java came under Dutch rule. The war had cost the Dutch Treasury 20 million florins, the lives of 8,000 Europeans and 7,000 Javanese who fought on their side. The number killed on Diponegoro's side has never been made known.

Dutchmen now settled down to develop the riches of Java. They made a mutually beneficial alliance with the Javanese aristocracy by restoring some of their prestige and giving them a share in their soaring profits. Javanese Regents acted as agents of the Dutch Government in a system which demanded either payment of the land rent (normally two-fifths of the crop) or the cultivation of crops ordered by the Director of Cultures. The structure of the Javanese system remained the same; the life of the people continued as before, only indirectly affected by the new money economy; vast plantations grew up mainly in and around areas where large towns already existed; the middlemen and the moneylenders continued to be Chinese in a period which has been called 'static expansion'. Dutchmen and, later, Dutchwomen, who came in increasing numbers, settled down in the towns. But five-sixths of the Javanese continued to live in 'desas'. The word desa, which is derived from the Sanskrit 'deca', means a village community. Most Javanese lived, and still live, in simple houses made of plaited bamboo; they ate their rice and they slept on bamboo couches; whilst Dutch-style houses were built in thousands on the outskirts of towns, the homes of the vast majority of Javanese remained simple, the kitchen equipped with wooden utensils, earthenware pots, tin and iron frying pans, kettles, and saucepans. Sanitation was practically non-existent; the river and the rice-field provided a convenient substitute, but also led to a very high incidence of ankylostomiasis (worms) and many types of skin and internal diseases.

For the most part, desas have changed very little from the time Jan Pieterszoon Coen built the town of Batavia (Djakarta) until the Republic took responsibility for their administration. Desas consist of groups of houses scattered among innumerable rice-fields like clumps of trees in an English park. The approach to most of them is along dirt tracks or along a higher ridge of soil between two rice terraces. Apart from the big plantations, rice-fields dominate the landscape as they do the lives of the people. Men and boys loosen the soil with buffalo-drawn wooden ploughs, simple, unchanged for centuries. They fix the intricate lines of bamboo tubes which carry water step by step from the edge of volcanoes down to the sea, and more than a quarter of

Java is artificially watered by this system. Small slender women sow rice in specially prepared seed beds of water which quickly become the brightest and greenest squares in the rice patchwork of Javanese landscape. They then replant them one by one and keep the fields weeded. After six months (or less in this fertile country), the water is drawn off, the landscape changes from terraces of green to bright gold as the rice ripens. The same women next cut the rice handful by handful with small curved knives; the men plough once more; the landscape changes to mirrored terraces of shining water; planting begins again in this cycle of rice-growing which led the first Indian visitors to call Java the 'Land of Gold'. Specially cooked rice is offered to the spirits of the desa, spread with flowers on banana leaves and placed under the waringin tree or on the graves of ancestors. Feasts called 'slametan' are arranged before the rice is planted and after the harvest and the special dishes are rice prepared with fish and meat and vegetables. When the rice is finally stored away in 'lumbungs', which are sheds built of wood or bamboo, and raised on poles for safety from rats, another slametan is held and dancing and singing and wayang performances accompany the harvest home.

The rice cultivators together with small craftsmen in wood and leather, the blacksmith and the tinsmith, food pedlars and small traders, make up the largest group in the desa; they are called 'wong tani'. The second group are the 'priyayi', the gentry, landlords (often absentees), the administrative people and the teachers. Each village has its Headman elected by the village assembly; he is responsible for arrangements about land-holding, he is consulted about ploughing and sowing, the selection of seeds, the irrigation canals as well as personal problems; he collects taxes for the Government which are passed on to the District Commissioner, who passes it on to the Treasury official. At the top of this complex administrative pyramid in Dutch times stood the Dutch Governor and the Dutch Resident. Below the Governor and Resident came the Indonesian Regents, usually members of the Javanese aristocracy, whose ancestors had lost their independence in the later years of pacification. Below the Regents, of whom there were seventy-six, came the

Wedonos, in charge of five or six districts, and the Assistant-Wedonos, in charge of fifteen to twenty villages; they were all Indonesians. Every month the Regent called these officials to a Regency Conference, in the Regency capital; the Dutch Assistant-Resident supervised the proceedings which were largely confined to the Regency budget, public works, market places and carriage and entertainment taxes. Even in the Native States, as they were called, where the Sultan was head of Djogjakarta, and Susuhunan of Surakarta, Dutch Governors were attached to them. The extent of their power is amusingly illustrated by Amry Vandenbosch's story of the visit of the King and Queen of Siam to Java in 1929. One of the Javanese princes gave a lavish dinner in their honour.

'The Governor, however, exercised a control over the issuance of the invitations, with the result that 250 European guests were invited by the Governor and a mere handful, since there was room for no more, were invited by the prince himself.'[7]

The Sultan was hereditary; the Regents were semi-hereditary, their sons or their near relatives usually being selected by the Dutch Government as their successors. The Dutch system thus preserved the Javanese feudal system. 'In fact,' Madame Subandrio (the daughter of the Regent of Paduruan in East Java whose family were Commissioners of the District and sub-district for nearly a century) writes,

'the organisation of civil administration which employed the "priyayi" (gentry) as Regency, District and Sub-district Commissioners, and other Netherlands Indies Government Agents, was based on the feudal structure of the Javanese community. Even the introduction of welfare measures, such as the reorganisation of agriculture, cattle breeding, the introduction of village banks, rice stores, schools etc., as recommended by the so-called Ethical Policy from the beginning of the century, has been carried out with "gentle pressure" from the "priyayi" administrators together with the help of the Village Board which was still held in patriarchal reverence by many of the population. . . . On the whole, modern economy and rural administration have both been influenced by the old conditions and traditions, with which they both have to reckon.'[8]

In the last fifty years of Dutch rule, Java was the island where the greatest external changes were made. The soil was so fertile that although there are more than a hundred volcanoes strung like smoking temples from west to east across the island, about 65% of the land was cultivated. Many good roads were built, chiefly by forced labour, to serve the plantations of coffee and sugar, rubber and tea and the forests of teak. Railway lines, good ports, deep harbours helped to make Java one of the richest trading areas in the world. An abundance of cheap labour from a population which increased from $28\frac{1}{2}$ million in 1900 to 41 million in 1930 was an essential part of colonial economy for the Dutch as it was for Britain and France in their colonies.

Unlike other Western colonial powers, the Dutch, over-crowded in their own land, increasingly settled down in Java, building Dutch-style houses in and around existing Javanese towns. Few of them lived in or had much contact with the villages; they were concentrated in twelve of the largest towns, all with a population of over 50,000. In the 1930 census, 64% of Europeans (largely Dutch) lived in these twelve towns; 47% of Orientals; 38% of the Chinese, and only 4% of Javanese. Javanese towns thus became the most Europeanized of any towns in Asia, presenting an extremely unbalanced picture to the visitors who rarely visited any other island than Java.

Djakarta itself, the capital, stands on the site of an old pre-sixteenth-century harbour town then known as Sunda Kelapa, the chief port for the Sundanese Kingdom of Padjadjaran. The Sultan of Banten changed its name to Djajakerta—'Glorious Fortress'—and here the Dutch established a trading post whose name they shortened to Jakatra. British and Dutch, then keen trade rivals, fought for its possession and razed most of it to the ground. When the Dutch won the battle, they built a new town, calling it Batavia, and their fortress is still one of the sights of the city. The Chinese, at one time restricted to a part of the town, still remain concentrated in the crowded streets of Glodok with their bazaars and shops and popular restaurants. Canals cross and criss-cross the whole city which has now been expanded far beyond its original site in large suburbs, built in Dutch style, and with vast business houses and administrative buildings—churches, hospitals, schools, modern shops—which give to parts of Djakarta the appearance of a provincial Dutch town. To the Indonesians it was always Djakarta and when the Dutch left the city in March 1942 and the Japanese became temporary rulers, the name 'Batavia' was dropped. By special decree on the day after sovereignty was transferred, the city was formally called Djakarta again.

Bogor is the second town in West Java which everyone visits, not for its historical associations, but because its situation at the foot of the mountains provides in half an hour a welcome change from Djakarta's steamy, monotonous heat. One of the many first-class roads in Java as well as a modern railway connects these two cities. The journey, like almost any other in Java, is through rich country; terraced rice-fields with their unforgettable greenness and the constant sound of water trickling through bamboo pipes. Originally the capital of the old Sundanese Kingdom of the twelfth to the sixteenth centuries—the people still speak the Sundanese language—its site inspired the famous Dutch Governor-General Van Imhoff (1743–50) to build there a large country estate and residence. He called it Buitenzorg (Sans Souci), and the name remained until 1942, although the Sundanese always thought of it as Bogor. Later, a Dutch Professor of Natural History chose it to build a Botanic Garden which became the most famous in the world. Here, in 1821, tea seeds from Japan were first planted; seeds from China gave a better crop, and in 1873, seeds from Assam proved the best of all. Here too, ten years later, the first specimens of the Brazilian rubber tree, *Hevea brasiliensis*, were planted. Subsequently, both crops were so highly developed and so widely grown by Dutch planters that from these experiments in Bogor, Java became one of the richest areas in the world in tea and rubber. Today, Bogor is a modern city with famous museums, herbariums, and scientific institutes. The large mansion which belonged to successive Dutch Governors-General is now a residence of President Sukarno.

East Java presents the same kind of picture. The ancient city of Semarang was the capital of Mataram, whose Sultan ceded it to the Dutch for money, rice, and security. With the development of plantations of tea, coffee, sugar, rice, maize, and tobacco, the Dutch made this the chief port in Central Java and today its harbour and railways sprawl along the coast for three miles and for at least a mile inland. Surabaya, second only to Djakarta, was a strategic site ceded by the local ruler to the Dutch in 1618 in return for their assistance against the Sultan of Mataram. By the time it was evacuated by the Dutch in March 1942, it had become a great naval base, an industrial centre, and the harbour for vast exports of sugar, coffee, and tobacco. Outside Surabaya, a small town when the modern city was still only a fishing village, is Grisec, a place of pilgrimage for Muslims throughout the island. For it was here that the Muslim priest, Maulana Malik Ibrahim, first made converts to his faith. He was an Arab who died in 1419; his grave still stands near an ancient mosque which has one of the few tower minarets in Java. His sacred kris (sword) is preserved there. But the town itself seems derelict and haunted—the mansions which the Dutch merchants built for themselves are now used by enterprising Chinese as nesting places for the birds which make the famous birds'-nest soup.

The city which is dearest to the hearts of Javanese is not one of these busy, prosperous, commercial, Europeanized centres, but Djogjakarta, relatively smaller, quieter, and far more typical of the island. This part of Central Java was a centre of Hindu-Javanese civilization from the fifth to the ninth centuries and in the countryside round Djogjakarta, between the Merapi mountains and the Indian Ocean, the history of the island can be read in early Hindu temples, and in one of the most famous Buddhist monuments in the world, Borobodur. Made with black lava blocks, each cut about two feet long and one foot wide, Borobodur was constructed round the upper part of a hill. The site was brilliantly chosen probably about A.D. 770, in the centre of a plain. On terraces, approached through elaborately carved gateways, the story of the Buddha's life and the virtues of his followers is told in bas-reliefs and sculpture. On the highest terrace, over four hundred identical statues of the Buddha are enshrined in separate undecorated stupas, impersonal and dramatic. In every direction, fields of rice stretch to the distant mountains, to volcanoes wreathed in bluish-grey smoke.

The elegant beauty of Borobodur was unknown from the days when Buddhists hid it in the ground to protect it from the Muslim invaders, until it was found by an English colonel during the British interregnum. Sir Thomas Raffles, with his absorbed interest in Javanese culture, had the monument excavated, lava block by lava block, and restored to its original site and splendour. No wonder that the people of Djogja, as the town is often called, have a special regard for Raffles. 'Does the name of this street—Djalan Malioboro—mean anything to you?' a Djogjanese asked me as we walked down the road that leads from the Sultan's palace to the rice-fields. 'Nothing,' I replied, 'except that I have never seen it before.' 'It dates from Raffles' days,' he answered. 'It was named after the British soldier, John Churchill, Duke of Marlborough. In our ears the word sounded like Malioboro. When the Republic came we changed many names, Julianaweg, for instance, became Djalan Sjahrir—but we kept Malioboro in honour of Raffles.' Another Javanized English phrase, also dating from the interregnum, is 'Garudo Pati', which is how the words 'Garden Party' sounded to an Indonesian ear.

From dawn till midnight Malioburo Road presents the life of Djogjakarta and the countryside stretching from the Merapi Mountain to the Indian Ocean. As dawn breaks, a procession of men and women, mainly women, arrives with produce for the market and shops. Women, with rutted faces, raggedly dressed, carry bundles of food, fruit, fowls, vegetables heaped on their backs so that they appear permanently doubled up. Some of them will squat on the wide pavement, display their goods around them and stay till midnight when the crowds begin to thin out. In the early morning as shops open, sarongs and kabayas in mellow browns and blues specially loved by Djogjanese are piled high up on the pavements like piles of newspapers; stacks of locally made cigarettes; kitchen utensils, large flat baskets of rice, knick-knacks, trays of Djogja silver, all kinds of haberdashery and large black hairpins; vegetables washed and tied in bundles or piled in heaps; mandarins and mango-steens and the auburn-haired chestnut-like rambustan, and in their seasons durians with the sweet-sour-caramel-custard-vinegar flavour without parallel and without equal; sandals and slippers; books and writing paper and fountain pens and pencils; bunches of carnations, asters, azaleas, gladiolis, sun-flowers, and red cannal lilies. And I once saw anklungs stacked on the pavement; they were enough for an orchestra, and must have been made locally from bamboo tubes graded to make an unusual percussion sound when shaken. When night falls, tiny oil lamps surround these pavement stalls and business is sharper than during the long hours of sunshine.

By the time the shops open, the second procession has begun; this time they are students, walking or on bicycles. For Djogja-karta is now a university town where five thousand young men and women crowd in buildings which were once the Sultan's palace. They come from all parts of Indonesia. Djogja was the Republic's first capital, the centre of political struggle and the first university where all the teaching is in Bahasa Indonesia. Here the Republican Parliament met in the large building which in Dutch times was a theosophical headquarters. In a side street, next door to the main post office, the Republicans broadcast to the world under the title of 'The Voice of Free Indonesia'. Here, President Sukarno was sworn in as the first President of the Republic of the United States of Indonesia, and here the first generation of Republican civil servants had responsibility for running a central administration. Many who are now working in the bigger, noisier, Europeanized city of Djakarta talk nostalgically of those early times in Djogja, days when the idealism of nationalist struggle had not changed into a period of political victory and competition for ministerial and other posts. Many who watch queues for Western-style palace-cinemas showing the cheaper sensational Western films and dance halls featuring Western dance orchestras in Djakarta, Bandung, and Surabaya, feel that Djogjakarta is still the centre of their own culture. 'You must go to Djogja,' they say, 'if you

34

want to see a performance of wayang, or Javanese dancing, if you want to buy fine batik or handsome silverwork.' So Djogjakarta seems to combine the past and the present, Javanese culture and Republican ideals; it is an Indonesian town, not a Dutch suburb. Even when the Dutch ruled the country, this town was always included as a show place where tourists could 'study native life at its best', as the guide books described it. To the colonial Power this meant feudal glory and subservient craftsmen; to the Republican Javanese there still seems too much poverty, but the craftsmen are no longer subservient.

By comparison with Djakarta, the streets of Djogjakarta are almost rural; the stream of official cars, the traffic of business and the crowded trams are absent; the people have the more careless, sometimes ragged appearance of peasants and the few who are richer often dress in the old-fashioned clothes of Javanese aristocracy; they are the equivalent of Victorian gentlemen. But there are many signs of change that show Djogjakarta is moving with Republican times; the crowded university where once the Sultan held court; the medical centre from which Dr. Kodiat's team of nurses go forth every morning to inject thousands of poor men, women, and children in the surrounding villages where framboesia afflicts a high proportion of them; the dancing school in the Sultan's palace where more than five hundred children learn Javanese dances that only the Sultan's family could perform in Dutch times; and the town's Assembly elected from the people with the Sultan as a member—a revolutionary change from the days when he was a reigning prince with complete power over his subjects whilst he himself owed allegiance only to the Dutch. The Republic has made its impact more healthily than in the more Westernized cities of Java, and modernization does not spell disintegration and conflict between the new and the old.

Around Djogjakarta as elsewhere in Java, the towns and the villages are densely overcrowded. It seems impossible to make any big changes in the standard of living unless and until more people are able and willing to move to the other islands where land and raw materials await development, where thousands of acres of rich land are uninhabited. A colonial Power could escape the consequences of the unequal development of these three thousand islands; the Republic cannot do so. The Dutch were not prepared to use their surplus wealth and officials for the 'outer islands' as they were called; such surplus went to the mother country. But the Republic must pay attention to islands other than Java.

NOTES

[1] Extract from Captain Travers' Journal of the voyage, quoted in *Memoir of Sir Thomas Stamford Raffles*, by Lady Raffles, p. 277. John Murray, 1830.

[2] Ibid., p. 286.

[3] Ibid., p. 286.

[4] *History of the Netherlands East Indies*, by E. S. de Klerck, vol. 2, p. 124. Published by W. L. and J. Brusse, N.V. Rotterdam, 1938.

[5] Ibid., p. 158.

[6] *Singapore Chronicle*, November 10th, 1825. From *Notes of the Indian Archipelago and Adjacent Countries*, by J. H. Moor (editor, *Singapore Chronicle*), p. 154. Published Singapore, 1837.

[7] *The Dutch East Indies*, by Amry Vandenbosch, 1941 (third edition, 1942), pp. 155–6. University of California Press.

[8] *Javanese Peasant Life*. Thesis submitted for Academic Post-graduate Diploma in Anthropology, University of London, by Hurustiati Subandrio, 1951, pp. 182–3.

CHAPTER III

SUMATRA FOR ENTERPRISE

SUMATRA is twice the size of Britain, thirteen times the size of Holland, and its population is just about the same as that of Greater London. The island is so long, and east so effectively divided from west by high jungle-covered mountains, that any story of it involves a separate consideration of the hinterland of its four main towns: Palembang in the southern part of the east coast and Medan in the north, Kutaraja at the northern tip and Padang in the west, on the shores of the Indian Ocean. In Dutch times there was little contact between these towns. They looked outwards to the west, to Malaya and to Java, for their importance was based entirely on the riches of their immediate hinterland. Between Medan and Palembang, a distance of about 600 miles, the land remains mainly swamp and jungle and a flight from Palembang to Padang takes the traveller over almost uninterrupted green jungle forest.

For the favoured few—civil servants, traders, and the occasional foreign visitor—Garuda Indonesian Airways brings the whole of Sumatra on to the screen of experience. Every morning Garuda planes fly from Djakarta to Palembang, 300 miles away. The name 'Garuda' was suggested by President Sukarno; it signifies the mythological bird which carried the Hindu god Vishnu safely and quickly on all his journeys.

Palembang

The tobacco-fields were a dark apple green as the plane brought me over them one morning in the spring of 1951. Here and there were large brick buildings, drying-houses for tobacco. Green jungle, green mangrove swamps, green plantations; the colour never changed, only the shade. There are tigers on the edge of the jungle, and if Garuda, carrying human, not

37

godly, passengers, had dropped us into the green entanglement
of trees and creepers, we might have had the good fortune to
fall to the accompaniment of trumpeting elephants. But we
landed safely on a thin red airstrip, narrow and isolated in a
clearing originally made by the Japanese in 1942. A red sand-
stone road led into Palembang, about ten miles away. On both
sides the jungle grew down to the edge, lining the road with
large green treeferns, purple rhododendrons, yellow and red
hibiscus.

Overlooking the town, which wanders alongside the River
Musi and its straggling tributaries, a hospital and a Resistance
cemetery stood proudly defying the jungle. The hospital was
the first to be built by civic authorities; in a town with 300,000
inhabitants, the only hospital accommodation had previously
been provided by the military and a Catholic Mission. A simple
stone monument, painted with red and white stripes—the
national colours—stood, unadorned and impressive. One part of
the cemetery was now full and wooden crosses told of the death
of men who had fallen in 1947 when Dutch troops tried to re-
occupy the country. Newly made graves were covered with elaborate flowers of silvered lilies and wreaths; they paid tribute
to guerrilla fighters whose bodies had only recently been
recovered from their temporary homes in the jungle.

Many wars have been fought for the possession of this town,
with its waterways, its face open to the China Sea, and its
strategic site controlling the Java Sea. It was one of the first
places the Hindus colonized. In about A.D. 683 Palembang was
the capital city of the Sriwidjaja kingdom which became the
great naval power of Western Indonesia. Apart from a very few
Buddhist statues, in stone and in bronze, and the oldest inscriptions of which the date is known, Palembang today shows no
trace of its earliest and its medieval history. Chinese, Indian,
Portuguese, Dutch, British, and American traders, and in that
order, have all contributed to its present prosperity; it is now
the largest city in Sumatra and the centre of oil refineries, ship-
building, rubber-milling, coffee-growing, with rich tin-mines in
the nearby island of Bangka.

The history of Palembang, as indeed of Sumatra, after the

conquest of Madjapahit by Muslims from South India, is mainly the struggle between British and Dutch for its possession. It was not only the richest and most accessible part of the island, but it controlled the Straits of Malacca, the shortest sea-route between Europe and the countries of the Pacific. With his eye on the rich tin ores in Bangka, Raffles was able to play off the Sultan against the Dutch and to strike with him a profitable bargain; the islands of Bangka and Billiton, and with them the whole tin production of the archipelago, were ceded to the British. When Holland and Britain agreed on their respective spheres of influence in 1824, these tin islands were handed over, not to the Sultan, but to the Dutch Government.

The Sultans of Palembang were difficult people to subdue and the Dutch had to meet their resistance as well as that of the organized guerrillas in the uplands. Most famous of them was Sultan Taha who came to power in 1858. He refused to acknowledge Dutch sovereignty on his accession whereupon the Dutch Resident organized a military expedition. When he refused to climb down, his Kraton was occupied and he himself escaped to the interior. When his son refused to succeed him, the Dutch Resident found a tame uncle who was willing to obey him. But the people were unwilling to accept him; 'The inaugurated prince', Mr. de Klerck writes, 'had simply been appointed as an agent or representative of the Sultan, thus a mere jackstraw of a dethroned prince'.[1] Sultan Taha and his son continued to resist Dutch pressure until 1886, when the Crown Prince agreed to become Sultan of Palembang. But a few years later, he refused to co-operate with Dutch officials with the result that he was compelled to abdicate. The Dutch Resident, finding no suitable successor, took over the administration of the sultanate himself in February 1901. His rule extended only over the town and a short way up the river. To extend their rule, a Dutch military expedition was sent to the interior. But there they came across Sultan Taha again and discovered that his authority was still acknowledged by the people. Dutch troops were reinforced but resistance continued until 1904, when the Sultan was killed and his brother died.

Palembang soon became a boom town. British and Dutch

capital were both poured into the development of oil-wells in its vicinity. By 1912, production was already over the million-ton mark, and at this point, Americans succeeded in investing their dollars. The Standard Oil Company was given a concession and formed the Dutch Colonial Petroleum Company. Production increased so rapidly that by 1938 the Palembang oil-fields contributed over five out of the total eight million tons figure for the whole of Indonesia. Meanwhile Bangka and Billiton had a similar boom period in tin production.

When the Japanese invaded the country, Palembang was one of the first targets. Eight hundred parachutists were dropped to surround the installations. Many of them were killed. Later, when ships landed thousands of Japanese troops, they found machinery had already been destroyed. But it was put into action again, and, for the rest of the war, the Japanese depended primarily on Palembang for their oil supplies.

Palembang is still a very prosperous town, and the main commercial centre as well as the capital of South Sumatra. The 'show place' is Pladju across the river. Here, oil refineries and a vast housing estate appear like a modern industrial city dropped into the middle of swamps and rivers ambling in all directions down to the sea.

Medan

From Palembang, Garuda Indonesian Airways flew 600 miles north-westwards, crossing the Equator about half-way, until the plane landed me in Medan, the second large town on Sumatra's east coast. It is a lonely journey over swamps and jungle which stretch almost up to the long mountain midriff of the island. When the mountains come down nearer to the sea, about a hundred miles south of Medan, the scenery changes to seemingly endless miles of tobacco plantations.

'Is this a Dutch provincial town?' I asked myself on arrival in Medan. Round the main square, the hotels were Dutch-owned and run, and palatial offices carried well-known Dutch names—the Java Bank, Nederlandsche Maatschappij—and a few English ones. Banks were the size of city halls, and churches might have been lifted up from Dutch towns, and outside the

city's centre tree-lined streets ran, straight and tidy, between
the Dutch-type bungalows built for Europeans. A stroll round
the Mosque—probably the grandest in Indonesia—on a Friday
morning soon dispels the illusion that this is a European town, as
thousands of Indonesians, all wearing their black velvet caps,
make their weekly visit to chant the Koran and say their prayers.
A few streets away, in Indonesia's largest market, all the trade
seemed to be in Indian or Chinese hands, and Indonesians
merely their customers. The same was true in hundreds of small
shops piled high with textiles from India and Japan and sold by
Indians, and of food and fruit shops where industrious Chinese
were the salesmen. Business, business, business in main streets
and side streets. Only one solitary person seemed withdrawn
from money-making. He was an Indonesian boy with a stall of
book oddments, guide books, a few ancient Penguins (*The Merchant of Venice, Richard II*, and *Julius Caesar*, priced 6*d.* now selling for a rupiah—the equivalent of 1*s.* 6*d.*) and a variety of dic-
tonaries and grammar books. The boy was learning English
whilst passers-by thumbed his wares. He seemed very glad to
treat me, not as a customer, but as someone on whom to practise
his few English words.

The centre of Medan on a Sunday morning is like a Dutch
provincial town. Banks and offices are closed, Europeans walk
solemnly to church and on their way home sip iced drinks
on the wide verandas of Dutch-owned hotels. The Chinese are
never still; vendors pad quickly through the streets with a
variety of foods, hot and cold, cooked and ready to cook, cakes
and ice creams, sweetmeats wrapped in small neat strips of
banana leaves. Their shops are piled ceiling-high with dried
fish in grotesque shapes, their shelves with sauces and teas and
tins of fruit. One Sunday morning I found an Indian salesman
who had time between his sales of expensive brocade for ceremonial kains (the Indonesian skirt), floral silks and organdies for
kabayas (a kind of blouse-jacket) to describe events in Medan
during the war.

When Singapore fell, Sumatra lay open for the Japanese army.
They crossed over from Malaya in March 1942. Suddenly, on a
Sunday morning, the Indian told me, hundreds of Japanese

appeared in the streets on bicycles. Chinese shopkeepers at once put up their shutters and scuttled off to the countryside. Many Indonesians greeted the Japanese with the word 'Banzai'—welcome. The cyclists were followed by troops in armoured cars and other motorized vehicles and treated as 'liberators'. Dutch residents were rounded up and taken off to internment camps. Their palatial offices and all town buildings were taken over by the Japanese army which moved in and settled down. As time went on, most Indonesians realized that the Japanese were as anxious to run Medan for the Japanese as the Dutch had been to run it for Dutchmen. But many worked in the various Ministries, others joined up with the army.

The division of opinion on this question of co-operation is still real and arguments still take place between those who worked with a certain enthusiasm for their temporary rulers and those who realized that a new chapter had started in their struggle for independence. Most Indonesians, however, were agreed that the Japanese were often crude and uncivilized in their everyday relations. This was what had struck my Indian informant. 'They seemed to consider it their right,' he remarked, 'to slap everyone they met on the face. In the second year,' he continued, 'they forced us all to work for them in the fields. We tried every trick to escape and always worked as slowly as possible when the Japanese guards were absent.' I heard a similar story from a Pakistani student in a Mission College. When the Japanese advance guard entered Medan he cycled off to a small place, Siantar, about fifty miles away, and found a job in the office of a Dutch firm. But the Japanese caught up with him, and within a few weeks his Dutch employers were taken off to an internment camp and the office was used for the administrative staff of the army. The Pakistani stayed on. 'This was a good experience,' he added. 'The Japanese were extremely efficient, and I learnt office technique. From time to time we were all forced to work in the rice-fields; we went out in groups as if we were under military discipline. As time went on, they became more and more cruel and if they suspected any lack of enthusiasm for their cause they simply beat up their victims. Every one of us had to make three bows to their Emperor as we entered the building. The end came very suddenly. When the British arrived in 1945 we welcomed them until we realized that they were bringing back the Dutch army. Still,' he concluded, 'the Dutch never behaved like the Japanese. Many people used to think the Japanese were the most advanced of any Asian nation. They know better now. The Japanese could never again win the respect of the countries they occupied.'

Plantations of tobacco and rubber, palm and tea stretch for miles round Medan, to the north and the south and the west. Their rich crops explain the palatial offices in this town which was only a swampy village less than a hundred years ago. But in the middle of that village Mynheer Nienhuys lived in a small hut making experiments in growing tobacco. He found that the fertile soil of Deli, as this part of East Sumatra is called, was perfectly suited for his purpose. In 1863 he obtained from the Sultan of Deli a ninety-nine-year concession for a thousand bau. Six years later, the Deli Maatschappij was founded and the tobacco rush had begun. Exports of tobacco which were worth just over $3\frac{1}{2}$ million florins in 1870 had soared to 32 million florins by 1900. The Deli company had built a railway and the harbour of Belawan was already under construction.

Like a gold rush, the tobacco rush introduced many new problems into lands which had not before attracted capital. To begin with, Europeans persuaded a number of local Sultans to give them concessions. The Sultans were not always unsuspecting and unworldly in their contracts with the foreigner, and they cared as little as he did for the rights of the plantation workers. Their extravagantly decorated palaces are as striking a testimony to their personal benefits from the tobacco rush as the palatial offices of Deli Maatschappij. In twenty years, 170 tobacco concerns were started in Deli, each one of them the result of local concessions. The tobacco rush brought with it abuses associated with every rush. The problem was one of cheap labour in an area where population was very thin. The Coolie Ordinance of 1880 (revised in 1889) applied to the east coast of Sumatra, and similar Ordinances were drawn up for other parts of the island. Workers had to be recruited under a contract and registered by an official. But one of the clauses, known as the Penal Sanction, led to the appalling conditions which subsequently became the subject of an Inquiry by the International Labour Office. When workers, recruited mainly from China and Java, had finished their contracts which were often signed in ignorance of their real meaning, they were virtually bound to renew them. As a rule they hadn't enough money to return home, and if they tried to escape, as they often did, they could then be brought to justice, as the process was termed. In practice it meant that they had no option but to stay on in the plantations. Coolie agents were often as unscrupulous as slave-traders. At last, Colonial Minister Cremer (whose own fortunes had been made in Deli) was challenged in the Dutch Parliament by Van Kol, an engineer in the Public Works Department in Indonesia, who, after being dismissed for political reasons, had become a Socialist M.P. He read out advertisements of coolie agents who undertook to export shiploads of 'prime quality labourers, carefully selected, sturdy, young, physically sound and strong'.[2] The Minister dismissed the charges as unwarranted gossip. But he was forgetting the possibility of Dutchmen in Medan taking action. The 'Indische Bund' organized a public protest meeting against these coolie agents and the agitation was sustained by a well-documented pamphlet, *De Millioenen uit Deli* (*The Millions from Deli*). The author was a Dutch lawyer, Mr. van den Brand. When conditions were still as disgraceful a year later, he returned to the attack in a second pamphlet, *Nog eens de Millioenen uit Deli* (*The Millions from Deli Once More*). Finally, Socialist agitation secured the setting up of a Commission by the Government. Mr. van den Brand's accusation that thousands of Chinese coolies and coolies from Java were living in conditions of slavery was completely confirmed. In 1904, the Government imposed labour inspection, a model form of contract was drawn up, the police service was improved, and a Court of Justice established in Medan. Five years later, official agents were appointed to obtain Chinese coolies from abroad, either through the Protector of Chinese in Singapore or through an official bureau in Swatow, whilst men who were recruiting coolies in Java were now placed under supervision. But the Penal Sanction remained, and in

1931, only about one-quarter of the imported labourers were free or 'non-contract'.

Pressure then came from unexpected quarters to improve the conditions of workers on tobacco plantations. In the United States, which was the best market for the famous Deli cigar leaves, the Blaine Amendment to the Tariff Law of 1930 prohibited the entry of any products made by any form of forced labour unless they could not be made inside America in large enough quantities to meet their needs. And, in the same year, the question of labour contracts with penal sanctions was placed on the agenda of the International Labour Conference in Geneva. The plantation owners, seeing the red light, announced their intention of employing only free labour in the future.

Hadji Agus Salim (one of the most widely known Indonesian nationalists) was appointed by the Dutch Trade Unions as their representative in the Workers' Section of the Committee on Forced Labour set up by the I.L.O. The Dutch Government had Javanese princes as their advisers; Raden Djajadiningrat and Raden Adipati Ario Soejono shared the honour between them. Hadji Agus Salim pointed out that although the Dutch Government had now declared its intention to abolish forced labour, public opinion was still needed to ensure that such intentions were fulfilled. His main attack was directed towards the local chiefs whose revenue depended on the number of persons subject to forced labour, and the absence of any measure of control that only fit adult inhabitants were called out. He described conditions in South Sumatra:

'We have here', he said, 'the regulation forced labour four times a year, each period being of nine days, of which two days are for travelling, to and from the work, 42 kilometres away from the village—a total of 36 days. Then there are four kinds of emergency cases, 7 days each, which makes 28 days. Then there is village work, five times a year, three days each, which makes 15 days. Then there is the so-called *koeli bacha* (full moon work) for the repair of roads and cleansing of growths, the repair of bridges and ditches along the minor roads, all within the border of the "marga" that is the territory of a chief. It takes 7 days each time and may come to 10

45

or even 12 days sometimes so that we can take for that 84 days. Then fifthly for carrying the post the period is 2 days. The rounds vary between 1 kilometre and 27 kilometres. It may occur that a man is called out every month. We will put it at 10 times a year making 20 days. Then there is porterage for chiefs of which there are 6 kinds.'[3]

The speaker went on to say that he himself had been in Palembang in 1928 and had found by investigation that 100 to 150 days a year was no exception for this kind of forced labour, which would not be made honourable and just by simply calling it a substitution for a tax as the Dutch had done. 'It has been *heerendienst* or *service du seigneur*, since its beginning a service laid by the sovereign master upon his subject, as his slave and his serf.' It was an institution which the Dutch Government continued on the grounds that otherwise local labour would not be forthcoming for the chiefs through whom they ruled. Economic pressure, world opinion as reflected in the I.L.O., plus a growing criticism of forced labour among Dutchmen as well as among Indonesian Nationalists persuaded the Dutch Government that the system of Penal Sanctions must end by 1946. They took steps to bring this about. But by 1946, many unforeseen, unimagined changes had taken place. The Republic was already in existence, and, although it was under heavy fire from Dutchmen, its Constitution laid down the responsibilities of trade unions in protecting the workers. Hadji Agus Salim became Foreign Minister in Dr. Hatta's Cabinet in January 1948, which lasted until the transfer of Dutch sovereignty in December 1949. He was then appointed an adviser to the Foreign Ministry in which post he remained until he died in November 1954.

Today, plantation workers in Deli belong to one of three trade unions: S.A.R.B.U.P.R.I. (Union of Estate Workers' Organizations), P.E.R.B.U.P.R.I. (Federation of Estate Workers' Organizations), and the much smaller S.B.I.I. (Islamic Labour Union). The plantations, many of them neglected and some of them destroyed during the post-war efforts of Dutchmen to reimpose colonial rule, were returned to their owners, with the exception of about 230,000 hectares of land which were given to the people for farming. About 80% of the pre-war planters, unwilling to face the changed conditions, returned to Holland. Younger men with a different background, who have not experienced the profitable days of the Penal Sanctions, have taken their place, and an increasing number of Indonesians are being given responsible positions in administration. The trade unions are strongly organized, and it was with a trade union leader that I visited plantations near Medan. We started off in a car along a track parallel to a narrow railway line now practically derelict. We soon dumped the car and then walked through stretches of young tobacco plants which were being sprayed one by one by girls and women. How picturesque it was; dark brown girls and women in a variety of coloured, sometimes ragged, kains and kabayas, the dark green tobacco leaves, the bright blue sky, and in the distance the bluer mountains. To these very photogenic workers, the main problem was the cost of living, the cost of textiles, and crowded homes. Not one of them had been to school. They all belonged to a trade union.

'Would you like to see where they live?' the Chairman asked me. We walked on for another mile and for the first time I knew the meaning of the phrase 'housing lines'—a phrase used in Asia by Western traders to describe the barrack-like rows of houses in which their workers live. I used the word 'barracks', but no army would allow its soldiers to live in such conditions. The place swarmed with women and children, fowls, chicken, and mangy dogs. The 'houses' consisted generally of one small room in which families lived and slept. Immediately alongside these hovels were open sewers; a few feet away a line of blocks of stone criss-crossed with dried wood served as kitchens. The women and children were ragged and dirty. Their conditions were very like those of the first coolies who were imported. The 'houses' were the same sheds, thrown together in the days of the tobacco rush and the boom in rubber. The contrast with the two tall blond Dutch planters who arrived at that moment was unforgettable; they appeared like two stars from an American musical comedy in their smart, neat shorts and their large floppy hats. We exchanged pleasantries; how

47

beautiful the countryside, how pleasant the eternal sunshine and how healthy the tobacco plants! But times were difficult: the men asking for more and more wages and doing less and less work; the Government placing more and more restrictions on trade, and more and more difficulties on sending home enough money to their wives and children in Holland. Presumably, as a European, I was on their side, and would sympathize with the hard lives of Dutch women. Dead silence met my suggestion that any of these women who stood around us in those wretched homes would be more than satisfied with a quarter of the amount planters were sending home. They replied: 'They don't know any better. They don't want anything else. They have hospitals a few kilometres away which they don't use.' The Chairman of the trade union reminded the planters of the efforts made by A.V.R.O.S. (The Association of Planters) to keep down wages, of the millions of florins taken as profits in the past. He had the better of the argument. It was clear that these two planters were well aware of the power which trade unions had in the Republican regime. It was true that the women could take their undernourished scabby children to a hospital. But it was miles away, and they had not yet understood their rights nor their privileges. In 1950 and 1951 owners of estates were building new hospitals or extending existing ones; the Deli Maatschappij, for example, had spent 8 million rupiahs on a hospital. The pressure of trade unions had already begun to have results in terms of social welfare as well as in wages and hours of work.

I wondered whether conditions were better on plantations run by British firms, and, finding that there was a British-owned rubber plantation in the district, I asked whether we could 'drop in' on the planter. It was a smallish plantation employing about 3,000 workers. They all belonged to a trade union, and the Chairman of the branch was warmhearted in his welcome. The planter lived within sight of his office; his residence with its fresh green lawns was like a well-kept English country house, comfortable but not large, a house, not a mansion. He offered to show me any statistics that would interest me. To my reply that I liked people so much more than figures, he took us to the clearing on the edge of the plantation and pointed out three very good individual houses built of bamboo and brick such as we had seen in hundreds driving through plantations owned by the Indonesian Government. 'This,' he said, 'is how all the workers will be housed. 'When were they built?' I asked. 'We've built these in the last year,' was his answer. With thinly-disguised reluctance he then accompanied us to another part of the plantation where all but the inhabitants of those three attractive houses still lived. The contrast was pronounced. Again the same 'housing lines'—probably the sheds built originally to house coolies from China or from Java in the early days, when rubber prices boomed, but not as highly as they boomed in 1951. The same open sewers, the same ragged women and scruffy children. Overcrowding was shocking. People invited me into their 'homes' which consisted of one small room in a long line of similar rooms all similarly housing men, women, and children.

It would be foolish to make any generalizations from such a limited knowledge of planation conditions. The trade union officials assured me that they were not at all exceptional. The larger plantations, they pointed out, were often better because more money was available for housing and other amenities. But the tremendous difference between the best living conditions on estates in East Sumatra and the poorest in Amsterdam remained.

Atjeh

Two roads lead northwards from the main square in Medan; one leads direct to the port of Belawan through which all its trade passes, and where a frequent passenger service runs to and from Singapore; the second wanders through miles of plantations, rubber, tobacco, palm trees, and fields of pepper, and passes, as its first town, the 'Coventry' of Sumatra—Pangkalan Brandan. But in this case the inhabitants set fire to it themselves in 1946 rather than let the Dutch troops occupy it, as they believed was their intention. I heard the story from the man who was then in charge of the Indonesian army in that district. The Dutch troops were only three kilometres away alongside a river which was the demarcation line between the two armies.

Pangkalan Brandan was an important riverine town with oil refineries. The news came through that the Dutch were planning to attack it, and three British soldiers who deserted from the Dutch army confirmed this in their story to the Indonesian officer. I tried to find out who these British soldiers were and what happened to them but without any success.

The Indonesian army local command took the desperate decision to evacuate the town and then to set fire to it to prevent it from falling into Dutch hands. Orders were given to the whole civilian population to leave and within two days without any loss of life 50,000 people had disappeared into the surrounding jungle villages. The next step was even more desperate; the army poured oil from the local refineries over the town and then set it on fire. The Dutch troops retreated further behind the cease-fire line, deciding not to take the risk of occupying the burning town.

We walked through lanes of ruins which the jungle would soon reclaim. A new town is now growing up in small clumps of houses and on the day we were there in spring 1951 we were shown the first oil plant to work again. We arrived—unannounced—at a very critical moment when the men were wholly concentrated on the first trickles of oil. We slithered up and down oily steps and a foreman explained the achievements of the men in remantling this oil-refining plant.

Along the road—there was only one road, of course, throughout the whole of North Sumatra, if by road you mean a modern highway—we smelt burning rubber. It isn't a pleasant smell as I knew to my cost when we called in to see Indonesia's first rubber remilling factory. The two young foremen were ex-guerrillas, and most of their workers had fought in the resistance movement. They were all trade union members with a forty-hour week. The factory, alongside a river, consisted of one large building like an English barn covered with corrugated iron. The latex was in heaps on the floor; men had collected it from the kampongs (villages) around, often buying up poor-quality, rather dirty latex which the big rubber merchants generally considered not worth while. The whole industry, which is a very big one in Indonesia, is in the hands of the Chinese, who have nothing to learn in the art of making a bargain. Gradually, Indonesians hope to build up their own industry. We sat down on bundles of rubber sheeting already packed for export like pieces of honeycomb. Bottles of orange crush appeared as they seemed miraculously to do on any and every occasion. 'Could I tell them the story of British trade unions?' these young rubber-milling pioneers asked. 'Did I know what happened to the three young English soldiers who deserted to their side?' 'Why had British troops helped the Dutch to come back?' Production figures must have fallen that afternoon. There was a happy team-spirit in this factory. 'Come back next year,' they suggested, 'and you'll see our mills extending far back into the jungle.'

In another village I came across a highly ingenious factory in a shed about forty feet by twenty. There was no equipment except a small printing machine hand-worked, and a hand machine such as knife-grinders used to wheel around English villages, turning a handle and running water from a small can on to the roller. In this Sumatran kampong, a young man who had been an engineer before the war, had collected a group of young men, also guerrillas, and set up a factory to make slate books. In the river nearby, the bed was covered with a fine ferrous dust; this was collected and then used as a coating for paper. The result was a book which took the place of a slate. 'The Atom Age Invention', the engineer called it, and the factory was named after Kartini, the daughter of a Javanese Regent, who pioneered for women's rights at the beginning of the century.

The road led on through more plantations, and followed most of the coastline until it reached Kutaradja, the capital of Atjeh, on the extreme northern tip of the island.

The Achinese have the reputation of being the toughest fighters, the most independent people in Indonesia, and the least attracted by reason. They were the last to be conquered by the Dutch, and it took expedition after expedition for nearly forty years to bring the country nominally under Dutch rule. Their country—the northern part of Sumatra—was the western gateway to the Indonesian archipelago. It was the nearest point to

Malacca in the fifteenth century when the throne of that kingdom was occupied by a Muslim, Mohammed Iskandar Shah. The result was that Atjeh was the first part of Indonesia to be converted to Islam. Their fierce devotion to Islam led Sultans to make 'holy wars' on other parts of Sumatra, until at one time their rule extended over almost the whole of the island. They combined religious fanaticism with a flourishing trade in pepper and they were powerful enough to resist the first of the European traders—the Portuguese. The Dutch who followed secured the right to build a fortified trading post in Kutaradja, but they were unable to make any journeys into the interior.

When Britain and Holland signed the Treaty of 1824, a special clause was inserted by which the Dutch agreed to respect Atjeh's independence. For fifty years, the Sultans and the Dutch Governors-General were usually at loggerheads; both countries were involved in profitable slave-trading expeditions to and from the Nias Islands along Sumatra's west coast; both tried to extend or to consolidate their positions in the interior and along the east coast. To the Dutch, the Achinese were pirates, slave-traders, and fanatical Muslims. To the Achinese their struggle combined trade with a holy war for the Prophet against Dutch infidels. The British, now busily occupied in developing Singapore, were not enthusiastic about Dutch policy; Lord Palmerston instructed his representative Distrowe to protest against 'encroachments of the Dutch', and in 1841 he regretted 'the hostile spirit and tendency of the proceedings of the Dutch authorities in the Indian seas with respect to British commerce'.

Disagreeable exchanges between these two empire-builders in Malaya and Sumatra ended only in 1871 when the Treaty of Sumatra rescinded Britain's special position in Atjeh and gave the Dutch a free hand. Atjeh now acquired additional significance by the opening of the Suez Canal, and the Sultan of Atjeh made advances towards Turkey, France, Italy, and the United States. British and Dutch Governments both saw potential rivals on the Asian horizon. Dutch authorities in Batavia organized several expeditions to Atjeh with the avowed object of putting down piracy. The Sultan's palace in Kutaradja was captured, the coast of Atjeh was blockaded, and still the Sultan and the people did not bow the knee to the Dutch Governor. In 1877, after vainly trying to win over some of the mountain chieftains, the Dutch tried to gain control of the valley of Atjeh at the head of which stood Kutaradja. Achinese guerrilla bands led by Teunku Ditiro and Teuku Umar and assisted by the ulamas—Muslim priests—continued the war in the mountains for the next ten years.

Teuku Umar then unexpectedly went over to the enemy. He defeated a number of local chiefs, but at the end of three years of this curious alliance, he returned to fight with his own countrymen, taking with him men, rifles, and cartridges. His decision proved to be a turning-point in the war.

Dutch policy now began to change towards large-scale, concentrated military operations. This was largely the result of a long and extremely detailed report on Atjeh by a Dutch scholar-agent, Professor Snouck Hurgronje, Professor of Islamic Law and Religion in Leyden. Posing as a Muslim, and adopting the name of Imam Abd al Gaffar, he spent six months in Mecca. The Atjeh war was then—in 1885—at a critical point for the Dutch, and in Mecca Muslims from all parts of the world discussed it with the disguised professor in terms of a 'holy war' against Dutch infidels. The Achinese boasted of their successes to their fellow-Muslims, and claimed that thousands of infidels had been destroyed.

Professor Snouck was ordered out of Mecca at a few hours' notice suspected of being a spy. He returned to Holland to write his report *De Atjehers*. He put forward the theory that the only way to defeat Atjeh was by large-scale military operations. His ideas were confirmed by Major van Heutz, another famous Dutchman associated with the Atjeh war. The professor and the soldier won the day. Military expeditions were increased, and slowly the war turned in Holland's favour. Teuku Umar was one of the toughest opponents and his death, in an ambush in 1899, was a serious loss to the Achinese. Van Heutz—now military and civil Governor, with Professor Snouck Hurgronje as his adviser,[4] subjugated the east coast, imposing fines and penalties on villages as leaders surrendered. He then turned to the west coast, adopting the same policy. The end of the war seemed in sight early in 1903 when the Sultan of Kutaradja surrendered, acknowledged Dutch sovereignty, and instructed local chiefs to desist from further resistance.

Van Heutz left Atjeh to become Governor-General of the Netherlands East Indies. His successors carried on the war to pacify districts where fighting continued, and to consolidate Dutch rule in others. When the Achinese began a well-organized campaign in 1907 along the north coast, the situation was so critical, and the methods of suppressing it caused such a storm of criticism in Holland, that Governor-General van Heutz returned himself to make an investigation. Tobacco plantations were booming along the east coast and he was shrewd enough to advise a more conciliatory policy which would lead to developing the rich tobacco land of Atjeh. Nevertheless, guerrilla bands supported by ulamas continued resistance until 1912.

On a balance-sheet of Dutch rule in Indonesia, Atjeh would probably show the smallest return. The Atjeh war alone cost over 4 million florins. Very few Dutchmen settled in a country where they were extremely unpopular. Until the end of their rule—in 1942—a garrison of Dutch troops was always maintained in Kutaradja.

In March of that year, Japanese troops landed; they spread out into two sections, one marching down the west coast to Singkal, the other taking the east coast to Idi. They occupied the two roads leading into the interior. When the Japanese troops left in 1945, the Dutch did not return. For the Achinese, Dutch rule ended in 1942.

The Japanese occupation which followed did not alter the structure of Achinese society. Like the Dutch they played off one group against another. The two largest groups which struggled for power were the uleebalang and the ulamas. The first were hereditary chiefs, appointed by the Sultanates; they were chairmen of the 'adat' (customary law) courts of justice and the religious heads in their respective districts. They were mainly feudal in outlook. The second, the ulamas, were fanatically religious, and wanted to see a society based on Islamic laws. They were opposed to the position of the uleebalang both as chairmen of the courts of justice and as religious heads. The Japanese, again like the Dutch, based their authority on the administration of the uleebalangs. When they left in 1945, conflict between the two groups was renewed and the ulamas proved to be the more powerful. The Central Government of the Republic, recognizing this situation, appointed ulamas in many government posts.

It was characteristic of Atjeh that orders from Djakarta were felt to be an interference in their own local affairs. And it was with great difficulty that the Achinese were persuaded to become part of the province of North Sumatra. In 1951 I never met an Achinese who did not speak with greater fervour than the most fervent Scottish Nationalist of the need for a greater measure of self-government. The government officials in Djakarta did not pay enough attention to the problem. Certain steps were taken in the very important matter of communications. Air and road services were built up between Medan and Kutaradja and other roads planned which would help to develop Atjeh as well as make administration easier. But all the schemes, whether they materialized or remained blueprints, did not satisfy the Achinese, any more than they solved the problems of social struggle or religious fanaticism.

In September 1953, a rebellion was launched by Tengku Daud Beureueh, Chairman of the religious group of ulamas as well as Military Governor in the early days of the Republic. He announced that henceforth Atjeh must be considered as part of the Indonesian Islamic State proclaimed by the leader of the Darul Islam, Kartosuwirjo. Militarily, the Central Government had the situation under control by the beginning of 1954 and Tengku Daud Beureueh's forces were reduced mainly to guerrilla bands in the mountains. Politically, promises were made to review plans for regional autonomy. Economically, new proposals were made for developing the resources of Atjeh. But the fact remains that the people of Atjeh are not yet convinced that a central authority is necessary for efficiency and that it does not necessarily conflict with individual freedom. The ulamas still fight for an Islamic State. The uleebalangs still hope to retain their feudal structure. The problem still remains of how to build a stable Atjeh which feels an integral part of the Republic.

Padang and Benkulen

The road from Medan on the straits of Malacca to Padang on the shores of the Indian Ocean passes round one of the most famous beauty spots in Indonesia—Lake Toba. In 1951, men were busily repairing roads and bridges, not because of heavy traffic, nor because high plateau walls descending sharply into the lake had fallen in, but because guerrilla bands had destroyed them in 1949 to stop the oncoming Dutch troops. Here and there in the villages tidy little cemeteries with simple wooden crosses and red and white flowers commemorate their courage in this, the last battle for their independence.

Lake Toba is the home of the Bataks, the second largest group in Sumatra. At the beginning of the nineteenth century German Missions started schools among them—there are about a million—and 80,000 of them are Christians. In many villages, a small tin-roofed church takes the place of the mosque, and, in Medan, the Bataks have their own church, built in German style with a Batak minister. Like the Menangkabau, Bataks still have communal houses, with curving roofs decorated at each end with horned heads, and totemistic carving. A traditional village consists of a small compound in which several of these long houses form the centre. You climb up a tree trunk notched to make steps, into the long house where each family has its own allotted space. Young men usually have their own long house. In the centre of the compound there is an open platform with a saddle-backed roof where the village council meets; buildings where rice is stored and communally owned; smaller sheds where women pound the rice on large round stones. It was highly photogenic. But within a generation such villages will be looked on as merely picturesque survivals. Their long, dark, crowded interiors, lacking all privacy, will certainly not satisfy the children who greet you in overcrowded schools.

Beyond the Batak lands the Padang Highlands of West Sumatra stretch down to the Indian Ocean. For me Padang will always be associated with small buggies clattering along cobbled stones to the accompaniment of tinkling bells on small wiry ponies dressed in silvered or painted harness. Padangese are proud of their ponies, and no one is allowed to keep them on the hot streets for more than six hours a day. When money-shrewd Chinese wanted to introduce *betjas* (cycle rickshaws) into the town in 1950, the local council unanimously opposed it on the grounds that it was undignified for human beings to drag others along, even if they were riding on bicycles.

The Wali Kota (corresponding to our mayor) was a doctor by profession, a local leader of the resistance movement, and local history was his hobby. He reminded me of the close associations which Britain had had with Sumatra's west coast for nearly three hundred years. When Dutch and then British traders arrived in the seventeenth century the west coast was ruled by Rajahs under the Sultana of Atjeh. Dutchmen won her neutrality with presents of tin, whilst they fomented revolts against her among her vassals. Finally, the East India Company promised their protection to Padang in exchange for a monopoly of pepper. On no account, the Dutch Governor was told, must Englishmen be allowed to trade in this town; they must only be permitted to get wood and water. The three nameless stone graves which lie on the seashore today are commonly believed, the mayor said, to belong to three Englishmen who dared to challenge Dutch monopoly.

For more than a century, Dutch traders had only one foreign rival on Sumatra's west coast—the English East India Company which was able to gain a footing in a little swampy town to the south of Padang. Here, in Benkulen, they built Fort Marlborough to protect their trade in pepper, spices, and coffee. When the Netherlands East Indies was handed back to the Dutch in 1816, there were local difficulties, and it was not until 1818 that Sir Thomas Raffles, then Governor-General of Benkulen, arrived to make arrangements for the transfer of power. He assembled all the Company's slaves before the local chiefs, explained British policy to them and then presented a certificate of freedom to them all. He stopped compulsory coffee-growing and he put an end to cock-fighting farms. While at

Benkulen he wrote to Mr. William Wilberforce, saying how much he wished that some of his attention could be

> 'directed to the Malay, the Javan, the Sumatran, the Bornean, the Avanese, the Siamese, the Chinese, the Japanese, and the millions of others with whom I am in daily communication, and to whom the name of William Wilberforce, if not entirely unknown, is only coupled with that of Africa.'[5]

On the west coast of Sumatra he made many expeditions into the Padang Highlands, where Dutchmen had never considered it safe to wander. He was tremendously impressed, as the visitor is today, by 'the grandeur of the vegetation; the magnitude of the flowers, creepers, and trees, contrasts strikingly with the stunted and, I had almost said, pigmy vegetation of England'.[6] He made many friends among the Menangkabau, finding them extremely intelligent and independent people with a matriarchal society. He met Muslim priests known as Padris who were dressed in white cloaks. At that time, they were making a fanatical campaign against such customs as betting, opium, and strong drink, all of which they considered to be against the Koran. They were violently opposed to the return of Dutch rule, to which they ascribed many of these evils.

When Raffles reluctantly handed back the administration of Padang and Benkulen to the Dutch, the Padris led a rebellion against them. It was partly religious, partly political, and it had the support of the people. When Dutch troops were sent into the Padang Highlands they found every village turned into a fortification. Again and again, their expeditions made little headway. Padris were defeated in one district, but rebellion at once broke out elsewhere. After nine years—in 1832—when Lt.-Col. Vermeulen Krieger thought the enemy was finally defeated at a place called Bonjol, the Padris regrouped their forces once more and the Dutch fell back again. Everywhere they were unpopular; they polluted mosques, they requisitioned food from the villages, and reintroduced opium.

At this point a decision was taken in Batavia to organize a new offensive. Troops were sent from Java, but they too were defeated. Finally, Governor-General Van den Bosch himself disembarked at Padang at the end of August 1832 and yet another expedition was sent against the centre of resistance—Bonjol. Van den Bosch divided his army into three separate columns nicely timed to arrive simultaneously from different directions and then to surround the town. Only one column arrived, the others, as E. S. de Klerck describes, 'being delayed by unforeseen hindrances on the way, and had, moreover, to contend with the obstinacy of auxiliaries and coolies'.[7] Once more the Dutch had to fall back. Other parts of the Menangkabau territory were taken, but it was not until 1835 that a final campaign was planned against Bonjol. The fortress defended by Teunku Imam seemed invincible. Reinforcements from Java were needed again and again. Indeed, it was not until August 18th, 1837, after Teunku Imam had defended the fortress of Bonjol for two years and a half, that Dutch troops were able to enter. With the fall of Bonjol, Dutch authority was established in Central Sumatra.

Imam Bonjol—as Teunku Imam was called after his brave leadership—is the great hero among the Menangkabau. There are songs and poems about him, books written about him, and his photograph is the most popular in private homes as it is in public buildings. Side by side with him one finds not only President Sukarno, but Dr. Hatta; he was born in Bukit Tinggi, a town built by the Dutch as a fort against the Padris. They named it Fort de Kock, after their Commander. Other distinguished Republican leaders from this part of Sumatra are Sjahrir and Natsir (both Prime Ministers), Mohamad Yamin (at present Minister of Education), and the late Hadji Agus Salim. The Padang area is one of the political nerve-centres of the country, and the Menangkabau the most politically-minded.

A short walk across the wide green maidan in Padang provides a short, vivid history of the Menangkabau. Two simple stone monuments stand on the edge of the maidan. The smaller records the foundation of the Youth Movement in Sumatra in 1910; the other tells how, in 1924, the Sumatran youth were responsible for a United Youth Movement, established in Djakarta. When Japanese troops occupied the town in 1942, these two monuments were left standing. They equally well understood national susceptibilities when they destroyed the large Dutch monument which stood in the centre of the maidan as an unpleasant reminder of their final victory in the war with Atjeh. They acquired a certain popularity by pulling down the offending General and putting in his place a Japanese garden with a decorated bridge surrounded by cherry trees. Nearly four years later when British troops arrived with Dutch troops, the bridge was taken down, the cherry trees removed, and the maidan became a barracks. Today, the finest monument in Indonesia stands there as tall and as white as a lighthouse, proclaiming Indonesian independence. Three and a half steps lead up to it, symbolizing three and a half centuries of Dutch occupation. At one point they are gashed with a sword illustrating the short period when Japanese occupied the country. With a simple elegance, this Pantja Sila monument consists of five white pillars joined together, representing the five principles of the Republic: belief in God, sovereignty of the people, nationalism, social justice, and belief in the equality of all men. An undecorated globe stands over the five pillars. Around the plinth, carved in silver by two local artists, is the story of the Menangkabau. It begins with the favourite story of the buffaloes. In the days of the Javanese kingdom of Madjapahit, the Javanese coveted the rich lands of West Sumatra and sent an expedition in eight ships to conquer them. Their idea of conquest was original; let two buffaloes fight a duel, they said, and the winning buffalo would decide the ownership of the land. The Menangkabaus took a young buffalo from its mother, starved it of milk for a day and a night. They then fixed sharp knives into the brow where its horns had not yet grown. The Javanese produced a fine large specimen of a buffalo. When the fight began, the young one dashed to the old buffalo's belly, searching for milk, but finding no udders to suck, the young buffalo's knives gashed deeply into his rival's flesh, and he ran away. 'Menang Kerbau! Menang Kerbau!' the people shouted —'Our buffalo wins', in other words. Hence the name Menang Kerbau. The Javanese are said to have accepted the verdict, the people called themselves Menangkabau, and they then set out to conquer the whole of Central Sumatra. They fought wars with the Achinese who were then, as now, fanatical followers of the Prophet and the Menangkabau became their first converts. The story then describes another favourite, Ayam Kinantan the prize cockerel, and this passes on to the time when the Dutch came in boats and stayed to conquer through the Company— the Dutch East Indies. At this point the artists decided to picture the life of the Menangkabau people; their ceremonies, the charono and brass mats indicating their welcome to guests and their friendship for all. The story goes on to a period of struggle, with spears and cannons in the forests. Finally, the Republic built with materials from the jungle, by carpenters and other workers who also symbolize industry. On the columns of the memorial were poems by local writers. The first one, written for the guerrillas by Husmaina:

> 'For us in this peaceful country
> You were killed amidst great sufferings and difficulties.
> We will remember you
> In the soul of our nation,
> The symbol of heroism
> For ever.'

Another verse, also by a local writer, reads like this:

> '*P* The struggle of Padang and the countryside
> *A* At the end the betel nut returns to its stem
> *D* We celebrate the day with feelings of joy.
> *A* Ours is a memorial for the nation
> *N* The Republic of Indonesia is our holy ambition.
> *G* Hold firm and remain for ever.'

The first stone of the memorial was laid by a woman who lost three sons in the two Dutch military actions. Its two entrance steps represented these two wars in 1947 and 1948, and guarding them was the stone carving of a boy, naked, holding an empty bamboo pole, both symbolizing resistance which began without any arms or organization.

It was no accident that there were local artists, stone-carvers, silver-workers, and poets to create this Pantja Sila monument. Menangkabauers are famous throughout Indonesia for their intricately carved houses, silver filigree work, fine kris blades, and the magnificence of their weaving and jewellery. But local talent is encouraged in a modern art school in Kajutaname, a few miles from Padang, and an art centre in Padang Pajang further up in the Highlands. The Principal and Founder of both school and art centre is a remarkable teacher, named Mohamad Shafei. As a young man, he belonged to the Sumatran Youth Movement. Later, in Holland, he decided to dedicate his life to education and became the educational expert of the Nationalist Movement: his colleague, Dr. Hatta, was the politician. Mohamad Shafei then spent several years in Shantineketan, and Rabindranath Tagore's approach to life and his methods of teaching were the inspiration of the school in Sumatra. Mohamad Shafei trained boys to become teachers of weaving and painting, of carving and pottery. They usually came from villages in Sumatra, and they returned home to share their experience with others. For Shafei was an inspired teacher and his students caught some of his inspiration. When the Republic was proclaimed in August 1945, he was appointed the first Minister of Education. But his heart was in the school and he was never persuaded to leave it to take part in the political life of Djogjakarta—the then capital. Indeed, he only became a more active politician in 1954 when he spoke in Parliament on the question of greater regional autonomy.

The school, as I saw it, consisted of half a dozen studios dotted about amidst small lakes. There were now girls and boys from all parts of Indonesia—the first batch sent down by the Ministry of Education to be trained as art teachers. The original school, holding four hundred students, was burnt down in 1948. As Dutch troops marched up from Padang, the students set fire to their buildings and escaped into the mountains to become guerrilla fighters; the Dutch completed the destruction. The most prized exhibits in the school today are photos of this unusual trek; of school books Shafei wrote whilst travelling from village to village; of his aged mother who was carried on a bamboo stretcher by the boys; of students who lost their lives in guerrilla action.

Everywhere in the Menangkabau country there is an

atmosphere of prosperity and a high standard of cultural and social activity. In Dutch times, students had to go to Djakarta or to Holland for advanced education. But in August 1951, a new university was opened in Padang. Trade unions were well organized and meetings I attended in a number of town halls showed not only a high level of political understanding but an intense interest in foreign affairs. Women's organizations were making a great contribution in all kinds of ways; they ran special schools for training girls in domestic science; they ran illiteracy classes in the villages; they trained girls to become nurses.

It was not surprising to find women playing such an important part in the life of the community. For here, among the million and a half Menangkabaus, there are still many customs which were part of their matriarchal society. Take the question of property; when the woman dies her property is inherited by her daughter, or her daughter's daughters, and only in the event of her direct descendants on the female side having died out completely is it inherited by the woman's brothers or sisters, the former for the period of their lives only, the latter down the female line of descent. This possession of property is only one, though an extremely important, reason why Menangkabau women have a special reputation throughout Indonesia for their independence and their dignity. But there are other reasons too; divorce is easy and based on incompatibility. Men are often merchants and traders, travelling from town to town, whilst the women run the homes, work in rice-fields and in coffee and tobacco plantations.

In most villages there are still a few traditional houses, their roofs ending in horns like a Chinese temple, their outside walls and doors intricately carved. They were built for a clan, in days when families lived together. Indeed, these houses were like small villages with as many as seventy people living in them, all of them descended from the same ancestral grandmother. The system is now rapidly dying out, and although families still hold together, sons and daughters begin to want their own lives and to live outside the villages or in some other part of the country. And wherever they go, their qualities of toughness, of independence and great ability assure them a welcome.

NOTES

[1] *History of the Netherlands East Indies*, by E. S. de Klerck, Vol. 2, p. 284. Published by W. L. and J. Brusse, Rotterdam, 1938.

[2] Quoted from *De Desa Pekalongan*, by Burger, p. 5, in *Netherlands India*, by J. S. Furnivall, p. 353, Cambridge University Press, 1939.

[3] Proceedings of I.L.O. Conference, June 20th, 1929.

[4] Professor Snouck Hurgronje wrote *The Achenese*, giving a detailed study of their history, customs, language, and religion.

[5] *Memoir of Sir Thomas Raffles*, by Lady Raffles, p. 410. Letter to Mr. W. Wilberforce (September 1819).

[6] Ibid., p. 317. Letter to the Duchess of Somerset (July 1818).

[7] *History of the Netherlands East Indies*, by E. S. de Klerck, Vol. 2, p. 251. Published by W. L. and J. Brusse, N.V. Rotterdam, 1938.

CHAPTER IV

KALIMANTAN (BORNEO) FOR PIONEERS

KALIMANTAN is like a vast mansion—it is the third largest island in the world—with a few open doors; most of its rooms are closed to the family of Indonesia as they are to the outside world. I walked through some of these doors, Pontianak on the west side, Bandjarmasin on the south, and Balikpapan on the east, and strolled through some of the corridors which led, after two or three hundred miles, into the inner rooms.

West Kalimantan

The seaplane which took me over the Java Sea from Djakarta, nearly five hundred miles away, landed on the River Kapuas. Pontianak, its destination, is crowded and smelly. The woman Mayor told me that her two main problems were drains and drinking-water. Neither yet exists, except perhaps in a few larger houses round the Sultan's palace and in the superior homes of a few Europeans and wealthier Chinese who live on the left bank of the Kapuas. But most of the streets run between two canals which join the main river or flow out to the sea. Over these streams, muddy when the tide is high and slimy and black when it is low, are rickety wooden bridges leading to wooden houses, crooked and ramshackle. In the centre of the town, shops and bazaars are run by Chinese who make up one-third of the total population of 45,000. Not only is this the second most Chinese town in Indonesia—Singakawa has 80% Chinese—but there are many Chinese settled to the north and to the south, whilst in the riverine villages far into the interior, in Dayak country, bazaars are run by Chinese, and Chinese pedlars take round their goods in large containers hitched on to poles hanging from their shoulders. There are Arab traders too, but far fewer than Chinese.

D   65

Chinese traders first appeared in Kalimantan in the seventh century and they settled first in West Kalimantan in the fourteenth century. But the great wave of Chinese immigration was during the gold rush of the eighteenth century. They came in thousands and many of them settled down to mining, trading in coconuts, pepper, rubber, and sago. At first only the men came and they often took Dayak wives. Later on, when they began to arrive as small communities, they brought their wives and families with them. These Kongsis, as they were called, kept together in communities, and to this day the Chinese have their own quarters, their own schools, their own temples. They are self-contained and play little part in the affairs of the country.

The story of the foundation of Pontianak is an interesting one, the result of the combined efforts of Dutch and Chinese and an Arab named Abdur Rahman. He was the son of an Arab theologian, but early in life he preferred adventure on the high seas to a life of contemplation. Nonetheless sayings of the Prophet were an effective introduction to local chiefs. He traded from port to port without paying any dues, and finally, when his fortune was already considerable, he acquired the governorship of an Islamic settlement through marriage with a local princess. When Dutch traders arrived, he appreciated the new opportunities to add to his fortune and helped them to found a town on the then uninhabited shores of the River Pontianak. The river took its name from a local witch; some say that she had the unpleasant gift of emasculating all males by the force of her jaws, whilst others describe her as the ghost of a woman who died in childbirth and returned to earth to take revenge on women who unsuspectingly awaited with happiness the birth of their children. Be that as it may, the name Pontianak has unpleasant associations. When Abdur Rahman founded the town in 1772 he made himself the first Sultan of Pontianak. The Dutch East India Company at once recognized him and gave further assistance to the town by establishing a factory. They then burnt the rival town of Sukadana to the ground, thus forcing the inhabitants to move into Pontianak. With less powerful Sultans they made treaties guaranteeing monthly stipends and protection against piracy in return for promises not to carry on any negotiations with other European Governments or with America. They made sure of a monopoly of trade for themselves in West Kalimantan through treaties with chiefs in the interior; their territories would be administered by the Dutch and the revenues therefrom equally divided.

With their hold over the Sultans, Dutch traders set out, as they did elsewhere in Indonesia, to defeat all potential competitors. They purchased gold mines and bought the monopoly of diamond mining from the Sultan of Pontianak for 50,000 dollars. They tried to undercut the Chinese who did a considerable trade in their junks, bringing in cotton cloth and taking away gold dust, diamonds, tin, and rattan. When the Chinese retaliated by poisoning the wells, the Dutch could still fight on by the simpler methods of imposing heavy immigration taxes. By the time Dutch authority was established in 1855 after a period of so-called 'pacification', there were no less than 150,000 Chinese in West Kalimantan. They worked in the mines, they settled down to agriculture, and gradually they became the middlemen—traders in the bazaars in the small towns and in villages three hundred miles up the River Kapuas. They traded in rubber and coconuts, and in any goods from which their non-stop industry could extract a profit.

The Sultans of Pontianak remained true to their Dutch masters; it was a convenient and profitable alliance for both partners. To the Dutch, this form of indirect rule was economical; to the Sultans it brought riches and a share in the extravagant pleasures of the Western world without any of its social obligations. But the subjects of the Sultans remained in their small riverine villages, and, in the interior, the famous Dayaks lived on in their long houses, built originally for protection in days of tribal warfare. Sultan and Dutch ruler were almost equally remote to them. Occasional Dutchmen travelled up the Kapuas from Pontianak; scientists who explored the potential riches of the jungle; anthropologists, whose researches led far more to picturesque articles on the practice of head-hunting than to a study of the type of education and social welfare which would lead to a more economical and happier method of paying tribute to one's ancestors; missionaries, who contributed an elementary knowledge of medicine which was unquestionably valuable and tried to convert these animistic peoples to a Western religion. Their deep fervour was unhappily often combined with Christian arrogance. To the missionaries the Dutch Government entrusted education.

A few miles up the River Kapuas, in a lonely spot on the right bank which has the much-deserved reputation of being haunted, the Sultans of Pontianak lie in their ornate tombs; all of them, that is, except the present Sultan Hamid who is in prison in Java for his part in an unsuccessful coup against the Republic. 'That wicked old rascal', as an official guide book describes him, Abdur Rahman, the first Sultan, is there and Sultan Hamid's father, whose golden crown lies on his tomb in a tall glass case draped with orange satin embroidered with the Muslim crescent. He met an honourable death at the hands of the Japanese in 1943 when nearly 2,000 'intellectuals' were rounded up because they were suspected of planning a rising. Outside this sacred territory of the Sultans of Pontianak, the lesser fry lie in the oddest collection of wooden and stone sarcophagi, broken and higgledy-piggledy.

How, I asked, did Sultan Hamid behave on the rare visits which he paid to his ancestral home? 'Like a Dutch officer,' the woman Mayor of Pontianak replied.

We passed on to more congenial subjects, to happier places. Her Worship the Mayor showed me the settlement of two hundred houses built in Pontianak during 1950; they were neat, individual dwellings mainly of wood and bamboo in great contrast to the slums along the muddy banks of the Kapuas. Nor was this all; we visited a large space already cleared of jungle growth where three hundred more such houses were scheduled. Back in the Mayor's Parlour, this highly efficient woman—she was a Menangkabauer from Sumatra who had settled in Pontianak—discussed the plans which she and her Council had made for draining the town and supplying the people with drinking-water.

Since Pontianak is the capital of West Kalimantan, it is the administrative centre and here the Resident lives. At the May

Day demonstration in 1951, he was the chief speaker, and put some frank questions to his audience. What were they doing with their independence? Production figures were low; those who worked only four out of the seven rightful hours in a day were cheating the Republic of three hours' work; those who were stealing goods in the harbour were stealing from the Republic. And so on. The audience of about a thousand workers were in holiday mood. Chinese workers came on to the sports field playing rows of gongs hitched on to bamboo poles, and completed their band with a large drum carried in a sedan chair. Muslim workers were led by men with a model of a mosque in green and white paper with bunches of red and white flowers decorating its entrance. But the Village Rubber-growers Trade Union would have won the first prize for their purple and white paper model of a hand-pressing machine, which they carried on a *betja* (a pedicab rather like a gaily painted Victorian bath-chair hitched to the front of a bicycle). After speeches by local trade union leaders, whose main theme was the high cost of rice, sports began; climbing a greasy pole, throwing a dagger, lifting weights, and races.

On this May Day, 1951, we drove out through miles of palm trees; coconut palms with a tall graceful beauty which seems never to become monotonous. We halted at a tall black column, topped by a silver globe. It might have been a super petrol pump. But its customers would have numbered perhaps twelve in a day. It was, in fact, a modern, curiously unsuitable obelisk marking the Equator. As I stood, one foot in the Northern Hemisphere, one foot in the Southern, I saw rubber-pressing machines at work. Men were pressing latex through the rollers of these small, extremely practicable machines like washing mangles. They had collected the latex from rather small plantations of rubber, and the fluid stood in small tins. Their problem, they told us, was that of marketing; they were now planning a village co-operative as this was the only way of defeating the individual bargaining methods of the Chinese traders. The problem was the same for coconuts which grew on individual plots, usually divided by swampy streams. Picking and collecting coconuts could prove a dangerous occupation; those swamps

69

and streams were the favourite haunt of alligators and people described friends who were casualties from alligators as English people described casualties in the blitz.

Villages were very small and thinly distributed. They were mostly a few wooden houses built on thick wooden poles with a veranda facing the roadway. Behind, the jungle came down to the back door. Occasionally, where a larger clearing had been made, market towns had grown up and Chinese bazaars were packed tight with dried fish and sauces, sacks of rice, cotton sarongs, and the inevitable cheap knick-knacks. Inside their very simple homes, these cheap mirrors and cotton cloths provided a touch of gaudy colour. On the walls there were often photographs: of the family, of boys lost in guerrilla warfare, and of President Sukarno. He is a symbol of the Republic, a living, if rather tenuous link with the Government 500 miles away, across the Java Sea, in Djakarta.

The road—the only one leading to the interior—continues for about two hundred miles, between coconut palms, until it reaches the foothills of the mountains. From then onwards there is no way of travelling except by boat along the Kapuas which has a crow's flight length of 300 miles, but a winding length of just over 700. In the upper reaches of the river, in wide open valleys between the Upper Kapuas Mountains, a quarter of a million Dayaks have their homes. They have their own representatives in Parliament. They have their own organization, the National Council of Dayaks, with a membership of 120,000. Their aim, one of the M.P.s told me, is to develop a communal rather than a tribal consciousness as a step towards the larger self-consciousness as Indonesians. This means that instead of forty-nine different tribes, each with its own language or dialect, its own tribal customs, the Dayaks will become one nation. These forty-nine divisions, this Dayak, a teacher by profession, pointed out, had meant continuous inter-tribal warfare in earlier times. Inter-tribal warfare had ceased some years ago, and the National Movement now encourages the building of individual houses. The centre must be the family, rather than the tribe. This change was already happening before the war; the war-time experiences of many Dayaks who left their homes for the first time had challenged their old conceptions of life.

For the first time in their history the doors which education opens will open for these Dayaks of Central Borneo, not as a special privilege granted by missionaries however sincere and self-sacrificing, but as a right. In 1950, ninety-one new schools were built in the Upper Kapuas; simple wooden structures, barely furnished. Equipment was one problem and sufficient teachers the other. They managed to find teachers for all but nineteen of their schools; in those cases, the missionaries provided them.

Thus, in the few years of the Republic's existence, the people of Central Kalimantan, and especially the younger generation of Dayaks, have a wider horizon; they are no longer content to be anthropological specimens, nor slaves of the ruling Power. If the Central Government has the good sense to appreciate the potentialities of the Dayaks, their ability as cultivators, their liveliness in handwork and design, their craftsmanship in metal and wood; if they will take more seriously the need to plan the development of Borneo they can make more changes in one generation than the Dutch made between the day when they recognized the Sultan of Pontianak and December 1949 when they relinquished sovereignty for ever.

South Kalimantan

The journey from Pontianak, capital of West Kalimantan, to Bandjarmasin, capital of the whole of Indonesian Kalimantan, where the Governor resides, is a distance of only about 400 miles. But it takes less time to fly from Pontianak to London and back to Bandjarmasin than it takes to do this journey by land. The chances of reaching Bandjarmasin are certainly greater, for the land journey is impossible except in small boats up and down the great and small rivers which flow from the high mountains of Central Borneo, crossing miles of swampy country, dodging alligators on the way.

In Bandjarmasin itself, there are more rivers and canals than roads. The result is a town of great charm, always busy but always quiet. Shopping in a small motor-boat along the Kwin canal is an unforgettable delight. All the shops are on polder houses facing the water, and all the shoppers are in boats. Small craft dart here and there with their goods—coconuts, brightly coloured textiles, frying pans and kettles, durians, mangosteens, jack fruit, shaddock, oranges, lemons, melons, and pomegranates. I saw restaurants travelling up and down the canal with dishes of rice and fish and meat, all very tempting and clean; travelling refreshment bars, with trays of lemonade and orange crush; boats with trays of small sweet cakes, boats with furniture, and one modest boat with six packets of cigarettes.

The canal joins two rivers, the Barito, the longest river in Kalimantan, and the narrower, deeper Martapura. A favourite excursion takes you up the Barito to the Island of Flowers to pay respects to an ancient Sultan of Bandjarmasin. Never had a royal personage a more homely shrine. A pier of rusty corrugated iron resting perilously on four bamboo poles led to a small square of bamboo matting under a roof thatched with bamboos. Other visitors had been to the shrine earlier that morning in May 1951. Local Chinese, the guardian of the shrine told us, had come to ask for blessings on their business. We left a hunk of bananas on the matting, not, my companions assured me, to invoke the spirit of one of their Sultans, but to tempt the monkeys which lived in their thousands in the dense jungle growth of trees and creepers and elegantly twining lianas. As for mosquitoes, they were present in millions. And crocodiles roamed through the swamps.

The Martapura flows through similar country, but after a journey of about thirty miles, scenery and atmosphere both change rapidly. The silent jungle gives way to mountains which are rich in diamonds and gold dust. In the busy riverine town of Martapura, priceless gravel is placed in large slightly curving sieves and taken into small factories where the diamonds are cut and sorted. Twenty miles further up the stream, gold and coal are both mined, though no extensive survey has ever been made on which any real estimate of their value can be made.

The knowledge of these mineral riches led many traders to cast an envious eye on Bandjarmasin. But although Dutch traders were there in 1606, and Portuguese some time earlier, they found the local Sultans extremely unwilling to facilitate their travels into the interior. Contact, they feared, between Europeans and the Dayaks whom they oppressed might lead to trouble. The result was that first the Dutch and then the British merchants were murdered, and when Portuguese missionaries tried to spread Christianity among the animistic Dayaks they met the same fate.

Later, during the British interregnum, Raffles stressed the importance of Kalimantan's rich resources and the strategic position of Bandjarmasin. In a dispatch to Lord Minto he called Borneo 'not only one of the most fertile countries in the world, but the most productive in gold and diamonds'. The Dayaks he described as 'not only industrious in their habits, but particularly devoted to agriculture'.[1] The result was that Lord Minto appointed a Mr. Alexander Hare as British Resident in Bandjarmasin. He founded a colony there, partly with convicts from Java. Sir Thomas Raffles in a lecture to the Batavian Society expressed his view that 'as confidence increases, we may look to a more extensive intercourse with the rude and scattered tribes of the interior'.[2] But this did not happen. The Dutch returned to Bandjarmasin. Their first step was a treaty with the Sultan who agreed to exclude the British. Sultan Adam also conceded to the Dutch the right to appoint the successor to the throne. All went well for some years, since there seemed to be no commercial prospects of any importance. The situation suddenly changed when coal was discovered near Martapura. At this point the Sultan was no longer acquiescent and agreed only under pressure that it should be mined. But local labour was not available, with the result that slave labour was imported from Java. The mines proved to be far less of a proposition than the Dutch had originally anticipated. Further, they met with a great deal of resistance from the sons of the Sultan who were not prepared to comply with Dutch requests. The result was the so-called Bandjarmasin war, which lasted from 1859 until 1863. Up and down the River Barito and its tributaries, boats passed with men and supplies. The Dutch navy and the Dutch army took part in this war, but the local people knew the land and the water much better than the invaders, and rallied behind

Hidayat, the Sultan's son. After some time, the Dutch were able to make headway; they were better supplied and they built fortifications along the river banks. When Hidayat refused to surrender, Dutch troops chased him far into the jungles of the Barito River, and it was on his plebeian shrine of ragged bamboo matting that we had placed a hunk of bananas.

Other smaller rebellions against Dutch rule were organized in 1870 and suppressed only after the death of the leader, and again in 1883. Indeed, it was not until 1905 that resistance ended and Dutch mounted police banished from South Borneo the chiefs who were unwilling to submit to their rule.

In 1951, the Kalimantan Governor, Dr. Moerdjani, showed me the blueprints for draining a large area of swamps round Bandjarmasin. Within five years, this area of a million acres, he calculated, could produce enough rice to make up Indonesia's total rice deficit of 600,000 tons. His technical adviser was a brilliant Dutch engineer, Dr. H. L. Schophuys, who was then in Djakarta making the first purchases of dredging, ditching, and draining machines. The Central Government had allocated 16 million guilders for the scheme, but its allocation was held up because of a change of Government. The Governor, with a balance in hand from large sales of rubber and copra at boom prices, was not prepared to allow a Cabinet crisis in Djakarta to postpone the first drainage work, since the rains would soon start and a whole year would be wasted. In addition to rice, he and his team of young pioneering enthusiasts calculated, there would be enough fish in the lower canalized waters to supply the whole country. The problem was not only one of more machinery but of more labour, technicians as well as less skilled workers. This raised the further problem of the shortage of labour in Kalimantan and the need for the Government to treat the transference of labour from overcrowded Java with far greater urgency.

Bandjarmasin had other pioneers too. There was the young teacher who was now a Co-operative Society organizer. I met him on his way up-country, which meant up-stream, where groups of villages had been asked to send representatives to plan local co-operatives. There was the local Ministry of Information,

74

where young men and women were busily printing their pamphlets, designing posters, and distributing all kinds of literature to their representatives throughout Kalimantan; the Women's Organizations which were then holding their annual celebrations on Kartini day—Kartini had courageously advocated the education of girls and the right of women to have a career. I attended a committee meeting when women represented various organizations: P.E.R.W.A.R.I. (the main women's society), Christian women, Young Women, Housewives, Servicemen's wives, Girl Guides, Union of Dutch women, Muslim women, representatives from the Swiss, the Indian, and the Chinese women, the women's branch of the Partai Murba (a non-Stalinist Communist Party), and the women's section of the Union of Plantation Workers.

These women were responsible for running a kindergarten school and two ante-natal clinics. The Governor's wife happened to be a qualified doctor, and when she was not engaged in the local hospital to which she gave her services free, she attended these two clinics, one of them in a school hall, the other in the front room lent by the Chairman of P.E.R.W.A.R.I. Equipment was confined to a long table covered with a piece of white oilcloth, a weighing machine, and a few chairs. On the walls there were posters giving diet charts, urging cleanliness, demonstrating the right way to carry babies and the harm to their limbs if they were cooped up in a slendang (the long wide scarf which women wear and use as a shopping bag as well as a cradle).

Those clinics, so bare, so simple, were a memorable illustration of the new spirit which independence brings to the women of a country.

East Kalimantan

The modern housing estate which climbs the hills overlooking the Straits of Makassar is based on oil. For Balikpapan on the east coast of Kalimantan was only a small village in 1890 when experimental borings showed that oil was available in commercially valuable quantities. From that year dates the Royal Dutch Company founded by a Dutchman, Aeilko Jansz

Zijlker. A second prospector, a Dutchman named Munten, being unable to raise enough capital in his own country, won the ear of Sir Marcus Samuel in London. The result was a company which later became the world-famous Shell Company. The firm of M. Samuel and Co. had originally imported from the East, amongst other goods, shells for decorating boxes and other knick-knacks and selected the shell as their trade mark. 'Little did they think', stated the *Diamond Jubilee Book* of the Royal Dutch Petroleum Company, 'that this "Shell" would one day achieve a reputation which had very little to do with decorated boxes.'[3]

The Shell oil concessions out of which Balikpapan grew into a large oil centre, were incorporated with the Nederlandsch-Indische-Industrie en Handel-Maatschappij, and out of this grew the Royal Dutch-Shell group; the two, one Dutch, the other British, participated in the proportion of 60–40 in the N.V. De Bataafsche Petroleum Maatschappij known as the B.P.M. They were my generous hosts in Balikpapan in 1951.

The landscape of this oil town is like a surrealist painting. In the foreground, the greyish-blue sea. On the horizon, huge rust-red iron cracking plants, crumpled like corrugated cardboard. Feathery alang-alang grasses wave over the wreckage of retorts, and generator bodies lay slanting like the gongs which call people to pray in the mosque. There are lanes of scrap iron. On the hillside, the green jungle is already growing over red oil tanks as large as Nissen huts. The Dutch engineer who accompanied me on this expedition through a weird iron world was one of only three survivors of the eighty-four B.P.M. employees who destroyed their plant on January 20th, 1942. The Japanese were only a few miles away when the decision was taken to destroy the oil installations rather than let them fall into enemy hands. The place was in flames when they arrived. They caught seventy-eight Dutchmen, took them down to the beach and shot them, and marched on to Bandjarmasin.

During their occupation of Borneo, the Japanese needed oil and rebuilt some of the installations. In 1945 these too were destroyed, this time by Allied bombers. Today, Balikpapan is a brand-new town. Along the water's edge, between and beyond

the wreckage, enormous grey, silver, and white oil tanks glitter
in tropical sunshine. I liked the touch of scarlet, the colour of
the 'agitators' as tanks are picturesquely called where oil is
treated with sulphuric acid to improve its colour. There were
sheds lined with trays of paraffin wax which looked like ice
cream in frigidaires.

On the line of hills overlooking the oil refineries and the harbour, the B.P.M. had built more than 2,000 houses, graded
according to income groups. A modern well-equipped hospital,
the efficiency of which I had the misfortune to prove for myself,
schools, a community centre, and motor buses gave the impression of a modern town. The difference between 1951 and pre-
war days was illustrated in one small corner that had survived
two bombardments; here were the old housing lines; they were
the only physical eyesore.

The Dutch directors lived on their own hillside, furthest away
from the harbour. They complained of low production figures,
of a great deal of thieving in the workshops, and although they
had accepted the idea of Indonesian independence, and the
need for bringing more and more Indonesians into responsible
positions, they resented the uncertainty of their position and the
vagueness of official policy. They were critical of the Government's failure to deal firmly enough with bands of young men
who still were at large in the surrounding countryside, some of
them guerrillas who had not yet settled down to normal lives,
some of them young gangsters. How much these activities were
political and how much gangsterism it was extremely difficult
to establish. Leaders of the local non-communist trade union
admitted that these were real problems, not only for B.P.M.
but for the Republic as a whole which needed maximum earnings from their oil-fields, and that security was essential. In the
second trade union office I visited, where photographs of Stalin
were more conspicuous than those of Sukarno, these problems
were dismissed as Dutch propaganda. Perhaps there was an
element of truth in this, but it was by no means the whole
story.

A year later Balikpapan was linked with Bandjarmasin
by a new roadway. The next stage in bringing together the now

scattered people of Kalimantan will be a road from Bandjar-masin to Pontianak, across miles of country which were mangrove swamps when the first Dutchmen visited the island and mangrove swamps when the last Dutchman left it. There was in Borneo a greater sense of pioneering than I met elsewhere, and a greater need for it. The largest virgin forests, untapped mineral wealth—the Republic needs them both. But there are not enough men and women in Kalimantan to do the work. The problem for the Government in Djakarta is how to encourage more people from Java to live there. The Transmigration Bureau has not yet shown many results in this direction. Far more propaganda is needed to stimulate the Javanese to go to unknown Kalimantan. But they must be people who are chosen with some care, for the people of Kalimantan have their own pride and they do not always welcome Javanese who have a sense of superiority. 'Give us a little more time and more machinery,' men and women will say to you in Pontianak and Bandjarmasin, 'and we shall so improve our communications and develop our rich swamps that Javanese will want to live in this rich island.' This sounds good sense, but the fact remains that Kalimantan and Java are complementary to each other, and that with goodwill and a sensible psychology, the Government, so largely centred in Djakarta, can add great human and material riches to the country as a whole by giving it more of its attention.

NOTES

[1] *Memoir of the Life and Public Services of Sir Thomas Raffles*, by Lady Raffles, 1830, p. 61. Letter to Lord Minto.

[2] Ibid., p. 152. Address to the Batavian Society.

[3] *Diamond Jubilee Book, 1890–1950*, p. 15. The Royal Dutch Petroleum Company, The Hague, 1950.

CHAPTER V

SULAWESI (CELEBES), THE MOLUCCAS AND WEST IRIAN

SULAWESI

Minahasa

ACROSS the Makassar Straits the island of Sulawesi sprawls over the Equator. It has a shape so peculiar that it has been compared with a mutilated octopus, a spider, a scorpion, a pair of pyjamas hanging on a clothes line, an orchid, a two-legged giraffe, and the twisted palm of a hand. In the northernmost tip of this beautiful equatorial island where the sea is never more than seventy miles away, and the climate is kind and comfortable, the European is in a countryside which is reminiscent of the Portuguese Riviera. Here in the Minahasa, the towns and villages have names that are familiar. The buses which come down from the mountains with fruit and vegetables to the chief market town of Menado return to such places as Tondano, Tomohon and Passo. Every village has its church and school and on Sunday mornings men, women, and children appear in their best clothes, often European, and attend services where Indonesian pastors preach Christian sermons. For in the Minahasa about 90% of the half a million people who live there are Christians. This is not the only sign that these Minahasans have assimilated more Western habits than any other people in the Indonesian archipelago. Villages and towns have an orderliness in the streets. Houses are neat, with flower gardens in front and ferns in bowls along the veranda, and an American visitor would not be embarrassed by sanitary arrangements. The same Western atmosphere exists inside: furniture, religious pictures, texts and family photographs, a sewing machine and a family Bible. The Netherlands Missionary Society achieved greater results in the Minahasa than in any other part of Indonesia; most of its converts were made in the years between 1827 and 1860, by which time more than 100,000 Minahasans had accepted Christianity. In the beginning, the Dutch administration had the power to appoint all ministers, but in later years, when Christianity had become assimilated, the great majority of ministers were Indonesians. Today this is also true of officials. The Minahasan pastor who officiated at a village wedding I attended had the same ritual that a minister uses in any English village; the same questions to bride and bridegroom, the same short sermon following the placing of the ring on the woman's finger, even the same hymns. Two accompanying items were different; the music was played by an orchestra on bamboo flutes and drums, and a collection followed the ceremony to which the bride, in white satin, gloves, and wreath of flowers, made the first contribution. Yet it was unmistakably Indonesian; the God of the Christian Church, like the Prophet of Islam and the Hindu deities, had been assimilated by Indonesia. The Hindu deities were now worshipped only in Bali. The missionaries of Islam had won great victories for the Prophet in most parts of the country, but the Minahasa was off their main routes. Christian missionaries from the Philippines, when they were still a Spanish possession and again when the Minahasa was 'pacified' in the early part of the nineteenth century, had had an unchallenged opportunity to spread their faith.

The north-eastern tip of Sulawesi on which Menado stands is nearer to the Philippines than it is to the town of Makassar, 800 miles away in the south-eastern part of the same island. Spanish traders settled in the Minahasa in the seventeenth century, which fact probably explains why many of the local people have olive complexions and oval faces. The Dutch came later and built the present capital, Menado, which with its fort overlooks one of the loveliest bays in Asia. Working from Menado as a centre, Dutch traders were able to expand, incorporating other parts of the peninsula. Local rulers were generally found who saw in an alliance with the Western trader an opportunity to enrich themselves and to secure positions of authority. Thus, in 1679, a Treaty of Friendship was signed with the ruler of Minahasa by which the Dutch recognized the local rulers in Menado, Tomohon, and Tondano. What happened is well known in the Minahasa, though it is doubtful whether the story is commonly known in other parts of Indonesia.

More than a century after the Dutchmen's visit a war was fought in Tondano which local residents still discuss. The story is this. A Dutchman named Schierstein became Resident of Menado. A local man, Poelowang by name, became his right-hand man. It was profitable work. Poelowang played his own people off against the Dutch. When they wanted to see the Resident, he asked for a fee; if they hadn't enough money, he sent them off home to collect more. He took payment in rice and meat and chicken, none of which found its way to the Dutch, nor to the Resident. When the Resident visited Tomohon, following complaints about heavy taxation, no one was there to see him. Poelowang had two stories ready for the occasion; to the people he gave the warning that the Resident would arrest them and to the Resident he explained that these local would-be assassins were kept out of his reach. Finally, when trouble started, the Resident was afraid to report to his Governor in Amboina, since it was mainly due to his own lax behaviour. He therefore brought over troops from the nearby island of Ternate and set fire to the villages near Tomohon.

When Captain Elphinstone and his ships appeared off the coasts of Menado in 1806, the new Resident Durr made some efforts to resist. He tried to recruit Minahasans, but when Poelowang appeared acting as recruiting sergeant people refused to join; they believed that he would trick them and send them into the interior to collect taxes. The result was that the Dutch Resident was forced to surrender, and for a time the Minahasa was under British rule. A year later, Minahasans decided to fight the Dutch when the island was temporarily handed back. Their plan of campaign was worked out at a meeting of the heads of twenty-six districts, corresponding to the earlier distribution of clans. The centre of resistance was chosen—Swambi, a small village on Lake Tondano. Whilst this was to be the only place where fighting would take place, other villages were allocated their special roles, supplying food, munitions, and guns, whilst people from other villages had to act as spies on the Dutch. The password was 'Kumuru-a-Masa'. Meanwhile, the Dutch themselves were involved with the British. The Dutch Resident decided it was good tactics to deal with the internal enemy first and then with the foreigner. He therefore sent his troops into the district round Lake Tondano in January 1807. At first they were defeated. The garrison from Menado was brought in as reinforcement. On one occasion which is still talked about in Menado, the resistance movement made a surprise attack; on the night of May 30th, 1808, they surrounded the battery in Menado harbour, and stole its guns. When the guards started off to chase the enemy, they found the ground covered by the sharp points of bamboo sticks dipped in poison. The Resident then tried to contact the heads of districts, but they failed to respond. Finally, he sent for reinforcements from Ternate and Halmahera. The Minahasans still fought on against Dutch troops who had to wade through swamps already very deep, as the rains had begun. The war continued until August, by which time the Resident had acquired boats to transport his troops over the marshes bordering Lake Tondano. When they arrived at the wall surrounding the town, the Minahasans, men and women, still defended themselves. Only two days later, when General Serapong and General Koringking had both been killed together with many of their supporters, could the Dutch troops enter Tondano. At eight o'clock in the evening of August 2nd, 1809, the war ended. Many people were exiled to Ternate and Banda. Some escaped. The area was not 'pacified' until the early eighteen-twenties. From that time onwards, Dutch rule was hardly challenged, and if you tell a Minahasan that his province is called 'The Twelfth Province of Holland', you are likely to be told this story of Tondano.[1] But it is undoubtedly true that Dutch ideas were assimilated by the Minahasans, and like the Christianized area of Amboina, men from Minahasa were easily recruited to serve in the Dutch army. The considerable pensions which they received helped to add to local wealth, just as the Gurkhas in the British army take their savings back to Nepalese villages.

The Japanese paid special attention to this area, strategically important, and so rich in thousands of acres of coconuts and vegetables. Five hundred parachutists dropped near the airstrip and 6,000 more Japanese landed in the early days of January 1942. After three weeks' resistance, the Minahasans settled down to life under the Japanese, who were noticeably on their best behaviour. They introduced new methods of market gardening, even new vegetables, but their consideration was soon understood when they began to ship loads of food back to Japan.

On August 20th, 1945, five days after the surrender of the Japanese and three days after the proclamation of independence in Djakarta, the red-and-white flag was hoisted in Menado. Then Australian forces entered the town, shelling it heavily and burning out buildings which still scar the harbour front. In February 1946, when Dutch troops returned, local people proclaimed their independence, and for twenty days they resisted the return of their colonial rulers. After this initial opposition, Dutch rule was rarely challenged. For this area, as throughout its history, was remote from affairs in Java, and the Nationalist Movement had made only a slight impression. Not until the second Dutch military action in December 1948 did the local people express any strong Republican feelings. By this time it was quite clear that Dutch rule could never be restored. It would be foolish to ignore the fact that among the older generation there are still Minahasans who look back on Dutch times with a certain nostalgia. But among the younger people who have not grown up in the atmosphere of Dutch censorship, support for the Republic is real and loyal.

The Toradja Lands

If we use the analogy of the palm of one's hands to describe Sulawesi, then the Toradja lands make up the greater part of the palm. This is one of the least known parts of Indonesia, and in Dutch times almost the only visitors were missionaries, some of whom made a serious study of philology and ethnology. The Toradja lands naturally fall into three groups: the Sadang in the south, nearest to Makassar, the Poso in the north, and the Sigi in the west. Almost without exception, their villages are isolated, separated by steep ravines.

When Dutch troops succeeded in their expedition against Boni, to the south, in 1860, the local Commander wanted to march on into the Toradja lands and annex them. But the Central Government did not agree to the scheme until three years later, and by this time it was no longer practicable. The Sultans who ruled the Toradjas were left alone until 1905 when Governor-General van Heutz made up his mind to end once and for all any signs of resistance to Dutch rule. His expedition of two and a half battalions reached Sulawesi in July 1905. After occupying Boni, to the south, on the east coast, and Pare-Pare on the west coast, Dutch troops embarked to Palopo, the home of the Datu of Luwu who ruled over the Southern and Northern Toradjas. Local forces were commanded by a Toradja, Puang Tiku, on the 300-foot-high rock fortress Barupu. The fortress could not be stormed, and it was besieged for months. After two months, a new Dutch expedition arrived, and Puang Tiku surrendered only when the rock fortress was about to blow up. Two years later—in 1907—Puang Tiku was killed during an attempt to organize a revolt.

The Toradjas were left to themselves, except for the missionaries in whose hands the Dutch Government entrusted education. The result was that about 40,000 converts were registered by the Netherlands Mission Council. Two Dutchmen, Dr. Adriani and Dr. Kruyt, in addition to their missionary work, made a study of Toradja customs and languages. Around the coast the population is largely Muslim, but elsewhere they remain animists. Like all spirit worshippers, they have special ways of honouring the souls of the dead. The corpse is placed in a coffin and kept in the forest until only bones remain. The funeral procession then begins; the small box into which the bones are placed is carried with great ceremony and with all kinds of goods and valuables belonging to the deceased until the rock grave is reached. The box is laid in a crevice in the face of the mountain and death masks and figures are placed at the entrance. Buffaloes are killed in large numbers, according to the wealth of the family and its friends. Villages of the North and West Toradjas have small temples where skulls were kept in the days, until about fifty years ago, when head-hunting was a ritual. Heads were believed to have special qualities of healing and the spirits of brave ancestors were thought to live in them. Both this practice and slavery, which was also common, were forbidden by the Dutch and discredited by the missionaries. People were also encouraged to live along the rivers rather than in clusters of houses on the mountains, a policy which helped to build a more settled society.

The Toradjas are mainly agriculturalists, growing rice and coconuts, and hunting in the forests for bark, often used as clothing, for resin, and for rattan to build their houses. In villages where iron and copper are found, both are worked, and local smiths make agricultural tools and craftsmen make figures from copper. Their only trade in the past was in the products of the forest which were handed over to Dutch and Chinese traders appointed to collect it and to recruit labour. Roads through the interior were built by statute labour which was imposed for four days in each month. During the Japanese occupation a certain amount of road building brought the Toradja lands into closer contact with South Sulawesi. In the Republic, road building and schools are the two main considerations. In January 1952, a plan to build a road between Makassar and Menado which would pass through the Toradja lands was agreed in principle by the Ministry of Public Works. The estimated cost was 190 million rupiahs and the time taken to build it, five years. Whereas under colonial rule, isolated communities, like the Toradjas, were of no particular interest, except to the missionaries, the Republic is as much committed to their welfare as they are to the people of Java or any other island. The idea of belonging to the Republic is now spreading, especially amongst the younger generation of Toradjas. Perhaps one of the most striking changes which the Republic has brought about in the Toradja communities is the passion for education. In the winter of 1950–1 they collected enough money to send 500 boys and girls down to Makassar for advanced education. They were mostly in their middle teens and they lived in crowded boarding-houses or with families. They were among the liveliest people I met. Their great desire was to found schools in the Toradja lands. To do this they had come two or three hundred miles, girls and boys whose grandparents still believed in the worship of spirits in gardens, rivers, houses, trees, and in the skulls of fellow-creatures.

85

Makassar

Makassar, on the south-western limb of Sulawesi, is the Singapore of East Indonesia. But the excitement of a walk along the waterfront in Makassar is not the big ocean liners to and from all parts of the world, but three-masted ships which sail in and out of the Java Sea in to the Straits of Malacca, round the Moluccas, anywhere between the Philippines and Australia.

When Portuguese traders, the first Europeans to visit the island, arrived in the sixteenth century, they found Makassar was already an important trading centre for spices and cloves. Chinese junks were there bringing silks and porcelains for the Sultans, rich and prosperous gentlemen whose extravagant Courts were then, as they remained for centuries, in great contrast to the rattan hovels of the people. Makassar was the capital of the Kingdom of Gowa, and, adjoining it, was Boni, its rival. The Makassars and the Buginese (living in Boni) both had a type of society which was different from that in any other part of the archipelago. Kings were elected from a group of aristocrats who were usually hereditary and extremely powerful. These feudal lords could also get rid of the King, and their permission was necessary for participation in a war, or any public measure, including the spending of money. In Gowa, the King was chosen by ten counsellors; in Boni by seven. Women were eligible to election in every department, but if one were elected, an additional officer was appointed to give her the benefit of his advice.

The Makassars and Buginese were the most numerous as well as the most powerful people in Sulawesi when the Portuguese arrived. In their sagas, or galigas, as they are called, they hold in the greatest esteem a legendary hero Sawira Geding, their first chief. Indeed, their legends say that he immediately descended from the heavenly chief, Bitaru Guru. Raffles, a social anthropologist long before anthropology was a science, understood the significance of such sagas in the lives of people who were otherwise quite illiterate. He wrote a description of Sawira Geding, a figure who is almost entirely overlooked by the more prosaic Dutchmen.

86

'The people of Celebes', he said, 'have a tradition that when their celebrated Chief, Sawira Geding, was exploring the Western countries, he put into one of the rivers in Sumatra, where a considerable part of his followers deserted him, and running into the interior, connected themselves with the people of the country, and established the kingdom of the Menangkabu. These people were for the most part of the lowest class, employed by Sawira Geding in cutting firewood and procuring water for his fleet, and are represented by him to have been captives from the Moluccas, or savages from the interior of Celebes, and have the term Malaya, from Mala, to bring and aya, wood: Malaya, a woodbringer, or as we should say a woodcutter, and to this day the people of Celebes look down with the greatest contempt on a Malaya, and are in the habit of repeating the origin of the name.'[2]

The saga is interesting for two reasons: first, it shows that the Makassars and Buginese were traders and sailors in very early times, probably when the Javanese were still tilling the soil; secondly, the name has been chosen for the new university in Makassar. Like the new university in Djogjakarta named Gadjah Mada, a national hero, the name Sawira Geding is chosen because of its association with a period in history before the Europeans arrived on the scene.

The Portuguese, when they arrived, were completely absorbed in their search for spices and cloves. British navigators followed, and in due course Dutch traders arrived to stake their claims. By this time the then Sultan of Makassar had himself learnt to appreciate the advantages of being a middleman in spices and cloves, obtaining them at his own price from the people and making the best bargain he could with Dutch traders. The Dutch, as was their custom, tried to secure and hold a monopoly; in the instructions sent to their first Governor-General in 1609, they laid it down that the trade of the Moluccas, including Amboina and Banda, was to be retained 'wholly, absolutely, and entirely in the hands of the United Company and that no particle of it shall be left to anyone but ourselves and to those whom we think proper'.[3] The reference of course was to the British who, as one historian remarks, 'had been following the Dutch round the Archipelago, pursuing them like gadflies'.[4]

The Dutch won, first of all against the Portuguese and then the British. With the whole resources of the State behind them, the Dutch East India Company was able to organize considerable military expeditions against Gowa. Commander Speelman's men were tough against a tough enemy. More than 5,000 Makassars died for want of food, 400 were taken as slaves, and then the assault on Makassar began in earnest. The Sultan, after two months of bitter fighting, signed the Bonjaja Treaty with the Dutch in 1667. The Dutch gained all they wanted; a monopoly in piece-goods and Chinese ware, to the exclusion of all other European nations; the restriction of all trade to the East by Makassars except with a Dutch permit; duty-free trade for the Dutch, and their money made the currency; a large war indemnity, 1,000 slaves; the razing of fortifications; the giving up of all claims to Moluccan islands.

Sultan Hasan Udin had signed the treaty, but he made one more effort to resist. He was defeated by reinforcements which Commander Speelman brought from Batavia; his fortified palace was ransacked, and in its place the Dutch built a fortress, called 'Rotterdam'. It still stands today on the waterfront, like an orderly Vermeer interior set in a Gauguin landscape.

With their garrison in Makassar, the Dutch could make expeditions for slaves, spices, cloves, or simple conquest. The Sultan of Gowa was defeated, and the Sultan of Boni was pro-Dutch. Buginese troops were used to pacify other islands. But conditions never remained stable for any length of time; Sultan intrigued against Sultan; the Dutch played one off against the other; there were raids from Boni into Gowa and vice versa, sometimes local, sometimes assisted by the Dutch. The Company made Makassar its chief trading centre. Feudal conditions remained and still exist in some areas. The British interregnum did not make any great impression on these outer islands, and when they were returned to Dutch rule in 1816, no substantial changes had been made.

When the Dutch took over from the British, they found local Sultans difficult to manage. The Sultana of Boni, a spirited lady, had the original idea of ordering all her ships to carry the Dutch flag in reverse. The result was a military expedition against her in 1859. A year later, the capital was taken, and Boni lost its independence. As each Sultan succeeded to the throne, he, or she, had to sign again a treaty with the Dutch Government. When it came to the turn of Sultan La Pawowoni Kraeng Segeri at the beginning of this century, he refused to give up import and export duties, and was finally banished. Never again did the Dutch risk having a Sultan in control of Boni; in 1905, they just considered it as conquered territory, and set up a Council assisted by a European director.

In Gowa, as in Boni, feudal lords proved troublesome to the Dutch; they asserted their independence, they quarrelled over spheres of influence, over a variety of trading problems. Having subdued Boni, the military expedition now turned to Gowa, where the Sultan refused to appear before the Governor of Makassar to explain his behaviour. Fighting continued spasmodically for some time, the Dutch adopting the tactic of occupying the country district by district. In 1911 Gowa too was incorporated in Dutch territory. By this time, the island of Sulawesi had come under Dutch administration.

Sulawesi was part of the area known as East Indonesia. The Governor was represented by a High Representative of the Crown in Makassar and by a Mayor in Menado. The two parts of the island had little contact with each other, nor with the Toradjas lands which lay between them. Until an air service was started just before the war, there were no communications linking north and south, except by sea. No railways were built, and roads were mainly local, radiating from Makassar for a distance of about 100 miles and rather more from Menado. The Makassars and the Buginese continued to be great traders and sailors. In their boats and praus they took away nutmegs and cloves, sandalwood and tortoiseshell, copra and rattan, sea foods, and sometimes a bird of paradise. On their return journey they carried cargoes of rice, cotton goods, oil, coal, tobacco, glassware, hardware, and knick-knacks for the bazaars.

The boats and the praus usually belong to the Makassars and Buginese who sail them, but their masters are Europeans and Chinese, whose headquarters are in the large warehouses on the waterfront. Chinese, who make up about 20% of the local population, run most of the bazaars, though the gay hand-made baskets and hats and mats are made by the local people and in the villages around Makassar. The Makassars and Buginese are very distinctive in appearance and their sarongs are the gayest of any in the Republic, bright red and bright purple, and large patterning of flowers that look like long-spiked dahlias and chrysanthemums. They have an astonishing gift of weaving mats and baskets, and hats that look like para-sols. From rattan, which grows in the local forests, they make furniture and mats and pile them up on the pavements under the shade of tamarind and canarium trees. In the quietest part of the city, away from the busy harbour front, the Dutch built many beautiful houses for their officials and an elegant Resi-dence for their High Representative of the Crown. Japanese officials took them over in 1942, and made Makassar their mili-tary headquarters. When the Japanese left, Australians and Americans took over.

The possession of this town was obviously of major impor-tance to the Dutch; to hold Makassar was essential to their plan of reconquering south-west Sulawesi. When Dutch troops arrived to take over Makassar, then held by the Australians, Republican supporters organized a powerful resistance. The Dutch immediately rounded up local political leaders, and in-terned or exiled them. The worst massacre in the history of Sulawesi happened at the end of 1946. It was carried out under the instructions of a Dutch officer, Captain Westerling, who has written an astonishingly frank account of the atrocities he himself ordered. Eye-witnesses described to me four years later how people were tied together in bundles of fifty, taken out into the marshy land on the outskirts of the city and thrown into vast pits. The number of Captain Westerling's victims is unknown; local people believed it to be not less than 30,000. The Dutch Government was forced to appoint a Commission to go into the matter of the brutalities committed by their troops, but no report has ever been published. Westerling's troops surrounded villages where resistance was suspected. People were arbitrarily snatched away and often shot at sight.

The pacification of South-west Sulawesi robbed the country of most of its political leaders, and of progressive men and women who were experienced in local administration. In their place the Dutch found representatives of the feudal system who saw in collaboration the opportunity to maintain their own position. These included the Rajah of Boni and the Rajah of Luwu.

Dr. van Mook now made Makassar the most important city in East Indonesia—an area which covered all the islands, large and small, east of Java. Here he concentrated his organization and here the Parliament of East Indonesia held its meetings. And it was here that the main K.N.I.L. Dutch Colonial troops were stationed. They remained, a source of provocation when it was quite clear that the transfer of sovereignty to the Republic was only a matter of time. Indeed, during the period of The Hague Conference which planned that transfer, a young Indonesian, Wolter Monginsidi, was executed by the Dutch authorities in Makassar for the part he played in organizing bands of guerrillas in the surrounding mountains. But that is not the end of the tragedy of Makassar.

When The Hague Conference was over, Makassar was once again the scene of trouble. Dutch-sponsored men were still in the Government of East Indonesia; 10,000 K.N.I.L. men under Dutch command were still in local camps. Trouble started when the Republican Government announced in March 1950 that units of their army were to leave for Makassar for garrisoning purposes, making clear that this was not a political decision but a routine movement. But Dr. Soumokil, who had been Attorney-General in the Dutch-sponsored East Indonesian State, saw this announcement as a threat to the existence of the remaining Dutch authority, and gave his secret support to a mutiny among sections of the K.N.I.L. troops. Before the Republican troops could land in Makassar, Captain Andi Aziz led the mutiny, attacked the troops from Djakarta, and took control of the city. When President Sukarno denounced this captain as an outlaw, and ordered him to Djakarta, he at first refused. When he finally arrived there, he was arrested. The rebels in Makassar then surrendered and Republican troops landed on April 19th and restored order. Meanwhile, Dr.

Soumokil escaped in a Dutch army bomber to the South Moluccas, and started a rebellion in Amboina. No one who described the affair to me believed that the Dutch were not actively responsible for the rebellion. The situation in Makassar continued to be extremely unsettled. The Republican Government set up an Emergency Government in the city following the rebellion, stating that the administration of South Sulawesi should be democratized, and that the local feudal rulers should adapt themselves to the new situation in line with the wishes of the people. One more effort was made by pro-Dutch elements, assisted by K.N.I.L. troops, to regain power. In August 1950, fighting broke out again in Makassar. It was short-lived; the Republican Government took prompt action and a Military Mission from Djakarta arrived together with military observers attached to the United Nations Commission on Indonesia, still in the country. They repeated views already given to the Dutch Government, that the real source of the trouble in Makassar lay in the continued garrison of K.N.I.L. troops. The matter would then have been settled if the Dutch High Commissioner in Djakarta had not sent, on the instructions of his Government, a destroyer to establish contact with the Dutch Commander in Makassar. The Republican Government was not even told of the decision, and naturally considered this action as a violation of their sovereignty. Fighting continued in Makassar for some months, and it was not until February 1951 that law and order were restored in the city and, with few exceptions, in the surrounding areas.

This sequence of events in Makassar was a potential threat to the security of the Republic in South Sulawesi. There is no doubt that it had the effect of slowing down many plans in commerce and social welfare, in building up an efficient administration and in education. In May 1951, there were many empty boats in the harbour; some of the big commercial houses on the waterfront were closed down; the Sawirageding University was silent, as the five Dutch Professors left the city at the time of the Soumokil-Aziz rebellion.[5] Guerrilla bands still roamed about in the mountains; some of them were ex-K.N.I.L. men opposed to the Republic; many of them were young men who found that type of life easier than settling down to a job, and some of them were just gangsters. The rebellion was still fresh in people's minds and I rarely met anyone who did not refer with horror to the Westerling massacre and to the fact that he had been allowed to land in Singapore.

There were many signs of consolidation in South Sulawesi. Trade unions were already organized; political parties were active, including a very lively branch of the Socialist Party. A Conference of Women's Organizations showed how seriously the women are playing their part in many branches of social welfare. I heard civil servants discuss with a representative from the Ministry of Social Welfare in Djakarta the problems of health, and the co-ordination of activities with such bodies as the Ministry of Information. In other words, Makassar was becoming an integral part of the Republic.

It would be unrealistic to ignore the elements in South Sulawesi which make for instability. There is, for instance, the struggle of feudal families to maintain their power. There are armed gangs of young men who have never yet settled down to a normal life. The army is confused by political rivalry. And, during the rising which started at the end of 1952, the leader, Kahar Muzakkar, called his army the 'Tentara Islam Indonesia' (Indonesian Islam Army) and contacts between him and the Darul Islam were known to have been established.

In South Sulawesi, as in Atjeh, the Central Government has paid too little attention to local needs, and in 1955, men like Tengku Daud Beureueh and Kahar Muzakkar can still find supporters in local guerrilla warfare. It is also very doubtful as to whether enough is done in the way of rehabilitation if and when the Government troops have forced a surrender.

THE MOLUCCAS

Eastwards of Sulawesi most of Indonesia's 3,000 islands lie scattered over an area as large as Europe. In these tropical seas islands have a beauty which is almost monotonous in its unvaried landscape; coconut palms which stand as upright as a lighthouse or bend as gracefully as the body of a Balinese dancer; clusters of banana trees, their ragged parchment leaves catching the tenderest breeze; sago palm, bamboo, and the surprising cocoa tree; nutmeg trees like large shrubs in an English parkland; gardens of cloves and fields of coffee plants; paddy-fields, pepper and maize plantations. Around every island men fish; sometimes alone with cast-nets, sometimes in teams with drag-nets. In some islands they catch turtles, and collect birds' nests, popular with the Chinese. The inhabitants are physically alike; they are descendants of Buginese, Makassars, Javanese, Malays, Portuguese, Dutch, and Chinese, who have traded in these islands for centuries.

The Moluccas vary in size from tiny atolls to islands which are 200 miles long. Across the Molucca Straits, Nature has created a freak reproduction of Sulawesi, so that we can describe it as the little mutilated octopus, the little spider, the little scorpion, the little pair of pyjamas hanging on a clothes line, the little orchid, the little two-legged giraffe, or the twisted palm of a little hand. It is in fact an island with the musical name of Jilolo, though a Western atlas may give it the more prosaic name of Halmahera. To the north of it is the island of Morotai, which was changed almost overnight by American bulldozers from an unknown land of sago and coconut palms to one of General MacArthur's most famous air bases. The jungle has since reclaimed the airstrips and today creepers and lianas twine round bulldozers, tractors, wrecked aircraft and tanks.

Of the small islands near Jilolo, Ternate and Tidore have played a role in Indonesian history. It was the Sultan of Ternate who entertianed Sir Francis Drake and signed with him a commercial treaty aimed at securing an ally against the Sultan of Tidore, then in league with the Portuguese. But it was left to the Dutch traders to stay longer on these island stepping-stones. The result was that they finally extracted a treaty (the Bongay Contract of 1667) from the then Sultan of Tidore, who abandoned all his claims to the Moluccas and to islands east of Lombok. The Contract became the basis of Dutch relations with other Sultans in East Indonesia and marks the complete success of the attempts of the Dutch East India Company to establish a monopoly of the spice trade.

By the time the Dutch Empire was transferred to the British at the beginning of the nineteenth century, these spice islands had lost some of their importance to Java. The Raffles period broke Holland's monopoly, and introduced a more enlightened rule. When the country was transferred to Holland again, there were popular risings which do not claim any major attention in Dutch history books but which are the landmarks of national struggle in the minds of the people. In May 1951, the death anniversary of a local leader was celebrated in the Moluccas. It was at this celebration that I heard the story of the Pattimura Rebellion of May 1817, presented in speeches and songs in broadcasts and in tableaux written specially for the occasion.

This was the story. In the Moluccan island of Saparuwa, when the time came for it to be transferred from British to Dutch rule, the headmen secretly called a meeting in the town hall to organize resistance. The meeting formed itself into a council of action; the captains of units were called 'pattimura' —hence the name of the revolt. Matulesiah, who had been a non-commissioned officer in the militia created by the British, was chosen to be Commander-in-Chief. Other people who were present included Christina Marta Tyahohu, the daughter of King Abuwo. Her special role was to make contact with the King of Bali and other royal personages. On May 15th, 1817, at four o'clock in the morning, the war started. The first objective was the Dutch garrison in Durstede Fort. This was taken by surprise; the Resident and his family (except a small son who was allowed to go back to Holland) and the entire garrison were killed. Before praus with reinforcements could arrive on the scene, the Pattimuras had won several important positions. The first expedition against them was a failure; most of the Dutch officers were killed, and only thirty privates escaped; reinforcements were brought in from the nearby island of Amboina; they too were defeated. The rebellion then found support in Amboina, Ceram, Haruku, and Musa Laut, and the fighting included a naval battle with the Dutch Admiral Buyskes. Towards the end of September the revolt had assumed such serious proportions that a considerable expedition was sent out which finally landed in Saparua in November. The

95

Pattimura, E. S. de Klerck records, 'had to be driven out of their entrenchments, and then attacked in their fortified villages, one of which, called Ulat, was a veritable bulwark'.[6] At this point the Dutch accepted defeat and negotiations were started with Matulesiah. But, according to the story told me in 1951, this was only a trap. The Pattimuras, believing the war was won, held a feast to celebrate it. In the middle of these jollifications, at which Matulesiah and Christina Marta Tyahohu were both present, Dutch troops surrounded the building and made many arrests. On December 16th, at seven o'clock in the morning, Matulesiah and his Pattimuras were hanged in front of the Dutch fort. Their corpses were exposed to the people and then thrown into the Banda Sea. As for the heroine, she was exiled to Java, but she died before reaching there, and was buried at sea.

The Dutch had won a military victory, but conditions remained so unsettled that three years later a committee was appointed to make an investigation. Their proposals, which included the abolition of forced deliveries of cloves and nutmegs, and the mitigation of forced labour, were not adopted and the situation grew worse. The result was another rebellion in 1829, but as plans leaked out beforehand, it was soon suppressed. And the monopoly system, which was the chief cause of trouble, was re-introduced by the Dutch. It was not until 1864 that conditions on the island were so bad that the Dutch Government was compelled to end monopoly and to discontinue forced labour and the compulsory delivery of cloves.

Two years later, the Government of the Moluccas was divided into three separate divisions with Residents in Amboina and Ternate and an Assistant Resident in Banda. They had little authority beyond the coastlines of most of the islands. But the Dutch were now far more interested in Java, where conditions were easier, communications easy, the soil fertile, and cheap labour abundant. Never again did the Moluccas achieve any significance; they were never raised to the status of a province 'because of the backward social conditions prevailing in most of its territory'.[7]

Apart from an occasional scientific expedition, the Protestant missionaries were almost the only Dutch people who stayed for any length of time in any of the islands. Many of them have a distinguished record in both medical work and the provision of schools. In islands such as Amboina, where Islam had never gained a foothold, most of the inhabitants became Christians. Many Amboinese, for example, are third-generation Christians belonging to a Church which is now largely Indonesianized; the ministers are almost all Indonesians and in 1935 the Indonesian Church was given self-governing rights, except in the case of finance. This common religion with the Dutch led in Amboina, as it did in the Minahasa, to a subtle integration which has had extremely important political consequences, and it may not be accidental that these two areas supplied most of the recruits for the Dutch army in pre-war days. Again, some thousands of Amboinese and Menadonese fought in the Royal Netherlands Indies army in the post-war period when the Dutch tried to regain control. To which it must be added that the areas which have created problems of law and order in the Republic have included Menado and Amboina. It seems to be true that where missionaries achieved the greatest success, they also created a difficult problem of divided allegiance.

This factor has helped to delay the consolidation of the Republic, and for that reason alone, it warrants attention. One of the many unfortunate clauses in the Round Table Conference Agreement stated that the Royal Netherlands Indies army (K.N.I.L.) should be dissolved by July 26th, 1950. Republican delegates weakly accepted Dutch excuses that transport difficulties would prevent them from dissolving this colonial army before that date. Now a large proportion of these 65,000 soldiers came from Amboina, from Minahasa, and from Timor. When July 26th, 1950, arrived, 26,000 of them had joined the Indonesian army, 18,750 had been demobilized in Indonesia, and 3,250 left for Holland.[8] This meant that 17,000 ex-K.N.I.L. men with the status of Dutch soldiers, under Dutch officers, remained in the country. The Dutch had not forgotten the technique of playing one area off against another; men from the eastern part of Indonesia were paid higher wages than those from Java and other areas. Professor George Kahin, who was in the country during this period, says that the men from

E   97

Christian areas were often told by the Dutch that 'in an Indonesia where the Republic was dominant their own Christian areas would be controlled by Mohammedan Javanese'.[9]

The K.N.I.L. army proved to be a centre of and a focal point for discontent and disaffection. The most serious incident among many happened in Amboina. On April 25th, 1950, a group of Amboinese, with the help of some Dutch officers, proclaimed the Republic of the South Moluccas, which was to be separate both from the East Indonesian State still in existence and from the Republic of the United States of Indonesia. From the outset, the Indonesian Government naturally regarded this as an act of rebellion, but its policy was to find some peaceful solution rather than to take military steps to suppress it. A Cabinet Mission, led by Dr. Leimena, an Amboinese Christian who was Minister of Health, left two days later to go to Amboina, but failed to open negotiations. The Dutch military command, then responsible for K.N.I.L. troops, issued an order to the rebel soldiers to withdraw from the movement. Not only was their order disobeyed, but the Commander of the Dutch Armed Forces who was sent from Indonesian Timor to order the troops back to their barracks, assisted in striking the Dutch flag and the hoisting of the 'national flag of the South Moluccas'. The rebels were naturally encouraged to continue their rebellion. Meanwhile, a second effort was made to find a peaceful solution; a brotherhood mission of Amboinese in Java tried, but failed, to reach the island. Finally, in July, troops were sent to nearby islands, and in September they landed in Amboina, meeting with considerable resistance on the part of the 'Green Berets' as the rebels called themselves. Some of them who surrendered, accompanied by an Indonesian army officer, went to their colleagues to seek a peaceful solution. This too failed, and the officer was murdered. Fighting continued until November 1950, when organized resistance was overcome. The Indonesian national flag was flown in the town of Ambon, and the Government settled down to send clothing, food, and medicine through the Indonesian Red Cross. A prominent Amboinese, Dr. Latuharhary, was reappointed Governor of the Province of the Moluccas, and the situation gradually became normal. The

Governor had a constructive programme to offer: it was a plan for the economic rehabilitation of the South Moluccas by a company in Djakarta for which the Ministry of Economic Affairs had agreed to allocate a capital of 1 million rupiahs.

The Amboinese in Holland are fertile soil for Dutch propaganda against the Republic, and keep alive the separatist tendency which has not yet been entirely overcome. The factors of geography and lack of communications still exist in Republican days as they did in the bygone days of warring Sultans, of British-Dutch rivalry and of Dutch rule, and the older generation of Amboinese still have their roots in the Dutch system and their psychology is still orientated towards The Hague. The younger generations growing up in the Republic now have, for the first time in the history of these famous spice islands, an opportunity of being part of their own country. Slowly the Government in Djakarta is winning their loyalty, and helping them to feel an integral part of the Republic. But there are dangerous separatist elements which still cling to the idea of a Republic of the South Moluccas, and even in 1955 stability has not yet been achieved in this area.

WEST IRIAN (WEST NEW GUINEA)

The word 'Irian' is used by Indonesians to describe the island, shaped like some mythical animal, sprawling across the Equator to the north of Australia. In the vernacular language 'Irian' means 'hot country' ('iri' stands for land, and 'an' means warm), and the word is in common use amongst the literate part of the inhabitants. The name 'New Guinea' by which the island is generally known is derived from a Spanish-Latin word.

The island is divided about equally between West Irian (still Dutch-controlled) and Australian New Guinea. It is with West Irian that we are concerned. Twelve times the size of Holland, about as large as Japan, this country has been so far removed from the industrialized world in space and time that their first glimpse of it was General MacArthur's Superforts in 1944. So little was it known that when American and Australian planes surveyed it in the war against Japan, they discovered that there were four times more people living there than Dutch official figures had suggested; a million where 250,000 was the usual estimate in Dutch publications.

'Of the population of New Guinea,' the Dutch stated in an official report,

> 'only a fourth part has been brought under administration which involves, amongst other things, that the far greater part of the population is still in a very primitive state, owing to which it is unable to express itself politically.'[10]

The same report introduces the research of geologists and zoologists, linguists and anthropologists, naturalists and biologists, to substantiate Dutch claims to West Irian. But research must be applied, and the fact remains that of the million people living in West Irian, only a quarter of them have had any contact with Dutch administration; that of the remainder, the great majority consist of tribes speaking hundreds of dialects, living nomadic lives, with no money economy, making payments with a kind of sea-shell, rarely wearing clothes or, when they do, wearing only a loincloth made of labu fruit (a kind of pumpkin). They are described as being

> 'one of the three most prolific centres of primitive sculpture in wood, the other areas being Negro Africa and North-West America . . . wood is used as a raw material for practical purposes everywhere, and ornamentation of utilitarian objects, with engraved patterns, often filled in with colour pigments, or, in many parts, decorative designs carved in open work, is more common than in any other part of the world. In fact, throughout the vast island there is hardly any implement, ritual or profane, without a plastic or linear decoration of some kind. But even utilitarian objects are mostly adorned with motifs derived from the mythology, religious beliefs, ancestor-cult or magic of the tribes . . . The primitive art of West Irian', the same writer continues, 'clearly reveals Indonesian influence.'[11]

Perhaps the most distinctive Papuan object is the korwar, a wooden casket for the skull of an ancestor shaped out of a piece of wood and elaborately carved. The skull, which is believed to have magical power, is modelled and painted in white and red and human hair is added to complete the effect. Papuan exhibits in the museum in Djakarta have a collection of these korwars and of such other characteristic objects as highly decorative bead-work and carved birds used in totemistic dances and religious rituals.

Like their art, the customary laws which govern the lives of West Irianese also show an Indonesian influence. In the coastal areas, people claim the right to possess the soil 'from the sea-shore to the mountains', and their ideas of usufruct and rights of property are similar. The village headman has extensive rights, differing according to areas; sometimes his permission is needed to catch fish or to hunt pigs, and he is entitled to a certain proportion of the products of forest, lake, or sea.

In the interior, especially in the mountain areas, there are many tribes speaking hundreds of dialects of which only the name is known. Like the people in the interior of Sulawesi, Kalimantan, and Sumatra, they have had little contact with the coastal people and many of them are still living in Stone Age conditions. To colonial rulers they were of no significance; they were living in thousands of small villages too remote to be accessible, they were peoples producing nothing that was economically worth while; they were, at the most, scientific specimens. To the Republic they are human beings, citizens who can only transform their Stone Age lives when freed from colonialism. Republicans, President Sukarno once said, do not advance arguments touching the question of 'intelligent-or-not-intelligent, Irian-having-the-same-blood-as-we-or-not, Irian-being-grown-up-or-not' but 'on the question colonialism or non-colonialism, independence or dependence'.

Thus, when West Irian was transferred to the Republic with the remainder of the territory known as the Netherlands East Indies, Dutch policy was, and is still, considered as colonial in this respect. In the Round Table Conference Agreement, it was stated

'that the status of the residency of New Guinea shall be maintained with the stipulation that within a year from the date of transfer of sovereignty to the Republic of the United States of Indonesia, the question of the political status of New Guinea be determined through negotiations between the Republic of the United States of Indonesia and the Kingdom of the Netherlands'.

That was in December 1949. Negotiations held in Djakarta and The Hague have so far failed, whilst a Joint Commission which visited West Irian in 1950 could not agree on a Joint Report. In 1955 no settlement is in sight.

Dutch concern about West Irian is a matter of prestige and strategy. Without this territory, they have no land to call their own in the whole continent of Asia. With this territory as a foothold, there is always the danger that it may be used as a springboard against the Republic. Meanwhile, it is a source of trouble between the Dutch and the Indonesians who naturally regard the question as one of colonialism or non-colonialism.

During the long period of her occupation West Irian was never of any importance to Holland. Indeed, for most of that time, Dutch policy recognized the right of the Sultan of Tidore to his claims over this territory. In the earliest days of the East India Company, the Board of Seventeen wrote to one of their agents that in these 'wild areas there was nothing to be done that would bring profit to the Company'.[12] In 1660 they made a 'Union and Eternal Alliance' with the Sultan which gave them the opportunity of exerting their influence whenever they so chose. The Dutch East Indies Company

'was not directly interested in this island. What did matter to her', the Dutch admit officially, 'was that it could not be used as a stepping stone for British or Spanish intruders, a danger to which its situation—so near the splendid spice-islands—was apt to contribute. In exchange for this favour all the Company expected of Tidore was that it would check the Papuan piracy.'[13]

Dutch policy remained completely indifferent until 1761 when the Company was alarmed by an English boat signalled on the north coast. A century of indifference again followed until 1826, when rumours went round that the English were considering a settlement on the south coast. Two years later, a secret treaty with the Sultan of Tidore acknowledged and de-marcated his rights. Still Dutch interests remained extremely limited, casual, and spasmodic. Only when a potential rival appeared on the scene, or when a Sultan seemed to be develop-ing thoughts of independence, did the Dutch awake to this out-post of their Empire. The country was outside the main stream of world affairs. 'Its remote situation,' the Dutch state officially, 'its inhospitable character, the absence of tangible promises of riches of the soil quickly to be realized, all these are factors which have contributed to it.'

Both Germany and Great Britain began to stake claims for that part of the island of New Guinea which the Dutch had never considered within her sphere of influence. When German newspapers advocated the occupation of the eastern half, the Government of Queensland simply proclaimed the annexation of the territory without waiting for the approval of the Govern-ment in London. Whereupon, Germany occupied the northern part, and in 1884, a year later, a treaty was signed demarcating the boundary line between Germany and Great Britain. After the First World War, Australia acquired north-east New Guinea as a mandate; today, it is virtually an Australian colony. Meanwhile, in 1895, the boundary lines between Dutch and British territories were defined in a treaty.

Thus, it was not until the turn of the century that the Dutch made any pretence of occupying or administering West Irian. The only impact Holland made was through Moravian Brethren who carried on missionary work in face of extremely difficult physical and psychological conditions, and usually without any encouragement from The Hague. There were occasional expe-ditions in search of rare tropical flowers, insects, and animals, and geological expeditions in search of oil and gold. Most fre-quent of all was the fowling of birds of paradise by traders who made fortunes from selling their feathers in the salons and palaces of Western Europe.[14] In 1899, when the Dutch Government established direct rule over West Irian, the inhabitants of the country were almost as little known as they were in 1660 when the Dutch East India Company declared itself to be 'Lord of the Papuans'.

There is a certain irony in the fact that the largest number of immigrants to West Irian were political prisoners exiled there in 1926 and 1927 after the abortive Communist rebellions in Java and Sumatra. Far up the Digul River thousands of men and women lived and died in appalling malarial swamps, from which no escape was possible. Boven Digul acquired such notoriety among Indonesian nationalists that the phrase 'to be digulled' was used to describe the worst form of exile. Dr. Hatta and Sjahrir were among those who were later 'digulled'.

In the 'thirties, a new rival to Dutch monopoly appeared on the horizon. Japan was now a rising Power, and the thinly peopled, undeveloped territory of West Irian attracted her interest. The 'Great Asiatic Society' founded in Tokyo in 1933 included West Irian in its ambitious programme. In the following year when negotiations were taking place in Djakarta on the subject of oil, the head of the Japanese delegation openly advocated joint exploitation of West Irian; they had already secured a foothold in several agricultural and forestry concessions, and for experiments in cotton-growing. When permission was sought to import a thousand Japanese families, the proposal was turned down, not because the Dutch did not require more workers, but because they suspected Japan's desire to build a naval base. In the Japanese Parliament questions appeared on the order paper suggesting that settlement in West Irian might be the best solution of their over-population problem.

The strategic importance of West Irian became clear as soon as Japanese bombs fell on Pearl Harbour. Situated at the intersection of two oceans, the Pacific and the Indian Ocean, and of two continents, Asia and Australasia, it was destined to play a vital part at the beginning and at the end of the war with Japan. Even in the First World War the Germans had recognized the value of West Irian harbours; their raider, the *Emden*, was hidden in Fak-Fak Bay for overhaul whilst the Australian navy searched for it in vain for a month. In the Second World War, it was the last line of defence for Australia, whilst General MacArthur used Hollandia as an advance base from which his troops began their island-hopping campaign which took them step by step to the shores of Japan.

One of the first results of West Irian's involvement in the war was an unexpected development in the self-consciousness of the people living round the coastal areas. It had its origins in a mythical, rather than a political belief, that one day the Millennium would arrive, when the Messiah would appear on earth and introduce a happiness that would be eternal. The same kind of idea was present in other parts of Indonesia, particularly in Java, where it was known as Djojobojo, and in East Irian where it was named Vailala. A more clearly defined idea was embodied in the Mansren Movement which was related to the prophet (Konoor) who ruled over a happy country. During the Japanese occupation it assumed considerable proportions, and some hundreds of its members were murdered by Japanese troops. When American and Australians arrived in 1945 after dropping leaflets from aeroplanes promising freedom and a higher standard of living, many Irianese believed the Millennium was about to begin.

In addition to these symbolic movements, groups of people worked politically in a number of coastal towns. The most important of them was in Serui in the north, led by Silas Papare. He refused to collaborate with the Japanese and lost his job with the Dutch New Guinea Oil Company as a result. In May 1944 he made his first contact with the American army, and from that time onwards he gave valuable assistance; he found out and passed on to the Americans such information as the number and position of Japanese troops, their arms, and munition dumps. He was sent ahead of General MacArthur's landing to make investigations and to prepare people for the attack. He led groups of the people's army in their fight against the Japanese, and finally joined the Australians in their decisive attack on Morotai in February 1945.

When the Proclamation of Independence was made in Djakarta in August 1945, politically minded people in West Irian believed that their struggle, not only against the Japanese, but against Dutch colonialism, had ended; that Indonesia, from Sabang (in Atjeh) to Merauke in West Irian, would be free. When the return of Dutch troops with S.E.A.C. showed that this was not so, political activities increased in West Irian as they did elsewhere. Groups were organized here and there, led in a number of instances by men who had been released from the prison camp of Boven Digul at the beginning of the war. A battalion of Papuans revolted in Hollandia in December 1945, and joined up with ex-Digulists to organize against the Dutch. A year later, a rebellion on a considerable scale was planned; it was prevented at the last moment by Dutch authorities sending home to Sumatra all those men who had been banished to Boven Digul in 1926-7 for similar activities.

The movement now became co-ordinated in the Partai Kemerdekaan Indonesia Irian (Indonesian Independence Party Irian), whose aim was the liberation of West Irian and its inclusion in the Republic; its flag was the Indonesian flag and President Sukarno was acknowledged as their leader. It is undoubtedly true that this movement has not yet extended far into the interior, that thousands of men and women, living in Stone Age conditions, have not yet heard the word 'Merdeka' (Freedom). But the essential fact is that the environment of nationalism has been created in West Irian and that whilst the rate of its growth cannot be forecast, the inevitability of its growth is certain. Dutch colonial policy in these circumstances is doomed to failure. Their claim to West Irian on the grounds of their ability to administer the territory will not stand the most superficial analysis. The argument that West Irian 'does not belong to Indonesia in ethnological, linguistic, geological, zoological, and botanical respects, that anthropologically, too, there are fundamental differences with the Indonesian people', does not carry any conviction, especially in a country where diversity is such an outstanding characteristic. No more convincing is the argument that since

'80% of the population of this area has not yet been brought under administration and therefore is neither in a position nor capable to exercise its right of self-determination, and because the remaining 20% of the population has, on the whole, not yet reached such a stage of development that it would be possible to give it at this juncture already such a share in the independent administration of its affairs that this could be qualified as full self-government'.[15]

To these arguments Dutch apologists add the need for some part of the world where their overpopulated islands can find relief, and where Eurasians can feel free to build new lives for themselves and their families.

Left to themselves the Indonesians and Dutch might have evolved some mutually satisfactory arrangement; the Dutch, for example, might have acknowledged Indonesian sovereignty over West Irian, and the Indonesians might have agreed to joint development projects. But even West Irian cannot remain outside the stream of world politics, and Australia, increasingly concerned with power politics and military strategy in the Pacific, has entered the stage of Indonesian-Dutch negotiations from the wings. Under Australian pressure, the Government in The Hague has hesitated to come to those terms which realistic Dutchmen, in business circles in Holland as well as in Indonesia, have supported in private, if not in public.

With the active encouragement of Australian official circles, the attitude of the Dutch about West Irian has hardened. In April 1954 the Dutch Government said that it was not prepared 'to negotiate on the political status of West Irian' and during discussions later on that year on the ending of the Union Statute, they refused a proposal to put it on the Agenda. At this point the Indonesians decided to raise the matter in the United Nations, and it was discussed in the Political Committee. A Resolution asking the General Assembly to call upon Indonesia and Holland to resume negotiations on West Irian with a view to achieving an early agreement on the political status of the territory, and inviting the Secretary-General to assist the parties in implementing this Resolution, received the support of 34 countries (14 voted against and 10 abstained). But when the General Assembly discussed it, the 8-nations Resolution failed to get the necessary two-thirds majority. Nevertheless the issue had been brought before a forum of world opinion, and it could no longer be regarded as merely an internal dispute between Indonesia and Holland. In Indonesia, the West Irian Organization set up in 1953 under the direct supervision of the Prime Minister, has become an important affair.

The problem of West Irian therefore remains like a

thundercloud in the Indonesian landscape, liable to break at any time with disastrous results. Unsettled, it is a threat to Indonesian stability; as an integral part of the Republic it would reinforce that stability, as well as that of South-east Asia, and would give the peoples of West Irian opportunities of development which are inconceivable under the belated paternalism of Dutch colonial rule.

NOTES

[1] The story is told in detail in *Sedjarah Perang Tondano* (1807–9), by H. M. Taulu. Published in Menado, 1937.

[2] *Memoir of Sir Thomas Stamford Raffles*, by Lady Raffles, p. 238. Letter to Mr. Marsden (1815).

[3] *Dutch Activities in the East*, edited by Nihar-Ranjan Roy. The Book Emporium, Calcutta, 1945.

[4] *Netherlands India*, by J. S. Furnivall, p. 27.

[5] It was reopened in 1953.

[6] *History of the Netherlands East Indies*, by E. S. de Klerck, Vol. 2, p. 96.

[7] *The Dutch East Indies*, by Amry Vandenbosch, third edition, 1942, p. 131. University of California Press.

[8] The last troops left Indonesia in June 1951.

[9] *Nationalism and Revolution in Indonesia*, by George Kahin, p. 453. Cornell University Press, 1952.

[10] *Report of the Committee New Guinea (Irian)*, 1950, Part II. Text of the Netherlands Main Constituent, p. 65. Published by the Secretariat of the Netherlands-Indonesian Union, 1950.

[11] *Primitive Art*, by Leonard Adam, pp. 152–4. Penguin Books, 1940. Enlarged edition, 1949.

[12] *Report of the Committee New Guinea (Irian)*, 1950, Part III. Text of the Indonesian Main Constituent, p. 10.

[13] Ibid., Part II. Text of the Netherlands Main Constituent, p. 25.

[14] This was banned in 1923 because of the abuses associated with it. Fowling was then allowed only if indigenous (Papuan) fowlers were employed. Breach-loading guns were prohibited.

[15] *Report of the Committee New Guinea (Irian)*, 1950, Part IV, appendixes, p. 43.

CHAPTER VI

INDIVIDUALISM IN BALI

THE island of Bali has an individuality which is not unlike that of Ireland. Novelist, poet, the doggerelist, the painter, and the camera-man have lavished praise on their landscape and their women which is none the less embarrassing because it is so richly deserved. Legends, now violent and warlike, now graceful and imaginative, take the place of factual records of their earlier history. In both countries, religion has remained unchanged for centuries; Hinduism has made as few concessions to Islam as Catholicism has to Protestantism. The Irish, in their colder, greyer climate, and bleak stony soil, have not achieved the luxurious festivals of the Balinese; cabbages, potatoes, and shamrock are a poor, although a genuine, substitute for the exquisitely arranged offerings of golden rice, pineapple, and champak which Balinese offer to their Hindu gods. In another respect too, Irish and Balinese have their likenesses; history has made rebels of both of them. Dutchmen, like Englishmen, complain that they are the most difficult people to handle. This is one of the reasons why the whole of Bali was not pacified until 1914, by which time the Dutch considered that 'Balinese resistance was sufficiently controlled, and the army was replaced by a police force'.[1] Not until that date could the Dutch reorganize the government of the island by keeping or putting in power those who were willing to act as puppets.

Long before the first Dutch ships visited Bali—towards the end of the sixteenth century—the island had been sometimes under the rule of Javanese kings and sometimes independent. The most important Javanese conquest of Bali was directed by the famous General Gadjah Mada, the first man, as we have already seen, to unite the whole Indonesian archipelago. He himself went to Bali to subjugate the ruling king. His victory in

1343 brought Bali under Javanese rule, but the Balinese have many stories of their revolts against the Madjapahit rulers. When the empire came to an end, partly for internal reasons, partly because of the success of Muslim conquest, an event occurred which had the result of stabilizing Hindu society. Bali has retained it until the present day. Although Hinduism in Bali was introduced direct from India, it was consolidated when the Javanese Court, with its priests and artists, escaped from the Muslim invaders and settled down on the south coast of Bali, their last remaining colony. There, the King's son proclaimed himself as King of Bali—the Dewa Agung. He divided the island into regions over which his relations and generals were appointed as governors. They gradually became independent kingdoms, and Bali had nine kings instead of one. Bali was never conquered by the Muslims. Its culture was enriched by artists and intellectuals from Java, and the art, the religion, and the philosophy of Hinduism have remained practically unaltered ever since those days in or about 1520. When Javanese rulers, filled with enthusiasm for their new religion of Islam, tried to conquer Bali, they were defeated.

The Dutch traders who discovered Bali fell victims to its charms. The King's hospitality to Cornelius Houtman and his fleet in 1597 was such that it tempted some of the sailors to desert and settle down in this 'paradise on earth'. They were impressed by a society in which the King had 200 wives and an unlimited number of slaves. They returned to Holland to pass on the exciting discovery, and Admiral van Semskerk was almost immediately dispatched on a mission to Bali with presents for the King. The King responded by presenting the Admiral with a beautiful Balinese girl.

Bali had no immediate economic interest for the Dutch traders except in the plentiful supply of slaves. In this the Balinese and Dutchmen settled down to an extremely profitable trade and they were more or less agreed as to their respective spheres of capture. The best prices were usually obtained in Batavia. In those days, Dr. Vlekke writes,

'The European citizens never went out without their escort of slaves, one of whom carried the pajong or sunshade . . .

Only Governor-General Van Riebeeck (1709–1713) had the exotic idea of taking along an escort of beautifully dressed slave girls riding on donkeys when he drove out to his country home outside the city.'[2]

An official statement of 1778 gives the number of Balinese slaves sent to Batavia as 13,000.

When Sir Thomas Raffles was Governor-General he paid a visit to Bali. The usual price of a male slave, he recorded, was from ten to thirty dollars, of a female from fifty to one hundred. He added his hope that 'this disgraceful traffic will soon be entirely annihilated'.[3] He proceeded to abolish slave-trading in the face of strong opposition from the Balinese as well as Dutch traders. When the island was handed back to Holland, slave-trading was resumed. During the Java war, E. S. de Klerck writes that this happened 'under the euphemistic label of enlistment, for it was the need of recruits which prompted the Government to send a representative to Badung. When recruits were no longer wanted, Bali was again left to its own devices.'[4]

But only a few years afterwards, a Dutch expedition secured the control of North Bali. It was an old Balinese custom that any ship which ran ashore should be confiscated with all its passengers and its cargo. When a Dutch ship ran ashore on the north coast in 1846, and the Balinese Rajah, when asked, refused to give up his rights, the Governor-General decided to send an expedition. The land forces were 400 Europeans, 100 Negroes, and 700 natives, 600 auxiliaries, and a landing party of 600. The Balinese, E. S. de Klerck records, 'were reckoned among the bravest, best disciplined and organized native foes the Dutch army ever had to fight against in the Archipelago'.[5] The Balinese lost more than 2,000 men in the battle for the fortress near Buleleng in June 1848. A second expedition having failed to defeat Balinese resistance, preparations were made on such a scale that De Klerck says 'never before had so strong a force been pitted against a native enemy'.[6]

The war lasted until June 1849 when the Rajahs of North Bali at a special Assembly in Badung agreed to acknowledge Dutch authority, refrain from relations with other nations, not allow other Europeans to settle in Bali without permission of the Dutch Government, pull down their fortifications, help the Dutch in time of war, check piracy and slavery and waive the shore rights. In return for this, their first victory in Bali, the Dutch agreed not to occupy the land and to refrain from interference in its internal affairs.

The war for North Bali was over, but the most important element of victory lay in the fact that Dutchmen were now able to use their influence in dividing Rajah from Rajah. The Dewa Agung (the highest Rajah) still considered himself the ruler of the island although he nominally owed allegiance to the Dutch Government. By playing one Rajah off against another, by sending expeditions when local rebellions occurred and by placing their officials in important positions, the Dutch were able to establish themselves in North Bali by the end of the century, and the states of Buleleng and Jembrana were brought under direct rule.

The conquest of South Bali began in 1900 when the Rajah of Gianyar asked for Dutch protection against a powerful alliance of neighbouring Rajahs. Protection turned out to be annexation, and a prelude to Dutch victory over the whole area. The final stages of Balinese resistance are still described by eyewitnesses or their children. Vicki Baum has based her novel *A Tale from Bali*[7] on such documentary evidence. The excuse for the large military expedition which landed in Sanur on September 15th, 1906, was the unwillingness of the local Rajah to pay compensation for a Chinese steamer wrecked off the coast and then looted by his subjects. When the navy bombarded Den Pasar and defeat was inevitable, the Rajah led his priests, his generals, his relations into a 'puputan', a 'fight to the end'. Men and women, armed with spears and krisses, met Dutch troops in the long avenue in the centre of Den Pasar. When the Rajah was shot dead, his wives stabbed themselves over his body. Entranced women threw handfuls of gold coins to the troops with terrifying requests to be killed. On the Dutch side, only one man, a sergeant, lost his life; he was stabbed by a woman. The Dutch won, 'but their victory tasted of a terrible moral defeat'.[8]

Two years later, only one independent Rajah remained—

the Dewa Agung of Klungkung; others had been eliminated by force or had taken their own lives rather than surrender. After another puputan in the main street of Klungkung the Dutch won their last victory. The army stayed on till 1914 when their place was taken by an armed police corps. Administration followed the general pattern adopted by the Rajahs. Those who were willing to do so became puppet Regents with Dutch Controllers who were nominally advisers.

Dutch visitors now began to appear in the island—generally in the eastern half, since the western part is mainly scrub and desert and almost uninhabited. Like their countrymen nearly 300 years before, they too succumbed to its beauty and set out to put Bali 'on the map'. The tourist boom of the 'thirties was the result. Shiploads of visitors arrived in Sanur, on the beaches which had echoed Dutch shells only twenty years earlier. They were shepherded from temple to temple, from beauty spot to beauty spot, from Dutch hotel to Dutch hotel, in Dutch buses and Dutch cars, from Chinese and Dutch souvenir store to souvenir store. The K.P.M. shipping line hired dancers from the villages to perform to the Balinese gamelan.

The K.P.M. built Western-style hotels in Den Pasar and Singaradja; in such 'beauty spots' as Kintamani. The K.P.M. representatives bought paintings and carvings and hand-made jewellery from Balinese painters and craftsmen and sold them to tourists. Anything that proved popular, irrespective of its artistic merits, was commissioned in quantities that forced Balinese artists to become mere copyists, mass producers of hand-made goods.

Bali became one of the world's most fashionable tourist centres, a paradise for escapists in the difficult days of the 'thirties. There were exceptions, of course; artists who appreciated the highly developed art forms in dance, in painting, and carving; writers who were attracted by the beauty of Balinese landscape and the everyday life of the people in their homes and their temples. But to the majority of foreign visitors, Bali was a pageant, queer, unusual, exotic, and full of colour. Few of them understood the significance of Balinese culture, the unique blending of animism and Hinduism. The Balinese

themselves, convinced that theirs was a heavenly island, specially
blessed by the gods, felt superior to the foreigner and looked on
the Dutch as barbarians; their chief desire was to maintain their
own culture, their religious practices, and their Hinduistic
system of caste society. Thus, when Dutch missionaries began
to penetrate Balinese life, introducing a bleak austere Christianity, Balinese representatives moved a resolution in the Volksraad asking the Government 'to refrain from giving either direct
or indirect support to propaganda of a religious nature'. The
Balinese religion and social order, they maintained, were so
integrated that any form of Christianity would disturb its equilibrium. Dutch missionaries pointed out that Bali was already
open to tourist traffic, commerce, the movies, Western administration, science, and education, so why, they asked, should
Christianity be excluded? These foreign influences, they argued,
could only disintegrate Balinese society, whereas Christian
missions would have the effect of a great spiritual revival.

The resolution was accepted in 1932, but the issue still remained undecided ten years later when Dutchmen in Bali, as
elsewhere, were interned and the island was occupied by
Japanese troops. The Balinese were as incomprehensible ·to
their new invaders as they were to the Dutch. These had an
initial but shortlived advantage in so far as they were Asians.
But they failed to make any impact on Balinese society and
remained as aloof as their predecessors had been from the
Balinese families behind their thatched mud walls.

Bali was reoccupied in March 1946 by Dutch troops led by
an Indian division. Fighting between Republican forces in Bali
and the Dutch continued until the middle of 1948. The island
remained under a state of 'war and siege' ('staat van oorlog en
beleg'). Support for the Republic increased although there were
suspicions because it was declared in Java and Javanese Muslims
might challenge Hinduism. And there were Rajahs in the Rajah
Council who having won their position under Dutch rule, were
now afraid that it might be challenged by the more dynamic
political elements in Java. Dr. van Mook found people willing
to co-operate with him in his federal schemes until the second
military action exposed the reality of Dutch intentions. A

Dutch-sponsored federal state was Dutch colonialism in a new guise. The Balinese Prince, Anak Agung, who served as Prime Minister in the Dutch-sponsored state of East Indonesia resigned and played a decisive role in subsequent talks between Republicans and Federalists.

Today, Bali still retains its own individual system of society and Hinduism remains deeply rooted in the lives of the people. But there are signs of tension and of change. The first impression which strikes the visitor landing in Den Pasar concerns an announcement written in large letters like this:

ANNOUNCEMENT

IT IS PROHIBITED TO ANYBODY TO MAKE PHOTOGRAPHS OF BALINESE WOMEN WITHOUT BREAST-COVERING OR NUDE, DONE ON PURPOSE OR ACCIDENTALLY, AS IT IS CONSIDERED UNDIGNIFIED AND HUMILIATING TO THE BALINESE WOMEN IN PARTICULAR AND THE INDONESIAN NATIONALITY IN GENERAL.

RESIDENT OF BALI

The same poster was placed in a prominent position in the Bali Hotel some fifteen miles away in the town itself. I heard the story of the announcement from a Balinese woman. In Dutch times, when thousands of tourists visited the island, they invariably photographed or filmed or described the women who were, as Sir Thomas Raffles had described them more than a century earlier, 'fairer than the women in Java, and wearing no covering above the waist, the natural beauty and symmetry of their shape is neither restrained nor concealed'. The twentieth-century tourists, armed with cine-cameras, popularized Balinese women as magazine covers the world over. Dutch guides lost no opportunity of publicizing their photogenic colonials. Film producers and script-writers from Hollywood and elsewhere had exploited the natural beauty of Balinese girls, their well-balanced features, golden-bronze skin, their firm uncovered breasts, and their slender bodies. Whilst this was tolerated with varying degrees of contempt in colonial days, the attitude of Balinese women began to change when the Republic was born. Matters came to a head in 1950 when a foreign photographer persuaded young Balinese girls to pose for him and then published the photographs with sexy captions familiar enough to the Western reader but crude and undignified in Balinese eyes. The Kaepala Daera—the administrative head of the island— agreed, under pressure from the women, to prevent any recurrence of this incident. The result was the announcement on the aerodrome and in the Bali Hotel, signed by the Resident, acting in his capacity as representative of the Governor of the Lesser Sunda Islands, of which Bali is the best known.

Some of the Balinese women on the local People's Council wanted to take more drastic steps; they suggested that the Central Government should prosecute anyone who photographed women without breast-covering. They put the proposal before President Sukarno when he paid one of his frequent visits to Bali to see his mother, a Balinese woman. Now the President is a connoisseur of painting and by no means narrow-minded and puritanical. He told the women that this was not a matter of laws. They must decide for themselves whether or not they wished to be photographed. The Venus de Milo, he added, had superb beauty; neither she nor the image of Sita, so pure, so perfect, aroused any sexual feelings in him. He left the women to settle this problem themselves.

The glamorization of Balinese women has obscured the part they play in everyday life. In the street in Den Pasar where the famous puputan (fight to the end) had taken place, I saw women cementing the sides of a sewer; two women were painting the outside of a house; others were making furniture from bamboo poles. Outside the town, they were mending roads. They all belonged to a trade union and worked a forty-hour week. None of them had been to school but several of them attended a mass illiteracy school (P.B.H.) in their village. In the markets, women did most of the work; they sat behind piles of coconuts, durians, pineapples, papayas, all beautifully arranged and clean; they cooked food in tall black saucepans like coal scuttles; they sold spices and vegetables; they made piles of slices of fried bananas, fried fish, and little sweetmeats of fried coconut wrapped in strips of banana leaves. They walked here and there through the crowds carrying piles of merchandise stacked high on their heads. They carried young porkers in their arms and one of them held a basket on her head with twenty-four fowls arranged like rolls round a plate; they were alive though they had long since given up squawking for their freedom. In the centre of the market, women sold gay cotton materials, arranged with a natural grace and sense of design on platforms slightly raised from the floor.

This gift of design which all Balinese women seem to possess is lavished on offerings they make to the gods, especially on feast days, and there are many such days in Bali. They cut out intricate, stylized patterns in palm leaves; they plait figures in rice straws; they build pyramids of fruit and flowers; they make rice cakes and paint them in gay colours and geometrical patterns; they fill large plaited baskets with all kinds of sweetmeats wrapped in neat little green strips of banana or palm leaf held together with tiny thorns. At the entrance to the temple, tall bamboos bend gently, their stems decorated with bits of cloth, tiny bundles of rice and flowers. The best of everything is showered on the gods; in their homes many women begin the day by making an offering of food, or fruit, or flowers to the household gods which live in tiny houses like dovecotes. Were they, I wondered, or did they only seem to be, indifferent to the dust and muddle in which they lived, these Balinese women with such a wonderful sense of colour? Their compounds, where as many as a hundred people live together, hidden from the roadway by mud walls, were far from beautiful; pigs and fowls and pi-dogs routed round between and under the mud and bamboo houses raised slightly from the ground. Women do all their cooking in a primitive mud stove or even on fires contained in four stones built in a square. Their household possessions are reduced to a minimum; to possess a magnificently handwoven sarong with gold thread for feast days is every woman's ambition; they find expression in the temple rather than in their simple homes.

The Balinese woman has definite rights. The money she earns from sales in the market, from weaving, or selling pigs and fowls belongs to her. She is responsible for her own debts and she is often the family banker. It was not so surprising, after all, that President Sukarno listened seriously to the protests of

Balinese women against the treatment they felt they had received at the hands of an enthusiastic foreign camera-man.

Whilst women express much of their natural artistic talent in their religious ceremonies, in weaving, and, while still girls, in dancing, the painters, sculptors, writers and musicians are traditionally men. They belong to all classes; their art is hereditary, usually anonymous and sometimes communal. In one compound two boys sat carving Balinese heads now on sale in most bazaars in the cities of South-east Asia; a model head was on the wall and the boys copied it, as their father and their grandfather had done before them. Indeed, they belonged to the seventh generation of woodcarvers. The father lamented this kind of mass production by hand, which had been encouraged and made profitable by the tourist traffic. Individual work, he said, found a far smaller market, and the Chinese middlemen who owned the shops would not take the risk of buying it. But his heart was in creative, not imitative work, and he belonged to a group of artists who aimed at building an Institute of Balinese Arts in Den Pasar where individual work could be exhibited and sold. In another village I walked across ricefields to see a painter. I had no appointment; he would not have expected one. His life was spent in a village composed of houses behind long mud walls thatched with bamboo grass to keep the mud together when the rains came. He might be walking through the rice sawahs or bathing in the village pool. He was, in fact, sitting beside a half-finished painting, drinking tepid orange crush. He had chosen as his subject a temple festival and tall bamboo stems decorated with orange flowers were the centre of the picture. His two sons, aged nine and eleven, were already artists; one, as his paintings showed, had a remarkable sense of form; the other, more impulsive, sometimes careless, his father remarked, had an equally good sense of colour. The father had broken away from the traditional Balinese painting of gods set in a Balinese landscape. The two sons were still painting in the traditional style where design covers every inch of the canvas.

One of the great joys of Bali is the discovery of communal life and art in every village. In one village we found a group of old men and boys making the instruments of a gamelan orchestra.

Their work was a labour of love for the village. We wandered into the bamboo shed and sat down with the craftsmen. We were given tea out of old and very cracked cups and one of the boys immediately ran over to a wayside stall conveniently opposite, and brought back bananas, peanuts, and small green parcels of rice. The oldest man, like his father and his grandfather, was an expert in the trompong. This is the instrument which stands in the front row of the orchestra; it consists of twelve or ten balls or rather bowl-shaped gongs, and the musician strikes them with a tiny mallet. These metal gongs were not made in this tiny impromptu workshop but were tested and assembled there. The old man had a precise ear for their tone and when he was satisfied with them they were fixed into a carved wooden framework which was then painted red and gold. Other craftsmen were making genders; in an orchestra, the gender is made of metal keys, treble and bass, and, sometimes played with one hand, sometimes with two, corresponds to the first and second violins and the double bass in a Western orchestra. Against the wall stood several gongs. Craftsmen were painting the wooden frames from which they are suspended at the back of the orchestra. When the elaborately decorated trompong for the front of the orchestra and its younger brother, as it were, for the back (known as the reyong) were ready, when the genders and the gongs were completed, there would still be the drums and the bamboo flutes and the two-string violin (known as the rebab) to build. And then it would be the pride of the village, used for all ceremonials in the temples, at marriages, and other feasts. A gamelan orchestra means as much, if not more, to a Balinese village as our own village choirs and orchestras combined; most Balinese will know neither the gramophone nor the radio. It is the combination of tone dissonance and harmony in the gamelan orchestra which gives it its special beauty. The difficulty of the transposition of Western and Balinese themes, apart from its undesirability, is one of scale; it consists of five notes which correspond to our E F G B C. I have heard melodies in a gamelan orchestra played by the flute and the rebab which might perhaps be adopted by our own English flute. They would convey the haunting impression of the gentle Balinese melodies.

Between and alongside the three roads which lead from South to North Bali, the majority of the million Balinese live in villages. Most villages have the same pattern; family compounds behind long mud walls topped with grass through which a large hole is the only entrance. In the centre of a hundred such compounds, there are communal buildings, usually a temple, an assembly hall, a market, a platform for cockfights (the most popular pastime for men and boys), a rice barn, a shed with the wooden kulkul or drum to summon people, and, to complete the picture, a large wairingin or banyan tree which is considered sacred. Schools are now becoming a familiar feature. Outside the village stands a cemetery, a temple for the dead, and a field where there are kepul trees which have the same associations as cypresses have in the West. Funeral ceremonies are very important events in Bali; a family will keep a corpse lightly interred in the earth near their home for months until they can do it justice, with an elaborate procession, with rich offerings to the gods and a grand feast. When the day arrives for cremation, the body is placed in a wooden tower which is often as high as sixty feet. Ribbons and floral decorations and tiny mirrors hang from the sides. At the temple the priest is ready to recite prayers. The body is taken from the tower and after being washed in holy water, it is transferred to a wooden cow hewn out of a tree trunk. Men of the village make the cow, and decorate it according to the dead man's status; if he is a Rajah, the cow is painted gold.

Before the wooden cow is burnt, offerings are made; coins which are a ransom to the lord of hell, and chicken which will teach the soul how to fly to the Hindu heavens. When the ashes are cold they are collected in small bowls and another and last procession begins to the sea, or the nearest water. The family has honoured its dead and assured its happy reincarnation.

All Balinese temples have the same form, though there is a great variety of style in adornment. A split gateway, of which the inner walls have no ornament nor architectural detail, leads into the first court, the 'djaban' (outside), and a decorated gateway leads on into the inner court, the 'dalam' (inside). The second gateway is smaller and similar in design to the split gate if its two sides were joined together. It is raised above the ground on a stone platform and was originally designed for the use of the gods and the kings; to the right or to the left or on both sides smaller and lower entrances are designed for the lesser fry. Temples are dedicated to different gods who have their own feast days. Local artists redecorate the temples when they become shabby. I recall one dedicated to Durga, the goddess of death; village painters had recently appeased her with brightly coloured friezes of flowers and animals, and, most surprisingly, a line of motor-cars. It was just another illustration of the unselfconscious contribution which modern Balinese make to their ancient gods.

In the north of the island Singaradja, the administrative centre of Bali, seems another world although it is only a hundred miles away. This was the first part of Bali to be conquered by the Dutch, and the grander part of the town which lies on the hillside might have been transferred brick by brick from any town in Holland. Here the Governor lives; Bali is only one of his charges, since his district extends over the Lesser Sunda Islands. Here too is the home of the Resident of Bali. He and his Balinese wife, and the Governor, who was Javanese, and his wife were an extremely able quartet, imaginative and practical. Better health, better communications, new productive outlets for the artistic ability of people who are mainly illiterate—these were the main problems on their agenda. One scheme was already well under way by which local doctors working with W.H.O. and U.N.I.C.E.F. officials are trying to eliminate framboesia. For in some of the islands near Bali this terrible disease, which eats deep into the flesh, has such a grip that there are villages where 70% of the population are infected.

Near the Governor's Residence, a block of modern buildings included a cinema, a co-educational school, and a library. They were the work of Bali's leading author—I. Goesti Njoman Pandji Tisna—who had the original idea of using the proceeds of the cinema to launch the library and school. He had other ideas too; near his home on the seashore, he was just preparing a house for use as a students' hostel, as a centre for conferences and discussion groups. His novels were popular, and were often based on Balinese folk-tales. But he was as much at home on the land as he was in his study surrounded by rice-fields and orange groves. One of the first conferences, he told us, would discuss ways and means of using the mountain lands of Bali. He was an interesting example of the integration of modern scientific ideas with Balinese culture. How, young Balinese ask, can a synthesis be found between old and new? How can the natural artistry of the Balinese find new forms, new designs, new patterns of dance and song? How, in other words, can the wide horizons of modern education, and a growing literacy, deepen Balinese culture, not cheapen it? Such questions are inevitably raised by the present course of social developments. Religion and art are probably more closely integrated in Bali than in any other country. This helps to preserve the social system which maintains feudal lords at the expense of peasants crowded together in the flimsiest, most primitive houses. The older generation of Balinese, the enchanted foreigner explains, 'will feel it an honour if some decrepit Rajah compliments them by taking a fifteen-year-old daughter for a twentieth wife; still stone-carvers will carve palace walls for a Rajah if he cares but to summon them, and they acquiesce merely for the reason that "it has always been so" and receive nothing for their labour'. But the same foreigner adds, however, that 'the younger generation say—and they are probably right—that such things do not make for self-respect in the people'.[9]

The truth is that Bali cannot escape the social changes which are taking place elsewhere in Indonesia; the younger generation of Balinese would not if they could. Many Western visitors try to reconcile the irreconcilable; they want the Balinese to retain their belief in mythical monsters and the power of gods to rule their lives, but simultaneously they want to remove the prevailing fears of village people in such 'foreign magic' as vaccination. The villager who seeks to appease evil spirits by gifts of rice and fruit and flowers arranged with exquisite skill and natural artistry will refuse to allow his children innoculation against smallpox or injections to cure them of framboesia. The doctor's needle has none of the beauty of temple offerings, but it saves life and prevents the disfigurement produced by so many diseases in Bali. The modern doctor makes no appeal to the artistic sense which is so attractive in the Balinese character. The maternity nurse cannot immediately drive away the fear of 'leyaks', witches who are supposed to suck the blood of young or unborn children.

To the difficulties which this unique pattern of religion and animism, of artistry and ritual, presents in Bali the answer is probably 'Education'. A visitor to Bali today cannot but be impressed by the keen interest taken in more than a hundred new schools, and in the steps taken to increase literacy. In practically every village there is now a building, often little more than a bamboo shed, which has the letters P.B.H. over the doorway. P.B.H. stands for Pen Brantas Buta Huruf Unum (fight against illiteracy). I often stopped to have a look at these schools; in most of them the only equipment was a blackboard and a few desks or benches, and sometimes a picture on the wall of President Sukarno. The teachers were often the local priests round whom the villagers collected after working from dawn till sunset in the rice-fields. Judging from the writing on the blackboards education was mainly concerned with the ending of illiteracy. And there the problem begins, not ends. This aspect of education seemed to me to be thoroughly understood by some of the young Balinese officials working in the local Ministry of Information in Den Pasar. In May 1951, a group of young painters and woodcarvers, writers and silverworkers met frequently to discuss such questions as the following: 'How can we maintain the artistic skill which is so important a part of Balinese life?' 'How can we retain those qualities which are fundamental to our Balinese art whilst developing it and introducing new subjects and maybe, new techniques?' 'How can we rescue our artists from the habit, already stimulated by the pre-war tourist traffic, of repetition, so that our carved Balinese heads have acquired the dullness of mass production?' 'How can we improve our appallingly low standards of social conditions?' 'How can we encourage our womenfolk to desire a fuller life than that which is provided by the rice-field and the temple?' 'How can we reconcile modern hygiene and modern medicine with the practices and superstitions of the accepted religions of Hinduism and animism?' 'Can we maintain the beauties of our dances based on the old epics of the Ramayana whilst teaching people the social and moral concepts embodied in the Pantja Sila—the five principles of the Republic?' 'Can we retain the individuality of Balinese culture whilst we encourage people to feel themselves an integral part of Indonesia?' The fact that such questions were asked by the younger generation of Balinese was in itself a reflection of the revolutionary changes the Republic had made on Balinese psychology.

Bali alone of the Lesser Sunda Islands is famous, but the Governor of this province thinks of Bali as only one among many of the islands in his charge. When he and his wife visit the islands, strung between Bali and Australia like a necklace of irregular lapis lazuli, they have to consider the needs of just over two million people. This in itself is a new outlook towards islands which were among the least known of the 'Outer Provinces' of colonial times. Lombok, Sumbawa, Flores, and the western half of Timor—all of them were a happy hunting-ground for slave-trading until nearly the end of the last century. Lombok was the bone of contention between Bali and the ruling power in Makassar. Balinese Rajahs who controlled the western part of the island for a considerable period were responsible for the conversion of the western half to Hinduism. The original people, the Sasaks in eastern Lombok, are Muslims. Dutch expeditions did not succeed in pacifying the people— about 25,000 Balinese and 320,000 Sasaks—until 1902 when the last garrison was disbanded. The island of Sumbawa was even more difficult to subdue; as late as 1908, the inhabitants still resisted, and one of the epics of the Lesser Sunda Islands is the revolt of the village of Saparua in March 1908. Only when its leaders were hunted down by Dutch troops and captured could any Dutch administration be imposed. In the case of Flores, reports were made in 1887 that gold was to be found. But a mining expedition that landed on the south coast two years later had to withdraw because the local population were hostile, and even a military expedition of 500 men failed to make any headway. Some years later—in 1907—Dutch mounted police forced their way into the interior, terrorized the people, and installed Dutch civil officials. Flores suddenly acquired fame in 1933, when President Sukarno was exiled there by the Dutch Government for his nationalist activities. The story of Timor is similar, but in this case the Dutch had to deal with Portuguese who were there first, as well as with a succession of difficult Rajahs; the issue was not finally settled until 1914 when the frontiers were agreed.

These islands all have their special interests; Lombok with its fields of pepper; Sumbawa is famous for its sandalwood, its horses, and handwoven 'ikat' fabrics; Flores where women make their own thread and weave it into a special dark 'ikat'; Timor, the largest of them all, is known for its horses, its fields of maize, and for a great variety of dances and songs.

Under Dutch rule, Catholic Missions were given a free hand in most of these islands; education and social welfare were made their responsibility and on Timor and Flores many converts were made and local men were trained to become priests. These Missionary Societies had contracts with the former Dutch East Indies Government which expired on January 1st, 1953. When the Governor from Bali visited the islands in 1951, he reported that there was excellent co-operation between the Republican authorities and the missionaries who were fulfilling the requirements of present-day education. With the shortage of teachers in the Republic, it seems likely that the Dutch arrangement will be continued.

When the Governors of the Republic met at a conference in Djakarta at the end of 1952, a report from the Lesser Sunda Islands showed how times have changed. In each island, fifty houses had been constructed; there was a new hospital in Timor; an oil factory and a weaving factory were under construction in Flores; roads and bridges and irrigation works were already started in a number of places. The problems were training personnel and communications. More doctors, more teachers— indeed this is invariably the demand that reaches Djakarta from places such as the Lesser Sunda Islands which have moved from their backwater under Dutch rule into the main stream of government under the Republic.

NOTES

[1] *Island of Bali*, by Miguel Covarubbias, p. 37. Published by Cassell & Company, Ltd., 1937.

[2] *Nusantara*, by Bernard H. M. Vlekke, p. 174.

[3] *The History of Java*, by Thomas Stamford Raffles, Vol. II, Appendix K, 'Account of Bali', p. ccxxxiv. Black, Parbury and Allen and John Murray, 1817.

[4] *History of the Netherlands East Indies*, by E. S. de Klerck, Vol. II, p. 319.

[5] Ibid., p. 320.

[6] Ibid., p. 322.

[7] *A Tale from Bali*, by Vicki Baum. Published by Geoffrey Bles, 1937. Reprinted, May 1942.

[8] *Island of Bali*, by Miguel Covarrubias, p. 35.

[9] 'The Clash of Cultures in Bali', by John Coast. *Pacific Affairs*, December 1951.

PART TWO

Indonesian Pattern

CHAPTER VII

THE PATTERN OF INDONESIAN CULTURE

ANY Sunday morning in Djakarta a stream of bicycles and a good proportion of the city's 18,000 betjaks (a kind of taxi-tricycle) stop outside the museum in Merdekalaan. Indonesians call it the 'Rumah gadjah', the elephant house, after the solitary bronze elephant which stands on a pedestal in the gravel entrance. He has stood there since 1871 when King Chulalongkorn presented him to the city. On his return journey to Siam he presented a smaller elephant to the city of Singapore; the British placed him in front of the Raffles Museum.

Inside the Rumah gadjah men, women, and children stroll around. The gamelan orchestra is the chief magnet. The audience crowd the passages and surround the players themselves. Ancient statues make convenient vantage points for boys and girls; Hindu gods and goddesses and large stone Buddhas are cool props for warm bodies in the humid heat. Never did an orchestra give a regular Sunday morning performance in such a dramatically historical setting as in this inner court of the museum; four statues of the Buddha, from the Borobodur, the greatest of all monuments in Indonesia, stand in the front hall leading to the inner court where men in ceremonial dress play the gamelan; facing the court is a huge statue of the seventeenth-century King Aditgawarman in the form of a demonic Buddhist deity. In his left hand he holds a cranial cup, in his right a sacrificial knife. 'This is all very fine,' an official said to me. 'The museum has come alive since we became independent. In Dutch times it was often a dead place where students came. Now we are busy all the time, especially on holidays. What a good sign! But we need twice as much space to show our exhibits properly, to say nothing of hundreds more which are hidden away in cupboards and brought out only at the request of a specialist.'

Through the rooms of the museum, the instruments of the gamelan echo, insistent, repetitive, haunting as they are in the villages of Java and Bali. In Djakarta the modern dance band has already established its hold and this Sunday morning performance is one of the few opportunities of hearing Indonesian music. When it ends, the crowds then begin to make imaginary tours round their own country. Few of them will have had any opportunity of visiting any other island than Java, and an enormous relief map of all Indonesia, skilfully modelled by a Dutch draughtsman, is a popular exhibit. Behind it a Javanese artist has painted portraits representing the types of people who live in the 3,000 islands between Sabang in the west and Merauke in the east. Here, for the first time, Borneo and Celebes, Bali and Sumatra, the Molucca Islands and West Irian (still under Dutch rule) become real. There are models of finely carved houses from Sumatra and of long houses from the Dayak territory in Borneo; carvings in wood and stone from Bali; highly decorative masks from almost every part of the country; bead ornamentation from Borneo and clothes made from the bark of trees from Celebes; totem poles from West Irian, and skulls, product of the one-time customary head-hunting, highly and gruesomely tattooed. A magnificent collection of wayang figures, illustrating characters from the Mahabharata and Ramayana, reminds us, like the statues of Brahma, Vishnu, and Siva in the entrance hall, that Indonesian art owes much of its inspiration to Hinduism. A collection of ceramics, earthenware pots, ceremonial vases and dishes all found in the Indonesian archipelago points to the early visitors from China who settled down in the country. A much smaller collection of indigenous Indonesian art shows that the people were skilled in casting bronze, painting burial stones, and decorating glass beads before Hindus or Chinese arrived in the country. An Indonesian writer in the magazine *Indonesian Review*, describing this period of his country's history, says that prehistoric times are considered as 'ending with the coming of the Hindus to Indonesia in the second or third century A.D. when history as recorded by inscriptions chiselled in stone and other written sources began. . . . It is this pre-Hinduistic civilization that formed the ancient Indonesian civilization. It is therefore incorrect to say that our pre-historic ancestors were savages, or that the Hindus were the bearers of civilization to Indonesia.'

In this prehistoric collection there are skulls which belonged to some of the oldest known human beings, and some—the *Pithecanthropus erectus* and the *Homo Modjokertensis*—which belonged to an early form of human being. 'Indonesia', as an American anthropologist, Professor Raymond Kennedy, writes, 'is the anthropologist's Garden of Eden. No older human remains than those of Java Man have ever been found anywhere in the world.'

In less distant days, but still in stretches of time which we cannot specify, many peoples have lived in these islands; some of them, such as the ancestors of undeveloped peoples living in parts of Australia today, exist only in such islands as Timor and Flores; others, who are now practically unknown in Indonesia, passed on to the Melanesian Islands; others, who are small in stature and Negroid in type, like their common ancestors in parts of Ceylon, Malaya, and the Philippines, still live in the remotest part of Sumatra, Timor, and West Irian, where they escaped from later migrations. Of those later migrations which peopled the Republic as we know it today, the two that arrived separately and then intermingled were the Malays and the Mongoloid visitors from the north, from Yunnan and from Tonkin.

This racial mixture of Malay and Mongoloid was already established when the first Indians arrived in the first century A.D. and it has changed very little since those days. For at least 700 years, Hindus travelled along the coasts of the Indonesian islands; they were traders and teachers but they were not colonizers. Their conquest was one of ideas, of the religious beliefs of Buddhism and Hinduism, of artistic conceptions in sculpture, dance, and music. In the seventh century a Chinese pilgrim who visited Sumatra on his return from paying homage at the Buddha's birthplace in India, wrote:

'Many kings and chieftains in the islands of the Southern Ocean admire and believe [in Buddhism]. . . . They investigate and study all the subjects that exist just as in the Middle

Kingdom [Madhyadeça in India]; the rules and ceremonies are not at all different.'[1]

These early Hindu immigrants enriched the existing languages, adding a wealth of Sanskrit words so that many words in the Javanese vocabulary can be traced back to them and any Indian visitor to Java today constantly finds himself comparing the words he hears spoken and the literature he reads with similar words in his own language. The same is true of the Malay language which is the basis, as we shall see later, of Bahasa Indonesia, the language of the Republic. For centuries, indeed until the coming of Islam in the fifteenth century, Indonesian culture was known as Hindu-Javanese; in Sumatra, and scattered among the other islands, traces of cultural development, in inscriptions, in architecture, in the subjects of dance and literature, all show the same origins. The Hindus settled down in the country; they were never colonials, groups of foreigners with their loyalty to and deriving their authority from their country of origin. With the Javanese nobility they gradually developed the kind of feudal social caste-system which still exists in Bali today. They constituted the priestly caste from whom Javanese imbibed their religion, blending Hinduism with their own animistic and mystical ideas. As an economically more advanced people, they developed commercial contacts within the existing system of more or less autonomous desa communities. They gave to the culture of Java a new inspiration and a great liveliness. But the coming of Islam, followed by three and a half centuries of Dutch rule, broke the personal links between India and Indonesia. When Pandit Nehru forged these links again by his visit to the country in 1950, an Indonesian writer paid this tribute:

'Pandit Nehru's visit to Indonesia reminds us of the old Hindu migration into the Archipelago during the second or third century of the Christian era. Many centuries separated these two events, but actually there is a close connection between the two ... The same lot has befallen these two nations. Having suffered from colonial oppression at the hands of Western peoples, they have attained freedom and independence after a stubborn struggle against their oppressors.

Both the Hindu migration and Nehru's visit are two historic events for Indonesia. The very history of Indonesia, that is to say, history as found in records, began with the Hindus' migration; prior to the coming of the Hindus one could only speak of the prehistorical period. The so-called Hindu period of our history comprises three-quarters of the entire historical period of the country. It was the time of development into a much higher civilisation, of establishment of new Empires, the beginning of trade relations with foreign States.'[2]

Whilst Java owed so much to Hindu influence—even the name Java is derived from the Hindu Jawa-Dwipa, meaning millet island—the Hindu cultural influence contributed far less to Borneo and Celebes, and seems not to have gone further than this last-mentioned. These islands were larger in territory and practically inaccessible, except round the coastal areas, compared with the small compact island of Java. Traders from Java in the Hindu-Indonesian period established outposts and, in the case of Sumatra, tried, at one time successfully, to make it part of their empire. But Sumatra, with its long coastline, early became a commercial power, trading with the Asian mainland across the straits of Malacca, and benefiting as the first port of call for traders from the Indian continent. The largest communities of Indians today live in Sumatra; the majority being still traders. The Sumatrans pride themselves on their tougher individuality as compared with the aristocracy of Java and on their wider range of international contacts. In Kalimantan, furthest away from India, Chinese traders, during this Hindu-Javanese period, captured coastal trade, settling down in communities and making trading centres where Hindu influence was less decisive. Chinese culture, though flourishing in China itself, did not have any marked influence in Indonesia. Chinese came and stayed as traders. In the general pattern of Indonesian culture, it is true to say that Indonesians absorbed, adapted, and transformed Hindu ideas of religion, of art, of agriculture, of many social customs, moulding them into a shape which is only now beginning to acquire a recognizable individuality.

The study of pre-Hindu Indonesia has acquired a new significance among Dutch as well as among Indonesian scholars.

In the thirties, a younger generation of Dutch experts such as Van Leur (he died in a Japanese concentration camp), Bosch and Rassers began to revise existing ideas of the Hinduization of Indonesia, and to formulate new and sometimes unexpected theories. What, they asked, was the cultural heritage of Indonesia independent of foreign influence? What part of it was of Hindu origin and what types of Hindus were responsible for its introduction and extension? They came to the conclusion that there was a wealth of indigenous traditions which had been obscured by colonial research, and that historical continuity could be proved in specific types of indigenous law and communal organization. Ancient animistic beliefs continued regardless of Hindu, Muslim or Christian domination whilst customary law was very slightly changed by the legal concepts of these three main origins of cultural influence. In an article, 'The Hinduization of Indonesia reconsidered' (*The Far Eastern Quarterly*, November 1951), Justus van der Kroef, Instructor in the Department of the History of Civilization, Michigan State College, has thus summed up contemporary study on this subject.

'The chief value of this entire body of new investigation of the so-called Hindu-Javanese period lies in the integrity of Indonesian society as it existed before the Hindus established contact with the Archipelago and long after that contact ended. This continuity of native forms of civilization attains, especially at this time when Indonesia has achieved her national independence, a new significance. The historiography of Indonesia has long been coloured by the colonial attitude which the Dutch injected into their studies of the East Indian islands, creating the impression that Indonesia was a *tabula rasa* on which foreign cultures wrote their text. . . . There is a need for an "Indo-centric" rather than a "Europe-centric" point of view, for a recognition of the uninterrupted continuity of native civilizations in Indonesia not in terms of "an isolated, stagnated East, but a strong East, a richly coloured tapestry with only a small unevenly interwoven Western pattern".'

The Muslim traders, who followed the Hindus in the

thirteenth century, were men with a dynamic faith. From the time they arrived in Atjeh, in the northern part of Sumatra, still the most fiercely Islamic part of the country, they set out to proselytize all whom they met, to expand the dar ul-Islam, the territory of Islam. Unlike the Hindus, they formed no special groups, they had no caste system, they based their beliefs on one God, and it was the duty of the whole community, aristocrat or beggar, trader or rice-cultivator, to spread the same teaching, the faith of Mohammed. The faith was not only a religious belief; it embodied a system of law, a social pattern, a doctrine applied to every aspect of personal behaviour. Islam rapidly made many converts, especially in coastal areas where Islamic merchants combined their faith with trade. In Sumatra and in Borneo, Chinese help was solicited against the invasion of Islam; the peoples of Central Borneo and part of the Moluccas were never converted. But elsewhere, and after varying degrees of resistance, Islam could claim for itself the adherence of the great majority of people, the main exceptions being those who lived in the interior, out of contact with any foreign influence, and the whole island of Bali.

Bali is a social phenomenon of great interest. After being under the rule of Javanese kings in Hindu-Javanese times, it became independent; it was then conquered again, once more independent, and yet again conquered. Finally, when the Javanese kingdom of Madjapahit fell to the forces of Islam, some members of the ruling class and some artists and priests escaped across the four miles of water dividing the two islands, to Bali. Their Hindu-Javanese culture and their religion combined with the culture and the animism of the Balinese to give to Balinese life its individual qualities. Today, Bali remains overwhelmingly Hindu. This produces fascinating problems within the Republic which is unified for the first time in Indonesian history; problems involving religious beliefs, though the Constitution provides for religious freedom; problems of education in a society with differences of caste; cultural problems among people who have probably the highest degree of artistic sensitivity of any in the world; problems of social and political significance in a society which still retains many feudal characteristics.

Outside Bali, among as many as nine-tenths of the people, Islam is the accepted religion. In most villages in Java and Sumatra and in the coastal areas of the other islands (with the exception of Bali) the mosque is a feature. In the cities they are as large as cathedrals; in the villages they are often little more than bamboo shacks—the equivalent of tin huts which sometimes serve as village chapels and mission-rooms in England. These mosques are often indistinguishable from dwelling-houses except that they always have a washing pool outside, sometimes a tree trunk cut into a rectangular piece of wood hollowed in the middle and used as a call on special occasions, and always a kind of hide drum used to call people to prayer at noon and at dusk. It is a curious, dramatic, primeval call, without tone, without note, but impelling and authoritative. It signifies the power of Islam, the magnet of its religious and social beliefs. But the dances and the songs which Indonesians perform and sing to celebrate Islamic festivals have a Hindu background and often illustrate the Hindu epics—the Ramayana and the Mahabharata. Similarly many of the customs associated with marriage and death have their origin in Hindu society. The wedding clothes of an Indonesian Muslim bride are similar to those of a Hindu girl. When an Indonesian Muslim dies, a pot of incense is kept burning near the bed on which he lies, just as it is in the case of a Hindu.

When Islam was first introduced by Muslim traders from Gujerat in the thirteenth century, it was readily adopted by traders in the coastal areas of Java and Sumatra and by rulers in the Courts. It was superimposed on existing Hindu beliefs and social customs. They continued, especially in the interior, which was not converted to Islam until two centuries afterwards. Later, contacts with the Muslim world, with India and with Turkey and Arabia deepened belief in the social and political aspects of Islam. The basic inequalities implicit in Hindu-Javanese society were reduced; the princely families of Java retained their power, but the teachings of the Koran gradually led to a more humane treatment of those whom Hinduism relegated to a low caste; the individual, however poor he or she might be, was in direct relationship with the Prophet; a new

group of teachers arose, not belonging to some prescribed, un-
alterable caste as in the Hindu priesthood, but freely chosen in
a village because of their knowledge of the Koran, or, in later
years, because they had made the pilgrimage to Mecca. Special
schools gradually sprang up where men studied the Koran for
years and then themselves became teachers.

Islam is an everyday religion, placing little, if any, emphasis
on artistic experience. Its influence was therefore much greater
on the social structure of Indonesian society than on the pattern of its culture. It had a humanizing influence which Indonesians compare with that of Christianity in the Western world.
Unlike Christianity in the West, or Buddhism in China and
Burma, it did not create any artistic awakening in Indonesian
life. The main pattern of Indonesian culture was Hindu-
Indonesian when the Muslims arrived; when the West first made
contact some three centuries later, it was very little changed
and three and a half centuries of Dutch rule did not make any
basic difference in the arts of the country.

The Portuguese introduced Christianity to some of the islands,
notably Amboina, where St. Francis Xavier worked in 1546.
A small number of Indonesians were converted. Here again, the
Indonesian ability to adapt other ideas is evident in those parts
of the country where Dutch churches, even to some extent the
Roman Catholics, have become an integral part of Indonesian
life. But whilst the artistic expressions of medieval Christianity
in the Western world were of great significance in its cultural
development, the God of the white ruler did not inspire any
similar yearnings in the minds of his Indonesian followers. In
the Christian parts of Indonesia, Christianity had other influences, not unimportant in the pattern of Indonesian life.

In the few scattered parts of the country—in Central Sumatra, in the Minahasa, and in some of the Moluccan islands—
where Christianity has about two million converts, Indonesians
adapted some of its precepts to their own society. This is very
striking in the Minahasa, where the Netherlands Missionary
Society carried out a systematic campaign from 1827 till 1860,
by which time they had made more than 100,000 converts. Today, the Western visitor easily compares this area of Sulawesi

with the Italian part of Switzerland; the scenery is rather similar, the villages in the mountains are bright with flowers and the land spaced out with market gardens, houses are spick and span with pots of ferns and flowers on verandas and window sills, their sanitation is unobtrusive, their pigs and fowls have learnt to choose the back rather than the front garden, many names have a Western ring (Tomahon, Menado, Tondano), the bells of the village churches peal at appropriate times, and the girls wear white frocks complete with wreath and veil when they are married.

Yet it is generally true to say that neither Islam nor Christianity, the two external influences in Indonesia since the downfall of the Hindu-Javanese kingdom of Madjapahit, has made any striking changes in the cultural life of the country.

Where then do we find the influence of the West on the pattern of Indonesian culture? A Dutch ethnologist, Dr. F. H. van Naersen, lecturing in his capacity of Rector of the Agricultural College at Wageningen, on 'Culture Contacts and Social Conflicts in Indonesia', makes a suggestion, which many Indonesians would probably accept:

> 'The West succeeded—not without conflict—in freeing itself much sooner than the East from the oppressive grip of traditionalism and conservatism, but when it conquered the Orient and controlled parts of it as colonies, or otherwise, either politically or economically, it did not allow the subject peoples freely to acquire from Western culture what they wanted and to experiment with it at their own risk as they saw fit. In other words: whereas Hinduism and Mohammedanism opened up their cultures to the Indonesians, the West withheld from them the precious treasures of their own hard-won civilization. The freedom of thought and action remained a monopoly of the West.'[3]

Few Asian writers have yet made any evaluation of the influence of Western rule during four centuries. Indeed, in the spring of 1955, there is only one such work—*Asia and Western Dominance*: A Survey of the Vasco da Gama epoch of Asian History, 1498–1945. The author—Sardar K. M. Panikkar—has this to say of Dutch rule:

'The Dutch alone of the European nations in the East carried out a policy which systematically reduced a whole population to the status of plantation labour, without recognizing any moral or legal obligation to them. Cringing and *kowtowing* in China, humble and reverential before Japanese officials, they were tyrannical beyond belief to the people from whom they derived their greatest profit. Lacking the spiritual enthusiasm of the Portuguese, or, generally speaking, the wide human interests of the British, at least in areas where they exercised direct political authority, or the sense of cultural mission to which the French laid claim, the Dutch held firmly to a theory of possession and exploitation, without accepting in the least degree any obligation for the welfare of the people over whom they had acquired control. When they were forced to change their policy during the course of the next century, it was not out of any conviction, but by the strength of the movements outside Holland and Indonesia.'[4]

This summary is one which many Indonesians would endorse, and with which a few Dutchmen might express sympathy. The Dutch East India Company was founded in the 'golden age' of Dutch culture, in the great period of Dutch painting, but the non-profit-making enterprise of cultural exchanges, or of cultural penetration, played no part in the activities of its officials. They occasionally sanctioned the work of missionaries to convert the infidels.

When the Company ended in disgrace at the end of the eighteenth century, and the Government in The Hague became responsible for the administration of those parts of Indonesia they controlled, conditions changed. In the interval—from 1811 to 1816—Raffles had introduced Liberal ideas; 'Raffles', J. S. Furnivall writes, 'had gone further in the Liberal direction than their own most advanced reformers [Dutch] had ever thought possible. By this time Liberalism was in the air, and the new Dutch Government attempted a compromise between their old traditions and the new policy of Raffles.' In the second half of the century, when Liberal ideas gained influence in the home country, the Government's policy in Indonesia changed too. Enlightened Dutchmen in Indonesia courageously exposed the abuses of the culture system. One of them, Dr. W. R. Baron van

Hoevell, a preacher in Batavia for ten years, went further; he advocated secondary and higher schools as well as a training school for Indonesian officials. He wanted a free Press and representation for the Indonesians in the States General. Because he was far ahead of the great majority of his compatriots in Indonesia, he was practically forced to resign. Later, he became a member of the Second Chamber in The Hague, and the Dutch historian Vandenbosch writes of him:

> 'He attacked the abuses of the culture system and demanded that the first consideration of colonial policy should be not how much the metropolitan country could get out of the East Indies, but how much it could do to raise the material and intellectual interests of the colony.'[5]

Dr. W. R. Baron van Hoevell was followed by a famous reformist, E. D. Dekker, who resigned his post in the Civil Service at a critical moment to stimulate Dutch public opinion against the Culture System. His book, *Max Havelaar*, written under the pseudonym of Multatuli, is often called the Dutch *Uncle Tom's Cabin*. It aroused so much public interest and concern that after fierce parliamentary battles in the eighteenforties, the decision was taken (in 1848) to make Ministers responsible to Parliament and not to the Crown. The Queen's speech read from the throne in 1901 struck a moral note:

> 'As a Christian Power the Netherlands is obligated in the East Indian Archipelago to regulate better the legal position of native Christians, to lend support on a firm basis to Christian missions, and to imbue the whole conduct of government with the consciousness that the Netherlands has a moral duty to fulfil with respect to the people of these regions . . .'

This moral attitude, which often proved good business at the same time, inspired what is known as the 'Ethical Policy' of the Dutch Government and led to the recruitment of many idealistic civil servants who gave a lifetime of disinterested service to their East Indian colony. To them must be added a long list of Dutch scholars in many fields of research who described the variety of languages, peoples, and stages of civilization, the flora and fauna, the Buddhist, Hindu, and Islamic influences in Indonesian culture.

The Dutch bibliography of Indonesia is interesting; no branch of knowledge, except the psychology of colonial peoples, seems to have been overlooked, the authors are among the most distinguished experts in their fields of work. In the museums of Holland, notably in Leyden and in Amsterdam, you may find the most detailed and the best arranged collection of exhibits ever arranged by a colonial Power of its colonies; its textiles and woodcarving, silver work and weaving of all kinds; wayang figures and jewellery; statistics of the products on which the lives of Indonesians as well as Dutch people depend, rubber, tin, cinchona, coffee, and tea; diagrams of schools and hospitals. But there is no sign of the fact, uppermost in the minds of all politically conscious Indonesians, that colonial peoples increasingly demanded the right to rule themselves, and that those who dared work openly for this right—men like Sukarno, Hatta, Sjahrir, and Natsir—were imprisoned and exiled, just as the British Government imprisoned Mahatma Gandhi and Pandit Nehru. And for the same reason.

This colonial relationship, the natural psychology of those who governed and those who were governed, was inevitably reflected in the cultural impact of the Dutch on Indonesia. Basically it was a relationship of superior and inferior which in more recent times was disguised and sometimes sublimated into that of parent and child. The Dutch decided what would be suitable for the 'native'. In the days of the Company, and as late as 1850, an official British manual says:

> 'Government concern for native education was limited to the native Christians in the Moluccas, but the necessity for a larger supply of native officials possessing a certain amount of education induced the Government to start some twenty schools in which the sons of the native aristocracy were trained. Before many years had passed public opinion began to realize the duty of bringing education and development within the reach of all natives irrespective of whether they were to become servants of the administration or not, but it was not till 1872 that a general scheme for native education was set on foot.'[6]

By this time, Dutch educational policy had passed through various stages. At first Indonesians could enter schools for Europeans, but when the number of applicants increased rapidly the Government began to erect schools for the people. 'Governor General Rochussen', Vandenbosch writes, 'was fully convinced of the disadvantages, principally of a political nature, which can proceed from such mixed education.' By Government decrees 'admission of natives to the European schools became exceptional. The Government did not close the schools to natives entirely, out of fear of the offence it would cause, but it did close them to the Chinese.' With the growth of Liberalism in Holland, policy changed; European schools were opened to Christian Indonesians and the children of Regents, and in 1872 (the date mentioned in the quotation from the British Government's *Manual*), European primary schools were theoretically open to all, but the qualifications included higher school fees and a command of Dutch. Two years later, the first Indonesian was admitted to a secondary school—he was the grandchild of a Javanese prince. But secondary education remained very limited, whilst university education was not made available in Indonesia until 1924, the theory being that Indonesians should go to Holland for higher education. The Dutch made no racial discrimination; education, and it was usually of a very high standard, was available to the Indonesian aristocracy; indeed, for obvious financial reasons, it was substantially limited to them.

In the ten years before the war, rapid strides were made towards providing elementary education, especially in Java and in Sumatra; the Outer Islands, as the Dutch called them, were practically ignored. Yet Professor Vandenbosch, writing in the late nineteen-thirties, thus summed up the position:

> 'The extent of the unfinished educational task can be determined only in relation to a given objective. If the goal is the provision of the entire East Indian population with a three-year-school type of education, 30% of the task has been accomplished; if the goal is a general six-year-school type, 20%; and if the objective is a seven-year-school type, the East Indian Government has only achieved 15% of its stupendous task.'[7]

This quotation from one of a number of enlightened Dutch writers suggests that even in the field of education, Dutch influence was limited to a small proportion of the population. Yet it was through education that the main influence of Dutch rule was exerted. There was little direct cultural impact, but the growth of education helped an increasing number of Indonesians to acquire a knowledge of their own history, even though it was through the eyes of Dutch scholars, and it introduced them to the culture of the Western world, again through the medium of Dutch. Apart from school reading, the Dutch Government organized a Bureau for Popular Literature, publishing Indonesian classics and folk-lore, translating Western stories, and encouraging Indonesians to write stories themselves, and to contribute to magazines. Libraries were organized, especially in the larger towns; they increased from 700 in 1912 to 2,334 in 1937, and in that year they had a circulation of 1,834,268 books.

Education was the catalyst of nationalism. So long as the Indonesian mind was unaware of the outside world, of the great social forces which were changing the society of the Western world, the rule of the foreigner was unchallenged. Adat—the Arabic word for 'customary law'—was undisturbed. Horizons widened by Western education implied a challenge to the *status quo*. Indonesian intellectuals inevitably acquired a new prestige among their own people and began to acquire a new confidence in themselves. This knowledge of their own intellectual gifts led to a demand for a share in the government of their own country, the first important rift between ruler and ruled. Western education did not have the effect, as many Dutchmen anticipated, of creating closer cultural ties between themselves and their colonial people. Indeed, one Dutch Professor of Sociology puts forward the theory that it had the opposite effect, heightening national consciousness, and lessening respect for the Dutch language as a social factor.

'The true nationalist', he says, 'is a non-co-operator; he no longer aspires to a job in the government service. Indonesian women with self-respect care less and less for employment as housekeepers in the service of Europeans. Eventually even marriage with a European has little attraction any longer for many Indonesian women. Thus a new scale of values is seen to be gradually projecting itself across the old colonial scale. Further, in common with education, this new scale of values affected the position of women and the young. In the capacity of Westernized intellectuals and fellow-fighters in the nationalist struggle, the womenfolk and the young could often win for themselves a social prestige which conflicted with traditional Indonesian ideas. In this sense, too, Western education, by which many young girls profited, had a revolutionizing influence on Indonesian society.'[8]

It was natural that this increasing awareness of themselves led to an examination of their own cultural heritage and to a deeper sense of the centuries of stagnation which characterized Indonesian cultural patterns and social structure. The challenge was met by young intellectuals who were no longer willing to accept *in toto* the methods or the content of Western education. The leading exponent of this revolutionary doctrine was a Javanese aristocrat, Ki Hadjar Dewantoro. He spent six years of his life in exile, dismissed from his country for nationalist propaganda. When he returned to Djogjakarta in 1922, his mind was already clear, his decision taken. He founded the first Taman Siswa school in Djogjakarta. The words literally translated mean 'students' garden', but Dewantoro was using them in a more symbolic sense. 'No imitation of the Western world, but construction from the bottom up of a civilization initially Javanese, later Indonesian', was the basis of his teaching. 'Everybody', he said, 'who learns a foreign language, gains access to a new world.' He wanted to help his countrymen to absorb into their own national lives those elements of knowledge and of beauty with which education had made them familiar. He and a group of Indonesians who rallied to his support refused to take any financial support from the Dutch Government. Teachers were paid only a subsistence wage—about one-quarter the salary paid by Government and mission institutions—but they always had a fine group of people who worked for the ideal, and by 1940 there were 120,000 pupils in Taman Siswa schools as against 66,000 in the corresponding Dutch-aided schools.

They were more than schools in the ordinary sense of the word; they taught the traditions of Javanese as well as of Western culture, they revived the arts of the country, its gamelan music, its painting, its literature, and its dancing. They were the cultural expression of nationalism, and the great majority of those young men and women who are playing an important part in Indonesian life today, especially among the Javanese, were pupils in Taman Siswa schools. The cultural awakening which is so marked a feature of the Republic—in painting, above all— is due, in large part, to the work of Dewantoro. 'A craftsman who makes beautiful and useful objects is much more valuable than a clerk' was one of his slogans.

Dewantoro encouraged self-expression and originality, a pride in tradition, and a willingness to choose or reject all that was valuable in their own culture and to integrate with that which was valuable in that of other civilizations. His emphasis was on artistic, rather than on scientific, values of life, and his views, comparable perhaps with those of Tagore, still influence the programmes of education in the Republic.

It is too early to see how Indonesian culture will develop; how much it will continue or build on its own traditions, and what it will assimilate from other cultures, both Western and from other Asian countries. The Dutch who occupied these islands in their own golden age, the age of Rembrandt and Franz Hals, grew rich in one generation on the products; they became a nation of burghers famous for comfort rather than artistic achievement. The Indonesians lost their inspiration, except in Bali, when Hindu influence ended and the rule of the Muslims began. Only when a new national consciousness developed in the last century did signs appear of a renaissance. The Taman Siswa schools canalized these yearnings for self-expression. Today Indonesians are free to build a new culture. What they have achieved and the pattern of the future are subjects which are described in a later chapter.

NOTES

[1] *A Record of the Buddhist Religion as Practised in India and in the Malaya Archipelago*, by J. Takakasu. Oxford, 1896.

For a longer account of this period, *Nusantara*, by Bernard H. M. Vlekke, 1943, is the most rewarding in the English language.

[2] *Indonesian Information*, July 1950.

[3] *Culture Contacts and Social Conflicts in Indonesia*, by F. H. Van Naersen, 1946.

[4] *Asia and Western Dominance*, by K. M. Panikkar, p. 118. Published by George Allen & Unwin, 1952.

[5] *The Dutch East Indies*, by Amry Vandenbosch, p. 60.

[6] *A Manual of Netherlands India*. Compiled by the Geographical Section of the Naval Intelligence Division, Naval Staff, Admiralty. Published by H.M.S.O., 1920.

[7] *The Dutch East Indies*, by Amry Vandenbosch, pp. 215–16.

[8] *Effects of Western Civilisation on Indonesian Society*, by W. F. Wertheim, Professor of Sociology, University of Amsterdam. Paper prepared for the 11th Conference of the I.P.R., 1950.

CHAPTER VIII

ISLAM, MARXISM AND NATIONALISM

THE last chapter showed the lasting influence which Hinduism exerted on the diverse cultures of Indonesia. Most powerful among the peoples of Sumatra, Java, and Bali, its impact was less in Kalimantan and Sulawesi, where it was confined to the coastal areas, whilst in the further territories of West Irian the majority of people remained in what was virtually a Stone Age period of development. The social pattern of Islam was gradually imposed on Indonesian society as it existed in pre-Hindu times, and it was not effectively challenged until the basic ideas of Marxism penetrated the young Nationalist Movement during the First World War.

The nationalist idea, in the sense of self-government, was scarcely discernible in the seemingly static society of Indonesia until the beginning of the twentieth century. At that time, the Dutch seemed firmly established as the permanent rulers of the country. They themselves had gradually introduced more liberal ideas into their administration, and at the turn of the century their Ethical Policy implied the dual objectives of economic development and certain measures of social welfare.

The Dutch system of 'indirect rule' had been based on an alliance of local rulers with the colonial Power. It was profitable to both partners. It developed a common interest in the *status quo*. In their first contacts with Indonesia, the East India Company had made treaties with the local rulers, just as the British did in the case of the rulers of Indian states. From the end of the eighteenth century when the Government took over the administration, until 1907, when a new policy was formulated, there were 282 native states of which four were in Java and the rest in the Outer Territories. These states were indirectly governed, although the power of the local rulers diminished until, as one Dutch writer describes it, the contracts between them and the Government

> 'really became mere acts of investiture, whereby the Government invested the vassal in his office only under certain conditions, and promised to maintain him in it only so long as these conditions were lived up to.'[1]

Outside Java, where for economic reasons the Dutch concentrated their efforts and intensified their rule,

> 'the relationship with the native states was punitive in character; interferences with them occurred only when international complications threatened . . . There were in the Outer Territories a number of small states which had not been brought formally under Dutch jurisdiction at all.'[2]

The new policy, as stated by the then Governor-General van Heutz, included the extension of Dutch influence in areas outside Java, new relationships with the rulers of native states, and an insistence that they should introduce much-needed reforms in their areas. For the long contracts (treaties) with the Dutch, a Short Declaration was signed by local rulers, recognizing the sovereignty of the Netherlands, and agreeing to execute and maintain all regulations issued by the Queen or the Governor-General. The Government in Batavia thus assumed a far greater measure of responsibility for local administration, and the local rulers—the sultanates—owed allegiance to the Dutch, although they themselves still maintained their privileged position in the areas they controlled.

Within about ten years, 250 Indonesian rulers had signed the Short Declaration with the Netherlands East Indies Government. 'In 1910', Dr. Vlekke wrote, 'the Indies showed a very different picture from that which they had presented in 1870. Peace ruled everywhere, and the administration of Batavia had become highly efficient. Economically, the country had developed amazingly.'[3] The time was ripe, he suggested, 'for modern methods and new ideas'. In The Hague, many enlightened Dutchmen, both in and outside the administration, began to feel a perfectly genuine 'concern' for the welfare of those millions of men whom they ruled. The days of crude exploitation were over; a paternalistic colonialism took its place. This change of attitude was influenced by several outstanding men of the time: Mr. Th. van Deventer whose article 'A Debt of Honour' argued that the Netherlands were bound 'in honour' to refund for social welfare some of the millions which had been acquired in Indonesia; Professor Snouck Hurgronje, famous for his studies of Islam, who wrote 'The Indonesians are imploring us to give them instruction; by granting their wish we shall secure their loyalty for an unlimited time'; Professor van Vollenhoven whose research on Adat law was responsible for Dutch juridical policy, and many other scholars who began to study the peoples of Indonesia, their religions, their customs, their dances, their village societies. For more than two centuries Dutch interests had been almost exclusively that of trade. At the turn of the twentieth century many Dutchmen became aware of an Indonesian civilization, and their conscience was awakened to a sense of responsibility towards it. 'The period between 1900 and 1917', Dr. Vlekke wrote, 'became an era of increasing care by the government for the native inhabitants of the Indies.'⁴ During the same period 'the economic progress was such that the reformers saw most of the material obstacles to their plans removed'.⁵

This is the background of Dutch policy as seen through Dutch eyes. But what was happening to the Indonesians themselves? Modern ideas could not be kept in watertight compartments, influencing Dutch opinion but having no impact on the small number of Indonesians who came in contact with the outside world. By the time Dutch opinion showed some sympathy with Indonesian culture, Indonesians themselves were emerging from their own isolation; they were asking for equal treatment and self-expression. During those last years of pacification which led to the *Pax Nederlandia*, Indonesians discussed their rulers inside the closed walls of the kratons which presented an outward, but misleading calm, and in the Islamic schools where few Dutchmen penetrated. The idea of self-government was not yet alive amongst the most advanced. Kartini, a Javanese woman who is acknowledged as one of the earliest Nationalists, wrote to a Dutch school friend in 1900:

'With heavy hearts, many Europeans here see how the Javanese, whom they regard as their inferiors, are slowly awakening, and at every turn a brown man comes up, who shows that he has just as good brains in his head, and a just as good heart in his body, as the white man. But we are going forward, and they cannot hold back the current of time. I love the Hollanders very, very much, and I am grateful for everything that we have gained through them. Many of them are among our best friends, but there are also others who dislike us, for no other reason than we are bold enough to emulate them in education and culture. . . .'[6]

'Oh, now I understand why they are opposed to the education of the Javanese. When the Javanese becomes educated then he will no longer say amen to everything that is suggested to him by his superiors.'[7]

A year later she described how 'influential men in the Government, with the Governor-General at their head' were 'strongly in favour of spreading the Dutch language among the natives'. And the reason? She expressed it as a 'means of bringing the Javanese nearer to the Hollanders; so that these last may seem, not as strangers, but as loved protectors'.[8]

Kartini was an exceptional personality, a Muslim who had certain Christian sympathies. She rebelled against the Islamic convention of polygamy, and she believed in the education of women. But in a wider sphere progressive ideas were alive in Islamic schools, among men who had made the pilgrimage to Mecca, and, most of all, among young Indonesians who came into touch with the teachings of the Egyptian Mufti Shaik Muhammad 'Abduh. This Islamic theologian made Cairo the centre of modern Islamic thought round about 1900. He started a magazine in 1900 called *al-Manar* (*The Lighthouse*) which one of his disciples, Rashid Rida, edited after his death five years later. Egyptian teachers visited Indonesia, and for an increasing number of Indonesian intellectuals their first contact with the outside world was acquired in the al-Azhar University in Cairo. Here, they discussed the adaptation of Islam to the new scientific trends of Western thought; the superstitions which were often embodied in Islamic practices; decadence among the mujahids (mullahs); the use of Latin characters and of other languages than Arabic in Islamic ritual; reforms in the Islamic educational system; the use of European clothing. While Dutch scholars were preaching the need to preserve adat laws and were constructing an extraordinarily complicated system of nineteen adat law areas to maintain the variety of legal and social customs throughout the country, leaders of thought in Islamic circles—and 90% of Indonesians are Muslims—were discussing their modernization. The Abduh Movement aimed at the restatement of Islam in terms of social values and worked for a more progressive Islamic society, not for the perpetuation of adat laws. It played an important part in the history of Indonesian Nationalism and the Muhammadijah, formed in 1912, became its most widely organized expression. It was more than a religious organization. It took up such issues as the need for reforms—in marriage and funeral ceremonies; it was responsible for special schools, hospitals, and libraries and it pioneered in the education of girls. The Friday sermon in the mosque was now given in the regional language which brought religion nearer to the masses. By giving Islam a social and ethical programme and by linking social progress with the mosque, the Muhammadijah also helped to develop the political consciousness of Indonesians and strengthen the nationalist idea.

The Muhammadijah was the expression of social ferment.

'The middle-class Indonesians', Professor Wertheim wrote, 'felt strong traditional emotional ties with Islam such as most Europeans feel with Christendom. Moreover, in a colonial country there was all the more need to distinguish oneself from the foreign overlords. What this Indonesian really needed was to be able to call himself an Islamite without having to feel ashamed of his faith in the presence of Westerners; to profess a faith, that is, which harmonized with the modern age and his own aspirations as a man of his time.'[9]

Thus, the modern tendencies in Islam contributed to the main stream of national awakening, and led, as a later chapter will show, to the formation of the Masjumi, the largest party in Indonesia today.

Parallel with the growth of Islam as an expression of Nationalism came events in other parts of Asia which gave it greater significance. The year 1904 is a landmark in the history of Nationalism throughout colonial Asia. 'In Atjeh,' Dr. Vlekke records, 'the party hostile to the Dutch braced itself for a last stand when the news of the Japanese victories over the Russians first brought home to them that an eastern race might have a chance of success in war against the men of the west.' The myth of White superiority was challenged, and the result was a greater self-consciousness, a deeper self-confidence. Within a few years the Nationalist Movement in Indonesia, as elsewhere in Asia, became a political force.

In 1906 and 1907, a retired doctor, Dr. Wahidin Sudirohusodo (Djogjakarta), visited many parts of Java to persuade young intellectuals to co-operate with him in setting up a scholarship committee. He knew from personal experience the poor living conditions of most Javanese. He believed that they could be improved only if more people with a scientific education realized their responsibility. On May 20th, 1908, he set up the 'Budi Utomo' (the Noble Spirit) with members from the Faculty of Medicine. Students from the Teachers' Schools in Djogjakarta, Magelang, and Surabaya started branches in their own areas, and in October at a congress in Djogjakarta, the organization elected officers and a committee. Its activities were restricted to the cultural sphere, since, by a Dutch Government Regulation of 1854, the setting up of a political organization was prohibited. Its appeal was limited, and its membership was confined mainly to Indonesian civil servants and intellectuals in Java and Madura.

Three years later an organization was formed which had a much wider support. The Sarekat Dagang Islam (Islamic Traders' Association) arose from a judicious blending of economic and religious motives. Javanese cloth merchants, alarmed by the competition from Chinese entrepreneurs, made Javanese trading interests their objective. Politically they stood for a self-governing Indonesia within the Dutch Empire. Parallel with the growth of Sarekat Islam, the idea of Nationalism was taking shape. In December 1912, Ki Hadjar Dewantoro, Dr. Douwes Dekker, and Dr. Mangunkusumo founded the 'Indische Partij' at Bandung. Its aim was frankly self-government, and it was the first open challenge to Dutch authority. The result was that these three men were exiled. But their place was taken by three Dutch Socialist officials, Sneevliet (he was executed by a Gestapo firing squad in Holland in 1942), Brandsteder, and Dekker, who formed a Socialist association in Semarang in 1914, just before the outbreak of the World War.

Sarekat Islam was by this time a powerful mass organization with a membership of 800,000. Its conferences—in Bandung in 1916 and in Djakarta in 1917—showed the pressure of Socialist ideology. The Socialists were a Marxist group within an organization based on Islam. They attracted a considerable following among the more politically minded members during the First World War. In 1913, the resolutions passed by Sarekat Islam urged social reforms but did not express hostility to Dutch rule. In 1916, the slogan had become 'Co-operation with the Government for the welfare of the Indies'. At the National Congress in Djakarta in 1917, a demand was made for independence 'by evolution, not by revolution', and a number of young Marxists, led by Semaun, who were destined to play leading roles in the political life of Indonesia, attacked Dutch rule, and introduced a Marxist analysis of society. The leadership of Sarekat Islam in 1917 was composed of Muslims who had come into the Nationalist Movement through Islamic organizations. They reflected the modern trend in Islam which was described earlier; their views had a social-religious background, and whilst they were struggling for independence, they were not working for any change in the pattern of Indonesian society. H. O. S. Tjokroaminoto and Abdul Muis, two outstanding leaders, belonged to the Javanese ruling class from which, as we have already seen, Dutch rule had found many willing allies until the days of national wakening. Staunch Nationalists though they were, they were then demanding recognition as equal partners rather than a complete break with Holland.

It is against this background that a change in Dutch policy must be interpreted. The national awakening, the Russian Revolution and the impetus it provided to social ferment throughout the world, the popularity of Sarekat Islam, the growth of Marxist ideas, all these were signs that changes must

153

be made in the East Indian Government. In Holland the Dutch Socialists added their demands for a greater measure of democracy in colonial government. The result was that in 1918 the 'Volksraad' was established. This 'Council of the People' had a minimum of thirty-nine members, of whom the Chairman was appointed by the Crown; of the others, the Governor-General appointed five Indonesians, fourteen Europeans and foreign Asiatics, and ten Indonesians, nine Europeans and foreign Asiatics were elected by indirect suffrage. The Volksraad had only advisory powers, but it was given the rights of free expression, of petition and questioning. For the first time, Dutch authority was challenged on its own territory. The Governor-General who opened it on May 18th, 1918, made history; never again could Dutch rule acquire absolute control in administration.

'Officials of the old school', Amry Vandenbosch wrote, 'dreaded the opening of the Volksraad, since they knew they would not feel at home under the new conditions. Where formerly they commanded, they would now have to emerge from their offices and studies into the glaring publicity of an assembly to explain and justify their actions. Their fears were more than justified, for such a storm of criticism broke loose in the first sessions as to sweep them off their feet. The Government, shocked by all this criticism, unprepared and overwhelmed, made only feeble replies. Hardly had the Volksraad been brought under control when news of revolutionary movements throughout Europe led to a second outburst, even more severe than the first. On November 18 a member of the National East Indian Party made a very critical speech in which he defended the right of revolution. When that same day the Government received news from the Netherlands of attempted revolutionary disorders there it apparently became frightened, for the Governor-General, without consulting either the Council of the Indies or the Minister of Colonies, sent a hastily prepared statement to the Volksraad promising far-reaching governmental reforms.'[10]

These were known as the 'November promises'; some of the changes they implied did not take place until 1925. The Volksraad provided a platform for agitation by Nationalists who formed a National Faction presided over by Moh. Husni Thamrin; they demanded a better system of administration, improvements in political and economic spheres. They were a parliamentary group working ultimately for independence by legal, non-revolutionary means.

Meanwhile, Nationalists were divided, not on the ultimate objective of independence, but on the methods whereby it might be achieved. When the Sarekat Islam Congress was held in Surabaya in 1921 this division of opinion led to a split. A section of its members were still prepared to co-operate with the Dutch whilst fighting for self-government; others, mainly those who were Marxists as well as Nationalists, considered such co-operation as a betrayal of the independence movement. Semaun, leader of the Marxist group, had been chiefly responsible for transforming the Social Democratic Association into the Perserikatan Kommunist di India (known as the P.K.I.) in 1920. They now formed a Communist group inside Sarekat Islam. P.K.I. speakers criticized Sarekat Islam as a capitalist body; the real division in society, another argued, was along class lines, not those of religion. This Marxist challenge in an organization founded by devout Muslims was taken up by Hadji Agus Salim who smartly retorted that the Prophet had expounded historical materialism twelve hundred years before Karl Marx was born. He carried the day. A resolution was passed forbidding members to belong to the P.K.I., with the result that Communists withdrew from Sarekat Islam.

Although well-known Communists like Semaun, Darsono, and Alimin withdrew from Sarekat Islam, they already had a central organization in the Indonesian Communist Party which directed the activities of its rank and file members. By 1923, most of the branches of Sarekat Islam were under Communist leadership. Thus whilst the leaders—Hadji Agus Salim and Abdul Muis—were in favour of parliamentary tactics, the local branches frequently supported revolutionary action in the form of strikes. The right-wing leaders met the situation by a purge of the organization, and the formation of a new one called Partai Sarekat Islam Indonesia (P.S.I.I.). The left-wing group formed a rival body called Sarekat Ra'jat Merah (Red People's

Union) which at once threw in its lot with the P.K.I. The P.S.I.I., led by men who were Muslim Nationalists, moved nearer and nearer to Pan-Islamism, and organized a series of 'All-Islam Congresses'. In a country which is predominantly Muslim, this policy secured a good deal of mass support, but it was non-political, and many of its leading members at that time were prepared to fall in with Dutch plans to increase Indonesian participation in the Government.

This issue of co-operation became more and more hotly contested as the Dutch increased Indonesian representation in the Volksraad. In 1925 they passed a new Constitution extending its powers. From being a purely advisory body it now became co-legislative; its assent was necessary for the budget; it was able to amend Government measures and to initiate legislation; to ask·for information but not to ask a question which carried the right to a written answer leading to a debate and a vote of confidence. Left-wing Nationalists, both Communists and non-Communists, saw in this change only a device to counteract the growing political consciousness of groups of Indonesians. Others considered the change in Dutch policy as a victory for the Nationalist movement and believed that gradually they could win effective control. The issue was one which faces all Nationalists; in India, in somewhat similar circumstances, the Indian National Congress, united under Gandhi's leadership, adopted the policy of non-violence. In Indonesia, Islam and Marxism were to a certain extent competing ideologies; the challenge to those nationalists who saw progressive Islamic ideas as the foundation of the State came from nationalists who were already consciously working for a Communist revolution.

The Fifth World Congress of the Comintern formulated a policy of revolutionary activities among the colonial peoples of Asia, and the P.K.I. at two conferences in Djogjakarta and Surabaya at the end of 1924 worked out the application of this directive.

The Communists themselves were not united on the policy they should pursue. In Indonesia, as in China, two groups struggled for leadership. One group, led by Alimin and Musso, was prepared to follow Comintern directives, whether they were suited to national conditions or not. The second group was led by Tan Malaka. After continuous agitation, Alimin and Musso succeeded in winning over the Executive Committee of the Communist Party to their policy. At a meeting held in the Prambanan Temple, outside Djogjakarta, in October 1925, the decision was taken to organize a revolution aimed at the overthrow of Dutch power; the date selected was June 1926, and the first blow was to be struck by the railway workers. Tan Malaka, the Comintern representative for South-east Asia and Australia, was in Manila at the time; he strongly opposed the idea, and before it could materialize, he wrote a pamphlet to show that it was premature and he had it circulated to Communist Party members in Java and Sumatra. When the rebellion was launched in November 1926—it had been postponed because of difficulties of organization in the Communist Party—it was quickly suppressed. Failure was attributed partly to Tan Malaka's counter-agitation, but the history of the revolution suggests that the masses of workers in the cities and on the big plantations, where the Communists had been able to exploit worsening conditions, were largely indifferent. Metal-workers and dock-workers struck in Surabaya and were supported by tram- and railway-workers. There were strikes in West Java, Central Java, and along the west coast of Sumatra in the district of Padang. In Djakarta the Communists seized the telegraph office and held it for several hours. In West Java and in Bandung, Dutch troops fought with Communist forces, and the situation was not under Dutch control for some weeks. In January 1927 a strike was organized in the coal-mining area of Sawahloento and Siloenkang in the hinterland of Padang. In the middle of the small town of Siloenkang today, in a square surrounded by markets, I was taken to see a memorial to the men who fell in the clashes with the Dutch police. 'We had guerrilla fighters even in those days,' my companions from a nearby weaving shed told me.

The Dutch launched a counter-offensive in June 1927 ostensibly because they had information indicating a third outbreak. In Holland itself, Indonesian students were suddenly visited by Dutch police; documents were seized purporting to provide evidence of connections between them and the Javanese P.K.I. leader, then in exile in Moscow. In Java and Sumatra several thousand people were arrested and many of them sent to the malarial swamps of New Guinea. The Dutch Government had given its Governor-General full powers to intern any Indonesian subject without trial. Thousands were seized on the grounds of being politically suspect. Dutch internment orders were so ruthless that a new word was coined to describe people who were sent to New Guinea, as 'di-Digulkan' (to be di-gulled, after the name of the worst camp Boven Digul). Many nationalists died in Boven Digul. Many were still there at the beginning of the war in the Pacific.

This was a turning-point in the history of Indonesian nationalism. The P.K.I. went underground; a new leadership emerged among young men and women who were deeply moved by the events of 1926–7. They began to hate Dutch rule, to think and feel as nationalists first and foremost. An ideology of nationalism developed which provided a united front. After 1927, there was only one issue, that of co-operation or non-co-operation with Dutch rule. The very fact that in the nationalist movement the concrete goal of an organization, Professor Berg writes of this period,

'is less of a stimulus to participation than the opportunity to express feelings of solidarity and grievance and instinctive opposition to foreign influence in many respects, renders it impossible to keep political, social, religious, Pan-Islamic, apologetic, and cultural action absolutely distinct.'[11]

In this second stage of the nationalist movement, which lasted until the Japanese interlude, all these factors played their part. Youth groups, until now called 'Young Java', 'Young Sumatra', 'Young Celebes', 'Young Ambon', now came together as one organization—'Pemuda Indonesia'—in Bandung on February 7th, 1927. The 'Pemuda Muhammadiah' (Young Muhammadans) was formed. Scouts had their own organization; some of its branches were affiliated to Pemuda Indonesia; others to Pemuda Muhammadiah. Young Nationalist teachers joined the Taman Siswa movement and Nationalists sent their children to these schools in Java and Sumatra in rapidly increasing numbers.

Indonesian women in December 1928 held their first Congress in Djogjakarta and decided to federate existing organizations. Until this time, women's groups—notably the Putri Merdeka (Independent Women) formed in 1912— were primarily concerned with education. Some of them had founded Kartini Schools for girls. But the Union of Indonesian Women, which was formed at a time of widespread political activities, provided a platform on which an increasing number of women could play their part in the independence struggle. Thus, the nationalist idea was written into every type of organization, trade union, cultural, religious, youth and women.

Nationalism was now the unifying factor. As a political concept, it owed much to Western thought, but it was more than a political concept. It was the self-consciousness of people under colonial rule, inevitable, inescapable, sweeping across boundaries of class, of religion, rousing illiterate peasant and intellectual, unsettling industrial worker and aristocrat, bridging regional differences, and ultimately welding the most diverse peoples into a common struggle. Differences of ultimate objective are overshadowed until the nationalist struggle is won. But there is a wide variety of difference as to the tactics which are adopted. They are all fundamentally concerned with the degree of resistance to the colonial power.

Dutch policy, after the oppressive, ruthless treatment of those who took part in or sympathized with the rebellions of 1926–7, now became increasingly paternal. More money was spent on education and social welfare; co-operative societies were formed; more posts were provided for Indonesians in the administration and more seats in the Volksraad. With every concession to nationalism, Indonesians were found who regarded this as a victory for co-operation. They were gradualists who, in many cases, developed a vested interest in Dutch rule. The narrower alliance of rulers in power at the beginning of the century was now widened to include a much larger section of society, the middle class. Dutch rule was challenged by those who were unwilling to co-operate, and non-co-operation became the slogan of nationalism.

In this new phase of nationalism, Sukarno played a leading part in Indonesia whilst Hatta, Sjahrir, and others were working together in Holland. Revolutionary methods had been tried by the Communists and had failed. The problem was how to achieve independence by other means. Those nationalists who were working in Holland—they were mainly students—and those whose political activities were carried out in Indonesia, made no concessions to Dutch rule; they were united in their idea of independence though the road they must travel seemed long and bitter. But the Dutch had shown such ruthlessness in dealing with the rebellions of 1926–7 that men like Hatta, in Holland, and Sukarno, now the leading figure in the movement in Indonesia, began to plan for a long struggle. They never turned back from this time until independence was won. Their names, together with many others—Sjahrir, Sjarifuddin, Sartono, Kusuma Sumantri, Nazir Pamuntjak, Ali Sastroamidjojo, Abdulmajid, Djajadiningrat, Dermawan Mangunkusumo, Subardjo, Setiadjit—to mention only a few of them, were well known to Indonesians; they were political heroes who were to spend many years in prison or in exile. They were freed by the Japanese in 1942, and at once were the acclaimed leaders. For this reason alone, Dutch propaganda that men like Sukarno, Hatta, and Sjahrir were Japanese stooges, and that the Republic was 'made in Japan', was as dishonest as it was misleading to the outside world unaware of Indonesian nationalism.

The first world contacts which these Indonesian nationalists made for their movement were in February 1927 at the Conference of the League against Imperialism in Brussels. It coincided with the large-scale arrests and deportations in Java and Sumatra. The Indonesian Delegation consisted of Hatta, Semaun, Nazir Pamuntjak, and Subardjo. Jawaharlal Nehru and K. M. Panikkar were there from India; Ernst Toller and Otto Lehmann-Russbuldt from Germany; Ellen Wilkinson, Harry Pollitt, Fenner Brockway, Reginald Bridgeman, and George Lansbury from England; Henri Barbusse from France; Katayama from Japan; a delegation of twenty-five Chinese;

Edo Fimmen, Roger Baldwin, and Willi Munzenberg; delegations from Indo-China, Egypt, Persia, from every part of Africa, from Mexico and Latin America, from Korea, Italy, Austria, and Czechoslovakia. Men and women who have played such important roles in the history of nationalist struggles, whose names are now so familiar as Prime Ministers and Presidents where independence has been won and as political leaders where it is not yet achieved, met in Brussels. They gave it a significance which the most optimistic could not have imagined.

Dr. Hatta contributed the first speech about Indonesian nationalism to an international gathering. In September of the same year he addressed the Conference held by the Women's International League for Peace and Freedom near Paris. Hatta came from the advanced political group in Sumatra and was already politically active before he left his home in 1921 to study in the Commercial College in Rotterdam. He was Treasurer and Secretary of the Padang Branch of the Sumatran Youth Association from 1917 to 1919 and then Treasurer of its Central Office. In Holland, he was Chairman of the P.I. and editor of its paper *Indonesia Merdeka*, and it was in this capacity that he spoke in the Palais Egmont. He gave an outline of Indonesian resistance to Dutch rule and of the development in the twentieth century of a conscious nationalism.

'How could a tiny country of 7,000,000 people,' he asked, 'whose prosperity is completely dependent on colonial wealth, fulfil its so-called historical duty to educate a people seven times as large? But is it really true that Indonesia is not yet mature enough for independence? We stand by our declaration that the Indonesian people possesses the capacity to govern itself. From oldest times have the political institutions of the Indonesians been built up on the principle of self-government, even down to the smallest villages. The Indonesian people has a natural feeling for democracy. As far as the present situation is concerned already more than 80% of the colonial civil servants are Indonesians.

'We have only to replace the tiny upper stratum of high civil servants, made up entirely of Dutchmen, and then we are at our goal. And for this we have sufficient intellectual capacity. Moreover the top Dutch civil servants themselves recognize that the Indonesian administrators, from Regents down to the most minor officials, possess excellent administrative qualities. It is a fault of the colonial system itself when, in this situation, morale is lacking because it is not permitted for people to express their opinion freely. But that is only the logical consequence of the education system of Dutch colonial policy, which consists as far as possible of creating a slave mentality. This situation will alter the moment the Indonesians have the right to take charge of themselves. There is no question of a too early independence for Indonesia. Even the Dutch in the last few years no longer put this question. The reality? The reality is that Holland will not give up her colonies as her prosperity depends on them. It is egoism that forces her to maintain this regime of force. On the other side no one can demand of us that we give up our right to national independence. The future will teach us how we shall receive this "summmum bonum" of mankind.'[12]

His account of Indonesia's struggle made a great impression on all those who heard it, and at the end of the Conference the following resolution was passed:

'The Congress against colonial oppression and for national freedom resolves:
'after hearing the statements about the general position in Indonesia and considering that:
'1. the purchasing power of the Indonesian population has decreased since the war by at least 15%;
'2. the wages amount to about only 15% of the wages of Europeans;
'3. all organizations and parties which are fighting for the improvement of this shocking position are forcibly suppressed; among other things through the suppression by the Assembly of the Sarikat Raiat (People's Party), the Railway Union, and others;
'4. the so-called democratic reforms are in themselves only a means to still worse slavery and deception of the people by Dutch Imperialism;
'5. the political terror of the Dutch administration describes every action as "communistic" or "Moscow inspired";

162

'6. the foreign policy of "Neutrality" which Dutch Imperialism is following in the Far East satisfies the interest of none of the imperialist powers, rather it awakens in each the desire for the possession of the strategically important Indonesia, whereby Indonesia today, in the possession of Holland, has become a factor in a new World War—which danger can only be avoided by the revolutionary freedom movement in Indonesia.

'In consideration of this the Congress resolves that the Independence movement has become a vital demand for the Indonesian people, as well as of the greatest interest for all mankind.'[13]

Hatta and his colleagues played a decisive role in the history of Indonesian nationalism whilst they studied in Holland. Their organization, the Perhimpoenan Indonesia (Indonesian Union), became increasingly political after 1927 and although most of its members were not then, and did not subsequently become, Communists, they were Marxist in outlook and they continued to co-operate with the League Against Imperialism until 1929. At that point the Communists who controlled it insisted on complete acceptance of their views, with the result that many leading Socialists resigned.

Meanwhile, in Indonesia itself a new organization with which the P.I. was in touch had been formed after the suppression of the Communist rebellions. The leader who emerged at this time was a young engineer who, in his middle school days, had written political articles under the name 'Rima'. His real name was Sukarno. In the Technical School in Bandung he had formed a Study Club which published a magazine, *Indonesia Muda*. His flare for political work, combined with great ability as a writer and a public speaker, made him a natural leader. On July 4th, 1927, he, together with members of the Bandung Study Club, formed the Partai National Indonesia (Indonesian Nationalist Party). Its object was uncompromisingly 'Indonesian Merdeka' (Independence); its political tactic was non-co-operation; its basic idea was the building of an Indonesian nation run by Indonesians. Meetings were conducted, not in Dutch, but in the Indonesian language. The new Indonesian anthem, *Indonesia Raja*, was sung at all their meetings. Sukarno was an impassioned orator with a powerful mass appeal, and the P.N.I. rapidly attracted members. It had a simple message which was taken to the villages by Sukarno and his colleagues—Sartono, Ishak, Anwari, Ali Sastroadmidjojo, and Sunarjo were the most active. They helped to spread and to deepen political consciousness among the masses more effectively than any other organization, and in due course it was able to gather together in one Federation all the Nationalist groups. For the first time the nationalist movement, whose membership was largely concentrated in Java and Sumatra, had achieved a unity of purpose.

The Dutch authorities became alarmed and in December 1929, Sukarno and seven other leading P.N.I. members were arrested, tried after seven months' detention, and then sentenced to varying terms of imprisonment. Their leaders in jail, the P.N.I. members became divided as to the tactics to be adopted. Some believed that co-operation with the Dutch might achieve most results. Others, and they were the majority, agreed to disband the P.N.I. and join a new organization called Partai Indonesia (Partindo). Its objective was independence, its tactics were non-co-operation, but it was more moderate than the P.N.I. had been. A smaller group, which was opposed to this cautious policy, was called Golongan Merdeka, and it was strengthened in 1932—when Sukarno was still in prison—by the return home from Holland of Dr. Hatta and Sjahrir. The name of the Golongan Merdeka was changed to Pendidikan Nasional Indonesia (Indonesian National Education Group). Hatta (then thirty) became Chairman and Sjahrir (then twenty-three) was his right-hand man. Both of them believed in building up well-trained, politically conscious cadres as an indispensable framework for the national movement. They were temperamentally different from Sukarno who was a natural propagandist, stirring audiences with his passionate appeals. Hatta and Sjahrir, returning, as they had done, from a Europe where Fascist ideas were beginning to find roots, were not only primarily educationalists but they were also international in their outlook. They realized, for example, that among

164

the Dutch themselves there were men like Dr. H. J. van Mook, Professor J. H. S. Logemann, J. A. Jonkman, and Mr. van der Plas who did not believe in the old-fashioned concept of colonialism. Their bi-monthly magazine *De Stuuw* (*Forward Thrust*) was a platform for progressive opinion in Holland at a time when the pro-fascist Vaderlandsche Club was attracting support in Djakarta.

When Sukarno was released from prison he had more sympathy with the Partindo than with the Pendidikan Nasional Indonesia, and after trying unsuccessfully to unite these two political groups, he threw in his lot with Partindo. Again, his leadership, for he was at once made Chairman, helped to attract a large membership. By the middle of 1933, it had fifty-six branches and at least 20,000 members. Once more the Dutch decided to remove this threat to their power, and Sukarno was arrested in August 1933, exiled to Flores Island and then to Benkulen on the west coast of Sumatra, where he remained until the Japanese released him in 1942. Within a few months Hatta was also arrested and then Sjahrir. They were exiled to Boven Digul; this was already a large internment camp, the 'home' of thousands who had been exiled there in 1926–7 after the Communist rebellions. Sjahrir and Hatta were transferred to Banda Neira in 1936, and, like Sukarno, they remained Dutch prisoners until the Japanese challenged Dutch rule.

Again the National Movement had lost its most outstanding leaders. Political activities were suppressed and a severe censorship imposed on correspondence and publications. In these conditions, divisions were inevitable and the next stage of the Movement is characterized by a large number of parties and a confusion of aims. The same main tendencies were there; those who believed that co-operation with the Dutch was a means to self-government and those who were firmly opposed to any co-operation. The main organization was the Parindra, formed by the fusion of the Budi Utomo, the Indonesian Study Clubs, and a number of smaller parties. With Dr. Sutomo as Chairman, its activities covered both political and social work. Some of its members joined the Volksraad and constituted a legal parliamentary opposition. In 1936, this group put forward a motion demanding self-government within the Dutch Empire with Cabinet Ministers responsible to the Volksraad. They asked the Netherlands to call an Imperial Conference to discuss the best methods by which self-government would become effective. The motion was accepted by a majority of the Volksraad and it became a petition to the Crown. But it met with no response. The Queen of Holland, in common with the colonial rulers of Britain and France, failed to recognize the signs of the times in Asia. The more radical nationalists who had been prepared to co-operate in the Volksraad—A. K. Gani, Amir Sjarifuddin, Sartono, Mohammed Yamin, Sanusi Pane, and others—formed a new political party, the Gerindo, which advocated self-government. Once more a party grew rapidly and enrolled thousands of members, chiefly in Java and Sumatra.

Finally, in 1939, when the threat of Fascism and war affected the whole world, political parties were brought together into one organization—G.A.P.I. (Gabungan Politik Indonesia, i.e. the Federation of Indonesian Parties). It reached a much higher level of joint political action than any preceding organization, and it showed a livelier sense of political strategy. In September 1939 it revived the rejected petition and issued a manifesto calling for a parliament with two chambers, elected by and for the people, to which the Government would be responsible.

Events in Europe were quickly reflected in Indonesia. In August 1940, when Holland was already overrun by the Nazis, the Nationalist Movement in Indonesia demanded (1) that the Volksraad should be transformed into a parliament based on election, each political group having representatives, and (2) that the Chiefs of Departments should be transformed into Ministers who should be responsible to parliament. This time, the Volksraad took the demand seriously but with no sense of urgency. It established a committee in September 1940, under the chairmanship of Mr. Visman, whose task it was to collect reports from all political parties.

The Report of the Visman Committee, published in 1941, proved to be the last official Dutch report on Indonesia. Its members—three Dutch, three Indonesians, and one Indonesian-Chinese—gave an account of the country between the

First and the Second World Wars; it discussed the views of many political organizations which were interviewed. 'One of the deepest impressions retained from the hearings', the Report states, 'was the general urge among non-European representatives for complete equality with the European.'

The Visman Report reflects the degree of support which nationalist organizations had achieved. How far its recommendations might have been adopted, how satisfied with its implementation the nationalist movement might have been, belong to the world of speculation. Queen Wilhelmina, then in London, did not wait for the report to be published before making a pledge to Indonesia (on July 30th, 1941) that when once the Netherlands were liberated from the Nazis, steps would be taken to revise Administrative Acts to 'lay the foundation for a happier and more prosperous future for the entire Kingdom'.

The statement, like so many similar promises made to India and Burma, was too late and promised too little.

'We have been too late with everything,' one Dutchman wrote, 'too late with political reforms, and too late with recognition of Indonesian self-worth.'[14] Discussing the Indonesian revolution in retrospect, another Dutch writer stated:

> 'The refusal of the government even to consider the motions of Soetardjo (1936)[15] and Wiwoho (1940) and the petition Roep (1940), for example, is sufficient evidence that the government as late as the outbreak of the Second World War, entertained not the slightest notion of altering the basic subordinate position of colony to mother country. These, to name but a few, were the grievances, which no number of asphalt roads, tiled roofs, hygienic services, or adat law codes could alleviate.'[16]

But the Dutch in London did not, or could not, believe that the rule over their 'beloved Indies' was seriously challenged, let alone coming to an end. Yet they were fighting in Europe against Fascism, and in the Atlantic Charter they expressed democratic principles for which the Allies were fighting the war. Twenty-eight Indonesians in the Volksraad asked that the Government in London should explain what were its consequences for the people of Indonesia. The question was put on

167

August 26th, 1941. The tone of the reply, which was not made until November 13th, was obtuse and patronizing.

'The Charter', it said, 'lays down rules of conduct for the establishment of good international relationships. Although it does not concern itself directly with the international relations in the individual states, every Government accepting the Charter should also be willing to accept its principles as far as rules of conduct inside the state are concerned. As these principles were already adopted long ago, by the Netherlands Government, and, as far as appropriate, thereby executed within the Kingdom, adherence to the Charter does not represent a special reason for new consideration regarding the aims of its policy, more especially as far as the Indonesian population is concerned. It may be considered as generally known how much the Netherlands Government pursues a policy of ordered, free collaboration for all groups of the population and interests within the Kingdom, and how, through practical statesmanship, it tries to bring about the quickest possible development towards this aim.

'A post-war investigation of constitutional relations, for which purpose a conference of prominent persons from all parts of the Kingdom is to be held, will give the Government as well as those governed, an opportunity to form a clear idea of the stage of development which has been reached and to plan reforms.'

Nothing could have more clearly proved to the nationalist movement in Indonesia that the Dutch Government had not learnt wisdom from their bitter experiences in Europe. They professed democratic principles to the Western world, but never regarded them as relevant in the East. It was indeed a Charter of the Atlantic, applying only to White people.

This division, not only between theory and practice, but between Asia and the West, was implicit in the Atlantic Charter; its importance has been insufficiently recognized in the Western world. Indonesian Nationalists drew their own conclusion and all organizations joined together in a supreme body consisting of an Assembly called the Majlis Rakjat Indonesia (Indonesian People's Assembly). This was in effect a representative body for the movement. G.A.P.I. was part of it and so were the Federation of Islamic Organizations, the Federation of Government Officials, Women's Organization, Trade Unions, and Youth Movement. It represented the highest point of organization yet reached by the nationalists, bringing together on a common platform the right, centre, and left-wing elements in the political parties, and those who were first and foremost Muslims. The movement had developed through struggle, encountering splits and differences now of policy, now of tactics. For the first time followers of Karl Marx and followers of the Prophet were united in a common aim of independence and all other issues were secondary.

When Japanese bombs fell on Pearl Harbour on December 8th, 1941, a Nationalist Movement was thus already in existence; it was not created by the Japanese, as Dutch propaganda suggested. On the contrary, Dutch refusal to face the demands of Indonesian organizations had led to a common front with the single aim of independence.

NOTES

[1] *The Dutch East Indies*, by Amry Vandenbosch, pp. 148–9, 1944.
[2] Ibid.
[3] *Nusantara*, by Bernard H. M. Vlekke, p. 316.
[4] Ibid., p. 319.
[5] Ibid.
[6] *Letters of a Javanese Princess*, by Raden Adjeng Kartini, p. 43. Published by Duckworth, 1921.
[7] Ibid., p. 45.
[8] Ibid., p. 95.
[9] *Effects of Western Civilisation on Indonesian Society*, by W. F. Wertheim.
[10] *The Dutch East Indies*, by Amry Vandenbosch, p. 112.
[11] *Whither Islam*, edited by H. A. R. Gibb, p. 284. Article by Professor C. C. Berg on 'Indonesia'.
[12] *Das Flammenzeichen vom Palais Egmont. Offizielles Protokoll des Kongresses gegen Koloniale Unterdruckung und Imperialismus*, Brussels, 10–15 February 1927, pp. 140–1. Neuer Deutscher Verlag, Berlin 8.
[13] Ibid., p. 141.
[14] *Diogenes in der Tropen*, by J. H. Veenstra, p. 54. Amsterdam, 1946.
[15] Requesting dominion status for Indonesia.
[16] 'The Indonesian Revolution in Retrospect', by Justus van der Kroef. *World Politics*, April 1951.
[17] Ibid.

PART THREE

Transition

CHAPTER IX

JAPANESE INTERLUDE

DUTCHMEN in Indonesia seemed to have no idea of the feelings towards Japan which were common among those whom they ruled.

'Japan', Sjahrir wrote in internment, 'seems to be very popular in most of Indonesia, although most people do not dare to express their feelings. Japan, nevertheless, has the sympathy of most of the people, and the Japanese are the most popular foreigners in our country—no doubt because our people have come to know only their good sides.'[1]

Even when Japan attacked China in 1937, and the intentions of Japanese policy were no longer obscured, many Indonesians regarded the incident as further proof of Japan's invincibility and the impotence of the Western world. When Holland was overrun by Japan's ally, Hitler, they were secretly glad.

'For the average Indonesian', Sjahrir wrote, 'the war was not really a world conflict between two great world forces. It was simply a struggle in which the Dutch colonial rulers finally would be punished by Providence for the evil, the arrogance, and the oppression they had brought to Indonesia.'[2]

People in Java related Japanese bombs on Pearl Harbour to the Djojobojo myth that, after the white man was defeated, yellow men would come from the north and rule for a hundred days.

A strong element of mysticism in the Javanese character goes a long way to explaining the influence of the centuries-old Djojobojo prophecy and the belief that if the Japanese invaded Indonesia they would appear as liberators, not as conquerors. The prophecy runs like this:

173

'The Great Ordeal will all the more exterminate Java and all that is upon her. However ultimately although the nurslings are prepared the ordeal of the times, the Great Governor does not accept it. He longs to terminate the terrestrial purgatory endured during the period of the three Heru Tjakra. Assistance will come from Tembini Island, yellow of colour, small of height, they will occupy the country of Java. Their rule will last for as long as the age of Indian corn, then they will return homeward, namely the Island of Tembini. Java will return to her original state, to the hands of her own sons.'

In 1951 I was very interested to learn in Minahasa that the Menadonese, who welcomed the Japanese when they landed in 1942, had a similar prophecy; that they would be liberated from Western tyranny and placed under the benevolent rule of the messengers of the Great King in a white cloud which they believed stood for the Japanese fleet as it entered the harbour.

To the Dutch, Pearl Harbour had quite another significance. Queen Wilhelmina (already in London) remarked when she was informed of the event on the telephone: 'A bomb on Pearl Harbour is a bomb on Java.' When the *Prince of Wales* and the *Repulse* were sunk, the Dutch believed the situation to be hopeless; these were the only two Allied capital ships in these waters. Dr. van Mook, Dutch Governor-General, left for the United States to ask for assistance, but discovered that none was available. On his way back, he describes his feelings in these words:

'Walking through an orange grove I felt, for a few moments, the relaxation of being completely out of the war. If I ever understood isolationism, it was then; at the same time I felt that South-east Asia, the beautiful Indies, were doomed to fall under the Japanese terror. And that nobody could do anything about it.'

The Dutch Government showed neither self-confidence nor enthusiasm for the anti-Fascist struggle. This was sometimes interpreted by Indonesians as evidence that the Dutch, in order that they might hold on to their colony, were prepared to make a deal with the Japanese as the Vichy French had done in Indo-China. Many Indonesian nationalists were prepared to co-operate in resistance to Japanese Fascism as their colleagues in occupied Holland were doing in the case of German Fascism. The Executive Board of the Madjelis Rakjat Indonesia (Council of the Indonesian People) and other organizations passed resolutions to this effect, whilst Dr. Hatta made this appeal:

'Our people, with the exception of a small minority now in the armed forces, has not learned to use arms and bears no responsibility for its own fate. Yet it should not think that this war does not affect us. . . . If we are convinced that the Japanese aggression endangers our ideas, then we must resist Japanese imperialism. Even if we believe that Japan will probably win, it remains our duty to come to the defence of our endangered ideals. It is better to die standing than to live kneeling.'

The first serious attacks on Indonesian territory came on January 10th, 1942, when fourteen Japanese ships landed troops on the island of Tarakan, important because of its oil-wells. Parachute landings followed up by a large transport fleet then captured the Minahasa. Places of strategic importance fell rapidly; Pontianak in West Kalimantan (Borneo) on February 1st, followed by Sabang at the north of Sumatra, Medan and Palembang on the east coast of that island; Balikpapan, the oil centre on the east coast of Kalimantan (Borneo), after Dutch employees of the B.P.M. had courageously set fire to the plant. After the fall of Balikpapan, the Japanese gained control of the Makassar Straits and Bandjarmasin. In two sweeping movements from east to west and from west to east, they finally broke off any communications with Australia by landing troops on the island of Bali.

Java was now completely encircled. Major-General Sitwell with 8,000 British and American troops was in favour of fighting the Japanese troops as they landed on March 1st. But without consulting him, the Dutch Commander-in-Chief of Allied Forces on Java, Lt.-General Ter Poorten, surrendered in their name. The story is told in detail in the Third Supplement to the *London Gazette* of February 20th, 1948, in the Report on Air Operations during the campaigns in Malaya and Indonesia from December 8th, 1941, to March 12th, 1942. The author of the Report, Air Vice-Marshal Sir Paul Maltby, Assistant Air

Officer Commanding Far East Command, R.A.F., from January 12th to February 10th, 1942, and Air Officer Commanding R.A.F. in Java from February 11th to March 12th, 1942, tells the story frankly:

'At about 0900 hours 8th March, a rough translation of a broadcast by the Dutch Commander-in-Chief was received at British H.Q. at Tjikadjang. It had been promulgated in the name of all the Allied Forces in Java as well as in that of the Dutch. At about 1030 hours it was telephoned through in English by, it is believed, Colonel Gulik, the Dutch Air Staff Officer at A.H.K. who had come for the purpose to Garoet at the foot of the hills. It was to the effect that "all organized resistance" in Java had ceased and that troops were to offer no further resistance to the Japanese. Colonel Gulik said that the Dutch C.-in-C. had cancelled his instructions about disregarding surrender orders and that he intended his order to be obeyed. The last was quite unexpected.'

Sir Paul Maltby also writes in the same Report:

'Yet something might have been done but for the quandary in which the British had now been placed by reason of the Dutch Commander-in-Chief's broadcast. This had been promulgated on behalf of the British forces, as well as on that of the Dutch, but without consultation with the A.O.C. or G.O.C. and although the British intention to continue resistance was well known to the Dutch Commander-in-Chief.'

Within eight days, the centre of Dutch rule, built up with such energy during three centuries, collapsed to the bewilderment of the Javanese and the arrogant surprise of their new conquerors. Indonesians asked if the Dutch were brave enough to fight for the country they had made their own. Was it not more probable, more politically sophisticated people asked, that they were willing to collaborate with the Japanese, as the French had done in Indo-China? Whatever happened, Dutch prestige was certainly undermined by Lt.-General Ter Poorten's spectacular failure to defend 'tropical Holland'. If the Japanese can win so easily, young Indonesians began to argue, why should we ever again tolerate Dutch rule? There were, of course, political leaders who understood the nature of Fascism, whether it was Japanese or German. They knew that on the wider canvas of world history, Holland stood for democratic principles, that Dutchmen were fighting with the Allies against Fascism. But this interpretation of immediate events was only two-dimensional; thoughtful Indonesians who looked beyond war, saw a third dimension which was the defeat of both Dutch and Japanese, followed by independence.

Whilst this diversity of outlook had important results in so far as it largely determined the course of action which political leaders adopted, the general picture of Indonesian reaction to the Japanese was one of welcome. And in the first few months they did many things to arouse enthusiasm. Imagine, for instance, the proud pleasure of flying the red-and-white flag, which was forbidden by the Dutch; the excitement of singing:

> '*Indonesia tanah airku. Tanah tupmah darahku.*
> *Disanalah aku berdiri, Tjadi pandu ibuku.*'

(Indonesia is my country. It is the land of my birth. There I stand, Guarding my motherland.)

These words—the first verse of the National Anthem—were regarded as 'dangerous thoughts' by the Dutch, and people were forbidden to repeat them. I asked many Indonesians whilst in their country in 1951 what were their first feelings towards the Japanese who appeared in their towns in March 1942. With few exceptions, they recalled a sense of liberation, a sudden consciousness of themselves as adult human beings, no longer treated as children by paternalistic Dutchmen. 'My most vivid memory', one young Indonesian writer told me, 'was that the newspapers were now printed in Indonesian instead of Dutch, not just little underground leaflets but the daily Press.' Another impression which was often related was the mixed feelings of release, self-assertion, and even pity when Dutch arrogance changed to servility before the eyes of young Indonesians. This complex psychological reaction has been recorded by S. M. Gandasubrata, Resident of Banjumas (Central Java) from March 1942 until August 1945. On the day the Japanese army arrived, he says, 'all State officials of the rank of assistant district head and above, of all nationalities and departments, were assembled in the Seraju Valley Railway Hotel'. They all were asked to stand up in the sequence of their respective ranks. Dutch Resident Boots was first; the narrator, Gandasubrata, was second, and so on. Colonel Sato stood in front of them, proclaimed the names and ranks of his fellow officers after which the Dutch and Indonesians stated their names and their ranks. Japanese Major Kosi described the objects of Japanese occupation forced on them to pacify East Asia. They would 'help the Indonesian Nation free itself from the Dutch colonial prison. Eventually Japan would build a Greater East Asia for common prosperity.'

'Then', writes Gandasubrata, 'we were asked one by one whether we were willing to work with Japan to build Greater East Asia. Resident Boots answered: "I am willing." I do not know the reason why, but the answer given by Resident Boots of itself made my own easier. Why should I, as an Indonesian, not wish to join in helping to build Greater East Asia for our common welfare? Apart from that, instructions from the Dutch Government had requested us to continue our work in order to guarantee security and to lighten the sufferings of the people as long as the country was occupied by the enemy.

'All the officials answered "Willing". Then we were allowed to return to our respective offices and were asked to continue our work whilst awaiting instructions from the Japanese army.'[3]

The writer describes a journey he made with Resident Boots past a burnt-down sugar factory and then through deadly quiet villages, until they came to a broken bridge. Water pipes were destroyed, electric cables were hanging in the air, and nearby stalls showed signs of recent looting.

'How would we be able to repair all this damage?' he asked himself. 'The Dutch who had conceitedly called themselves "Lovers and protectors of the Indonesian people" had surrendered our fate to Japan in the midst of immeasurable wreckage and ruin.'[4]

Within a few months, most Dutch men (including Resident

Boots) and women together with many Eurasians were interned in camps where they stayed for the remainder of the war; they suffered every kind of humiliation and thousands died from starvation and sickness. Describing Resident Boots's arrest, Gandasubrata writes:

'Resident Boots and Assistant Resident de Klerk were interned. How did they feel? I do not know; I only remembered Resident Boots saying after the Dutch Government had surrendered to Japan: "Indeed, Regent, we should have given Indonesians dominion status fifteen years ago. Then all would have turned out otherwise." But there is no use in crying over spilt milk.'[5]

For the Dutchman, Japanese occupation meant internment camp; for Gandasubrata it meant promotion to take the Dutch Resident's place. But Japanese Military Government was superimposed on the colonial regime. 'The Commander of the Army of Dai Nippon', paragraph 2 of their Military Law read, 'holds the highest powers of Military Government and also all powers which previously were in the hands of the Governor-General.' And paragraph 3 continued: 'All governmental bodies and their powers judgments and laws of the previous government, are recognized as valid for the meanwhile, so long as they do not conflict with Military Government orders.'[6] The policy was clear, but to many Indonesians there came their first opportunity to hold top positions in administration. Further, and this was particularly true of the villages, young men and women were sent to Djakarta to follow courses in a variety of subjects, and they returned full of self-confidence. 'The self-respect which in Dutch colonial time was not visible among our people', the Resident writes, 'now grew little by little.'[7] Distinctions between Dutch and Indonesian in education disappeared. Whereas 'Holland for centuries had held the opinion that the Javanese could not become satisfactory soldiers . . . Japan was willing to invite the Javanese people to oppose the Allied attack together with her'[8] and the first Indonesian army in this way came into existence.

But this is only one side of the picture. When they arrived the

Japanese released many Indonesians imprisoned by the Dutch for their political activities. One of them was Sukarno. Hatta and Sjahrir had already returned from Banda Neira. Sukarno returned from his prison fortress in Benkulen (Sumatra) under police escort at the request of the nationalists in Java, supported by Hatta. They were not deceived by Japan's sudden embrace.

These three men met together. Sjahrir had already established contact with an underground movement organized by Sjarifuddin and Mangunkusumo. Sjarifuddin had started it with Dutch knowledge and financial help amounting to 25,000 Dutch guilders. He contacted the illegal Communist Party and many of its members became his most active, sometimes his most indiscreet, supporters. Sjahrir informed his two colleagues on this matter. Of Sukarno, he wrote that he

> 'had been treated rather roughly in Sumatra by the Japanese. He regarded them as pure fascists, and felt that we must use the most subtle methods to get round them, such as making an appearance of collaboration. He furthermore considered the future to be far from promising because he thought the war with Japan would last at least ten years. I presented the thesis that the war would be much shorter, and we must therefore develop our revolutionary aims. Neither he nor Hafil [Hatta] opposed this, and we agreed that they should do everything legally possible to give the nationalist struggle a broader legal scope, and at the same time secretly support the revolutionary resistance. We realized that the Japanese would try to capitalize on Rachman's [Sukarno's] popularity for propaganda purposes, and we agreed that political concessions from the Japanese for the nationalists must be pressed for in return.'[9]

These three experienced nationalist workers decided that in the next phase of their struggle for independence, Sukarno and Hatta should work with the Japanese authorities whilst maintaining contact with Sjahrir who would work with the underground resistance movement. The result was that throughout this Japanese interlude, Tokyo was able fully to exploit the fact that two Indonesian leaders were collaborating with them. After the war was over, when it was known that Hatta and

Sukarno were also in contact with the Resistance throughout, Dutch propaganda continued to mislead the world by calling the two Indonesian leaders 'Japanese Quislings'.

Sjahrir, Sukarno, and Hatta were agreed on their policy of resistance, but their appreciation of world events did not always coincide. Sjahrir always believed in the final victory of the Allied cause. Sukarno had a purely nationalist approach and interpreted the war in terms of a struggle between East and West rather than 'a war for democracy', as Allied propaganda described it. Educated in Indonesia, bitterly hostile towards the Dutch and the Western world of which they were a part, he had a certain respect, as a fellow-Asian, for Japan's impressive achievements and he believed that they would repeat on a grander scale their victories in 1904–5. Hatta was deeply anti-fascist and, as his companion-in-exile, Sjahrir, described him, 'a profoundly democratic individual' with genuine pro-Allied feelings. Indeed, just before they were released from Banka, Hatta, with the honesty which has characterized his whole life, wrote an article expressing his opposition to the Axis, and his support for the Allies. It was translated into several dialects and widely distributed whilst Japanese forces were already in sight of the coast of Sumatra. Hatta's position was difficult to sustain; it required courage and integrity of purpose. When the Japanese Military Government released him on March 22nd, 1942, he had refused to become an official in Japanese service. When, at the request of Sjahrir's underground group, he consented to become an Adviser to the Japanese Government, he made the condition that he was free to express his own views on matters of administration. He believed that the war would last for at least three years, but that ultimately the Americans with their far greater resources would emerge victorious. In the meantime, he believed that he could help build the framework of real independence as soon as the war was over. From April 1942 until October 1943, he ran an organization called Gunseikanbu Kikakuka Daiti Bun Situ from Pegangsaan Timur, Djakarta. He himself was in charge, and people told me that this was the only office in Indonesia where no Japanese clerks nor heads of departments were to be seen. Hatta was in constant touch with Sjahrir through such loyal underground workers as Djohan Sjaroezah, his secretary, who later became Secretary of the Djakarta branch of the Socialist Party. With much ingenuity, he was able to pass on Hatta's reports of Japanese plans and of the activities of those Indonesians who were giving their collaboration sometimes quite genuinely, sometimes because they were given good positions in Japanese administration. Sukarno himself was kept in touch with the underground movement by Hatta.

Meanwhile, we must see what was happening among the masses, so many of whom had welcomed the Japanese arrival in their homes and villages. To many Indonesians, especially in Java and Sumatra, the first result was an opportunity for the first time in their lives to fill the higher grades of administration. For, as the Dutch were interned, thousands of posts in Government Departments, both central and provincial, were left vacant, and the same applied to industry and commerce. Only a small proportion of the Japanese could speak any Indonesian language; their order that Japanese should become the official language in administration and throughout the schools met with obstinate resistance. Thus, posts vacated by the Dutch suddenly became available to Indonesians. In Dutch days, 92% of the higher positions were filled by Europeans, and 7% by Indonesians.[10] In the Japanese interlude, the great majority of higher positions were filled by Indonesians. The Heads of Departments, as I discovered in many offices, were Japanese, often men who did not know any other language than their own. They were forced to depend on their second-in-command, who was an Indonesian. Further, the Japanese had to train thousands of young Indonesians to carry on the work of the country; in industries with a war potential and in the armed services they exercised a strict control, but at no time did they have sufficient people of their own to take over completely. No wonder that many young Indonesians were swept into Japanese service, where they acquired self-confidence in running their own country. The opportunity was as welcome as it was unexpected. Sukarno and Hatta cleverly used the fact that Indonesia was now mainly administered by Indonesians as propaganda for the idea of independence. It must be said, however, that this applied most of all to Java and Sumatra, the main centres of Dutch administration and economic development as well as the areas where nationalism had had its greatest influence. For the same reason, underground resistance groups appeared first and became most highly developed in these two islands.

By the beginning of 1943, that is less than a year after the Japanese occupied Indonesia, people began to realize that the Djojobojo prophecy was at most only half true. The Japanese had come from the north, the Indonesians were already running their country more extensively than at any time for three and a half centuries, but the men, 'yellow of colour, small of height' had already been in the country for more than the 'age of Indian corn'. No one thought in terms of a renewal of Dutch rule and an increasing number of people began to take part in underground activities aimed at ending Japanese rule. Openly Sukarno and Hatta continued to co-operate. Sukarno, temperamental and a brilliant demagogue, was always before the public in his capacity of Director of the Central Headquarters of the Java Patriotic Association. He spoke on Hirohito's birthday and at ceremonies which celebrated Japanese victories. His hatred of the Dutch was now transferred to the British and Americans, and the Dutch are never tired of quoting one of his remarks: 'America we shall iron out, England we shall destroy.' But the Indonesian people saw in him a symbol of Indonesian independence.

The welcome which the Japanese received when they first landed was short-lived. An increasing number of men and women, especially young people, soon began to find ways and means of opposing these new foreign rulers. Whilst they were nominally in control, holding top positions, so few Japanese knew any Indonesian language that they were forced to depend on Indonesians who thus gained experience and above all, self-confidence. Japanese officials who demanded that every employee should bow three times to their Emperor as a morning salutation were often deceived in believing that this was a genuine acknowledgment of their authority. Many a Japanese who slapped the face of an Indonesian—and this was a very common incident—would have been surprised had he realized that his victim was comparing this crude behaviour with the civilized manners of their Dutch predecessors. But the result was not to make the Indonesian wish to see the Dutch return, but to reinforce his desire for self-government. Sukarno and Hatta, ostensibly Japanese collaborators, understood this and their speeches often implied it, although their subtle remarks passed over the heads of Japanese speaking from the same platforms. In his remarkable study of the Indonesian nationalist movement, George Kahin describes the radio speeches which Sukarno frequently made to the whole country, since the Japanese had built up a network reaching all the larger towns and, through 'singing towers', a considerable proportion of villages.

'In these, according to his instructions from the Japanese, he attacked the Allies, extolled the Japanese and called upon the population to support their war effort. An examination of these speeches, however, will support Sukarno's contention that "75% of their content was pure nationalism". Moreover they were full of subtleties and double talk which generally passed over the heads of Japanese monitors but were meaningful to the population, especially those of Javanese culture. Such talk made it easy for the peasant to equate "anti-imperialism" with "anti-Japanese".'[11]

Sukarno was much more impressed by Japanese victories than Hatta, who retained his belief in the Allied cause and concentrated his work, as far as possible, on preparing for the day when Indonesians would achieve independence. He worked, for example, with the Panitia Memadjukan Bahasa Indonesia (Committee for the Development of the Indonesian Language) where young writers and poets discussed the enrichment of the Malay language with scientific and literary words which it did not possess. He was also a member of the Kyukan Seido Tyous Iinkai (Research Committee for Traditional Laws and Customs) from November 1942 until September 1943 when it was dissolved. This work provided opportunities for underground members to gather together. It was a welcome change to Indonesian intellectuals from Dutch days; it involved a recognition of their nationhood.

The Japanese themselves saw the wisdom of promising self-government and of providing some outlet for nationalist feelings. In March 1943, all the Indonesian organizations in Java and Madura were merged into the P.U.T.E.R.A. (Poesat Tenega Rakjat—Centre of People's Power). Sukarno was the Chairman; Hatta, Vice-Chairman, whilst the two remaining members of the Board of four were Ki Hadjar Dewantoro, founder of the Taman Siswa schools, and Hadji H. M. Mansoer, a prominent Muslim leader. The P.U.T.E.R.A. was an umbrella organization which covered varieties of activity, all of them regarded by the Japanese as contributing to their war effort. Many of them did. There were, for example, the mobilization of Hei Hos who were conscripted into the Japanese army; P.E.T.A., consisting of soldiers who would defend Indonesia; the Seinendan, a youth corps; and the Keibodan, an auxiliary police corps. The effect of these military and semi-military organizations was the training of a large proportion of Javanese youth in Japanese methods of war. The largest group—the P.E.T.A.—had as many as 120,000 armed men in 1945 and they were the basis of the Indonesian People's army.

Japanese military authorities soon began to doubt the usefulness of the P.U.T.E.R.A. in helping their war efforts. Sukarno, Hatta, and other Indonesian leaders were only too clearly much more popular than the Japanese and from time to time youth groups openly expressed anti-Japanese sentiments. The Japanese disbanded it at the end of 1943 and set up a new organization called Djawa Hokokai; Sukarno was the Chairman, but the real control was in the hands of the Japanese Commander-in-Chief. To gain the support of leading Muslims, they formed a large Islamic organization called the Council of Indonesian Muslim Associations, generally known as the M.A.S.J.U.M.I. Thus, as far as Java and Madura were concerned, practically every type of organization was brought within the scope of Japanese propaganda. The result was not always what the Japanese expected. They gradually became aware of their unpopularity and they sensed the need to respond to Indonesian nationalism. In the winter of 1943, they allowed Sukarno to set up and to preside over a Central Advisory

Board, together with local boards in other parts of Java. The idea was that they should be consulted by the Japanese before any new measures were introduced. In November 1943, Sukarno and Hatta went to Tokyo and publicly expressed their appreciation of this move towards their self-government. Japanese propaganda at that time, and Dutch propaganda after the war, made great play with the visit and particularly with the rather lavish phrases Sukarno used in praising Japan's war efforts.

Whilst Java was naturally their main administrative centre, the Japanese paid a great deal of attention to the other islands. Sulawesi was an important territory for the Japanese and it was therefore worthwhile developing some of its riches. They introduced new methods of horticulture, even new vegetables such as the Japanese radish, in the fertile lands of the Minahasa; they taught new methods of planting upland rice and producing two harvests in the year; they reclaimed land and increased production of flax and cotton; they imported Japanese cows and improved the stock; they built the first paper mill in Menado; they developed mines; they built small ships and canal boats; they developed communications, building a new highway cutting across the Equator and introducing the Toradjas in Central Sulawesi to steamrollers and the preparation of asphalt; they started schools for training government officials, for post office work and agriculture, and trained engineers to become the managers of industrial concerns in Makassar, and sent batches of students to Japan. This was not philanthropic work; the Japanese increasingly needed food, raw materials, and minerals, as people in Sulawesi realized when they saw well-loaded ships leaving their harbours *en route* for Japan. But, meanwhile, Indonesians were gaining experience. And, even though they were forced to bow three times to Hirohito before starting their daily work, they believed it was a temporary enslavement, a belief that grew in 1944 as news of Japanese reverses in the Pacific began to trickle through to Indonesia. Further, under pressure from Sukarno and Hatta, the Japanese Prime Minister Koiso declared that Indonesia should be free. This declaration communicated by the Commander-in-Chief of the Japanese Administration in Djakarta was widely celebrated and demonstrations at which the red-and-white Indonesian flag flew and the National Anthem sung were reproduced in all Japanese propaganda, throughout the country.

The Japanese concentrated a great deal of their efforts on Sumatra, again an island rich in raw materials and with the largest oil supplies and refineries. They organized a Central Advisory Council of thirty members; fifteen were elected from provincial assemblies and fifteen appointed by the Japanese Military Administration. Twenty leading Sumatrans were advisers to the Council. The first President was Mohamad Shafei. He was one of the leaders of the Young Sumatran Youth in 1926, a colleague of Hatta and Sjahrir. In the nationalist movement he had long been an outstanding educationalist and when a student in Holland with Hatta he had pledged his life to the struggle for Indonesian independence.

In North Sumatra, a Provincial Council was formed in Medan; of the 210 members, 90 of them were appointed by the Japanese Military Administration and 120 recommended from various provinces. Political parties which were working under Dutch rule were dissolved and new organizations built up which held an inaugural meeting on July 31st, 1942; the subject, 'How to end British and American influence'. The Civil Service was greatly expanded and hundreds of young Indonesians had an opportunity of training which was to prove valuable when independence came.

The Japanese were beginning to lose some of their earlier confidence, though the course of the war was not publicized. Further, they were well aware of their own unpopularity. Even in Sumatra, especially in Atjeh, where military administration was running fairly smoothly, people began to resent Japanese propaganda methods, and the removal of crops from plantations to Japan or to other Japanese-occupied countries. There is, as yet, no detailed account of Japanese rule, nor of the growth of resistance in islands outside Java. But there are incidents which show that under the surface, people soon began to understand that Japanese occupation was a new form of colonization.

In Kalimantan (Borneo) in the spring of 1951, I heard the story of opposition in what is usually considered a politically 'backward' part of Indonesia. When Japanese troops landed in Pontianak, they blazed the slogan 'Asia for the Asiatics'. At that time there existed thirteen organizations, social, political, and religious. Their leaders met in secret and decided to watch events with a view to winning their independence. Local Sultans joined the movement. Within a month the Japanese ordered the liquidation of P.A.R.I.N.D.R.A. and other political parties. The leaders met again in secret and decided on their programme of action. The plan was to have a 'legal' front which was named 'Nissinkai' and the former President of P.A.R.I.N.D.R.A., Noto Soedjono, became its President. This too was soon liquidated. Another organization was then formed; the name was different—Pemoeda Moehammadyah—but the people were the same. Meanwhile, in South-east Borneo, with Bandjarmasin as its centre, a similar resistance group was formed and its leader, Dr. Susilo, made contact with Pontianak, and together they planned a general revolt. But the Japanese discovered their plans in South-east Borneo, and Dr. Susilo and his friends were arrested and executed. In Pontianak preparations were continued; arms and munitions were procured for the fighting groups, called Soeka-relas, and plans made for a revolt on December 8th, 1943, to begin with an attack on the headquarters of the Kempeitai. The plan also included arrangements for the future administration of the island and a provisional Ministry was selected. These plans were never carried out because the Japanese discovered them. Arrests began with twelve Sultans who were meeting in Pontianak. A reign of terror followed and thousands were carried off in trucks—'wagons of hell' they were called—to the marshes nearby and executed in batches. It was not until the summer of that year that the Japanese paper *Borneo Shimbun* announced the success of the Kempeitai in destroying the underground movement. In the course of several months they had executed most of the leaders, and 20,000 people had been rounded up from the villages and shot.

The next story comes from Menado where seven men were executed in 1943 for plotting against the Government and all wireless sets were confiscated. This was followed by an Espionage

Week. On the first day—July 12th—the Japanese went round in cars to distribute pamphlets telling people how to disable spies in their work. The second day, students in Japanese employment distributed propaganda in the art of counter-espionage against the United Kingdom, United States, and Holland. Day three was an occasion for a seventy-minute speech by a Japanese official; the next day songs were provided celebrating the destruction of spies, and on the seventh day, music was used to impress the sceptical population. Bands played 'spiritual music to increase the spirit of the people to destroy the spies of the United Kingdom, United States, and Holland'.

The line of the speech made by the Japanese Head of the Celebes Government shows the propaganda directives of that period in 1943. 'England and America', he said, 'were the enemies of Islam and must be destroyed. Roosevelt and Churchill were the enemies of justice. The Indonesians must return to the religion of Islam [presumably this was referring to the fact that Minahasa is almost entirely Christian]; Western influence must be entirely destroyed. Asia is for the Asiatics and not for the Western people. The betrayers of Indonesia must be destroyed. Enemy spies must be destroyed. The enemy of truth is the enemy of Asia and the enemy of Asia is the enemy of Islam. The rays of the Rising Sun will destroy England and America. Indonesians who favour the Dutch are betrayers of Indonesia.'

It was naturally in Java that resistance was greatest and most effectively organized. By the time the tide of war had begun to turn in favour of the Allies, Japanese Military Government was already publicly attacked and extremely unpopular. The case of the 'romushas', as slave labourers were called, is an example. These were men and women who were taken away from villages and forced to work in the fields or the mines or for the Japanese army. Many of the women were forced to be prostitutes, and some thousands of them died or went mad. As the conditions of these 'romushas' reached the public, opposition to the Japanese was often openly expressed. Dr. Hatta set up a new office named the 'Penolong Peradjurit Pekerdja' (Office for the Assistance of the Labourers) in Djakarta. He refused to have any Japanese officials, and they were not in a strong enough position to impose them.

Nothing that the Japanese authorities did in their temporary occupation of Indonesia created so much bitter opposition as the treatment of these 'romushas'. People, especially women, still talk about them as Europeans discuss Nazi atrocities in the territories which they occupied. The psychological atmosphere of resistance deepened in the minds of people who were not politically conscious; they were no longer impressed by Japanese propaganda and they became fertile soil for resistance ideas. In Java, the underground movement was well organized by the time the Allied counter-attack began in Burma and Japan's defeat became a matter of time.

Centres of resistance existed throughout the island. The most effective was that led by Sjahrir. His clarity of outlook, his political integrity and his correct analysis of Japanese and Allied policy won the allegiance of many young men and women who were destined to play decisive roles in the history of the Republic both in Indonesia and in the capitals of the world. A second group was led by Mohammed Natsir, another outstandingly able and honest Indonesian, coming like Sjahrir and Hatta from Sumatra; it took the form of study clubs which were organized openly as centres of nationalist propaganda. Natsir kept in touch with Sjahrir and other resistance groups. The Communists had their own organization, centred on the illegal P.K.I. which had been reinforced by members released by the Japanese when they first arrived, and by Communist sympathizers.

The Japanese authorities could not hide their defeats after Allied landings in West Irian (New Guinea). Resistance became stronger and Indonesians in the Japanese army began to rebel. Thousands of people were thrown into prison. The situation became more revolutionary as Allied troops moved across the Pacific in their island-hopping campaign. Japanese policy was confused. There were those, chiefly in Japanese army circles, who believed that the war against the Fascist Axis would become merged in a Third World War against Communism. The Soviet Union was not then in the Pacific war and this analysis of what might happen was not without some basis. Others, particularly in the navy, began to approach nationalist leaders; Sjahrir himself was invited to give lectures to the Ashrama Indonesia Merdeka (Association for a Free Indonesia) set up by Admiral Mayeda, Chief of the Japanese navy. Sjahrir, Hatta, and a number of others saw in these courses of lectures an excellent opportunity of training young Indonesians to prepare for independence which, they themselves were convinced, was already on the horizon. Admiral Mayeda's role is still a subject of controversy. He chose as his chief organizers Wikana and Subardjo; Wikana was a Communist working closely with the illegal P.K.I. and Subardjo was Chief of the Consulting Office on Political Affairs of the Japanese naval headquarters in Java. In the early 'twenties he was active in Communist-sponsored organizations, but, although he continued to hold Marxist views, the focus of his political loyalty was obscure. The Ashrama Indonesia Merdeka provided Marxist training for some hundreds of young Indonesians and, as Sjahrir himself writes,

'quite a few of those who took the courses later became capable fighters for our freedom and our republic'.[12]

The reason why Admiral Mayeda sponsored this organization and gave it his active support is analysed by George Kahin who discussed the subject with many who took part in it as well as with Dr. Nobutaka Ike, Japanese Professor in Stanford University.

'Sjahrir was convinced', he writes, 'that the primary purpose was to penetrate and eventually control the P.K.I. underground through the youths trained in these schools';[13]

later, under Subardjo's leadership, they would be

'controlled and turned against Britain and America, the powers most likely to invade Indonesia'.[14]

All Socialists did not accept this explanation; one of the leaders in Surabaya believed that

'their object was limited to splitting the P.K.I. and detaching part of it'.[15]

Others, including Hatta, were convinced that

'Mayeda and many of the naval officers under him were genuinely sincere in their desire for Indonesian independence. . . . Several Indonesian intellectuals developed close acquaintance with them and were surprised at the depth of their knowledge of Marxism. Some of them were convinced that these officers were Communists with a strong International bias.'[16]

It must be remembered that the U.S.S.R. was not yet in the Pacific war. A Japanese view quite widely held expected an alliance between Japan and the U.S.S.R. against the United States. Dr. Nobutaka Ike says that

'by mid-1944, navy officers, particularly intelligence officers, stationed in Indonesia must have realized that Japan could not win the war. There appears to have been a rather widespread belief among both Japanese army and navy officers that, if Japan was defeated, it was probable that a Communist revolution would break out in Japan. Conceivably, they reasoned that in case of such a revolution, Russia would throw her support to Japan. . . . Anticipating the rise of a Communist regime in Japan and the possibility of an alignment of Japan and Russia against the United States, it might not seem illogical for them to endeavour to equip potential Indonesian leaders with pro-Communist leanings.'[17]

Whatever was the reason for the co-operation of Japanese naval officers with Indonesian Nationalist leaders, one point emerges clearly from this period, namely the need to make concessions to the widespread demands for independence. On January 3rd, 1945, the Japanese Military Administration announced:

'1. With regard to preparations for East Indies independence the Army will immediately enforce the following measures:
(a) Enlarge the scope of the institution of political participation by the native.
(b) Establish a general affairs bureau and a Central Council.
(c) Strengthen and increase membership of Provincial Councils.

(*d*) Plan to expand the scope of appointments to the Military Administration and to strive for appointment of native employees.

(*e*) Inculcate spirit of national rule.

2. Train personalities who are to become future leaders and intensify present systems absolutely essential to education of future citizens.'

Meanwhile, on March 1st, 1945, a Committee of Investigation for Indonesian Independence (Badah Penjelidik Usaha Persiapan Kemerdekaan) was set up in Djakarta with Sukarno and Dr. Hatta as leading members. Its first task was to draft a Constitution for Free Indonesia 'in the future'. How near or how far that future might be, none of the sixty members could know, but they had no doubts that when the war was over there would be an Indonesian Republic. By July 1945, general agreement was achieved on the main lines of a constitution and a similar Committee was then formed in Sumatra, with Mohamad Shafei as Chairman.

Concession after concession to Indonesian Nationalism was based on Japan's knowledge that defeat was now practically inevitable. In March 1945, the Allies were winning the war. With the defeat of Germany, events moved quickly in the Pacific; island after island was lost to American and Australian forces under General MacArthur, and although Japanese propaganda tried to hide their defeats, the underground movement in Indonesia was well-informed. Wireless transmitters and receivers were well organized; Sjahrir's own home was a secret wireless station and sets were placed inside the university and elsewhere, in buildings often run by Japanese Military Administration. Thus, all leading underground groups in Java, and to a lesser degree in Sumatra, were well aware that Australians had landed in Tarakan and Balikpapan (East Borneo), whilst on the western front, which was under Admiral Lord Louis Mountbatten's command, Mandalay was recaptured on March 20th and Rangoon on May 3rd. The advance of the Fourteenth Army through Burma was clearly the prelude to an attack on Malaya and then on Sumatra. When the U.S.S.R. came into the war on August 9th, the defeat of Japan was already in sight.

Indeed, the Government in Tokyo had already put out a number of feelers, designed to lead to surrender without too big a loss of face.

At this point, the Indonesians were allowed to form a Committee, known as the Panitia Persiapan Kemerdekaan Indonesia (Preparatory Committee for Indonesian Independence), on which every part of the country was represented. Now for the first time, nationalist leaders came together from Sumatra, Celebes, Borneo, the Moluccas, and the Lesser Sunda Islands, and a representative was appointed from the Chinese community. The Japanese were still thinking in terms of home rule —Dokuricthu, as they called it. Among the Indonesian leaders there was a difference of opinion; some believed that this was all they could obtain; others, not yet convinced that Japan's defeat was certain, still thought in terms of co-operation with Japan, and preferred it to any alliance with the Western Powers. The idea of returning to Dutch rule was out of the question.

On August 8th, General Terauchi, Commander-in-Chief of Japanese Forces in South-east Asia, called Sukarno, Hatta, and Radjiman to his headquarters in Dalat, near Saigon. Before they left, Sjahrir had a conference with Hatta. They discussed the desirability of making as sharp a division as possible between themselves and the Japanese so that they would be forced into open conflict with them. This political strategy would eliminate possible differences of opinion between the underground movement and those who had collaborated. As soon as the delegation left Java, underground leaders were informed that the moment for which they had waited and prepared might arrive at any time.

During their absence in Saigon, Sjahrir had a report that the Japanese were on the point of capitulation. When Hatta returned on August 14th, he was able to give Sjahrir the news that the Japanese had agreed to set up an Assembly to declare a Republic, and that the date selected was August 19th. Sjahrir replied that this was 'a swindle, because their surrender would be announced at any moment, and they could no longer be in a position to call such a convention'.

There were differences at that time between Sukarno and Hatta on the one hand, and Sjahrir on the other. Sukarno and Hatta did not yet believe that the Japanese situation was desperate; neither did they appreciate the political implications of a Republic which seemed to be set up by the good graces of the Japanese. Sjahrir and his colleagues were convinced that a Proclamation of the Republic must be made by the Indonesians themselves, and the resistance organizations were alerted to prepare for demonstrations and perhaps fighting if the Japanese tried to use force. The sign for demonstrations was to be the proclamation. Key people in Java were informed that the proclamation would be made some time after five o'clock on August 15th. But at six o'clock, Sukarno still asked for postponement. Meanwhile, thousands of people, and the whole student population, were congregating in agreed places. The situation became dangerous as at any moment the Japanese might have discovered what was on foot, and their police and army could have made wholesale arrests. Finally, when Sukarno again refused in the early hours of the fifteenth, a group of students together with the military kidnapped him and Hatta as well. They were freed on the sixteenth after Sukarno had promised to make the proclamation the following day. During the night of the 16th–17th of August, members of the Preparatory Committee met Sukarno and Hatta in Admiral Mayeda's house (now the British Embassy) in Djakarta. The Admiral, who certainly behaved as if he were in favour of an independent Indonesia, absented himself. In the early hours of the morning, the text of the declaration was agreed upon. At first members discussed adding their names to it, but finally it was agreed that it should be signed only by Sukarno and Hatta. On the morning of August 17th, 1945, Sukarno read a declaration to a small group of people outside his own residence. It was then broadcast by Indonesians who were working in the Domei Indonesian wireless headquarters. Locking themselves into a room in this Japanese building, they gave the news over the whole network of Japanese radio. The declaration read:

WE, THE PEOPLES OF INDONESIA, HEREWITH PROCLAIM THE INDEPENDENCE OF INDONESIA. ALL MATTERS CONNECTED WITH

THE TRANSFER OF POWER, ETC. WILL BE CARRIED OUT EFFEC-
TIVELY AND IN THE SHORTEST POSSIBLE TIME.
ON BEHALF OF THE PEOPLE OF INDONESIA,
SUKARNO.   HATTA.

With the proclamation of the Republic, thousands of men and women who worked secretly in resistance organizations and thousands more who had collaborated with the Japanese authorities could now show their real feelings. Civil servants, police, the army, and many organizations immediately declared their support for the Republic. Mass meetings were held in spite of the fact that the Japanese were everywhere. Leaders of demonstrations were prepared for an attack by Japanese military or police, but met no opposition. The Japanese knew that they were no longer even temporary rulers. Sukarno, who became the first President, issued an order to all civil servants to ignore orders from the Japanese; he announced that henceforth only the red-and-white flag of the Republic should be allowed to fly from all offices. The Rising Sun had set for ever. In some places a struggle took place over the flags; Japanese who had never before seen their flag hauled down made a last protest, and held out for some weeks in certain areas. Although their Government had now officially surrendered to the Allies, there were Japanese who still believed they could make a stand in Indonesia. Many of them were killed, many committed suicide. The long-pent-up feeling of Indonesians was expressed in many acts of violence; the Japanese had taught them well.

The first fortnight of the Republic, namely the period between the proclamation and the arrival of the first Allied troops, was inevitably a time of confusion. The resistance movement was strongest in Java; and it was there that the Republic was declared. News quickly spread throughout the other islands, but it was generally a few days after August 17th before the red-and-white flag was flying in Sumatra and Borneo, in Celebes, the Moluccas, and Bali. But the Republic was in existence. There was no going back from President Sukarno's declaration from Pegangsaan Timur.

Two days after the proclamation of the Republic, the Preparatory Committee divided the country into eight provinces:

West Java, Central Java, East Java, Sumatra, Borneo (now called Kalimantan), Celebes (now called Sulawesi), Maluku (Moluccas), and Sunda Ketjil (Lesser Sunda Islands). Governors were appointed from the local resistance leaders and local committees were set up on the same pattern as that in Djakarta.

The Japanese, taken by surprise, acted quickly. They immediately imprisoned Admiral Mayeda and his staff and then disbanded such organizations as the P.E.T.A. and the Hei Ho. The response to the declaration of independence was so overwhelming that they decided not to go ahead with their original plan to arrest Sukarno and Hatta. Young men trained in Japanese methods of warfare refused to give up their arms and clashes were common; in many areas, Indonesians were able to defeat Japanese units and take over control. In Djakarta, the newly proclaimed Republic won the support of the masses, and the leaders of underground organizations emerged to become members of the Komita Nasional Indonesia Pusat (Central Indonesian National Committee) which took the place of the Preparatory Committee for Independence. That is, all except Sjahrir. Sjahrir mistrusted Sukarno, fearing that he would take too indefinite a stand against the Japanese in his declaration of independence. The result was that Sjahrir and his group were not present when the proclamation was made. Sjahrir turned down an offer to serve in Sukarno's first Cabinet and made a tour of Java to judge for himself the general atmosphere. He found 'a large and strongly national front' in opposition to the now apathetic Japanese authorities, a sense of unity which 'reached greater heights' than he had imagined. Everywhere Sukarno was the popular hero and the unquestioned leader. When President Sukarno instructed all Indonesian civil servants to ignore Japanese orders, to obey the Republic of which he was the head, and to fly the red-and-white flag from all offices, the response was immediate and widespread. A people's revolution was born in the struggle of the flags.

'Where the Japanese did not show much resistance,' Sjahrir observed, 'the revolution was bloodless. Where fighting occurred—and this took place in areas where the Japanese had made themselves particularly hated—primitive instincts arose to the surface and blood baths and atrocities resulted. But the apparatus of government became republican.'[18]

Sukarno was the symbol of the Republic. Convinced that no other leader had mass support comparable with that which Sukarno had won during the Japanese occupation, Sjahrir returned to Djakarta and gave his allegiance to the Republican Cabinet though he was never a member. Most of its members were men who had held high positions under the Japanese and few underground leaders had been appointed. This caused a great deal of dissatisfaction, especially among the students and youth who had provided the driving force of resistance. Some of them believed that certain Cabinet members had collaborated with the Japanese as long as it suited their own purpose and then transferred their enthusiasm to the young Republic for no more laudable motives; others felt that some restriction should be placed on the powers of the President. Sjahrir shared these ideas with a number of young men who had worked with him in the underground. Together they organized a

'sort of joint executive bureau in the students' assembly hall to direct action in Batavia,' Sjahrir writes, 'and more decisions were made there than in Pegangsaan, where the Republican government assembled daily'.[19]

Finally, when the situation changed sharply with the arrival of British forces, this group round Sjahrir organized a petition to Sukarno urging that the K.N.I.P. (Central Indonesian National Committee) should be given real legislative powers jointly with the President. Hatta and Sukarno agreed to this change and in Sukarno's decree approving it, powers were delegated to a small permanently sitting body called the Working Committee, of which Sjahrir was elected Chairman. Members included Sjarifuddin (Vice-Chairman) and twelve others, most of them men with a fine record of anti-Japanese resistance. One of their first steps was the enlargement of the K.N.I.P. to 188 members fully representative of every part of the Republic. The K.N.I.P. was in fact the first Parliament and the Working Committee functioned as a Cabinet.

NOTES

[1] *Out of Exile*, by Soetan Sjahrir, p. 136. John Day & Co., 1949. Letter dated November 16th, 1936.

[2] Ibid., p. 219.

[3] *An Account of the Japanese Occupation of Banjumas Residency, Java, March 1942 to August 1945*, by S. M. Gandasubrata, Resident of Banjumas, p. 1. Data paper No. 10, Dept. of Far Eastern Studies, Cornell University, August 1953.

[4] Ibid., p. 2.

[5] Ibid., p. 3.

[6] Ibid., p. 4.

[7] Ibid., p. 10.

[8] Ibid., p. 15.

[9] *Out of Exile*, by Soetan Sjahrir, p. 246, 1949. Sukarno is referred to as 'Abdul Rachman', and Hatta as 'Hafil'.

[10] The remainder were filled mainly by Chinese.

[11] *Nationalism and Revolution in Indonesia*, by George McT. Kahin, Executive Director, Southeast Asia Programme, Cornell University, p. 108. Published by Cornell University Press, 1952.

[12] *Out of Exile*, by Soetan Sjahrir, p. 252, 1949.

[13] *Nationalism and Revolution in Indonesia*, by George Kahin, p. 117.

[14] Ibid., p. 118.

[15] Ibid., p. 118.

[16] Ibid., p. 118.

[17] Ibid., pp. 120–1.

[18] *Out of Exile*, by Soetan Sjahrir, p. 261.

[19] Ibid., p. 261.

CHAPTER X

BRITISH INTERLUDE

Taking the Dutch Back

WHILST Indonesians prepared to rule themselves, Dutchmen made plans to return to their colony. In Indonesian eyes the Dutch had forfeited their claims to rule when they failed to defend the country. In the eyes of Dutch prisoners in Indonesia as well as of Dutchmen in Holland, Indonesia was as much Dutch territory as Holland itself. The defeat of Japan in Asia and the defeat of Germany in Europe presupposed a return to the *status quo* in September 1939 with certain modifications.

Exiled in England, Queen Wilhelmina broadcast from London on December 6th, 1942:

> 'I announce that it is my intention, after the liberation, to create the occasion for a joint consultation about the structure of the Kingdom and its parts in order to adapt it to the changed circumstances . . . it will be possible to reconstruct the Kingdom on the solid foundation of complete partnership to carry fully their responsibility, both internally and externally.'[1]

In 1943 she visited the United States. Her Prime Minister (Professor Gerbrandy) records that:

> 'President Roosevelt, assured by Her Majesty that the Netherlands Government intended to conduct a liberal policy in the overseas dominions, ranged his great authority behind us in our plans to restore the kingdom in its pre-war form.'[2]

Towards the end of 1944 Japan's defeat had been considered certain. Dr. van Mook was sent to Australia with powers to assume charge of administration when the war ended. He set up a provisional Netherland Indies Government which was ready to move back into its handsome European-style offices in

Djakarta. Similarly, Governor-General Tjarda van Starken-
bergh Stachouwer (then a prisoner of war in Korea) would
return to his palace. The Volksraad would function again.
Heads of Departments were selected. Everything was worked
out with Germanic thoroughness—'even as in the case of the
Netherlands itself,' Professor Gerbrandy records, 'for a return
to the old tried and constitutional way, though with the aid of
temporary institutions and exceptional temporary powers'.[3] A
period of war-time organization, then a period of transition, and
finally complete rehabilitation; this was the Dutch plan, meticu-
lously worked out, detail by detail, by men who were completely
out of touch with reality in Indonesia.

Holland had been occupied by the Nazis as Indonesia had
been occupied by the Japanese. But there the parallel ended.
Japanese occupation, as we have already seen, provided Indonesians with opportunities of ruling their own country. Yet no
Dutchman seems to have taken into consideration the profound
changes in Indonesia. Was it reasonable to assume that Indonesians who had taken the place of high-ranking Dutch officials
would step back again if and when the Dutch returned? Would
Indonesians, refused permission to fly the red-and-white flag
during the days of Dutch rule, now haul it down and put up the
Dutch tricolour? Would Indonesian schoolteachers, now teaching in Bahasa Indonesia, return to the Dutch language? Dutch
policy was based on the assumption that Indonesians, like themselves, would be satisfied with some modifications of pre-war
Dutch rule.

It was assumed that the reconquest of Indonesia would be
carried out under the orders of General MacArthur. His
South-west Pacific Command included the whole of Indonesia
with the exception of Sumatra which came under Lord Mountbatten, Supreme Allied Commander, South-East Asia. In his
Report to the Combined Chiefs of Staff, Lord Mountbatten
describes a discussion he had in July 1945 in Manila:

'General MacArthur suggested that as he would now be
preoccupied with preparations for the assault on Kyushu
(Operation OLYMPIC) which was to begin in November, and
for the final assault on Honshu (Operation CORONET)

H*   201

scheduled for the spring of 1946, I should take over all the South-west Pacific Area south of the Philippines. But I was not prepared to assume full responsibility until Singapore was available as our main base: since the logistical, shipping, and minesweeping difficulties which this new commitment would entail would be insuperable so long as we were still entirely dependent on bases in India, Ceylon, and Southern Burma. I therefore replied that after the capture of Singapore and the opening of the Straits of Malacca—probably by October—I would be willing to take on this commitment, if asked to do so by the Combined Chiefs of Staff; on condition that General MacArthur's appropriate Intelligence files, as well as those members of his Intelligence staff who had specialized in the areas he would be turning over, were made available to me in ample time.'[4]

At Potsdam, Lord Mountbatten was told that 'the major part of the South-west Pacific Area would come within the boundaries of S.E.A.C. while the remainder would pass under Australian command'.[5]

Again, Lord Mountbatten asked for 'adequate advance Intelligence regarding these areas', more especially since he was asked to take over command as soon as possible after August 15th—less than three weeks later. Between these two dates—July 24th and August 15th—the atom bomb fell on Hiroshima. Thus, whilst plans were made for operations in Indonesia against Japan in the spring of 1946, the top planners in Potsdam were basing their plans on other assumptions.

'I was also told', Lord Mountbatten writes, 'in the greatest confidence by the Prime Minister and the President at Potsdam, of the intention to use atomic bombs against Japan at the beginning of August: it was expected that the Japanese would at once sue for peace, and the Prime Minister predicted that the war in the Far East would end by the 15th August.'

Mr. Churchill's assumption was correct; on August 14th Japan accepted an unconditional surrender; and that same day that part of the South-west Pacific command discussed at Potsdam passed into S.E.A.C. command. No major strategic decision could have been taken with so little preparation. General MacArthur seems to have divested himself of all responsibility. No effective liaison existed between the two Supreme Commanders, except through the slow channel of their respective Governments and Chiefs of Staff. No new operations in this area, strategically complicated by its island structure, had been contemplated until October. 'Now', writes Lord Mountbatten, 'my responsibilities were immediate and urgent, but neither the troops, the shipping, nor the Intelligence I had asked for were available to me.' To which he adds the astonishing footnote, 'Nor were they ever made available to me'.

Whether American Intelligence had made any appreciation of events in Indonesia is not recorded. For the Report which Lord Mountbatten presented to the Combined Chiefs of Staff and which His Majesty's Stationery Office published in 1951, does not deal with the post-surrender developments in Indonesia. If the general supposition is correct that such a section was in fact written, it is a pity that, in the interests of a complete documentation, it should not have been made generally available. The Command did not, in effect, close down until November 1946, whereas the Report as published ends in September 1945. What we know is that during those fateful days when General MacArthur was on his way to Tokyo, Sukarno and Hatta, following a conference in Saigon, described in the preceding chapter, had proclaimed the Republic of Indonesia. On the following day, August 18th, President Sukarno and Dr. Hatta announced:

'We hereby declare that the establishment of the State of Independent Indonesia, as required by the whole nation, is being carried out accurately. All who are ready to account for their deeds towards the nation are assisting in this. What we think necessary for the establishment of the State of Independent Indonesia is being carried out and will be finished within a short time. We expect the whole Indonesian nation to be calm, quiet, prepared, well-disciplined, and good.'

Within a few days the Constitution of the Republic was

adopted. A Central Indonesia Committee was appointed, then a Cabinet. Plans were made for the establishment of a National Army, and for a central as well as provincial administration. President Sukarno decreed that henceforth only the Republican red-and-white flag should fly from offices.

In this period of general confusion and uncertainty, any military decision had important political significance. To Lord Mountbatten, the vital point was whether or not the Japanese in South-east Asia would obey the Imperial Order when it was made, to lay down their arms. The possibility had to be considered that this undefeated fully equipped army of nearly three-quarters of a million Japanese might decide to carry on the war, thereby necessitating military operations, for which plans were not yet complete. Besides, there was the urgent problem of rescuing Dutch prisoners-of-war. What would be their fate if the Japanese decided to continue fighting, and how would they be treated by the Indonesians themselves? In Tokyo, General MacArthur, now Supreme Commander for the Allied Powers, gave orders on August 19th that 'the actual documents of surrender in theatres other than his own might only be signed after his own had been signed; and that no landing or reoccupation by military forces might be made until after the formal signature of the surrender document in Tokyo' (which was expected to take place on August 28th). By August 26th, Japanese policy was clear; delegates who arrived in Rangoon to sign the preliminary agreement[6] of surrender obviously intended to obey Lord Mountbatten's orders 'punctiliously'.

From a military point of view the situation was much easier than S.E.A.C. anticipated. The Japanese behaved with an excessive politeness that is often caricatured. To the first British officers who arrived in Indonesia, they immediately gave information about the 130,000 Dutch prisoners-of-war in Java. They meekly accepted orders, quickly changing their allegiance, showing no signs of the resistance or fight which S.E.A.C. had had to take into consideration as a possibility. The truth of the matter was that they were in no position to do so, since, as we have seen in the last chapter, the Indonesians were in control. The underground movement had planned for a rising against the Japanese to coincide with the Allied attack on Java and Sumatra. But when Japan surrendered so suddenly, Allied plans did not materialize; there was no occasion for the projected attack on Java and Sumatra. And the Indonesians who would have led the rising were now leaders of the Republican Government—proclaimed on August 17th. The question arises as to why contacts which would have been established with them in the event of a joint military effort were not made in the changed circumstances.

Two assumptions can be made: one, that political development had been insufficiently appreciated; and two, that those in charge of British policy, in London and in Singapore, had allowed themselves to be persuaded by Dutch authorities that the Republic was merely a Japanese time-bomb. The fact of Japanese acquiescence in the launching of the Republic was interpreted as Japanese support rather than as showing how strong were the forces of the Republic. Were Intelligence Reports so meagre, or did S.E.A.C. depend so exclusively on Dutch sources that S.E.A.C. headquarters was unaware of the considerable degree of control which had already passed into Republican hands even before the Japanese had formally surrendered to General MacArthur in Tokyo? The Japanese were themselves uncertain as to the policy they should adopt towards the Republic. Republican leaders were able to convince them that any effort to suppress it would inevitably lead to a bitter struggle and heavy casualties on both sides. They therefore acquiesced in the activities of the Republic as its influence spread over the country. In some instances the Japanese handed over areas to the Indonesians. But more often underground organizations, especially amongst the students, became involved in clashes with Japanese troops, risking their lives in attacks on arsenals and seizing military supplies.

Meanwhile, at the beginning of September, following a conference with Dr. van Mook, Lord Mountbatten instructed Field-Marshal Terauchi that he would be held responsible for maintaining law and order until the Allies took over the country. Again, it must be supposed that either Intelligence Reports from Indonesia were quite extraordinarily inadequate or that Dutch officials painted a misleading picture of the situation. One thing is certain; these instructions to the Japanese forces to maintain law and order gave serious offence to the Indonesians, then enthusiastically celebrating their newly formed Republic. They considered themselves as the new rulers, and it was on them, not on the Japanese, that responsibility for law and order lay. Further, they were given to understand that the intentions of S.E.A.C. were limited to the disarmament of Japanese and the release of Dutch internees. Most of the Dutch were still in concentration camps, many sick and all of them starving.

Sjahrir, who visited a number of Dutch camps at the time, wrote:

> 'Those of our friends who had drawn up the programme for us for underground work on behalf of democracy and freedom in the early days immediately declared their support of the Republic. In general the Netherlanders who came out of the camps were not inclined towards enmity against the Republic. It was clear, however, that they did not really understand what had happened. Most of them were physically exhausted and mentally deranged by their internment.'[7]

When he returned to Djakarta at the beginning of September he observed that people were 'definitely neutral if not friendly to the Dutch as they were released from the camps. On the other hand, Japanese were murdered daily and fighting against them was widespread.'

In these circumstances, and as a matter of military expediency, the Supreme Allied Commander cannot have neglected to consider establishing contacts with Republican leaders. And in fact he held a meeting in Singapore on September 28th with General Christison, Mr. van der Plas (Dr. van Mook's representative) and the Secretary of State for War (Rt. Hon. J. J. Lawson) who was at that time touring South-East Asia to see British troops. As a result of this meeting, Mr. van der Plas re-broadcast the proclamation made by Queen Wilhelmina in December 1942, and followed this with a broadcast of his own which was plainly intended to pave the way for contacts with the Republican leaders. This broadcast was repudiated by the Dutch Government; and indeed the

Dutch Governor-General (Mr. Tjarda van Starkenborgh Stachouwer) had resigned at the thought that any proposals should be made to the Indonesian leaders. Furthermore, Dr. van Mook had evidently been prevailed upon to meet the Indonesians, for his intention to do this was publicly repudiated by The Hague, and no meeting took place.

British troops arrived in Tandjong Priok (Djakarta) harbour on September 29th. Throughout September, Dutch prisoners-of-war were released, and many of them flown home. Lady Louis Mountbatten, Superintendent-in-Chief of the Nursing Division of St. John Joint War Organization, visited many of the camps and arranged for the welfare of these internees. Mr. Jack Lawson, M.P., the then Secretary of State for War, stated in Singapore at the time that Britain's obligations to her Allies would not involve fighting for the French against the people of Indo-China or for the Dutch against Nationalists in Java. General Christison, in charge of the landing, said a few hours later:

'We have no interest in their politics. British and Indian troops will not become involved in national politics. I intend to see the leaders of the various movements and tell them what we are coming for. Until a change is made in their political structure they must co-operate.

'I am stopping all Dutch troops coming until we are well established. We shall hand over all internal security to them when their forces come in, and then dispense with the Japanese.'[8]

When he landed, General Christison said that the Dutch administration at his 'urgent insistence' was meeting with Nationalist leaders. 'What form of self-government the Dutch are going to give them, I don't know. They will certainly have to give them something.'

The Republican Government naturally considered these statements as a friendly gesture. They knew that the British had refused to arrest their leaders as the Dutch requested. Therefore, President Sukarno ordered Indonesians to co-operate with the Allied forces in maintaining law and order. 'The Indonesian movement is not an anti-White movement,' he said, two hours before they landed. 'There is no anti-British feeling in Java. The Indonesians are fighting against the continuation of the Dutch colonial policy of exploiting the Indonesians.' Notices were posted at street corners in Djakarta saying in English: 'Indonesians will be hospitable towards everyone who respects their freedom.'

Republican leaders were reassured by General Christison:

'Our sole job', he said, 'is to rescue prisoners-of-war and disarm the Japanese. We are not going to interfere with the political position in Java. I have made it clear that we are not going in to put the Dutch back into power. I am going to keep law and order, and I shall expect the political leaders to co-operate with me. The Dutch Government must make a statement about the future status of the Netherlands East Indies. Mr. van der Plas, the Senior Dutch representative, is making strong demands to his Government. In the meantime I am doing my best to ameliorate the position by bringing together for the first time round a conference table the leaders of the Nationalist Movement and the Dutch Government representatives.'[9]

When British and Indian troops landed, they met with no resistance from the Republicans. Seaforth Highlanders marched along the two-mile-long straight road from Tandjong Priok into the centre of Djakarta. The red-and-white flag of the Republic flew from almost every building. Sometimes the Stars and Stripes flew with it, sometimes the Union Jack. But there was no sign of the Dutch tricolour. Only when the army reached its head-quarters, formerly occupied by the Japanese, did the Dutch flag reappear for the first time since March 1942. The Japanese had pulled it down; the British Commander hoisted it up again together with the Union Jack and the Stars and Stripes.

Unfortunately, the Cabinet in London was more closely in touch with the Netherlands Government than it was with realities in Indonesia. Within twenty-four hours of the landing of British and Indian troops, the Dutch had not only repudiated Mr. van der Plas's broadcast but their Embassy in London issued a statement saying that Sukarno and his followers were a puppet Government armed and aided by the Japanese.

'They do not represent a spontaneous nationalist movement, but are, on the contrary, a Japanese puppet government of a totalitarian character, dependent on the Japanese
military organization. They have been armed and are being
aided in every way by the Japanese. Sukarno received a
high decoration from the enemy. He was allowed to proclaim
his Indonesian Republic ten days after the Japanese surrender while Japanese military forces were still in control of
the island.'[10]

This statement was given the widest publicity and broadcast
by the B.B.C. It was mischievous and misleading. Yet Labour
Ministers allowed themselves to be influenced by Dutch misrepresentation. When Professor Logemann arrived from Australia on October 1st, he told the Cabinet that Sukarno was utterly
unreliable, one day a Fascist, and the next a Communist, one
day a friend of the White man, the next day a violent enemy.
In Singapore it became clear that the Cabinet did not appreciate the situation, nor the strength of the Republic. Lord
Mountbatten thereupon sent Lt.-Col. Laurens van der Post to
see Mr. Attlee; he had led a resistance group in Java during the
Japanese occupation, he had many friends among the Republicans, and was trusted by them. 'I have spoken personally with
Sukarno and other Nationalist leaders,' he wrote, 'and I have a
strong impression of their sense of moderation. But when riding
the tiger it is difficult to dismount.' He urged 'the human
psychological approach to these Indonesians, who are bewildered ·and easily deluded after three and a half years of
Japanese terror'. Mr. Attlee sent this South African officer to
The Hague to give the Dutch Government the benefit of his
special knowledge. But they turned a deaf ear. Colonel van der
Post's mission was a failure. Dutch propaganda continued to
call Sukarno a Japanese stooge, and to mislead the world by saying that the Republic was 'made in Japan'.

Dr. van Mook was one of the very few responsible Dutchmen
at this time who appreciated the revolutionary change which
had occurred in Indonesia, and on October 14th he told the
Press he was prepared to treat with all groups, including
Sukarno, when security was restored. The Dutch Government

immediately issued a statement to the effect that it must be due
to a misunderstanding. They had emphatically instructed Dr.
van Mook to the contrary. Professor Logemann followed with a
declaration that his Government was ready to offer self-
government within the Netherlands Union to Indonesians, but
that they were not prepared to discuss it with Sukarno. Foreign
Minister Dr. Subardjo replied that his Government would confer with Allied representatives, but not with the Dutch Government. Unfortunately the Cabinet continued to underestimate
the Republic. Mr. Attlee's first official statement on October
17th reflected Dutch misrepresentation:

> 'In Java', he said, 'we found that, outside Batavia, control
> had in fact been largely relinquished by the Japanese to an
> Indonesian independence movement. While we have had to
> take account of the existence of this movement, we must be
> careful about accepting its claims at their face value. It has
> been sponsored by the Japanese for two or three years and
> during this time the people of the territory have been cut off
> from all outside developments.'[11]

To which Mr. P. J. Noel-Baker, in reply to a question, added:

> 'H.M.'s Government of course recognizes no authority but
> that of the Netherlands Government in all territories which
> are under the sovereignty of our Dutch Allies.'[12]

Many Labour M.P.s felt that the Cabinet did not sufficiently
appreciate the revolutionary changes which had taken place
in the Far East. And, in October, sixty of them signed a statement on the situation in Indo-China and Indonesia, con-
cluding: 'We urge that the Dutch and French Governments
should negotiate with the existing provisional Indonesian and
Indo-Chinese Governments and accept their proffered aid to
disarm the Japanese troops without delay. We urge further
that the problems that arise from the termination of the war in
the Far East should be recognized as a concern of the United
Nations.'

On their side, the Indonesians put out many feelers. At a
Press conference on October 18th, Dr. Hatta rejected the
Netherlands proposal for partnership in the Netherlands Empire:

'Not for a moment will Indonesians countenance any form of colonial status, whatever new garb it assumes, or whatever fancy name is given it. War or revolution raging fiercely for years and years will be the only result. This may be the Dutch idea of bringing peace and order into the country, but certainly it will never end in Indonesia being brought under Dutch control.'

He welcomed van Mook, whom he described as 'edging towards the hard realities of life', and then repeated suggestions he had previously put forward to General Christison: (i) No more Dutch troops should be landed under Allied protection or otherwise; (ii) Dutch troops now in the country should be moved and should not function as part of the Allied Army of Occupation; (iii) Netherlands Indies Civil Administration (N.I.C.A.) should remain quiescent; (iv) until the Indonesian question had been reviewed by the world powers, the present Indonesian administration headed by Dr. Sukarno should be recognized as the *de facto* Government in the interests of law and order. The present uncertainty and conflicting aims of the four parties vested in whole or in part with the administrative power, the Indonesian Government, the Allied Army of Occupation, N.I.C.A., and the Japanese, make stable and orderly government impossible. And (v) the Allied army, with no Dutch element in it, should confine itself to its two proclaimed objectives of caring for prisoners-of-war and interning and disarming the Japanese. To a question which followed, Dr. Hatta said that he was willing to meet Dr. van Mook personally. But the best way was to submit the whole problem to an International Court. 'Provided we could state our case before it ourselves, we should accept such a Court's decision even if it did not give us everything we wanted.' President Sukarno appealed to international opinion and telegraphed to President Truman. As more and more British troops arrived, bringing back the Dutch army, he told General Christison that if the British continued their 'calculated policy to reimpose Dutch rule over Indonesia the ultimate result would be the drenching of Indonesia in a blood bath'. 'Your attitude is far from neutral,' he concluded, 'it is decidedly pro-Dutch.'

The situation now began to deteriorate. In a number of Javanese towns—Bandung, Surakarta, Djogjakarta, Semarang and Surabaya—Indonesians were fighting the Japanese to gain control. As Dutch troops landed under S.E.A.C. command, and as Dutch officials (Netherlands Indies Civil Affairs Administration) took over under S.E.A.C. protection, Indonesian feelings towards the Allies became increasingly hostile. The most serious trouble arose when Japanese troops were used by S.E.A.C. to fight Indonesians. Take the case of Semarang. Indonesians had suffered 2,000 casualties fighting the Japanese for control of this, the third largest town in Java. No sooner had they begun to gain control than Japanese troops were used by S.E.A.C. to get it back for the Dutch. The Dutch themselves were arrogant and trigger-happy. Many incidents occurred as groups of young Indonesians realized that far from the Japanese being disarmed, they were now fighting to regain control of Indonesian towns only to hand them back to the Dutch. It was at this point that serious atrocities occurred on both sides. Dutch women and children were attacked as they were released from prison camps, and Indonesians were shot indiscriminately.

The turning-point came when the second wave of British and Indian troops landed in Surabaya. Large-scale fighting occurred with heavy casualties on both sides. President Sukarno flew to the town and joined with Brigadier-General Mallaby in an appeal to Indonesians to stop fighting. A precarious truce was signed on October 29th; it arranged that firing should cease immediately; that order, except in two areas of the city occupied by the British, should be maintained by the Indonesians and that a liaison office should be established for carrying out the agreement. On the following day Brigadier Mallaby was killed in circumstances which have never yet been officially explained. General Christison, assuming that it was the work of Indonesian extremists, issued the warning:

'Unless the Indonesians responsible for the death of Brigadier Mallaby and the breaking of the truce surrender to my forces I intend to bring the whole weight of sea, land, and air forces under my command, with all the weapons of modern warfare, against them until they are crushed. If in this process innocent Indonesians should be killed or wounded the entire responsibility will rest with those Indonesians who have committed the crimes I have mentioned.'

In conditions which existed in Surabaya, such a statement was calculated to make talks more difficult. No one—least of all the Republican Ministers—condoned the death of Brigadier Mallaby, but an investigation into the incident was required, not a threat to Indonesians which could only have the effect of consolidating them against the British. President Sukarno intervened a second time.

> 'I learnt with the greatest regret', he announced, 'that fighting had been renewed, and that Brigadier Mallaby, whose bravery I witnessed and whom I honour, became a victim of the disorders. We have ordered a stop to the fighting and shall take appropriate measures to master the situation. I shall myself maintain close co-operation with the Allied army. If there is the slightest trouble, it will be enough to call me personally to settle it.'

Those who were on the spot realized perfectly well that the situation in Surabaya was extremely dangerous. On both sides, efforts were made to prevent an explosion. Two days after Brigadier-General Mallaby's death Dutch (Dr. van Mook, Mr. van der Plas, and Mr. Idenburg) met Republican leaders (President Sukarno, Dr. Hatta, and Dr. Subardjo) in General Christison's house. But before negotiations could begin, the Dutch Colonial Minister issued a statement that the meeting was against the direct orders of the Government. 'The Government', it concluded, 'is holding fast to its principle of "no dealing with the rebels".' Once more, Dr. van Mook's reasonableness and Lord Mountbatten's efforts to find some basis of agreement were defeated. 'Either the Dutch Government is being monumentally inept,' Ian Morrison wrote in *The Times*, 'or else it wants to put the whole conflict to the test of arms as soon as possible—or both. The most charitable explanation of their choppings and changings is that they will not face the facts.'

President Sukarno made a last appeal to Prime Minister Attlee on November 10th, urging him to stop British and Indian

troops from intervening on the side of the Dutch in Indonesia.
He appealed to Stalin whilst his Foreign Minister appealed to
Molotov to intervene on behalf of the Indonesian people 'in
this bloody battle'. In India, Mr. Jinnah urged that all Indian
troops should be withdrawn. 'One million Muslims in India',
he said, 'are watching with the utmost sympathy the struggle of
forty million Muslims in Indonesia to achieve freedom.' (His
figures referred to the population of Java, the centre of the
struggle.) Pandit Nehru tried in vain to get permission to go to
Indonesia. The Dutch were naturally opposed to it. The British
Cabinet turned down the request. 'The refusal to afford facilities for Mr. Nehru to visit Indonesia', Mr. Arthur Henderson
told Mr. Sorensen, 'was taken with the agreement of the
Supreme Allied Commander, in view of the present disturbed
conditions in Java which render it undesirable for such a visit
to be made.'[13]

Tension never relaxed after Brigadier Mallaby's death. Indonesians called for a 'Holy War' to drive the Allies into the sea.
British and Indian troops were bewildered, living in a city of
hostile people, charged with duties which were extremely un-
palatable to men who understood their role in the struggle for
independence. Orders dropped by British planes calling on Indonesians to surrender their arms were not obeyed, whereupon the
Fifth Indian Division immediately entered Surabaya. Then
naval and artillery fire, Thunderbolts and Mosquitoes, combined to destroy large areas of the city and to kill many men,
women, and children. Fighting continued for several weeks until
the city was occupied street by street. The front line ran through
the centre of the city; to Indonesian youth it was their Stalin-
grad.

The Battle of Surabaya was a turning-point in the war: to
the Indonesians it was a proof of their political unity and their
armed strength; to the Labour Government it suggested that
they must now intensify the war or make a bold political gesture.
Mr. Bevin and his colleagues were opposed to war and they
made strong representations to the Dutch Government. The
Dutch Labour Party was in effective control but there were few
Dutch Socialists who had the courage to admit—as Mr. de

Kadt did in *Het Parool*—that the only solution was 'the recognition of independence and an attempt to make an agreement as to co-operation between Holland and Indonesia on that basis'.[14] The Dutch Commander in Indonesia, Admiral Hellfrich, advocated an 'all-out' war and made no secret of his resentment of the restraining hand which S.E.A.C. imposed on him.

During this period—in the weeks following the Battle of Surabaya—a struggle between various political groups and personalities in the Republic led to the appointment of Sjahrir as Prime Minister on November 15th. He was a Socialist with a fine record of political struggle, a moderate conciliatory personality whom Mr. Bevin greatly underestimated. He was the best hope for a solution, yet the Dutch line of propaganda that he had no real following carried a great deal of weight in Whitehall. The real situation in Indonesia at this time was described in a Memorandum which a group of Indonesian officials attached to N.I.C.A. sent to the Dutch Government through the good offices of Dr. van Mook who was still on friendly terms with Republican leaders, especially with Sjahrir. Basing their remarks on investigations done by them 'individually and collectively on their own initiative, by visiting and obtaining information from Government authorities, officials, intellectuals, representatives of youth and women's organizations, common people and studying telegrams and reports' they reached the following conclusions:

'(*a*) There is normal functioning of public services, public traffic, mines, light and water, provisions, all things generally needed to establish social order in the difficult circumstances for the young but vital republic;

'(*b*) There is a republican form of State, accepted by all circles of the Indonesian population of Java, Sumatra, Borneo as well as certain parts of the Bigger and Lesser Sunda Islands while the principalities of Java and the self-governing lands of Sumatra loyally and strongly stand behind the Republic too; parts of the Arabic, Chinese, and Eurasian groups are also supporting the Republic;

'(*c*) That the "Indonesia Merdeka" (Independent Indonesia) inspired the whole Indonesian population;

'(*d*) There is no racial hatred but the conflicts must primarily be regarded as reaction against any form of re-colonization;

'(*e*) The fear that Dutch and other internees are in danger of life is unfounded, since in all places where the Allied troops have not yet arrived (such as Surakarta, Djogjakarta, and Malang) they are left alone and well looked after;

'(*f*) There has grown a change of mentality caused by the Japanese domination revealed in the first aim to reach an Indonesia Merdeka;

'(*g*) To regard this and to solely ascribe it to subversive Japanese activities would not only reveal lack of insight and good will; the Indonesian people would observe it as a misjudgment of their right to self-determination. (For the just analysis of the Japanese influence, see Sjahrir's brochure, *Perdjoangan Kita*, i.e. *Our Struggle*.)'

After giving a short outline of the history of the Nationalist movement, these young Indonesian officials in the employ of Dutch administration, twelve of the fourteen having doctors' degrees (and one of them being Dr. Ali Sastroamidjojo, the present Prime Minister), concluded:

'The undersigned [therefore] sincerely insist that the only solution for the Dutch Government lies in the recognition of the Republic. It is the only guarantee for the promotion of Dutch as well as Indonesian interests and it is the only way out of the present impasse and for the·prevention of further bloodshed.'[15]

This was only one of many signs that the roots of the Republic were growing deeper. Sjahrir had the confidence of wide sections of people. His Government dealt firmly with such difficult problems as that of extremists, many of whom he regarded as victims of Japanese rule, influenced by Japanese propaganda methods and mentality. His pamphlet, *Our Struggle*, written at this time was more than a political manifesto; it was a brave condemnation of moral deterioration during Japanese rule, of the dangers inherent in racial hatred; it suggested that in foreign relations the Republic could expect support from 'the Pacific giant America', that Britain was inevitably tied up with Holland, and that Dutch rule was the result of British power politics. It then outlined the case for Socialism with such cogency, clarity, and persuasion that it laid the foundation for all political thought and action.

Here was an opportunity for the Labour Government to make a political gesture; but either Mr. Bevin was being provided with misleading information by his representative in South-East Asia (Mr. (later Sir Esler) Dening), or else he was choosing not to take any notice of it. Whichever it was, the Foreign Office continued to act as if it was unaware of the balance of forces in the Republican Government, and remained hostile to any recognition of the Republic. At the end of November when the situation was still tense, Sjahrir told a Press conference that he was willing to have tripartite talks, even without waiting for the general situation to improve. But the day his statement was made, Professor Logemann, the Netherlands Minister for Overseas Territories, even without consulting Dr. van Mook, attacked the Republic in terms which ruled out any such talk. Professor Logemann had made what was tantamount to a declaration of war in response to Sjahrir's offer of negotiation. Mr. Bevin remained silent.

At this stage, a conference was held in Singapore at which military and political advisers were present. It would have been an intelligent gesture to invite Sjahrir to attend; if the Labour Government had insisted, the Dutch could scarcely have refused. The result of the conference was to extend Lt.-General Christison's mandate over the whole Indonesian territory. Sjahrir's reaction when informed of this decision was that 'if the British are going to bring more forces to start a large-scale action, then all Indonesians will resist to the best of their ability'.

When more troops began to arrive they were met by bitter resistance. Impartial observers at the time admit horrible atrocities by Indonesian gangs; one of the worst instances was in Java on November 23rd, when a Dakota with five British airmen and eighteen Indians made a forced landing. They were all hacked to pieces by a mob of young Indonesians belonging to a society originally sponsored by the Japanese. The Black Buffaloes, as they were called, were a law unto themselves, and their terrorist activities did a great deal of harm to the Republic; the Dutch could produce them as evidence of Indonesia's unfitness to govern. But that is only one side of the picture; Dutch troops and N.I.C.A. officials were themselves guilty of many murders, and the Republican Ministry of Foreign Affairs published daily lists of atrocities.

There was no complaint of the attitude of British and Indian troops. Many of them detested the duties they were called on to perform, and they were frequently critical of the arrogant, trigger-happy behaviour of Dutch troops and officials. But there was no excuse for British policy in setting fire to the village of Bekasi in retaliation for the deaths of R.A.F. men and Indians in Java. In the village of Tabang the Black Buffaloes murdered an English Red Cross girl and a Brigade Major who had bathed in a pool which was attached to a mosque and, as such, had religious associations, for Muslims bathe before taking prayers and alongside every mosque there are pools for this purpose. In Tabang, as in Bekasi, petrol was poured over buildings and bamboo houses and the area reduced to ashes; in Bekasi over a thousand houses went up in flames. For after burying the dismembered bodies of their comrades who had been murdered when a Dakota plane made a forced landing, British troops had set fire to the portion of Bekasi inhabited by terrorists. Four days later—on November the 17th—Lord Mountbatten laid it down as his policy that although everything must be done to ensure the security of British forces, retaliation must not be taken as a matter of principle. In the event of buildings being destroyed in future, warning must be given to the inhabitants and the opportunity given to them to remove their belongings.

The Bekasi incident roused such feelings on all sides that the atmosphere was charged and seemingly unsuitable for any further talks. Sjahrir expressed his regret to General Christison 'for the happenings that took place in Tjakoeng, Bekasi, and Ambarawa that were brought about by misunderstandings between the occupation troops and the people'. And he gave a statement to the Press reiterating the readiness of his Government to submit the Indonesian question to the United Nations and to abide by its decision even if it were unfavourable to Indonesia.

'If the Dutch recognize our right to independence,' he added, 'then we shall accept Dutch co-operation in the economic and technical spheres. We should even be ready to give them a privileged position in view of their special contacts and their long association with the Indies.'[16]

Such statements were ignored or ridiculed in The Hague, they were underestimated by those political advisers whose voices were heard in Whitehall. Again and again Sjahrir made conciliatory gestures, often at the expense of his position as Prime Minister. He formed a Peace Army to escort Allied transports from Djakarta to Bandung, a 150-mile stretch of road where many incidents had already happened. The Republic alone could guarantee safety, and this Peace Army fulfilled a very important role. So much was this the case that on December 22nd Sjahrir announced that he had accepted a British proposal that these troops should undertake the disarmament of 25,000 Japanese in East and Central Java. This was a wise request suggesting, as it did, a growing confidence in the Republic to maintain law and order. General Christison also arranged with the Indonesian Ministry of Transport to co-operate in checking up cars.

'When the British first arrived', Sjahrir said at this point, 'they were obliged to seek Indonesian co-operation, but they did it unofficially or through the Japanese. Three months later they were making their requests for co-operation directly and publicly. . . . We are prepared to co-operate on a basis of justice to seek the accomplishment of the tasks entrusted by the United Nations to British Forces and to maintain the general peace and security of the territories occupied by the Allies . . . Allied troops are exempt from politics and do not pursue political aims, whilst political affairs are solely the concern of the Indonesians and the Dutch.'

Sjahrir's statements, made on behalf of his Government, were in great contrast with Dutch behaviour. British and Indian troops were increasingly unwilling to carry out their task of reimposing Dutch rule. When Dutch troops made two attempts to assassinate Sjahrir, British soldiers saved his life and captured the would-be assassins. Lt.-General Christison tried to calm British and Indian troops in a circular addressed to all officers of the rank of Major and over saying: 'We must continually remind ourselves that the majority of the unfortunate Dutch are mentally sick.'[17] He was referring to the men and women who were released from internment camps. Dutch troops were so reckless that Admiral Hellfrich appealed to them to end 'aggression which is in complete disaccord with the dignity of military standards'.

Finally, at the end of December 1945, wiser counsels prevailed in The Hague and the Soviet Government announced its intention of raising the use of British troops in Indonesia on the agenda of the Security Council which was to meet in London in February 1946. Dr. van Mook arrived in London at Christmas-time. He met Mr. Attlee and Mr. Bevin as well as several Labour M.P.s who did not share the official British attitude towards the Republic. They suggested that Sjahrir should be invited to London, which was a reasonable proposal. But it met with no response.

Early in 1946, under pressure from the Labour Government, and faced with the possible condemnation of the Security Council, the Dutch Government finally agreed to take part in discussions. Sir Archibald Clark-Kerr (later Lord Inverchapel) relinquished his post as Ambassador in Moscow, and it was under his very able and friendly chairmanship that the talks were held. In April, Lord Mountbatten relinquished his post as Supreme Allied Commander and returned to England. The stage was now set for serious negotiations for the recognition of the Republic.

Recognizing the Republic

Negotiations, sometimes in Indonesia, sometimes in Holland, resulted in the signing of a truce on October 15th, 1946, and to the initialling of the Linggadjati Agreement precisely a month later. During this period of proposal and counter-proposal, the

Dutch Labour Government had been succeeded by a Catholic-Labour Coalition which was even less friendly disposed towards the Republic than its predecessor. In Indonesia the Republic had laid solid foundations of government over a wide area of the three islands on which sixty out of seventy million Indonesians lived. Outside Java, Sumatra, and Madura, Republican resistance still continued. In Bali it was not suppressed until the middle of 1948. In the Minahasa (North Sulawesi) and in Makassar (South Sulawesi) Dutch troops had met with widespread opposition; in the first case, Indonesian soldiers belonging to the Royal Netherlands Indies Army (K.N.I.L.) had rebelled and with local support maintained authority for a month; in the second case, the Dutch used a notorious terrorist, Captain Westerling, to pacify the country with the loss of life of thousands of Indonesians. Captain Westerling has written his own account[18] of the 'pacification' of South Sulawesi, an incident which greatly undermined any prestige the Dutch still retained, since he was acting officially on their behalf, co-operating with the Commander-in-Chief of the Dutch troops in East Indonesia. He found a great deal of support for the Republic—to him it was the equivalent of bandit activity. Village after village was surrounded by his troops, and men were picked out and shot on the spot. Any local rulers who were friendly to the Republic were removed and those who were still prepared to collaborate with the Dutch administration were given positions by which they believed they could still retain their rule.

But in spite of their large purchases of war equipment and thousands of tons of machinery at rock bottom prices—the whole American naval base at Hollandia in New Guinea was purchased for the dollar equivalent of £2,000,000—the Dutch did not succeed in gaining control in Java, Sumatra, and Madura. They, and British troops, limited most of their operations to areas round the bigger cities—Djakarta, Bogor, Bandung, Semarang, Surabaya in Java and Padang, Palembang and Medan in Sumatra. The Republican Government survived a number of crises, partly the result of Dutch unwillingness to consider terms which were acceptable to the left-wing members, partly because of internal struggles for power among those who supported Sjahrir and those who were prepared to plot with Tan Malaka for his removal.

Although there were many problems to be solved, Republican rule was being consolidated in the spring and summer of 1946. This was especially true of areas which had not been occupied by Dutch and British troops. Take, for example, Djogjakarta, which was the Republican capital. The first Dutchman to visit this city was a Labour Member of Parliament, Mr. Goodhart, who attended the celebrations of the First Anniversary of the Proclamation of the Republic (August 17th, 1946).

'I have the impression', Mr. Goodhart said, 'that public life is running normally. The large majority of the people are kind and friendly and I wish to emphasize the fact that I had no difficulty whatsoever. Everywhere I have had a warm reception. I came to Djogja against the advice of my countrymen because I have faith in the policy of the Republic and the way in which it is being carried out. I wanted to see for myself how things were in the interior.'

This is how he described the attitude of the man in the street:

'People are a bit curious to see me, and their curiosity becomes all the more when they discover I am Dutch. But there is nothing in their attitude to suggest hatred for me, nor can I see anything in their eyes to indicate mischief or maliciousness. I have been walking in the streets of Djogja for hours at a time, unalarmed and without a guard. I repeat that I have had no trouble or difficulty. On the contrary, I have been offered drinks and cigarettes by total strangers whenever I entered some public building. I have seen for myself the condition of the city here. There is no shooting, or plundering of houses, no murder and no disturbances. What has been told me in Djakarta about unsettled conditions in the interior is not true.'

Or take another example, this time the report of a semi-official Dutch mission led by Dr. P. J. Koets (Chief of Dr. van Mook's Cabinet), which visited the interior of Java at the invitation of the Republican Government:

'The general picture', he told the Press, 'was that of a society which was not in the course of dissolution but which is being consolidated. . . . I must add that I have had talks with many people whom I knew in former years, as well as with young people whom I met for the first time. Each time I asked "What is for you the essential thing that has happened during the last year?" . . . I received the same answer . . . "It is the feeling of human dignity." People now realize that they are capable of doing something. From conversations which went beyond superficialities I heard of the fear of a return to colonial status . . . Not so much because people feared economic exploitation or domination, or something of that sort, but rather because of a fear that they might lose again this new feeling which they had joyously acquired, which they had, so to speak, discovered in themselves, and which the people feel is something so precious that they cannot live without it. This is a reality of which we must be thoroughly aware.'

Visitors to Sumatra returned with similar reports. In Bukit Tinggi, for instance, conditions were now sufficiently consolidated to allow the barter of raw materials for ready produce between the Indonesian Government and the Allied Command. In the month of July alone, about 90 million guilders' worth of manufactured foods had been exported from Palembang in exchange for other articles.

From all sides came reports of Republican activities; an Indonesian State Bank was opened by Dr. Hatta in Djogjakarta on August 17th; and branches planned in Djakarta, Solo, Kediri, and Malang; plans were announced for increasing rubber and tea production in West Java; the first radio-telephone service was opened between Java and Sumatra; at Tjirebon, 50,000 peasants, all members of the Farmers' Organization, volunteered for a three-days' period to collect wood for locomotive fuel; in Solo, the local Arab community rejected the Dutch offers for participation in Dutch-sponsored political discussions and advised all other local Arab groups to give their loyal support to the Republic. Training courses in social welfare were started in Solo; two new high schools opened in Tjeribon and a secondary school in Rembang; production of quinine in West Java was increased; a Publicity Conference in Djogjakarta planned the distribution of newsprint and set up a committee to promote a film industry. The Republic had also established its first contacts with India, and after overcoming petty difficulties, put in the way by Dutch officials, dispatched the first consignment of rice to help India in the famine and was promised in return textiles and agricultural machinery. This was the occasion of a ceremony in Probolinggo where the port was stacked high with many thousands of sacks awaiting transport in the ship, the *Empire Favour*. At a given signal, in the presence of Dr. Hatta and members of the Indian delegation, a decorated lighter, bright with flowers and bunting and with the Indonesian and Indian flags flying side by side along the masthead, moved up the quay and made fast. The head winchman tipped a switch, his crane swung over, picked up a sack of rice and hoisted it towards the lighter. It halted in mid-air in front of Vice-President Hatta. Dr. Hatta placed his hands on the sack and guided it into the waiting lighter. Thousands of people watched this ceremony. Mr. K. I. Punjabi, representative of the Indian Government, told them:

'Words fail me to express the gratitude which India owes to the Republic of Indonesia for her generous offer of rice at a time when India's food requirements are causing concern throughout the world. It is a historical occasion, both for Indians and Indonesians, for Indonesia is exporting rice to India for the first time in modern history, and that at a time when India is in dire need of it. There is a saying that a friend in need is a friend indeed; that you have proved—not by mere lip sympathy—but by positive action which India cannot and will not forget.

'India, on her side, is aware of your requirements in textiles and other consumer goods; and as Your Excellency has been informed, India has undertaken to send twenty million yards of textiles to Indonesia, of which quantity five million yards are expected to reach Indonesian ports shortly.'

With the consolidation of the Republic, there were naturally those who doubted the wisdom of making concessions, believing that guerrilla activities were more effective than negotiations. How far support for the Republic could have been mobilized round a policy of armed resistance to the Dutch it is impossible to say. This was not an academic question in the Republic in the summer and autumn of 1946. Broadly speaking the Masjumi and the P.N.I. were in favour of a strong opposition to the Dutch, whilst the Socialist Party and the Communist Party were in favour of negotiations. Within the Socialist Party itself, however, there were two trends of thought, one headed by Sjahrir, the other by Sjarifuddin; Sjahrir was willing to consider a compromise—even an acceptance of Commonwealth status. Sjarifuddin criticized this attitude. Sjahrir's view prevailed. His general plan was to come to an agreement with the Dutch on the basis of the recognition of the Republic and then to clean the country of all collaborationist elements, to democratize the Government machinery; on the economic front he stood for a policy of nationalization for the big enterprises and the key industries as a step towards socialization. His policy was similar to that of the Labour Government. With Sjahrir advocating agreement, it is probably true that no political leader could at that time have secured a following for a policy of non-co-operation.

But there were many who doubted whether co-operation did not in practice mean that when the British troops left—as they were due to do in November 1946—the Dutch would not be in a strong enough position to challenge the Republic and gradually to undermine it. Dr. van Mook's activities during the long-drawn-out negotiations were a pointer to Dutch intentions. In spite of his earlier friendly relations with Republican leaders, his attitude had changed after the election of the Labour-Catholic Coalition Government. Whilst taking part in negotiations with Lord Inverchapel as Chairman, he now set out to build up a series of puppet states which would counteract the Republic. At Malino in July and at Pangkal Pinang in October 1946, Dr. van Mook held conferences of carefully selected delegates to discuss the formation of so-called autonomous areas. When the time came, he could use these puppet states to reinforce Dutch arguments in favour of Balkanization which was the real purpose of his federal policy.

Meanwhile a truce was necessary before these federal ideas could materialize, and this was signed on October 15th. Sjahrir had no illusions about the truce. He told the Press at the time that no political settlement was possible unless these conditions were fulfilled:

'(1) An exact definition of Republican territory.
'(2) A definition of the relationship between the Republic and the rest of Indonesia and consequently between the Republic and the Netherlands.
'(3) An agreement on military matters such as the number of Dutch troops to be stationed in Indonesia and an exact definition of their task.
'(4) The representation abroad of the Republic and cultural questions, as, for example, the language.
'(5) Principle on which future economic and financial relations would be based.'

The Linggadjati Agreement soon followed the truce: it was initialled by both sides on November 15th. It fell far short of Sjahrir's demands. But the Dutch envisaged it as expressing permanent relations between themselves and the Republic.

On paper the Linggadjati Agreement[19] accepted the Republic as an entity which in itself reflected the change in Dutch policy of a year before. To the Republic it gave recognition on a limited basis. Java, Sumatra, and Madura constituted the major areas of what had been the Netherlands East Indies, and accounted for sixty out of seventy million Indonesians. But even within these areas they had not yet control; the existence of 92,000 Dutch troops, mainly concentrated in those three islands, was in itself a potential threat to the Republic. They were pockets of hostility which prevented the Republic from settling down to its constructive tasks. Further, Dutch control of Borneo and the Great East provided them with a platform on which a battle of words or of arms could be planned against the Republic.

The truce signed and the Linggadjati Agreement initialled, British troops left Indonesia on November 29th, 1946. In the course of their fourteen months' stay, 600 had lost their lives, 1,320 were wounded, 320 were missing, and 600 had deserted, most of them Indians who had joined the guerrillas. As an army of occupation they were unexpectedly popular; many of them hated their task of reimposing Dutch rule, and their relations with the Dutch were far from cordial. Sjahrir voiced the feelings of many of his countrymen in this farewell statement:

'In all circumstances, however, even in unfriendly contact or in conflict with us, we learned to appreciate and to admire you. You introduced to our country by your personal qualities some attractive traits of Western culture—your politeness, kindness, and dignified self-restraint.'

President Sukarno voiced similar feelings when Lord Killearn (who had taken Lord Inverchapel's place) took leave of him. 'I thank you', he said, 'for the unruffled calm, patience, and integrity which you showed at all times, and I express the hope that your efforts may be crowned with success.'

Success, however, was extremely unlikely. With 92,000 Dutch troops in the country, armed with all the surplus British equipment which was transferred to them, on repayment, the 'hungry Dutch tiger', as one writer expressed it, 'has been allowed into the Indonesian house'.

Return to Colonialism

The dangers to the Republic inherent in the Draft Linggadjati Agreement quickly materialized; the Dutch began a series of demands for the interpretation or the elucidation of certain clauses which caused the Republicans to doubt their good faith. Five days after the initialling, Mr. Schermerhorn sent his interpretation to Sjahrir. The same day Sjahrir forwarded his interpretation to Mr. Schermerhorn; the issue at stake was whether or not the Republic could have its own representatives abroad. The Indonesians interpreted Article 15 as meaning that they could; the Dutch in subsequent letters put their own interpretation, van Mook entering into the correspondence with the new point that the representation 'in a strictly international sense will only become possible after the United States of Indonesia have been constituted'. With every instance of this kind, reactionaries in Holland (led by Professor Gerbrandy), and the more extreme people in the Republic (who had always distrusted Linggadjati), strengthened their position with the result that mutual mistrust deepened.

Van Mook simply went ahead with plans as if Linggadjati did not exist. In Bali on December 18th, 1946, seventy-five representatives of daerahs (regions) and a variety of social and economic groups were called together to draw up a constitution for a new state of East Indonesia. This new state would exercise certain local autonomy at once, but foreign affairs, defence, finance, trade, education and economic policy would still be run from The Hague. Van Mook found a weak Indonesian named Soekawati to be the President. The Republic naturally regarded this as an infringement of Article 2 stating that the Netherlands and the Republic 'shall co-operate to ensure the early establishment of a sovereign democratic state on a federal basis, to be known as the United States of Indonesia'. The Republicans interpreted this as meaning that they would have equal rights with the Dutch in creating an East Indonesia, or indeed any other state. Van Mook thought otherwise. He used the disingenuous excuse that Linggadjati had only been initialled.

By the time the agreement was signed on March 25th, 1947, it had little meaning. So strongly was this view held by Mr. de Boer, a member of the Commission-General, that he resigned a few days beforehand on the ground that his own Government by twisting and obscuring the interpretation of articles in the agreement had destroyed the objectives on which it was originally drafted. Two of the Commission-General's advisers also resigned; they disapproved of the Government authorizing the signature on the basis of mutually differing interpretations of the terms 'co-operation' and 'federal'. The Dutch assumed that they had sole responsibility pending the formation of the United States of Indonesia, whilst the Republic maintained that in the setting up of the projected federation they had joint responsibility and mutual consultation. Further, whilst the Dutch interpreted 'federal' to mean equal states with equal powers—the Republic, for example, with East Indonesia—the Republicans assumed that they had equal powers with the Netherlands.

Each side accused the other of truce violations. But it cannot be doubted that the presence of 92,000 Dutch troops in Java and Sumatra was the biggest single contribution to the tension which grew as the weeks passed by after the signing of Linggad-jati. To the Republicans they were a constant threat, and clashes between them and the T.R.I. prevented settled conditions essential for the consolidation of Republican rule. Why, the people asked, were the Dutch troops in the country if the Dutch Government meant peace and co-operation? The Dutch justified their troops by reference to a number of incidents in which their own nationals were attacked by Indonesian extremists. This confused cause and effect, since the most powerful incentive to young Republican extremists, some of them still under the influence of Japanese gangsterism, was the irritation at young Dutch soldiers making merry and acting as if they owned the country. Other reasons for the breakdown of relations were the setting up of puppet states by Dr. van Mook and the Dutch blockade which had disastrous results on Republican economy. This is how puppet states were organized. On May 4th, in Bandung, a Party formed for the occasion and known as the Sundanese People's Party (Partai Rajat Pasundan) proclaimed the independence of West Java where 12 million Sundanese people live; they have their own language and a local nationalism which under Dutch rule had been encouraged as part of their policy of 'divide and rule'. The proclamation on May 4th, 1947, was at once turned over to the Dutch army, who were asked to help set up a 'government' and hold a 'plebiscite' in the Sundanese part of West Java. The American writer, Charles Wolf, describes the incident:

'Actually the whole "movement" was a farce from start to finish. In the first place, the two top leaders chosen for the "movement" were the most impossible selections imaginable. Soeria Kartalegawa, the "President", had been widely regarded as a ne'er-do-well and Raden Mas Koestomo, the "Prime Minister" and spokesman of the group, had been released from a mental institution in Buitenzorg only a few months before the proclamation of independence! The Sundanese People's Party itself had had no contact whatsoever with the Sundanese people as such, since the organization had never ventured outside the Dutch-held cities of Bandoeng and Buitenzorg.'[20]

The movement was so palpably absurd that the Netherlands Government Information Service publicly dissociated their Government from it, and van Mook's headquarters unofficially expressed disapproval. Pasundan had been too blatantly carried out, the Dutch troops a little over-enthusiastic. Pasundan might be repeated anywhere, and the next time the troops would behave more discreetly.

A few days after the Pasundan affair, West Borneo was declared to be an autonomous state within the framework of the Federation, and in East Borneo, four Sultans signed an agreement to form a state. South and Central Borneo were planned next on the agenda of Dutch separatism; these two areas were to be called Great Siak. In none of these activities did the Dutch make any pretence of discussion with the Republic as agreed on in Article 2 of Linggadjati. The Republican Government protested in vain. Sjahrir himself maintained that the correct procedure was to hold plebiscites in the areas involved so that the people themselves could express their own wishes on the projected United States of Indonesia.

The second source of trouble was the blockade which was enforced by the Dutch Navy. Admiral Pinke, Commander-in-Chief of the Dutch Navy, seemed determined to destroy the Republic. The Admiral's high-handed interpretation of ordinances relating to trade with the Republic were such as to incur protests from the Governments of the United Kingdom and the United States. It was obvious that if all the ports of the Republic were blockaded, the only alternative was smuggling with all its inevitable evils of high prices and doubtful tactics. When protests were made, Admiral Pinke replied that he would lift the blockade if the Republicans would restore the pre-war property of Dutch and European business men and planters. The Economic Minister, Dr. A. K. Gani, replied that as an assurance of Dutch good will all troops should be withdrawn from the areas in Java and Sumatra which the Netherlands Government had recognized as *de facto* Republican territory. The Dutch replied that since *de jure* responsibility rested with the Netherlands throughout Indonesia pending the formation of the United States of Indonesia, and since they doubted the intentions of the Republicans on this question of pre-war European properties, they would not withdraw their troops until all foreign properties were returned. At this point the argument broke down. Two months after Linggadjati the vicious circle of charge and counter-charge, of provocation and incident, had closed in and on both sides an explosion was anticipated. Anyone reading the right-wing Press in Holland at that time, or listening to the speeches of ex-Prime Minister Gerbrandy, and other men in responsible positions, would be justified in saying that many Dutchmen wanted such an explosion. They were obsessed with the idea of blowing up the Republic once and for all. Finally, in the middle of May 1947, Prime Minister Beel and Minister for Overseas Territories Jonkman flew to Djakarta for a conference with their Commissioner-General van Mook. It was in fact a pre-war conference. Charles Wolf, describing this period, writes:

'Dr. van Mook himself had been convinced that, under the economic exigencies of the situation, force would almost certainly have to be used. Only Schermerhorn, the chairman of the Commission and the leader of the Labour Party, held out for continued discussions, and Schermerhorn's support was necessary if military action were not to signify the dissolution of the Catholic-Labour coalition and the fall of the Beel Government. By the time Beel and Jonkman returned to Holland in the last week of May, Schermerhorn too had agreed that if a final set of Dutch proposals were not accepted by the Republic in full, he would not oppose any subsequent action which the Government might deem advisable.'[21]

In other words, war was being planned in The Hague, where the right-wing parties had advocated it from the beginning, van Mook had been won round to this point of view, and the cowardly acquiescence of the Dutch Labour Party leader was promised. A Dutchman in the Government Information Service in Djakarta said to an observer at the beginning of June 1947 on his departure:

'It is too bad you are leaving at this time. You have seen the Dutch cowering for a year and a half now; if you were to wait just a little longer, you would see what we can *really* do.'[22]

The Dutch meant war. All that remained was a manoeuvre which would possibly put them 'in the right' with world opinion and the Republic equally 'in the wrong'. The British Labour Government might perhaps have been able to exercise some restraint; they were in the strongest position in so far as they had facilitated the return of the Dutch troops and had left with them large quantities of equipment. They were in the strongest position because their own policy in India was a powerful argument to use with the Dutch Labour Party then in a coalition Government with the Catholics. But their protests were half-hearted 'behind-the-scenes' diplomacy which had no material effect.

The Dutch farce began on May 27th, when the Commission-General in Djakarta presented Sjahrir with a document of 10,000 words. Van Mook made it quite clear that these words were 'final' in a covering note which ended:

> 'The Commission-General considers itself bound to demand that a reply to these proposals be given by the Republican Delegation within fourteen days. In case this answer is in the negative or unsatisfactory, the Commission-General sees to its regret no possibility of continuing the discussions and will have to submit to the Netherlands Government the question as to what is to happen further.'[23]

The document amounted to a demand for a surrender on the part of the Republic of all that they had won.

Dr. van Mook's proposals amounted to a threat: 'Federalize or we shall shoot.' The purpose of setting up his puppet states was always clear to the Republicans. By making their own interpretation of the Linggadjati Agreement the Dutch had gone ahead with their scheme to Balkanize the Republic. By an ingenious scheme of joint colleges for federal matters the Republic would be put in a position where it was virtually powerless. Here was the reason for the puppet states; by forming them, and then by finding stooges to act as nominal heads, the Dutch could be sure of finding a majority for their proposals. By making joint arrangements for relations with foreign Powers, they believed they could neutralize the *de facto* recognition accorded the Republic after the Linggadjati Agreement and the close relations established with Arab countries.

The Republican Government had no doubt as to the significance of this ultimatum; political parties and the Federation of Trade Unions (S.O.B.S.I.) rejected it immediately. Sjahrir, whose discussions with Jonkman convinced him of the probability of war in the event of the proposals being turned down, still tried to find another way out. He was aware that he could not carry his Cabinet with him; on the other hand, his standing was still high enough to warrant his own counter-proposals. He strongly criticized the general attitude of the Dutch towards the Republic; he refused to accept the proposal which gave the Crown the power of veto, the *ex-officio* chairmanship of the various administrative bodies and councils. He refused to commit himself on the proposals for the restoration of Dutch and other foreign properties unless and until the returning owners changed their policy regarding labour. The proposal of a joint gendarmerie he turned down on the grounds that 'the maintenance of peace and order within the territory of the Republic of Indonesia is a task of the Republican police, not that of the Netherlands army'. On the question of consultation for defence he said that this must be the concern of the Indonesian Government, but he added that Netherlands assistance in the form of equipment and technical skill would be welcomed after the representative Chiefs of Staff had agreed to a formula. Sjahrir had not in fact made any concessions, but in the note of June 8th he had kept the door open to negotiations. The less hostile Press in Holland treated his note as one which 'opens up a sombre vista'. Almost alone in extending goodwill to the Republic, *Het Parool* said:

'Now that Indonesia has replied to our Note in a spirit of goodwill, and clearly with the purpose of making a contribution to the final agreement, the Netherlands ought to reject outright every thought of the alternative of bloodshed.'

But before negotiations finally broke down, America intervened, presumably with Dutch collusion, in an effort to break the resistance of the Republic to a federal scheme which obviously would mean their undoing. In an *aide memoire* to the Republican

I*

Government, the Americans offered the bait of financial aid if and when the Interim Federal Government was formed:

'The United States Government', it stated, 'has viewed with increasing alarm the danger inherent in a failure to implement the Linggadjati Agreement. The United States must necessarily be concerned with developments in Indonesia, because of the importance of Indonesia as a factor in world stability, both economic and political. It wishes, therefore, to stress to the Indonesian Republic the sufferings likely to result from a further deadlock. It wishes also to point out the benefits which flow from a prompt agreement and a co-operative endeavour to overcome the problems with which Indonesia is confronted. . . . It is the expectation of the United States Government that establishment of an interim government on a basis of mutual benefits for both sides will provide the political stability essential to the development of a positive program for economic rehabilitation. The United States Government is prepared, therefore, after the interim government shall have been established and mutual co-operation along a constructive path assured, to discuss, if desired, with representatives of the Netherlands and the interim government (including representatives of the Republic and other constituent areas) financial aid to assist the economies and rehabilitation of Indonesia.'[24]

The American Note was regarded as having been sent to the wrong address; American pressure was needed most where the desire for war was strongest—in The Hague. The Dutch ultimatum presented only two alternatives: war or surrender. The offer of dollars therefore was tantamount to trading dollars for Indonesian independence. It is possible that the Americans believed their offer would strengthen Sjahrir's hands, and he was the only man in the Republic of any standing who believed that at the most he might reopen negotiations and at the worst he might gain time. He had resigned on June 10th after a vote of no confidence. He was asked to return. But he was now convinced that hostilities would eventually occur. He believed that when this happened he could best help the Republic on a world platform. On June 27th President Sukarno informed the Netherlands Government that the Sjahrir Cabinet had resigned, but that the Government of the Republic of which he was the head 'fully endorse what was put forward by her Delegation in her last letter June 23rd'. Events then moved quickly; Sukarno appointed Sjahrir as 'special adviser to the Government' on June 30th; on July 3rd he appointed Amir Sjarifuddin Prime Minister of a Coalition Government which had the support of the left wing of the Masjumi and the P.N.I.

A series of notes passed between the new Prime Minister and Dr. van Mook. At the last moment the Republican Government went to extreme lengths in the concessions it was prepared to make; the formation of proposed federal bodies for the regulation of economic affairs, the unconditional restitution of foreign property. But it still refused at all costs to accept the proposal for a joint gendarmerie.

Finally, on July 18th, deadlock was reached. And, two days later, on June 20th, 1947, van Mook informed the Republican delegation:

> 'The Netherlands Government, therefore, recovers its freedom of action and will take such measures that will make an end to this untenable situation and create conditions of order and safety which will render possible the execution of the above-mentioned programme as it is expressed in the Linggadjati Agreement.'[25]

He arrested the Republican delegation. He was then free to attack the Republic. Dutch troops moved into action on July 21st, 1947. The colonial war which it had been British policy to avoid had begun.

NOTES

[1] *Indonesia*, by Professor Gerbrandy, p. 59.

[2] Ibid., p. 95.

[3] Ibid., p. 63.

[4] Report to the Combined Chiefs of Staff by the Supreme Allied Commander, South-East Asia, 1943–5. H.M.S.O., p. 181.

[5] Ibid., p. 181.

[6] General Itagaki formally made his surrender in Singapore on September 12th.

[7] *Out of Exile*, by Soetan Sjahrir, pp. 260–1.

[8] *Christian Science Monitor*, September 29th, 1945.

[9] *Sunday Times*, September 30th, 1945.

[10] September 30th, 1945.

[11] *Hansard,* October 17th, 1945, Col. 1153.

[12] Ibid., Col. 1152.

[13] Ibid., November 12th, 1945, Col. 1879.

[14] *Het Parool,* November 26th, 1945. Letter dated November 17th, 1945.

[15] Memorandum sent by Indonesian officials of the N.I.C.A. (Netherlands Indies Civil Administration) to the Dutch Government, transmitted through Dr. van Mook. Published by *Perhimpoenan Indonesia* (London office).

[16] Press conference, December 4th, 1945.

[17] *Evening Standard,* January 15th, 1946.

[18] *Challenge to Terror,* by Raymond ('Turk') Westerling, pp. 83–115. Published London, W. Kimber, 1952.

[19] The Linggadjati Agreement was initialled on November 15th. It was above all the greatest common measure which Sjahrir could find at that period. The main points were the following:

(1) That the Netherlands Government recognize the Republic as the *de facto* authority in Java, Madura and Sumatra. The areas occupied by Allied or Netherlands forces shall be included gradually, through mutual co-operation, in the Republic territory. (Article 1.)

(2) The Netherlands Government and the Government of the Republic shall co-operate in the rapid formation of a sovereign democratic state on a federal basis to be called the United States of Indonesia. (Article 2.)

(3) Component parts of the United States of Indonesia shall be the Republic, Borneo and the Great East, without prejudice to the right of the population of any territory to decide by democratic process that its position in the United States of Indonesia shall be arranged otherwise. (Article 4.)

(4) That the Netherlands and Republican Governments co-operate toward the formation of the Netherlands-Indonesian Union—including the Netherlands, Surinam and Curaçao—and the U.S.I. which Union would have as its head the Queen of the Netherlands. (Articles 6, 7, and 8.)

(5) That the Netherlands-Indonesian Union and the U.S.I. be formed not later than January 1, 1949, and that the Union set up its own agencies to deal with matters of common interest such as foreign affairs, defence, and economic and financial policies. (Articles 9, 12, 13.)

(6) Directly after the agreement has been signed, the two parties shall proceed to reduce their armed forces. They will consult together concerning the extent and the rate of this reduction and their co-operation in military matters. (Article 16.)

[20] *The Indonesian Story,* by Charles Wolf Jnr., p. 108. Issued under the auspices of the American Institute of Pacific Relations. The John Day Company, New York, 1948.

[21] Ibid., pp. 117–18.

[22] Ibid., p. 118.

[23] Quoted from official text of Memorandum of May 27th, 1947.

[24] Appendix, 'Text of the United States *Aide Memoire* to the Indonesian Republic', delivered on June 27th, 1947. *The Indonesian Story,* p. 180.

[25] Appendix, 'Memorandum of July 20th, 1947, from the Lieutenant-Governor General to the Government of the Republic of Indonesia'. Quoted in *The Indonesian Story* by Charles Wolf Jnr., p. 183.

CHAPTER XI

INDONESIA AND THE UNITED NATIONS

The First Dutch Military Action

WHEN General Spoor gave the order to his troops to attack the Republic at zero hour on July 20th, 1947, he unwittingly made an international issue of what he had intended to be an old-fashioned colonial war. The Republic was now accepted throughout the world. India, now independent, was in a position to assist Indonesia. 'No European country,' Pandit Nehru said, immediately Dutch troops went into action, 'whatever it may be, has any right to set its army in Asia against the people of Asia. The spirit of the new Asia will not tolerate such things.' In Australia, the then Labour Prime Minister, Mr. J. B. Chiffley, gave his support to the Republic, and behind him was ranged a wide section of Australian opinion, in the churches, and, above all, in the trade unions which had already shown their willingness to help in 1945.

Pandit Nehru, to whom history will allocate a major role in the struggle for Asian freedom, appealed to Mr. Bevin to take action. Mr. Bevin moved only to the extent of expressing his keenest regret at the renewal of military action, and he would only commit himself to the remark that he could not give an opinion as to whether the Security Council was 'the best and most appropriate means' of ending the conflict. In the absence of a lead from Whitehall, India and Australia brought the subject before the Security Council under different Articles of the Charter. Like the British Government (with which Mr. Bevin said it was 'throughout in full consultation'), the United States Government considered it the better part of valour to by-pass the Security Council, and made repeated offers of its 'good offices' to the two parties. The Republican leaders suspected these 'good offices'; the Dutch welcomed them since no step could have suited Dutch colonial policy better than negotiations with the Indonesians behind the scenes of the United Nations. It was an internal affair, Mr. van Kleffens argued, and neither the peace nor the security of any other country was threatened by this 'limited peace action' of Dutch troops. He was helped by the British delegate, who refused to support a resolution calling for a cease-fire on the grounds that this would prejudice the legal aspect of the case; Article 2, paragraph 7 of the Charter, he maintained, precluded interference in the domestic affairs of member States.

The line-up of members was clear. Mr. van Kleffens could always count on the support of the Belgian delegate; the Chinese usually voted with him, although Mr. Tsiang sometimes took a strong personal line favouring the Republic; the British delegate invariably found excuses for the Dutch although Mr. Bevin made personal remonstrances behind the scenes. The Americans were generally on the same side as the British. Mr. van Kleffens at no time made out any case for the continuation of Dutch rule in Indonesia. His line was to denigrate the Republic, comparing it with Utah or New South Wales, or Parahiba in Brazil. He argued that a country which was 'not a State in the proper sense of the term' had no right to be heard and Sir Alexander Cadogan supported him. The Polish delegate's suggestion that Prime Minister Sjahrir be invited to the Council rostrum was accepted by a majority. Mr. van Kleffens, who should have been regarded as the prisoner in the dock, behaved as if he were the judge waiting to pass the death sentence on the Republic. He made the counter-proposal that delegates from East Indonesia and Borneo should also be heard; in the name of 'fair play' the delegates from Great Britain, America, France, and Belgium supported his misleading proposition.

Sjahrir, modest, disarming, eloquent, was the first Indonesian to address a world audience. He introduced his country, its culture, its history, its nationalist movement. He described without bitterness the period of Dutch rule and he gave a frank exposition of Indonesian policy during Japanese occupation. He concluded with a detailed account of Dutch policy in post-war years and an appeal to the Council to support the cause oɪ Indonesian independence and with it the peace and stability oɪ

South-east Asia. His speech was the highlight of the Security Council. His intellectual brilliance and political insight provided a sharply focused picture of a complex situation. Mr. van Kleffens, his urbane self-confidence undermined, asked the Council to wait for a telephone call he was expecting from The Hague; otherwise he was not prepared to reply at once to Sjahrir since he would be at a disadvantage. The telephone call having been received, he compared Sjahrir's 'rose-tinted glasses' with his 'uncoloured medium of stark reality', and repeated the old theme that 'Japanese ideology, Japanese methods, Japanese indoctrination' characterized the Republic.

Mr. Pillai, speaking on India's behalf, described foreign armies on Asian soil as 'an outrage against Asian sentiment' and warned his audience that if they tolerated this or remained inactive then the United Nations would cease to exist. His suggestion, repeated by the Soviet delegate, that the troops of both sides be withdrawn immediately to the positions they had occupied before the beginning of operations, did not gain the support of the Council, which passed a harmless enough resolution on August 4th, 1947, calling on both parties to cease hostilities forthwith and to settle their dispute by arbitration or other peaceful means.

The 'cease-fire' resolution did not meet the situation; each side accused the other of truce-breaking. The Russians wanted a Committee composed of representatives of all State members to visit the country. The Belgians wanted a request to the International Court of Justice to advise whether or not the Security Council was competent to deal with the matter. Finally, both suggestions having been turned down, the Council decided on August 25th, 1947, to ask those members who had consuls in Djakarta to prepare a report (America, Great Britain, France, and Belgium) and simultaneously offered its 'good offices' through a Committee of Good Offices (as it was later named) consisting of an Australian (chosen by the Republic), a Belgian (chosen by the Dutch), and an American (chosen by the Australian and Belgian). The Consuls, being on the spot, went straight ahead with their work. The Committee of Good Offices arrived in Djakarta two months later.

Whilst days of discussion at Lake Success had entangled the real issues in manoeuvres and legalities, the Dutch went ahead with their plans. General Spoor ordered his troops not to advance further in accordance with the cease-fire resolution, but before the Consuls started their investigation Dr. van Mook had drawn an imaginary line linking up the points which Dutch spearheads had reached. All the land behind them, he said, was Dutch-occupied area. There we are and there we mean to stay, was his policy. The Consuls who visited Java and Sumatra admitted in their report to the Security Council that 'there is no doubt that the continuance of hostile action is due to the decision of the Netherlands authorities to impose control . . . over the area defined by the van Mook line'. The Republican forces they described as having 'remained in their positions' and as being 'subjected to mopping-up operations'. The plain fact, as Mr. Pillai pointed out when one of the Consular reports was under discussion at Lake Success, is that 'the Security Council's resolution calling for the cessation of hostilities was obeyed by the one side and disregarded or circumvented by the other'.[1]

To the Republicans, the Committee of Good Offices seemed an endorsement of Dutch military action whilst its advisory activities—its terms of reference did not allow action or the initiation of action—seemed confined to persuading them to give up gracefully in the name of the United Nations those areas taken by military force between July 20th and August 4th. This was in fact what happened when as a result of the Committee of Good Offices the two parties signed the Renville Agreement on January 17th, 1948. The Dutch had won the day, and van Mook's demarcation line was sanctioned as the *status quo*. The area of the Republic was reduced to the rump of Java and Sumatra, whilst the political terms of Renville defined it as one member of a United States of Indonesia, a federation which would be incorporated with the Kingdom of the Netherlands in an overall Netherlands-Indonesian Union. Meanwhile, the Republic recognized Dutch sovereignty until such time as this was transferred to the United States of Indonesia and during the interval 'the Kingdom of the Netherlands may confer appropriate rights, duties, and responsibilities on a provisional federal

Government of the territories of the future United States of Indonesia'. One provision only seemed to imply a concession to the Republic—that 'within a period of not less than six months or more than one year from the signing of this agreement, a plebiscite will be held to determine whether the populations of the various territories of Java, Madura, and Sumatra wish their territories to form part of the Republic of Indonesia or of another state within the United States of Indonesia, such plebiscite to be conducted under the observation of the Committee of Good Offices should either party request the services of the Committee in this capacity'. But the plebiscite was never held; the parties were unable to agree as to whether the 'agreement' referred to meant the Renville Agreement or a future political agreement.

When the Security Council discussed the Renville Agreement, the Australian, Indian, and Soviet delegates expressed in varying degrees of forthrightness their dismay at the Republic's enforced retreat. The Australian delegate stated frankly that the Republic, as a result of its adherence to United Nations principles, 'now finds itself in a less advantageous position than it was at the time when it accepted the Security Council's offer of good offices'. Mr. Gromyko attributed Holland's victory to the fellow-feeling of American, British, French, and Belgian Imperialists, whilst his Ukrainian colleague simply called the Committee of Good Offices the 'Committee of Good Offices for the Netherland Usurpers'.

The Second Dutch Military Action

The United Nations had frustrated Dutch schemes for a complete come-back. But it had not changed the nature of Dutch policy. In Indonesia, General Spoor and Admiral Pinke had at no time conceived of nor desired any other policy than that of force; Lt.-Governor General van Mook, for reasons never yet explained, now believed that his Government should go straight ahead and destroy the Republic. If it continued to exist it would be only in the role of a very junior partner in a Dutch family of nations, owing allegiance to the benevolent House of Orange.

He now settled down to the building of a federal state, and found among Indonesians a number of opportunists to whom power, independently of its source, was purchasable, men whose services could be obtained for positions of authority, however nominal; he won the temporary allegiance of feudal lords who owed their position and their wealth as much to Dutch colonial influence as to their own aristocratic background, men who believed that their existence would be brighter if a *status quo* could be maintained under Dutch rule than it would be in a Republic where they must reckon with democratic forces.

In Madura, Mr. Tjakraningrat, head of the feudal family ruling the island for many generations, was put in charge of 'a free Negara within the United States of Indonesia', the result of a plebiscite which even the Dutch delegation and officials admitted had taken place when 'most of the people had not yet returned from the jungles where they took refuge, being afraid of Dutch aggression'.[2] Similarly, in West Java, whilst the area was still under martial law, Mr. Kartalegawa, a civil servant in the Netherlands Indies Government, suddenly appeared as leader of a mushroom party, 'The Sundanese People's Party', which staged a coup in Bogor, after which the local civil administration was offered to the Dutch Civil Service. When the Dutch-sponsored authorities arranged an election for a provisional representative Assembly, a Republican candidate, who had the temerity to stand, was elected as Chairman. On his election tour among the people he was asked such questions as 'When are we permitted to hoist our red-and-white flag again?' whilst Sundanese children sang the Republican song *Bung Karno and Bung Hatta are our leaders*. East Java was difficult to handle; too many people had followed events in Madura to fall into a similar trap. The Dutch Commissioner, failing to win local support for a conference, was helped out of his difficulty by the Dutch authorities in Djakarta who simply created a state of East Java by the easy process of an 'emergency ordinance'. Meanwhile, in Sumatra, similar tactics were adopted, and in the south and east parts of the island, Dr. van Mook found enough support from the local feudal aristocracy together with their own pensioned officers to set up a skeleton administration.

Van Mook now became more ambitious; he decided to organize an Interim Federal Government as referred to in principles attached to the Renville Agreement. Dr. Hatta put his sincerity to the test by expressing Republican willingness to co-operate, an embarrassing offer which was disingenuously side-tracked. Van Mook replied that such co-operation 'cannot be considered till a political agreement is arrived at'. This caused confusion on all sides; it made the work of the Committee of Good Offices almost impossible; month after month their activities were bogged down in hopeless efforts to reconcile two incompatible interpretations of the word 'interim'; the Republican Government interpreted this as referring to a period, on an analogy with British policy in India, which was transitional to a sovereign United States of Indonesia; the Dutch interpreted it as a transitional period to a return to the Dutch East Indies Government.

The Republic edged out of the picture and the Committee of Good Offices neutralized, van Mook went ahead and formed a United States of Indonesia without the Republic. From May 27th until July 17th, 1948, he held a conference in Bandung. The representatives of thirteen 'non-Republican States' were present; they were best described later by the Filippino delegate to the Security Council as 'initiated, inspired, abetted, sponsored, and actively supported by the Netherlands authorities'.

While van Mook federalized, the Committee of Good Offices stood weakly by, its sub-committees discussing a wide variety of social, administrative, and economic difficulties, none of which could be ameliorated in the absence of a political solution. It could only report or act or protest as a Committee, unanimously; the Belgian delegate could, and did, withhold his agreement to any criticism of Dutch policy, and it was only as the result of the Australian representative's insistence that any reference to the setting up of van Mook's federal states was made in the Committee's reports to the Security Council.

It was very much to the credit of Mr. Tom Critchley (Australian) and Mr. Coert Dubois (American) that they made a joint effort to end the deadlock which now arose. On June 4th, whilst Dr. van Mook was holding his conference in Bandung, they drafted and presented a confidential working paper to both parties. The Belgian member did not agree with the proposed procedure and reserved his position. The proposals were bold and realistic; the central idea was that elections should be held throughout Indonesia for a Constituent Assembly which would also function as a Provisional Parliament; the Netherlands and the Republic were to be sovereign independent States 'united in partnership on a footing of equality'; suggestions were made to meet the complex problems of the pre-federal period, political, economic, military, and financial. The Republic accepted these proposals as a basis for negotiation; the Dutch turned them down immediately, and on June 23rd broke off all negotiations on the trumped-up excuse that the working paper had been disclosed to the Press. Van Mook, who at all times considered the Committee of Good Offices an unnecessary interruption, then by-passed it by a personal invitation to Dr. Hatta to meet him in Djakarta—a meeting which was criticized by many of his Republican colleagues and deplored by the three members of the Committee. It had no results.

Mr. Merle Cochran then arrived on the scene to take the place of Mr. Coert Dubois. He immediately put forward new proposals to the Dutch and to the Republic; they were so secret that even his Australian and Belgian colleagues were only informed about them the next day. The Republic accepted them with certain reservations as the basis for discussion. The Dutch delegation, after delaying a reply for a month, proposed sixty-seven amendments. Thus the Committee of Good Offices continued as ambiguous spectators. They watched the drift towards war, they followed, through the detailed reports of their military observers, the growing clashes on both sides of the *status quo* line, they saw the economic disintegration of the Republic as the Dutch blockade was drawn tighter and tighter; they witnessed such provocative events as the seizure by Dutch authorities of the Republican Hospital in Djakarta, and the killing of a boy scout in Pegangsaan Timur where Sukarno had originally proclaimed the Republic. The boy was there, it is said, to watch a newsreel of Princess Elizabeth's wedding. The Committee's silence during the summer and autumn of 1948 gave point to

Mr. Malik's description of them as a 'toothless and powerless organ . . . used in defence of Netherlands colonial interests'.

Events now moved quickly and in directions outside the control of the Committee of Good Offices. Elections in Holland were fought on the Indonesian issue. A Cabinet was formed three months later, in August, which placed power in the hands of the more extreme members of the Catholic Party. The new Prime Minister, Dr. Beel, and the Minister for Overseas Territories made no secret of the proposed 'toughness' in Indonesia, while Professor Romme, the evil genius of this policy, told his Catholic People's Party Executive that the resumption of military action would be necessary before the problem was solved. Dr. Stikker, Foreign Minister, would have preferred a more moderate policy, but he showed his weakness in his advice to the State Department during a visit to Washington in September. His Cabinet, he said, was so precariously balanced that its very existence might be endangered if it were formally confronted with such a plan as that which Mr. Merle Cochran was then discussing with Republicans and Dutch in Djakarta. The plan in fact was the last chance of a compromise.

Political instability in Holland coincided with unexpected and dangerous political events in Indonesia. Republican morale was growing weaker; the Committee of Good Offices was in cold storage; the Dutch blockade meant terrible shortages of food and clothing. The hospitals were almost denuded of essential drugs, and bandages were made out of banana-palm leaves. In Djogjakarta, people were hungry and many were clothed only in gunny sacks. The population was increased by more than a million refugees from territories under Dutch control. Dr. Hatta seemed to be retreating from concession to concession. These were conditions in which revolutionary ideas found a fertile soil. The Communist Party line had changed (in March 1948) from one of united front to revolutionary tactics in Southeast Asia. In May, the Soviet Consul in Prague had indicated his Government's interest in the Republic by signing an agreement with a brilliant young Republican envoy, Suripno, who was not known at the time to be a Communist. In August, when Suripno was recalled to Djakarta to explain his activities, he took with him, disguised as his secretary, a Communist named Musso who had lived in Moscow most of the time from 1926 when the Dutch expelled him. After a series of political manoeuvres, Musso, Suripno, and Sjarifuddin led a rebellion against the Republican Government. The rebellion was quickly defeated. The Dutch Foreign Minister, then in Washington, offered Dutch support. In immediately refusing it on the grounds that this was purely an internal affair, Republican morale was considerably strengthened. Internationally, this Communist rebellion was a conclusive answer to Dutch propaganda that the Republic was run by Communists.

Dutch policy now concentrated on defeating the Republic by political and, later, by military action. In The Hague, an Emergency Bill was passed in the Lower House in October 1948 giving full powers to the so-called Interim Federal Government, initiated by Dr. van Mook. The Government was planned to come into operation on January 1st, 1949. By this time, those who were in favour of military action believed that the Republic would collapse as soon as it was attacked by Dutch military forces. There were those in the Dutch Cabinet who still wanted negotiations and Dr. Stikker, the then Foreign Minister, through Mr. Merle Cochran as intermediary, met Dr. Hatta and other Republican Ministers. But although they made far-reaching concessions, Minister for Overseas Territories Sassen, leader of the war group in Holland, described them as a sell-out to the Republic. The result was the recall of Dr. Stikker, and the appointment of a second Mission, this time led by Mr. Sassen himself.

He was accompanied by Dr. Stikker and by Mr. Neher, the Royal Commissioner in Djakarta. From the outset they behaved as if their object was to deliver an ultimatum. In The Hague, the British Ambassador made gentlemanly representations to the Dutch Government, expressing anxiety lest the Dutch launch their military campaign. In Washington, Republican representatives made a personal call on the South-east Division of the State Department, saying that they expected Dutch military action at any moment. What, they asked, would be America's reaction? 'That depends on the situation,' they were told, and the remark was interpreted as meaning that the kind of resistance the Republic made would determine the State Department's policy; that there would be no effective American intervention on Indonesia's side unless the Republicans demonstrated their capacity to make their resistance effective.

With Mr. Merle Cochran as intermediary, Dr. Hatta was persuaded to make far-reaching concessions to the Dutch Mission. He knew that the situation was desperate and he doubted the strength of the Republic to resist. On one point he was unwilling to give way—this was the vital suggestion of placing the Republican army under the ultimate authority of the Dutch High Commissioner during the duration of the provisional Government. But he went so far as to agree to a joint Netherlands-Indonesian staff under the chairmanship of a Dutch officer, provided their functions were purely advisory. Further, in the event of the Interim Federal Government calling on the assistance of Netherlands armed forces to meet an emergency, the Government of the Republic was prepared to accept Netherlands command over all forces in Indonesia. It was extremely unlikely that such concessions could have found popular support; indeed many Republicans felt that, acting under pressure from Mr. Merle Cochran, their Prime Minister had gone much too far.

Negotiations finally broke down on December 11th, when the Dutch authorities informed the Committee of Good Offices that 'negotiations under the auspices of the Committee at this stage are futile, as these would only lead to purposeless discussions'. Mr. Merle Cochran, at Dr. Hatta's request, made a last-minute effort to reopen negotiations. But the Dutch replied that a continuation of talks would be useless unless the Republican Government bound itself to accept immediately the Dutch point of view on basic issues, including the implementation of the truce. This ultimatum demanded that the Republican Government send its answer before December 18th, 10.00 hours Djakarta time, for relay to The Hague. Mr. Cochran, who had so successfully persuaded the Republicans to make one concession after another, felt that this was intolerable. In a letter couched in critical terms he told the Dutch delegation:

'You will agree, I am sure, that in such circumstances, I cannot in justice press Dr. Hatta for an immediate reply to a letter which calls not for a mere expression of willingness to resume negotiations but rather for surrender to the position of your Government on every material point.'

The Republic did not answer the ultimatum. At half-past eleven on the night of December 18th, Mr. Cochran was informed that the Dutch were terminating the truce. Before the Committee received this notice of war, the long-prepared attack was launched. Paratroops occupied Djogjakarta without any serious opposition. President Sukarno and six other Cabinet Ministers were arrested and taken to Sumatra. On the airport just outside Djogjakarta, forty-six Dutch transports landed with 900 commando troops. Within two weeks all the big towns in Java were in Dutch hands, with the exception of Kediri, and all the roads were under their control. In Sumatra they equally quickly occupied Bukit Tinggi and from this busy market town in the Padang Highlands they fanned out in all directions. The war, long and carefully planned, was on. The United Nations was presented with a *fait accompli*.

Asian Solidarity

The Security Council passed resolutions on December 24th, 1948, calling for a cease-fire. But the mistake was made, as in the first military action, of refusing to demand that Dutch troops withdraw to lines demarcated by the Renville Truce Agreement. The Dutch ignored it and their troops went on fighting in Java until December 31st, 1948, and in Sumatra until January 5th, 1949.

Meanwhile, Asian countries, recently freed from colonial control, regarded Dutch action as a challenge to their newly won independence. Pakistan, India, Burma, and Ceylon at once banned the Dutch airline, the K.L.M. In Australia, dockworkers boycotted Dutch ships as they had done in 1947, and resolutions from many progressive organizations, political and religious, began to flow into the United Nations. Pandit Nehru agreed to the suggestion of the Burmese Government that a Conference of Asian Nations should be called to consider joint action. Delegates from Afghanistan, Australia, Burma, Ceylon, China, Egypt, Ethiopia, India, Iraq, the Lebanon, Nepal, Pakistan, the Philippines, Saudi Arabia, Syria, and the Yemen together with observers from Siam and New Zealand met in Delhi and passed unanimously on January 23rd, 1949, a resolution urging the release of all political prisoners; freedom for the Republican Government to function freely; the formation of an Interim Government composed of representatives of the Republic and of non-Republican territories by March 15th, which should enjoy full powers of government including control over its armed forces, and freedom in external affairs; elections for a Constituent Assembly to be completed by October 1st; power over the whole of Indonesia to be completely transferred by January 1st, 1950, to the United States of Indonesia; relations with the Netherlands to be settled by negotiations between the Governments of the United States of Indonesia and the Netherlands; and, finally, in the event of either party to the dispute not complying with the recommendations of the Security Council, the Council should take effective action to enforce its recommendations.

The Security Council could not overlook the Asian Conference demands and on January 28th a resolution was passed which was almost identical with that in Delhi. The Committee of Good Offices was renamed the United Nations Commission for Indonesia and it was instructed to help both parties in implementing the resolution, whilst the Consular Commission (which had never been disbanded) was told to provide military observers, staff, and other facilities.

The blow which was intended to end the Republic had failed. Forces, internal and international, were released which could not be ignored.

Towards Independence

When the first bombs fell on Djogjakarta they ended a tension which was rapidly undermining Republican confidence. 'We would rather be blown to pieces than accept the Dutch terms' summed up the spirit of people though they were weakened by the blockade and knew that war meant even greater suffering.

Preparations had been made to meet the Dutch attack for which they had massed troops outside Djogjakarta. Dr. Sjafruddin, the Republican Minister of Economic Affairs, had flown a week before to Sumatra. When Republican Ministers were arrested he at once announced an Emergency Government with himself as Prime Minister. He gave the terms on which the Republic would meet Dutch authorities; the immediate release of the Cabinet Ministers; withdrawal of Dutch troops to the pre-December line; recognition of the Republic's sovereignty over Java, Sumatra, and Madura; formation of an all-Indonesian Government by popular vote free from Dutch interference, and the withdrawal of the Dutch army from Indonesia as soon as possible after the formation of such a Government. But the Dutch still believed they could defeat the Republic and their Commissioner for East Sumatra told the Republican prisoners that: 'The Netherlands Government no longer recognizes the Indonesian Republic as a political entity with its own territory and as a result does not recognize the position of its leaders.'

The Dutch, characteristically obstinate, still assumed that they could depend on the Federal States set up by Dr. van Mook. This proved their greatest miscalculation. Many Federalist Ministers had already realized that they were not only powerless, but that they were extremely unpopular. Therefore, when Djogjakarta was bombed, the Governments of East Indonesia and Pasundan (West Java), the most important Federal areas, resigned, while others refused to support Dutch military action. Van Mook's Federal Empire began to crumble. Even Dutch officials in Indonesia doubted the wisdom of military action and in February 1949 a group in Djakarta sent a document to The Hague boldly stating that, instead of bringing law and order to Indonesia, Dutch military action had brought large-scale terrorism and insecurity; that the people of Holland would be unwise to accept any optimistic view; that preparations were being made to extend guerrilla action; that the second military action had widened the gap between the two peoples. They recommended that the Netherlands should reach agreement with Republican leaders.

Military observers attached to the United Nations Commission soon began to report well-organized guerrilla resistance, systematic and co-ordinated.

The Emergency Government in Sumatra worked effectively as the core of military organization, with Colonel Hidayat as Chief of Staff and Territorial Commander of Republican Forces in Sumatra. General Sudirman held a similar position in Java. Both islands were divided into military territories under Military Governors who received orders from and reported to the Emergency Government. This strategy combined overall control with responsibility for local activities and for the transference from one area to another of specialist groups trained in various types of sabotage. This military organization was closely co-ordinated with the civil administration. Many Republican civil servants left their posts in the towns and carried on their work in the countryside. They had the fullest support from the people and they were able to administer justice, to collect taxes, to keep schools open, and to open new ones and to maintain their own Republican currency. The Dutch army was unable to give a strategic reply to these guerrilla tactics because their forces were insufficient to cover the whole area. The Republican guerrillas avoided pitched battles; clashes with Dutch troops were regarded only tactically, and even as incidental to the main strategic task of preventing them from benefiting from their reckless adventure. This widespread, centrally organized guerrilla warfare with its desperate scorched-earth activities was a tremendous surprise to the Dutch troops, and their morale soon showed signs of deterioration. Only a month after their attack, disrupted communications, the erratic delivery of supplies, and the system of payment of troops broke down in many places and instead of a quick victory the Dutch found themselves involved in a long-drawn-out war of attrition, living in the midst of hostile people. General Spoor, the Dutch Army Commander, in an interview given to the *Free Press* in Surabaya in January 949, admitted that conditions were very difficult for his troops, that it was not possible for them to occupy the whole country, since, if this were attempted, it would mean the dissipation of a small army over a large area. He also confirmed the Republican claim that its army units—the T.N.I.—had remained intact in many places. He understood perfectly well that if guerrilla forces received the support of the people it was hopeless to attempt the pacification of the country.

Responsible Republicans frequently deplored the enormous damage caused by scorched-earth tactics; rubber, tea, coffee, and palm-oil plantations were completely destroyed, oil-wells, factory installations, and electricity supply plants all fired with incalculable loss both short-term and for the future. Yet the Government and the people were agreed that even the loss of so much of Indonesia's wealth was preferable to the loss of their independence and their sense of nationhood.

Resistance was not confined to Java and Sumatra. In Bandjarmasin (South Borneo) a general rising took place immediately after the Dutch attack, and guerrilla warfare followed and rapidly increased. The leader was Hasan Basri, who had been Commander of the Division D4 of the Republican navy. In Bali and Celebes, the Dutch found it increasingly difficult to maintain their rule; local risings took place in Tabanan (South Bali) and in Makassar. In other words, as months passed by, the Dutch plan of a quick war, as advised by Mr. Sassen and his War Minister and enthusiastically adopted by General Spoor, turned out a failure. The road to colonial victory proved only a blind alley. Their policy had won the contempt of Asian nations mobilized as never before; their complete disregard of the Security Council resolutions of December 24th and 28th, 1948, and of January 28th, 1949, caused Dr. Jessup, the American delegate, to make the remark: 'Any military success achieved by the Netherlands military action would not affect a solution of the Indonesian problem.'

The Dutch Cabinet was divided; one group, led by Dr. Drees, the Prime Minister, maintained that wisdom dictated conditional compliance with the Security Council's resolution within the general framework of their plans to establish a United States of Indonesia. The other group, led by Mr. Sassen, Minister for Overseas Territories, suggested that the Security Council should be ignored and that they should go ahead with their military and political plans. On February 8th, Mr. Merle Cochran arrived at The Hague. He was fêted like a pro-Consul. But on

February 11th, it was Mr. Sassen and not Dr. Drees who resigned from the Cabinet. Otherwise the whole Government would have resigned after Mr. Cochran had shown them America's red light. They now knew that they could not depend on American neutrality, let alone support.

During these weeks, Republican Ministers remained prisoners firstly in a mountain resort in Sumatra and then in the island of Bangka. They were offered freedom to move if they signed a pledge to refrain from political activities. It was obviously a trap into which experienced political workers would not fall. Later, Sjahrir was released. President Sukarno and the others were given one room, twenty feet square, with six beds wired off like zoo cages. When Woodrow Wyatt, M.P., visited them in March 1949, the cages had gone but the windows were still wire-netted. They were offered freedom to go wherever they pleased, with only one exception—Djogjakarta. And they were invited to attend a conference at The Hague. To accept such an invitation without establishing contact with their Emergency Government was asking for repudiation. 'If they left for Holland without doing that', Woodrow Wyatt wrote,

'they would have no authority; and, if they were foolish enough to return afterwards, they would probably be shot as traitors for their pains. Nor would they have the slightest chance of ordering a cease-fire unless they had also re-established their administration in the capital. For the Dutch to pretend that this would be difficult is absurd.'[3]

Finesse is not the most outstanding Dutch characteristic. While they made one clumsy gesture after another, their prisoners made their own plans. With Sjahrir as a personal bridge and with the United Nations Commission as a valuable intermediary, Federal leaders visited Bangka Island. Anak Agung and Sultan Hamid, who had resigned their posts as Prime Ministers of East Indonesia and West Borneo respectively in protest against Dutch military action, now sought ways and means of associating themselves with the Republic. Sultan Hamid, reactionary, Dutch-minded, was an opportunist creeping on to the Republican band-wagon; Anak Agung was a man of considerable calibre who had already signified privately his support for the Republic.

The National Front of Republicans and Federalists

The Federalists were by no means an insignificant group. Van Mook's policy of creating fourteen Federal States had met with some considerable success, and the Federal Consultative Assembly, as their 'parliament' was called, was already a rival focus of power when Dutch troops launched their second campaign in December 1948. Federal States varied in size, from Billiton with a population of 100,000 to East Indonesia (Celebes, Lesser Sunda Islands, the Moluccas) with 10,000,000. Each had one vote in the Assembly. The Dutch had given them no real power, but the Republic nevertheless could not claim the allegiance of their leaders, while many people who were pro-Republican were in Federal jails.

There was a real danger that in some of the more politically backward areas, the Dutch could maintain a number of feudal rulers to whose status the Republican Government's dynamic youthfulness and radicalism were a challenge.

By their military action, the Dutch had stimulated Republican resistance, raised morale, and caused the Federalists to reconsider their position. Their talks with Republican prisoners convinced them that the conception of Dutch-sponsored Federal States was incompatible with the freedom of the country as a whole or with their own personal dignity. Such was the significance of the discussions in Bangka Island.

The Hague Government was bound to take into consideration this unexpected co-operation between the Republicans and the Federalists. And, with a shrewd sense of timing, the Dutch made an agreement with the Republican prisoners forty-eight hours before the General Assembly was due to meet. Two statements were announced from Bangka Island. The Indonesians announced that the President and Vice-President of the Republic had given personal assurances that they favoured and would urge their Government to adopt, as soon as possible after their restoration to Djogjakarta, a policy including (1) issuance of an order to their supporters to cease guerrilla warfare, (2) co-operation in the restoration of peace and the maintenance of law and order, and (3) participation in a round table conference at The Hague 'with a view to accelerating the unconditional transfer of real and complete sovereignty to the United States of Indonesia'. The Dutch statement said, amongst other things, that in view of the undertaking announced by Republican Ministers, they would agree to the return of the Republican Government to Djogjakarta, to cease all military operations, and to release all political prisoners arrested in the Republic since December 17th, 1948.

This Rum-Van Royen Agreement, so called after the two signatories, was the prelude to the Round Table Conference. A great deal of credit must be given to the United Nations Commission under whose auspices the Republicans and Dutch negotiators came together. But the vital factor which had changed the Indonesian picture was that Republican guerrillas now had the military initiative. United Nations military observers reported that over a large area only the main towns and roads were held by Dutch troops. Their conclusion was inescapable; political settlement was the only alternative to a prolonged and increasingly destructive war. There were Republicans who argued that now the military initiative was theirs, it was advisable to 'fight to the end'; otherwise they ran the risk of losing through concessions round the conference table all that they had won by their courageous resistance. Successful military action had transformed Republican morale.

With the active and patient co-operation of the United Nations Commission, Republicans and Dutch settled down now to the work of implementing the Rum-Van Royen Agreement. Both sides acted with a great deal of common sense through working groups; one dealt with the withdrawal of Netherlands forces from Djogjakarta, the formation of a Republican Police Force, and the transfer of public services; another group was concerned with public utilities, railways, the rebuilding of bridges, the reinstatement of telephone and radio communications, and postal facilities; a third group covered the supply of essential goods, medical supplies, and textiles, from all of which the Republic had been cut off by the blockade.

June 30th, 1949, was a red-letter day in the history of Djogja-karta. A beleaguered city was suddenly liberated. People were ragged and hungry after months of blockade. Many homes were bereaved by the deaths of guerrilla fighters. Many who had left the city with all they possessed on rickety ox-carts, now returned to find their homes destroyed. Yet victory was in the air. Ministers and officials returned from their guerrilla battle-fields to put the finishing touches on plans for evacuating Dutch troops. On June 30th, 1949, people watched in silence the departure of those who had made their city a place of terror and insecurity since the first bombs fell on December 18th, 1948.

Most moving of all those who returned was General Sudir-man. For six months he had acted as an inspired Commander-in-Chief of the Republican Army. He was in the last stages of tuberculosis, and painters and writers have described how he visited the troops and gave orders from a bamboo stretcher. He lived to see the last Dutch soldiers leave Djogjakarta. Today, in front of the building which served as a Republican Parliament, a large bronze statue honours his memory.

The change-over was quiet and orderly. Two thousand guerrilla fighters marched down the long Malioburo Street leading to the palace of the Sultan. His absolute refusal to talk with the Dutch was one of the many gestures which inspired popular resistance and made him a loved and respected hero. The time-table was fixed by the United Nations Commission, who ordered the guerrillas to keep at least 300 yards behind the withdrawing Dutch army. Sultan Hamengku Buwono, unarmed, dressed as a Major-General of the Republican Army, drove his own car along columns of guerrilla troops. This city of a million people which had seemed deserted only a few hours before, now came to life and the streets echoed with 'Merdeka'. The Indonesians realized that the Dutch had left never to return. Their departure was remarkably different from that of the British from India, where Lord and Lady Mountbatten were garlanded and British troops marched out with the Indian bands playing their regimental music. It was also unlike the leave-taking in Rangoon where the first Cabinet of the Union of Burma watched with undisguised sorrow the departure of Sir Hubert and Lady Rance. So might the Dutch have left their colony.

Djogjakarta was again beflagged on July 6th, to welcome the prisoners from Bangka—President Sukarno, Prime Minister Hatta, and their colleagues. The United Nations Commission, impersonally describing their return, said that 'it was greeted with noticeable enthusiasm on the part of the population'. President Sukarno told the enormous crowd which welcomed them, 'I am proud of the people's struggle. Our own strength and the international world has brought us back. Let us now continue to work for national unity.'

The newly restored Republic held its first Cabinet meeting·on July 13th, and Sjafruddin Prawiranegara, head of the Republican Emergency Government in Sumatra, who had returned in a United States aircraft, handed back his mandate to President Sukarno. A happy omen of what was to follow appeared in the form of a present of textiles and medical supplies from the East Indonesian Government. Then, on July 20th, an Inter-Indonesian Conference attended by Republicans and Federalists underlined the unity which was forged on Bangka Island. It was, as President Sukarno described it, a 'historic moment which would decide Indonesia's destiny for many centuries'. The audience consisted of twenty Republicans, sixty-six Federal delegates, and the United Nations Commission, the last group in the capacity of benevolent optimistic spectators. Some of the Republicans were famous guerrilla leaders, a price still on their heads, since the cease-fire had not yet been settled.

In Djogjakarta and in Djakarta, to which the conference later moved, a common programme was worked out, so that when the Round Table Conference began at The Hague some weeks later, Dutch negotiators were dealing with people who now spoke for the first time with one voice.

The Round Table Conference

War was officially ended on the night of August 10th in Java, and in Sumatra on August 14th, United Nations military observers supervising the cease-fire. Guerrillas often laid down their arms reluctantly; some of them escaped to the mountains with them. Many politically minded men and women were suspicious of the forthcoming meetings at The Hague. Hopes had been belied too often, and discussions had ended only in one-sided concessions. Sjahrir and his colleagues doubted the genuineness of Dutch intentions, and saw the conference against the background of the 'cold war', with American influence dominant in the United Nations Commission through Mr. Merle Cochran.

The Round Table Conference was officially opened at The Hague on August 23rd, 1949. Dutch delegates made hard bargains, and wasted weeks of time in discussing definitions and interpretations which could have been settled in a few hours.

Finally, after differences of approach, of temperament, and of fundamental outlook had caused crisis after crisis, the conference came to an end on November 2nd. Its achievements were these. The Dutch agreed to transfer unconditionally sovereignty to the Government of the United States of Indonesia before the end of the year. The new sovereign State would be a Federation consisting of the territory of the Republic and the sixteen non-Republican States. A Constitution was agreed upon. This new State was to be linked with the Netherlands in a Union headed symbolically by Queen Juliana. A Union Statute was settled.

Agreement was achieved on foreign relations and co-operation in international affairs; the parties agreed to promote their mutual relations in education, science, and culture.

In military affairs, it was agreed that all Dutch forces, numbering about 85,000 men, would be withdrawn as quickly as possible. After the transfer of sovereignty, Military Missions would be exchanged, whilst the naval base of Surabaya was to serve ships of the Royal Netherlands navy. These were dangerous concessions, as time proved. The last of the Dutch army left Indonesia only in May 1951. A Dutch naval command in Surabaya is a potential provocation, whilst in October 1952, the Dutch Military Mission proved a source of considerable discontent.

The social affairs clauses were bound to lead to trouble.

They arranged that at the time of transfer, the Republic would accept into its service all civil government officials at that time employed by the Netherlands East Indies Government, and also assure all rights and obligations of the predecessor Government in respect of those officials as well as former Government officials and their beneficiaries. For two years, as from the time of transfer of sovereignty, the Republic agreed to refrain from taking any measures which would unfavourably affect the legal position of those Government officials of Dutch nationality who were thus taken over. In some respects this was the most serious of all concessions. It meant nothing less than a potential fifth column throughout the whole administration of the Republic, including its Intelligence Service. It provided an outlet for Dutch resentment and there were many who took every advantage of it. It was an impossible alliance of officials, who were arrogantly experienced, with Indonesians eager to express their hard-won independence. Bad relations were inevitable, Indonesians were often humiliated where they needed self-confidence. Even if Dutch officials had had good faith—and there were many who had—the relationship inevitably led to confusion, often to unnecessary inefficiency. The Dutch may argue that their experience was indispensable, that there were too few trained Indonesians. To this argument there are two overriding answers: the most experienced, even the most efficient administration is undermined by bad morale; if there were too few trained Indonesians, the responsibility was largely the result of Dutch policy. A possibly satisfactory agreement would have been one which gave the Republic the chance of employing Dutch officials and the Dutch officials the right to choose whether they remained.

Financial and economic agreements were almost equally disadvantageous to the Republic. It assumed full responsibility for former Dutch East Indian debts and tied the economy of the Republic to that of Holland, with resulting restrictions on her economy and trade.

Finally, the Dutch insisted on retaining West Irian, using the weakest of ethnological arguments. Dr. Hatta made this concession during the last few days of the conference, believing that by holding out on this issue he risked complete failure. The arrangement that within a year of the time of transfer of power this question should be determined through negotiations has not materialized, and West Irian still embitters relations between the two countries. There are many who suspect that this compromise was encouraged by Mr. Merle Cochran in the belief that this area would thereby be more accessible to his country's strategic plans.

The Round Table Conference Agreement was welcomed by the United Nations, with the exception of the Soviet Union and her satellite countries, who regarded it as part of the machinations of the Anglo-American *bloc*, an effort to turn Indonesia into 'their own military base'. It was not popular in Indonesia and not everyone endorses Dr. Hatta's comment: 'Historically and internationally, what we have achieved is the best that could be achieved at this time.'

The last act in this long-drawn-out struggle for Indonesian independence was performed in Djakarta and The Hague on December 27th, 1949. In Djakarta, the Sultan of Djogjakarta, acting Prime Minister, took over civil and military administration at a ceremony in the Governor-General's Palace in Koningsplein, where, from now onwards, President Sukarno made his residence. The Dutch National Anthem was played for the last time and the Dutch tricolour then lowered. After a moment's silence the red-and-white Indonesian flag flew from the palace masthead and thousands of Indonesians cheered and sang *Indonesia Raja*. In Amsterdam, Indonesian and Dutch Prime Ministers signed the Protocol transferring sovereignty. Then Queen Wilhelmina, who had never set foot in her Asian colony, read the deed of confirmation from a large red leather book. She called the ceremony one of the most moving of our times. 'No longer do we stand partially opposed to one another. We have now taken our stations side by side, however much we may be bruised and torn, carrying the scars of rancour and regret.' Dr. Hatta accepted the charter of sovereignty and briefly expressed hopes for the future. The Queen leaned over and shook his hand. The carillon of palace bells rang out the *Wilhelmus* and the *Indonesia Raja*.

'Indonesia is my country,
It is the land of my birth.
There I stand,
Guarding my motherland.
Indonesian is my nationality,
Are my nation and my country.
Let us call together:
"Indonesia be one." . . .'

NOTES

[1] Report of the Security Council, October 27th, 1947.
[2] Report of the Committee of Good Offices.
[3] *New Statesman and Nation*, March 5th, 1949.

PART FOUR

The Republic

CHAPTER XII

THE UNITARY STATE

D R. HATTA returned to Djakarta to face problems unlike those of any other Prime Minister. Sovereignty was transferred, his country was recognized as an independent Power by countries in quick succession and the non-Communist world's Press acclaimed the Round Table Conference as a success for the United Nations, and a triumph for the sensible, solid people of Holland. 'The existence of free Indonesia in free association with Holland is perhaps U.N.O.'s major contribution to date to the well-being of the world', the *News Chronicle* wrote; the *Manchester Evening News* said that 'the United Nations gets so few bouquets, that its achievement in Indonesia deserves special notice', and similar comments appeared, acclaiming the United Nations, praising the goodwill between Holland and her ex-colony. The Indonesians who had had to wait so long for their independence began to ask questions when Dr. Hatta returned. Independence? Yes, but at what price? Ties with Holland, economic, political, military, cultural? West Irian still under Dutch rule? Dutch investments of at least $3\frac{1}{2}$ billion guilders in Indonesian key industries? A provision that Dutch civil servants must be retained for two more years? The Dutch army to stay in the country for six, seven, maybe twelve months? A Military Mission would remain for three years? The strategic base of Surabaya would be under Dutch operational control, and in West Irian, Dutch military and financial planners would have a free hand for a year? Further, by taking over the federal structure of administration, the signatories of the Round Table Conference Agreement had kept open the door to feudal leaders who had maintained their power by Dutch support at the expense of the Republic, men whose wealth was derived in part by association with the big financial magnates in rubber, tobacco, oil, and tin.

K*   265

Thus, whilst the carillon in Amsterdam rang out its chimes, the bells seemed muffled in Indonesia. The 'first, fine, careless rapture' of independence was tempered by disillusion, in some cases amounting to fear of results which might follow the compromises made at The Hague. Young men and women, still in the mountains, armed as guerrilla fighters, were prepared to go on fighting for a cause which they believed was betrayed. Others had no wish to settle down to the less exciting work of building a new country. There were those who questioned whether their leaders had made the most of their strategic position when face-to-face with their ex-rulers; others who suspected that the United Nations Good Offices Commission used their persuasive powers to the advantage of Dutch interests.

This was the atmosphere in which Dr. Hatta and his Government set out to build a new nation. Basically, it was the consolidation of loyalty to an idea, the welding together of people whose loyalties were fragmented. Rice-cultivators in Java must learn to feel that they belong to the same nation as the rubber-tappers in Kalimantan, the Batak village people must develop a common interest with those of the Toradja lands in Sulawesi, the Christians in the Minahasa with the strict Muslims of Atjeh and the devout Hindus of Bali. These are differences of background, of language and customs, of religion, differences which were useful to a foreign ruler but a handicap in a young independent country, just emerging from colonialism.

There were also immediate, far more complex political problems to face, problems of the transference of loyalty, of a psychological break from Dutch rule. The Republican idea was social as well as Nationalist in the minds of a majority of its supporters, especially among the youth, and they were the most articulate. Feudal families in Kalimantan and Sulawesi realized that they were challenged by the Republic, and to this social resistance we must add their local patriotism, their feeling that the Republic had been made in Java, although so many of its leaders were from Sumatra. In both cases there were seeds of disloyalty, seeds which with Dutch encouragement might bear dangerous fruit for Indonesia. Nowhere in the world was such a complexity of motives and allegiances to be found; my conversations in the spring of 1951 almost invariably led to a discussion of individual behaviour in the sequence of events which ultimately led to independence. Was he a Dutch stooge in pre-war days? Was his collaboration with the Japanese officials too cordial? A Dutch collaborationist? A Japanese collaborationist? A United Nations Good Offices Commission collaborationist? Did he support the Federalists, the post-war expression of Dutch colonialism? Would the Javanese, who naturally made up the majority of Republican supporters, try to dominate other parts of the Republic of the United States of Indonesia?

At the beginning of 1950, the Government was overwhelmingly concerned with a strong central authority as a solid foundation for the new Republic. When sovereignty was transferred, the federal Indonesian State was made up of sixteen partner-states and autonomous territories. How could a nation be built up on this basis of a divided administration, people asked? Could the single, independent, and sovereign Indonesian State materialize on a basis of division which was inherited, not only from Dutch colonial rule, but from the hated policy of van Mook after the war? There were, of course, men who had served in his administration, officials who had vested interests in a half-federal, half-unitary system; officials from Sumatra and Kalimantan, Sulawesi, Bali, and the Moluccas, who were afraid that in a centralized administration most of the plums of office would fall into the eager laps of Javanese. There were men, on an analogy with the United States, who considered that a federal system was desirable; the American Ambassador, Mr. Merle Cochran (who, as a member of the United Nations Commission, took more than a paternal interest in Indonesian affairs), was an active propagandist of this idea. Hadji Agus Salim, a veteran of the Nationalist struggle, and adviser on Foreign Affairs at the time, argued the case against federalism. 'In the United States', he wrote,

'the federal form was indicated by its historical development. The parties were the thirteen states, every one of which had existed as a separate colony, established by a separate colonial charter from the King of England and having a completely

267

separate administration. They only united in revolt against the mother country to secure their independence.'

The contrary was the case where Indonesian history was concerned; here,

'the creation of an increasing number of participating States and territories was purely artificial—a Dutch fabrication, aimed, originally, at avoiding the unconditional recognition of the sovereign Republic of Indonesia, and, subsequently, at the complete dismemberment of that Republic to enable the Kingdom of the Netherlands to restore their control over the former colonial empire in a less conspicuous form. Nothing in the historical development of Indonesia had ever indicated a tendency towards the formation of a federation of separate States and territories.'

This question of the form of government was the first one Dr. Hatta tackled on his return to Djakarta. 'True indeed', he said in a broadcast at the time,

'is the saying that the birth of a nation is like the birth of a child, that it is attended by labour pains. Mother Indonesia, too, had to suffer when giving birth to Indonesia Merdeka. A curious thing is that she had to suffer those pains not in childbirth but afterwards.'

The first of those 'pains' occurred when the Government commenced the process of building a unitary State. Up to the time of the Round Table Conference, the areas in Indonesia, other than those which were under Republican administration, were divided into six territories called States (negaras of Pasundan, East Java, Madura, East Sumatra, South Sumatra, and East Indonesia); nine territories forming autonomous constitutional units (daerahs of Mid Java, Bangka, Billiton, Riouw, West Borneo, Great Dayak, Bandjar, South-east Borneo, East Borneo), and other territories of which the status had not yet been determined. The 'negaras' and 'daerahs', many of them entirely artificial, were organized in the Federal Consultative Assembly, presided over by van Mook. At the Inter-Indonesian Conference in July 1949 the Republic and the Federal Consultative

Assembly had agreed that the provisional Constitution of the Republic of the United States of Indonesia should indicate clearly which territories would be the component parts of the Federation, and that the Republic should comprise territories recognized as under its control in the Renville Agreement. The Constitution which became part of the Round Table Conference Agreement made the stipulation that the Republic of the United States of Indonesia 'is a democratic state of federal structure', but added that the ultimate status of the territories forming the Republic of the United States of Indonesia should depend upon the desires of the inhabitants, expressed freely through democratic means. In other words, the effect of the Round Table Conference was that the Republic (proclaimed on August 17th, 1945, and reduced by the Renville Agreement to the rump of Java and Sumatra) was one state within the Republic of the United States of Indonesia. It was on an equality with the states created by van Mook—states which, as we have already seen, were organized with the express intention of defeating the Republic. Undoubtedly, Dutch negotiators at The Hague believed that if the Republic of the United States of Indonesia could be built up with this division, the Republic itself would cease to play a major role in the country as a whole. The other states in the Republic of the United States of Indonesia were far less developed politically as well as economically; they were mainly those 'native states' of colonial times where the local rulers had acted as Dutch representatives.

By the end of January 1950, it was clear that the continued existence of several states was no longer practicable, and in many parts of the country, especially of course in Java, people demonstrated their desire for a unitary change. Pasundan (West Java) was the first to demand liquidation and the transfer of authority to the Government of the R.U.S.I. When President Sukarno attended the first meeting of Parliament on February 15th he referred to this popular demand for the abolition of the federal constitution and announced the Government's intention of introducing a draft Bill 'to channel the claims and demands of the people along legal and peaceful ways'. Eventually, this Bill was promulgated as an Emergency Law in the following month. It provided that the initiative to realize 'political reforms' could be taken by each state, by the Government of the Republic of the United States of Indonesia, or by a territory without the status of a state. The suggestion was made that popular support or disagreement should be expressed either through a plebiscite or by a Council of Representatives set up for the purpose. However, the need for central government was urgent and on March 9th, by decree of the Federal Government, East Java, Central Java, Madura, Padang, and Sabang were incorporated into the Republic. With the exception of East Sumatra and East Indonesia, all states and territories had followed by the beginning of May; in the former, local leaders, who had supported van Mook's Federal States, stood out for an independent existence, while in East Indonesia the problem was complicated by an unsuccessful military coup led by Captain Andi Aziz of the ex-Netherlands Indies Army (K.N.I.L.) and supported by local federalists. Finally, at a joint session of the Cabinets of the Republic of the United States of Indonesia and the Republic of Indonesia, on July 20th, 1950, arrangements were made for transition to the unitary State structure of government. The whole territory of what had once been known as the Netherlands East Indies, with the exception of West Irian, was divided into ten provinces: West Java, East Java, Central Java, North Sumatra, Central Sumatra, South Sumatra, Kalimantan, Lesser Sunda Islands, Sulawesi, and Moluccas. This particular division was the same as that decided upon when the Declaration of Independence was announced in August 1945, except that Sumatra was now divided into three provinces. Two days before the celebration of the fifth anniversary of the birth of the Republic, President Sukarno proclaimed the establishment of the Republic of Indonesia as a unitary State in a ceremony in Djakarta, and then flew off to Djogjakarta to repeat the performance. Back again in Djakarta, he asked Dr. Hatta and his Cabinet to stay in office as a 'caretaker' Government until a new one was formed. The Constitution stated that general elections should be held for membership of the Constituent Assembly, one member to be elected for every group of 150,000 inhabitants. Meanwhile, the People's

Representative Council, the governing body of the country, consists of the Chairman, Vice-Chairman, and members of the House of Representatives and Senate, the Working Committee of the Republican Provisional Parliament, and the High Advisory Council. This is not yet a popularly elected body. It does in fact represent conditions as they existed in 1946, and, until a general election is held, it is impossible to say whether or not it is representative of the country as a whole. The issue is discussed later when we come to a description of political parties.

Problems of Administration

One of the most difficult problems the Government had to face after the transfer of sovereignty was that of building up a Civil Service. This involved not only the selection and training of young Indonesian men and women, but the integration of two sets of officials and two administrations which had functioned separately and antagonistically for five years; one consisted of Republicans fighting for their survival; the other of Federalists led by van Mook who planned a Federal Indonesia in which the Republic was only one unit. Two armies which had fought each other had to be integrated. Two forces of policemen who had been enemies, one trying to maintain order for the Republic, the other serving Dutch and Federalist rulers. And, apart from this highly charged problem of integration, there was an overall shortage of trained personnel inherent in every field of colonial administration.

Unlike the British Government in its relations with India, the Dutch regarded their 'tropical Holland' as an integral part of the mother country, qualifying gradually for a greater measure of self-government but never independent. The British, although they delayed independence, built up the Indian Civil Service which was ready to take over. In the Dutch case, scarcely any provision was made for Indonesians to be trained in any higher-grade position. Amry Vandenbosch (one of the Secretaries of the United Nations Trusteeship Committee at the San Francisco Conference, now Professor and Head of the Department of Political Science in the University of Kentucky) made this analysis of the distribution of posts in Indonesia in the year 1938, the last normal year of Dutch rule:

	Lower Personnel	Lower Intermediate	Purely Intermediate	Higher Personnel
Europeans	0·6	33·3	57·6	92·2
Indonesians	99·1	64·0	40·0	6·9
Chinese	0·3	2·7	2·3	0·8

'This table', he writes, 'indicates that the lower governmental positions were filled almost exclusively by Indonesians; that the intermediate positions were shared by the Indonesians and the Eurasians, with the lower intermediate positions filled predominantly by Indonesians, and the higher intermediate predominantly by Eurasians; and that the higher personnel was still overwhelmingly Dutch. . . . In the decade from 1928 to 1938 the Indonesians made considerable progress; but the significant fact is that aside from the important but semi-hereditary position of regent they had been entrusted with few highly responsible positions. Of the executive departments, only one had an Indonesian as director, namely the department of education. One large city in Java —Bandung—had an Indonesian mayor. It was not until the early 1930's that an Indonesian was elevated to membership in the Council of the Indies.'[1]

Van Mook himself appreciated the problem.

'. . . it is absolutely certain', he wrote, 'that Dutch policy since 1931 has become stratified in conservatism, which it seemed incapable of altering, even after 1937. It has been the chief malady of this policy that during an entire century it was unable to visualize the inevitable emancipation of the Asiatic colonies and the growth of nationhood in these areas. The thus resulting retardation of political development was not even so much expressed in the existing political institutions themselves but particularly in the insufficient absorption of Indonesians in the upper strata of administrative direction.'[2]

Just before the Japanese invaded Indonesia, the Visman Commission began to study political reforms. The Report,[3] published after Holland was invaded, noted that 'a matter of ever-recurring bitterness was the small number of Indonesians who are considered for the higher (administrative) posts'. 'The Government', one large Indonesian group added, 'should have more confidence in the ability of Indonesian intellectuals'; '78% of the Netherlands East Indies Civil Service consisted of Indonesians but they held only 7% of the positions for which an academic degree was required'.

Such was the background of administration when Japanese troops occupied the country after only a few days of Dutch resistance. The immediate result was that many Indonesians suddenly had to take over administration. The opportunity to govern had unexpectedly been forced upon them. A visit to many Ministries in Djakarta in the spring of 1951 showed, much to my surprise, how fundamentally the Japanese interlude affected the country. Well-qualified Indonesians who, under Dutch rule, were restricted to lower grades, walked overnight into chairs occupied by senior Dutch officials. This happened in the Civil Service, in post services, in railways, in the management of industry—anywhere, indeed, where Dutchmen had reigned supreme. Now that they were pushed off into concentration camps, the Japanese did not have sufficient personnel to handle the machinery of government, of industry, and agriculture. The result was that for the first time a considerable body of administrative officials had to be drawn from Indonesians. This was true throughout Indonesia, but it had the biggest effect in highly developed, over-populated Java.

When British troops arrived in 1945, taking with them the Dutch army, they found Ministries functioning in Djakarta, Indonesians running hospitals and the university, schools and business offices. There was a skeleton of administration; the standards were probably often much lower than the high standards of experienced Dutch civil servants. But efficiency is, in part, a matter of experience. Unfortunately, the interruptions caused by two military actions meant that it was impossible to consolidate administration until August 1950, when the unitary

273

State was formed. Many young men and women left Government posts to join the guerrillas, while others had to devote their time to propaganda at home and abroad. Republican administration had to depend on a small number of officials trained under colonial rule, and a generation of young men and women whose only experience was under Japanese rule. Thus it is a matter for surprise that the Civil Service is running as smoothly as it is, that every Ministry is engaged on two-year plans, five-year plans, ten-year plans which were unknown under Dutch rule. That there is inefficiency is not surprising; there are too many untrained people, two officials doing the work of one, overlapping, red tape, the hesitation of inexperienced officials to take decisions. Above all, there is a wide gap between first-class, often brilliant men at the top, and the next grade; it will take a generation to fill it. But, as a Dutchman said to me: 'This may be true; what is much more important is the fact that Indonesians are anxious to learn as they have never been before.'

Another point which struck me was the danger of too great a concentration of civil servants in Djakarta; Java received an undue proportion of attention in Dutch days, and Indonesians tend to make the same mistake. In Makassar and Menado, in Pontianak and Bandjarmasin, the complaint was often made that too few officials were sent from Java to help train local talent. There is of course another side to this picture; the resentment against Javanese who are not wholly emancipated from the feeling of superiority which comes from an old aristocracy on the one hand or from people who are conscious of their greater experience on the other. These are problems which Indonesians themselves alone can solve; outside assistance from the specialized agencies of the United Nations can make a contribution in the form of personnel, and by providing opportunities for scholarships and experience abroad. Foreign advisers, especially technicians, may temporarily fill some of the gap, but a remark frequently made to me in 1951 was that foreign personnel rarely knew the language; they understood nothing of local customs and background; their superior technical knowledge could not be effectively used unless they had the right psychological approach. In other words, Indonesians are extremely sensitive and they will not welcome United Nations paternalism. Dutch technicians and administrators are in the best position to assist, provided of course that they are free from colonial prejudices. I met some of them—Dutch officials whose loyalty to the Republic was beyond question, men who had accepted Indonesian citizenship and saw their lifework in the country; a Dutchman in East Sumatra developing light industries with pioneering zeal; a Dutch civil servant working as assistant to the Resident in Pontianak; a Dutch economist helping to train students in Makassar; a brilliant Dutch engineer throwing himself into the work of draining the marshes round Bandjarmasin with as much excitement and devotion as his compatriots showed when they drained the Zuyder Zee. To this list we might add Dutch officials who are employed in many Republican Embassies.

The Round Table Conference Agreement committed the Republic to carry over a considerable number of Dutch employees for a period of two years. They belonged to every department, including that of Intelligence. Like many other clauses, this prolonged the ties between two countries which were part of their colonial history. Where there was goodwill, the arrangement was not unhelpful; we have already seen how inadequate were the numbers of experienced Indonesians. But such goodwill did not always exist, and one of the present difficulties, especially in Djakarta, is the bad relations between Dutch and Indonesian officials. A great deal of criticism of administration comes from Dutch sources which can scarcely be called independent or objective. Only a new generation of Dutchmen who were not brought up in a colonial atmosphere is likely to judge Indonesians on their own merits, to take instructions from them as the rulers of their own country.

The special relationships between Holland and Indonesia which were born in history and partly reimposed by the Round Table Conference Agreement, will inevitably mean a larger proportion of Dutch officials than those of any other country. But there are fields of work in social welfare, in education, in financial and commercial administration where the knowledge and experience of other nationals might be invaluable. Foreign staff can supplement Indonesians for some time, but this is not a permanent solution. The field of administration extends over wider and wider areas of the country; the remotest villages of the Outer Islands will no longer be satisfied with less amenities than Java or Sumatra; inter-island trade and transport is already increasing; international relations demand representatives, cultural, diplomatic, commercial. The need for an efficient administration, both at the centre and in the provinces, will become greater. This calls not only for ability and training, but for a sense of service to the country, a disinterestedness which is not undermined by material advantages, and an integrity which will encourage a belief in popular democracy.

NOTES

[1] *The New World of Southeast Asia* (1949), p. 91. Chapter by Amry Vandenbosch on Indonesia.

[2] *Indonesia; Nederland en de Wereld*, pp. 14–15. Dr. van Mook, 1949.

[3] *Verslag van de Commissie tot Bestudeering van Staatsrechtelejke Hervormingen,* September 14th, 1950. Batavia, 1941. *Pacific Affairs*, September, 1943, contains a full summary in English of the Visman Report.

CHAPTER XIII

EDUCATION

I N his Preface to a pamphlet entitled *Mass Education*, the Secretary-General of the Ministry of Information, Roeslan Abdulgani, thus described the objectives of Mass Education:

> 'The Law governing Education and Teaching in the Republik Indonesia (Law No. 4/1950) . . . states that the aim of education and teaching is to produce able and upright men and women and democratic citizens, aware of their responsibility for the security and welfare of society and country.
>
> 'In our mass education we thus aim at changing the very mentality of our people. The mentality of the slave must go; in its stead must come the mentality of the self-respecting citizen, of the moral man, aware of his responsibility towards, and of his place in, the history of his people and his country.'

A revolutionary change towards education is reflected in this statement, a change based on the difference between independence and colonial rule. In the Republic education is necessary for the development of citizenship; it must be universal; the Toradjas in Central Sulawesi and the Kubus in Sumatra, Papuans living in the jungles of West Irian and Dayaks in the smallest riverine villages of Central Kalimantan need more, not less, attention from the Ministries of Education and Information. This outlook on education goes to the very core of independence in every country which has overthrown colonialism. There were, of course, a number of distinguished Dutch writers who were sensitive to the contradictions within colonialism, and to the temporary nature of paternalism. As the colonial power extended its rule and increased its vast commercial concerns,

'modern colonial government and modern colonial exploitation,' Dr. van Mook wrote, 'whatever the humanitarian at home or in the colonies might wish, became ever more intricate and demanded ever higher qualifications of administrative and economic efficiency. The number of civil servants, planters, merchants, bankers, and technicians in the overseas territories grew rapidly. And if some of them could see the independence of colonial people in the dim and distant future, the issue did not present itself as a practical proposition during their tenure of office as long as the claims of modernization continued to outgrow the slow spread of native education and experience.'[1]

The colonial power needed workers; as commerce flourished, so local labour had to be trained to fill the lower posts. The paradox of Dutch education was that it was functional, vocational to fulfil the needs of their development of the country's resources. That education should be vocational is beyond doubt, but true vocational education, which would enable colonial people to run their own countries and develop their own resources, defeats colonialism. Therefore vocational education was aimed, not at training people to become administrators, engineers, agriculturalists, etc., but to become second- or third-grade clerks. The small minority which could afford higher education had to go to a Dutch university, divorced from their own background. Van Mook and others were well aware of this problem; how 'particularly galling', as he wrote, it was for the 'budding nationalist' that

'every white child could get a full primary schooling of seven grades and that for a long time, the text-books, even in the vernacular schools, were written from a typically colonial point of view. The Indonesian student had to reach the University by a long, arduous, and expensive route, and only the incredible sacrifices his parents were willing to make to procure a university degree for him made it possible for him to reach it at all.'[2]

Until the 'twenties, Dutch official policy assumed that Indonesians desiring university education should go to the Netherlands, where they would receive exactly the same training as Dutch students. A change of policy then led to the opening of a Technical School in Bandung and a Law College in Djakarta.

In 1940 a Liberal Arts College was opened in Djakarta, and on the eve of the Japanese invasion the Volksraad had just approved a Bill to provide for a College of Agriculture and to unite the five existing colleges into a single university. University education was of a high standard, but it existed for a minute number of Indonesians.

'In 1938–9', Amry Vandenbosch writes, 'the three professional colleges had 81 graduates; 12 in engineering, 30 in law, and 39 in medicine. Of the 81 graduates, 40 were Indonesians, 21 were Chinese and Arabs, and 20 were Europeans.'[3]

The standards were high, 'too high', he says, 'and have too marked a Dutch orientation'. The proportion of students which failed was very large, especially in Technical Education. Mass Education also produced disappointing results:

'In spite of all the educational efforts since 1900, there are more illiterates in absolute numbers today than there were in 1900. The school-age population has increased more rapidly than the school-going population. According to the 1930 census only 6·3% of the native population was literate.'[4]

This very revealing calculation follows:

'The Dutch-Native Education Commission estimates that at the rate of progress being made in 1928 it would require 167 years to wipe out illiteracy. It has been estimated that it would take an expenditure of a billion florins for a quarter of a century to overcome illiteracy. In view of the conclusion of the Hartog commission that no child who has not completed a course of four years will become permanently literate, the fight against illiteracy becomes almost hopeless.'[5]

He was right; the fight against illiteracy is almost hopeless for paternal rulers. It can only succeed if it reflects a desire of the masses and a nation-wide sustained drive on the part of the administration. Whatever proposals Dutch educationalists might make, however much money Dutch Treasury officials might spend, they could not escape the dilemma of colonial education. As the same writer says of a Dutch Native Education Commission in 1927:

'The nationalists are naturally inclined to attack the educational system from both sides. On the one hand they complain that the educational system is too Western and has for its object the denationalization of the Indonesians; on the other hand, whenever a limitation of Western education is proposed the nationalists accuse the Government of wishing to deprive them of just that type of schooling which will most rapidly prepare them for self-government.'[6]

Dutch educationalists could not break the vicious circle. Colonial rule itself was based on an inequality of two nations, on the principle of Western superiority, on white management and coloured worker, on a supply of cheap labour. Mass education led to demands for better conditions, and ultimately for self-government. A temporary equilibrium could be maintained as long as higher education was practically confined to the local ruling aristocracy, since their interests, like those of the Dutch, were served by maintaining the *status quo*. However high the standards of Dutch education in Indonesia it inevitably failed in three respects. It was based on an alien culture and paid little attention to local culture. This criticism was confirmed by a group of American educationalists who visited Java and Bali in 1933 to make a survey of education at the invitation of the Netherlands East Indies Government on behalf of the Institute of Pacific Relations.

'Little', they wrote, 'that we have to suggest concerns improvement in educational methods judged by European standards. Our criticisms are against a system, however competent, which tends to disinherit a people from its own traditions and ways of life, which assumes that "progress" means Western civilization, which ignores all the beauty and expression and communal assets of the East.'

They regretted that people

'who are struggling so hard for education in a European tongue should be learning a language of so little world scope as Dutch. . . . If the people of the Indies were acquiring the use of English or French or German, they would be really entering the modern world with free access to almost the whole of literature and learning.'[7]

The second failure lay in the fact that as independence was never assumed by Dutch administrators, Indonesians were not trained to rule themselves. The results we have already seen in the chapter on administration. Dutchmen, like any other colonial rulers, thought in terms of making Indonesians into good brown Dutchmen, people able to fulfil the lower ranks of employment, industrial, agricultural, and professional. 'The most important influence the Dutch have had', a young teacher said to me one day, 'is to make us think like Dutchmen.' Thirdly, it did not go hand in hand with any serious effort to raise productivity, to develop a society which was 90% agricultural in line with twentieth-century standards, to provide for the methods of hygiene which bore some resemblance to the hygiene in Dutch villages, to encourage rural development. In the late 'thirties a liberal-minded Director of the Department of Education in the Indies, A. de Kat Angelino, wrote a long dissertation on the role of education in the desas. He did not regret that there was sometimes 'insufficient money to finance beautiful plans'; he wanted 'equilibrium between the producing capacity and the consumption of every organism, of the social organism as of others'. The well-equipped school and the highly developed teacher 'will not be a blessing for the Eastern village so long as the village itself has not reached the degree of development which enables it to absorb the pupils into its own life, socially, economically, intellectually, and politically'.[8] He and his successor—one of the few Indonesians to be given the position of Director—were responsible for increasing the number of children in desa schools from 700,000 in 1930 to 2,000,000 in 1940. But this achievement was unrelated to social and economic development; the desa in 1940 had changed very slightly from the desa in 1900. The problem was deeper than one of numbers, or of efficiency; it was primarily—to quote a Dutch sociologist— 'a question of the channels into which the process of social development is guided'.[9]

It was no accident that one of the first fields of work undertaken by the Nationalist Movement was in that of education. A Javanese aristocrat, R. M. Soewardi Suryaningrat, who came to be known as Ki Hadjar Dewantoro ('the teacher of all the gods', if literally translated), has already been mentioned in the chapter on nationalism. His study of Dutch educational methods convinced him that the type of education provided by Holland did not assume Javanese culture and therefore could not help in its development. He believed that the Western world was too materialistic, too intellectual. 'No imitation of the Western world, but construction from the bottom up of a civilization initially Javanese, later Indonesian. Everybody who learns a foreign language, gains access to a new world', he wrote, but the new world must be assimilated by and not superimposed on Javanese culture. His emphasis was placed on music and dancing, music being that of the gamelan, and dancing the traditional steps of Javanese dance. His teachers were people with a 'mission' in life; they were often paid little more than a subsistence salary, far less than the Dutch paid either in Government or in Mission schools. The Dutch did not oppose these schools; they tried the subtler method of offering subsidies. To take them would have undermined the basis of the Taman Siswa idea. 'The Indies', Dewantoro said, 'cannot expect to obtain satisfactory results from a system of education for which they cannot pay themselves.' He insisted on independence, and made the schools a 'cause' rather than a profession. By 1940, the idealistic work of Dewantoro and his associates had provided Indonesia with over 200 Taman Siswa schools where young people lived in communities reminiscent of Santineketan. From an academic point of view the standard was not always as high as that of Government schools, but it was self-expression that was the criterion, not technical distinction. It would be difficult to estimate the influence of Taman Siswa education on the present generation of young Javanese. They discovered not only the souls of their ancestors but an expression of themselves, of their own culture; they were inspired to work for independence.

When independence was finally won, the question arose as to how the Taman Siswa scheme of education could fit into the general pattern. There were those in educational circles who felt that their object was now achieved; they were part of the nationalist struggle, when self-expression was frustrated, and Dutch rather than indigenous culture formed the pattern of education. Now times had changed; education must fit into the Republican pattern, methods of teaching, conditions of training and curricula must all come under the same organizational umbrella. But this view did not prevail; there was, in the Ministry's view, room for variety, and scope for those who felt the particular appeal of Taman Siswa idealism. The result is that the Taman Siswa schools are the largest private educational institution in the Republic, and in the year 1951–2 Government subsidies were granted to 53 of their elementary schools, 64 lower secondary schools, 8 higher secondary schools, and 1 teachers' college. A leader of Taman Siswa, Mohammad Said, in a broadcast interview had this to say:

'Before we achieved independence Taman Siswa was mainly meant for the struggle for freedom. Now its efforts are directed towards giving that freedom content. That freedom must be filled with the consciousness of self-help, self-determination, self-confidence, and self-reliance so that Indonesia may be independent culturally and spiritually as well as politically. These are the alpha and omega of the Taman Siswa.'[10]

Whilst the Taman Siswa schools had a measure of continuity, the Republic was faced with many difficulties in the first four years following the declaration of independence. Many schools were closed down or burnt as the result of war, and the problem of planning educational schemes either at the centre or in districts temporarily under Dutch administration seemed insoluble. It was not until 1950 that the Republican Ministry of Education settled down to its task. It was at once overwhelmed by the demand for education. Gone were the days when an Indonesian could write:

'One of the hardest jobs of the East Indies Government has been to persuade the natives that learning was desirable. Mild coercion frequently had to be employed to inveigle parents into sending their youngsters to school.'

The Republican Ministry had no need to convince people of the need for education; their problem was how to find buildings, paper and pencils, books and blackboards, how to find enough teachers to make skeleton staffs. With a literacy rate of about 10%, among 78 million people, the emphasis on numbers is inescapable. Therein lies a certain danger. The content of education is quite as important as the number of school buildings, which is increasing at a tremendous rate. Enthusiasm is an impressive quality, but it must not be allowed to obscure issues common to all independent countries: What form of education will help the rice-cultivator to become a better rice-cultivator and a more fully developed member of his own society? Of what advantage is education to him if it proves a disruptive force which merely encourages a trek to the nearest town? When children leave school, what will they read? What will they hear on village wireless sets, and see on travelling cinemas?

The Republic has to deal with two quite separate problems of education for some years; the education of youth based on a ten-year plan by which compulsory education is envisaged by 1960, and mass education among adults, at least 80% of whom are illiterate. The second is the reponsibility of a Department of Mass Education in the Ministry of Education and Culture. In addition, the Ministry is concerned with such special schools as those dealing with different branches of science, and with rehabilitation schemes for young men who have not yet readjusted themselves to society after the experience of guerrilla life.

Every school building I visited in 1951 was vastly overcrowded; was it possible that less than half of the 12 million children between the ages of six and thirteen were still unable to go to school? There are far too few buildings, and a great shortage of teachers and practically no equipment. Yet figures for 1951 show how much has already been achieved in increasing the number of children at school. Comparative figures for 1944, when the Japanese still occupied the country, and for 1941 when the country was still under Dutch rule, are given as basis for comparison.

Although these statistics show a remarkable increase in the number of schools and pupils, there is still a tremendous shortage of buildings and staff. How inadequate schools are in every part of the country is plain to the visitor, inadequate at every stage of education. A district in North Sumatra is typical;

11,000 children were ready to attend a secondary school, and accommodation existed for only 2,000. The teachers, also far too few, do double shifts. In the morning it is no unusual sight to see a thousand boys and girls pouring out of scantily built, poorly equipped classrooms after their lessons. Temperature is already in the eighties and the sun still climbing. For the teacher

Type of School	Dutch Period (1941)		Japanese Period (1944)		1951[11]	
	Schools	Pupils	Schools	Pupils	Schools	Pupils
Elementary General	13,595	1,879,270	15,069	2,523,410	26,670	4,977,304
Secondary	94	19,338	55	21,433	889	236,927
Vocational	276	25,612	122	22,932	957	102,980

there is no afternoon siesta. Another thousand boys and girls crowd into the same classrooms and the teachers are there to greet them. They have a blackboard, sometimes an ancient map, and a small pile of reading books shared between three and four children squashed together in desks scarcely comfortable for two. Books are so scarce that in many classrooms I visited pages had been duplicated on sheets of thin foolscap paper. In some of the secondary schools I was often surprised to see boys in their late teens working with others five or more years younger. At first I assumed that either they were backward or that space forced this unfortunate grouping of such widely different age levels. The reason given to me was unexpected; they were boys whose education had been interrupted by Dutch military action in 1948. For months they lived as guerrillas with the result that when at last they returned to school, sometimes after a good deal of pressure on the part of local authorities, they were at least two years behind.

After the six years which in theory at any rate are given for elementary education, children can attend the S.M.P. (Sekolah Menengah Pertama, or Junior Colleges). Early in 1955 only 275 of them exist throughout the country and for this reason pupils are not admitted until they have passed a competitive examination. This Junior College course, and the S.M.A. (Sekolah Menengah Atas, or Senior College) last three years. In the Senior College pupils begin to specialize. Parallel with the S.M.A. colleges, there are Vocational Schools for the twelve to eighteen year group. These are the responsibility of the appropriate Ministry; the Ministry of Agriculture, for example, runs schools for Fishery (Tegal in Central Java), for Forestry (Bogor), Cattle-breeding (Malang), for Agriculture (Bukit Tinggi), (Sumatra) and Makassar (Sulawesi)). The Ministry of Defence has a Technical Aircraft School, and the Ministry of Health a Pharmacy School. Domestic Science schools for girls reflect the influence which independence has exerted among women. In the past a girl, on leaving school, if she had parents progressive enough to allow her this degree of freedom, would live a secluded life until her fate was settled in marriage—often at fourteen. Many girls coming from the same social groups today become teachers. In a training college in Djakarta for training young women to become vocational teachers in domestic science schools, there are 700 students, coming from all parts of the Republic. Some of them have come from areas with a strong adat (customary law) which they have had to break. They are in fact the first generation of emancipated young women.

At a higher level, where specialized courses are provided which are not catered for in the universities, there are Academies; the Police Academy in Sukabumi, Physical Training Academy in Bandung, Academies for Foreign Affairs, for Trade (Djakarta) and Academies for Plastic Arts and for Political Science (Djogjakarta). All these Academies were faced with similar problems, most important of which was the shortage of teaching staff. For, it must be remembered that in a country of nearly 80 million people, there were less than 1,000 who had received university education. They were men and women whose families, in Dutch times, could afford a tuition fee of 300 guilders a year (the average yearly income of the pre-war Indonesian family was approximately 100 guilders). They were men and women whose official language was Dutch, and who were now called on to teach in Bahasa Indonesia. Enthusiasm was a powerful incentive and many professors lectured at several faculties and academies as much as twenty hours a week and in three or four different subjects. A few examples will illustrate this point. Sixty-year-old Professor Purbatjaraka, then Professor of Sanskrit and Old Javanese at the Faculty of Arts, taught in the University of Indonesia as a full Professor, gave courses in the Moslem University, in an upper-form secondary school, and gave one course for teachers in Djogjakarta and another in Surakarta. Professor Djokosutono, then Dean of the Faculty of Law in Djogjakarta, lectured in his own faculty, at the Police Academy, and in the Academy of Political Science in four or five different subjects. Professor Pryono, then Dean of the Faculty of Arts in Djogjakarta, was also director of a girls' school for home economics, director of a school for secondary teachers, and leader of a course for high school teachers. And he lectured at the Police Academy in four, sometimes five, subjects. This problem of teaching staff is one which the universities are trying to solve.

The Republic has made great strides in university education. The Dutch were extremely slow in providing education of university rank, holding the view that Indonesians should go to Holland. Thus it was only in the last year of their rule—1940—that the Volksraad approved a Bill which would have united the five existing colleges into a single university. At that time there were Faculties of Law, of Medicine, of Literature in Djakarta; of Agriculture in Bogor, of Dental Surgery in Surabaya, and a Technical College in Bandung. Education was mainly in Dutch and the curricula similar to those in Dutch universities in Holland. In the early days of Japanese occupation all the existing colleges were closed down. Later those which had potential value in the war effort were reopened; the colleges of medicine in Djakarta and Surabaya (1943) and the Technical College in Bandung (1944). The Japanese opened several new colleges, a Veterinary College in Bogor and Pharmaceutical Colleges. When power was transferred to the Republic they built on these existing institutions, making the University of Indonesia in Djakarta the central body to which outside Faculties were attached. The President of the University of

287

Indonesia, Professor R. Supomo (Ambassador to the Court of St. James since June 1954), described some of his problems in his address on the occasion of the *Dies Natalis* in February 1953, and they are by no means solved today. There was, for example, the difficulty of increasing the number of Indonesians on the teaching staff. Of 107 professors, only 26 were Indonesians; 81 were foreigners, mainly Dutch. One way of training the future Indonesian staff, he suggested, was to appoint suitable students who had passed their candidates' examinations as student-assistants in their various fields of specialized work. While valuing the work of Dutch and other foreign teachers, he said that 'the Indonesianizing of the University was necessary in the interests of the country'. No one is likely to dispute that remark, but it is very easy to imagine the psychological as well as the educational problems that are involved.

Second in importance to the University of Indonesia in Djakarta, and first in the affection of the people, comes the Gadjah Mada University. It has a special interest which is nationalistic rather than academic. In January 1946, when Dutch troops were still fighting to regain control of the country, a group of prominent university men met in Djogjakarta and decided to set up a Committee for Higher Education. This led to the founding of the Gadjah Mada University three months later. The Sultan of Djogjakarta offered part of his Kraton as a university building. This was the Republic's first university on a national basis. From the beginning, all lessons were given in Indonesian. Students came from every part of the Republic to a university which had no ties with the past, no taint of colonial rule. In 1951 I was interested to find that more than 3,000 students crowded every part of the university; they were massed in hundreds under the elaborate Napoleonic chandeliers which in pre-Republican days lit up the dancers and the grand gentlemen of the Sultan's Kraton. The walls were still decorated in jade green and gold. Outside in the mango and pawpaw trees some of the students made overflow accommodation and sat like boys perched in trees sneaking a free view of a football match. Lecturers needed two loud-speakers for their lessons. Faculties of Law, of Literature, of Agriculture, of Medical

Science, of Technical Science as well as Teachers' College were all housed in this same compound. The Bacteriological Department met in one of the outhouses of the Kraton; its clinical chemistry room was formerly the old main gate to the Sultan's residence. The Pendopo, which was originally used for the Sultan's Council of State, was the general lecture hall. In an old ceremonial room, students studied physiology and optics; villagers from a small town nearby called Klaten, carried their equipment on shoulder poles and yokes when the department was forced to evacuate at the time of the second Dutch military action in 1948. When the Dutch marched into Klaten, students and employees and staff and villagers became smugglers and trekked along the road to Djogjakarta carrying with them all kinds of instruments disguised in packages. They travelled on foot, on bicycles, and on ox-carts. To complete the picture: the main women's ward in the hospital attached to the Medical Faculty was the Sultan's former living-room, whilst the nurses' office was formerly a ceremonial room dedicated to his ancestors. When a newly married couple belonging to the royal house first arrived, they were allowed to sit there on their wedding day, but it was generally used only by the Sultan when he wished to pay homage to his ancestors.

This hospital, and the polyclinic housed in what was formerly the carriage shed, with a neighbouring drug store which was store-room for a gamelan orchestra, were all free. In a city which has a population of over one million people of whom many are extremely poor, the clinic treated about 4,000 patients a month.

By the end of 1951 this problem of accommodation was taken very seriously by the authorities. A large area of about 100 hectares was selected on the outskirts of the city, and here a new modern building was planned. President Sukarno laid the foundation-stone on December 19th, 1951, of a university which will provide room for 10,000 students when it is completed in ten years' time. Meanwhile in 1955 there are 4,500 students in six Faculties. They take a special pride in being a national university and have so far fiercely resisted suggestions made in Djakarta that they should be united with the University of Indonesia.

From Gadjah Mada students return to their homes in every part of the Republic equipped to take their share in building the nation. Their academic standards inevitably suffer through shortage of equipment and overcrowding; nearly a million people live in this city which housed less than a quarter that number before the war. But so much history was made here that the town has a significance which will provide a magnet for students for years to come. Here was the first capital of the Republic where Parliament met and all kinds of political and commercial organizations made their headquarters; here, the United Nations Committee frequently came during the period following the Renville Agreement; here President Sukarno opened the first anti-illiteracy campaign and here he was sworn in as the first President of the Republic of the United States of Indonesia; here the people felt most the shortages of food and textiles which resulted from the blockade; here the Voice of Free Indonesia broadcast to the world, and every student in the Gadjah Mada University, man and woman, left their lecture rooms in December 1948 when Dutch planes bombed the city. Djogjakarta is indeed the political heart and the cultural centre of the Republic.

In June 1954 a University Act was passed which led to the foundation of four new universities. They were all named after national heroes: Purnawarman (in Bandung); Airlangga (in Malang); Adityavaram (in the Menangkabau district of Sumatra); and Hasanuddin (in Makassar). The present Minister of Education, Mohammed Yamin, combines drive and enterprise with a profound knowledge of Indonesian culture and history. The curricula of these new Universities provides for a training based on Indonesian rather than on Western traditions.

Apart from schools and colleges and universities which come under the Ministry of Education and Culture, or other Ministries in the case of vocational schools, there is a wide variety of education which is based on local initiative. First of all there is the natural pride in having local institutions where students may obtain higher education; secondly, as literacy increases the demand for education far exceeds the facilities which the Government has been able to provide. It therefore very wisely encourages private initiative with the result that a number of private institutions of higher education have grown up in islands other than Java; in Java itself the Government has concentrated too much of its attention. There is, for example, the Pantjasila University in Padang which specializes in Law. In North Sumatra a new university deals with Medicine and the Islamic University of Indonesia in Medan is an Islamic Theological Institution. These are not recognized as universities which can confer degrees, although this may develop in the future. But the Government provides facilities to obtain books and equipment and in some cases financial assistance is given to those institutions which are prepared to work within the framework of the official education programme.

Quite apart from official or officially blessed education, local people who themselves have had training are taking the initiative in training others. The visitor who travels round the country often stumbles on interesting examples. There was, for instance, the Bogor district where ex-guerrillas had built simple schools of bamboo in a great many villages where accommodation existed only for children. Most of these young men were boys in 1948 when they left their homes to join guerrilla groups in the mountains which stretch across the countryside like a theatre backcloth. Their leader, a schoolteacher, lived with his wife and family, moving from place to place evading the Dutch troops. In 1951 he was Bupati, an official post which is the equivalent of a Mayor over a large area. The influence of such men is tremendously valuable, deepening stability as well as helping to reduce illiteracy. A quite special contribution comes from the women. In their organizations which are widely distributed in Sumatra, Java, Sulawesi, and Kalimantan, and now extending over the whole of the country, women, generally from middle-class and aristocratic circles, make it their duty to have classes in their homes. I visited several domestic centres run by women's organizations where girls were given training in cookery and hygiene and elementary first aid; in some places, they had borrowed a building to run classes for small children not catered for by official schemes; they run Kartini schools for girls, named after the pioneer of women's education. Their work is recognized by officials, but a great deal of it is unobtrusive, outside, though supplementing, the more publicized blueprints or statistics.

Any survey of the campaign against illiteracy is inevitably more difficult to make. This work is under the direction of the Department of Mass Education, attached to the Ministry of Education and Culture. It calls for particular gifts of patience, imagination, and a sympathetic understanding of the undeveloped adult mind. Visitors to this Department in Djakarta, experts in this field of education, representatives of U.N.E.S.C.O., have all paid the highest tribute to the work carried out by a very small staff in insignificant offices. Publications for adults, graded carefully, with good follow-up books, all of them related to everyday life, planting bananas, separating rice seedlings, drying coconuts, and rubber-tapping, lessons in health and cooking, showed that relationship of literacy to life which must convince the adult that the struggle to learn is worth while. Coloured charts and diagrams and maps all seemed to me to provide a stimulus to illiterates who were intelligent but untrained, an encouragement to them to improve their own lot in their own villages.

The system of combating adult illiteracy is in four stages: (1) spell-period; (2) local post-literacy; (3) general post-literacy, combined with general courses and newspapers; and (4) the connection with various so-called prosperity services, such as physical culture groups, youth organizations, and boy scouts. The method of work has been carefully planned at the centre. An official instructor makes the first contact in an area with a film-unit. He shows a film describing the fight against illiteracy and stimulates not only curiosity but the desire to read and write. Simple posters are then put up, pictorial and related to the lives of the people, to rice cultivation and animal husbandry and personal hygiene. A few local people then form the nucleus of a committee of men and women who know the regional language, local conditions, and who inspire confidence. Literacy courses usually take at least six months. They have to be adjusted to a variety of local conditions; the busiest periods of rice-planting and harvesting must be avoided; special arrangements must be made for those who work in plantations. Then comes the problem of feeding the 'neo-literate', as he or she is called, with reading material. The Department issues four magazines in four provinces with a circulation of 15,000–30,000 copies a month and a news-magazine with a circulation of 250,000 copies. Last year a new privately owned magazine dealing with reconstruction affairs, the *Harapan* (*Hope*), was circulated among 50,000 teachers to give them additional information for their work against illiteracy.

People who are able to read and write are encouraged to attend Adult Community Courses which give them training connected with their own daily occupations. If they are literate, then they must apply their knowledge to raise better cattle and poultry and to prevent the spread of infectious diseases among their buffaloes or their fowls or in their rice sawahs. These Adult Community Courses also encourage the formation of small producers' and consumers' co-operatives and in time they will have an appreciable effect on the economic life of the countryside.

The Mass Education Department has had the closest co-operation with U.N.E.S.C.O. Delegates have attended Seminars and U.N.E.S.C.O. officials have frequently visited Indonesia. The ten-year programme is going ahead; the official figures of literacy are now: Java, 54·3%; Sumatra, 55%; Kalimantan, 33·3%; Sulawesi, 54·5%; Lesser Sundas, 55·5%; Moluccas, 20%.[12]

I was personally interested in the approach of Indonesian educationalists to the problem of their less developed countrymen in remote interior villages, isolated from the main stream of Indonesian life. I had an opportunity of discussing this subject with a young official of the Mass Education Department of the Ministry of Education. We were travelling hour after hour over what seemed to be the densest of dark green jungle in Sumatra. Yet somewhere in these forests, he told me, two young teachers from his Department wandered from clearing to clearing, returning to Djakarta every few months to make reports and to collect supplies of salt and textiles. They were working amongst the Kubu, a still largely tribal people living in South Sumatra. These men and women, of whom there are about 5,000, live nomadic lives, building simple houses of logs of wood stuck into the ground and tied round with rattan. They live mainly on fruit and small animals which they trap with spears made of bamboo or wood. When they make small clearings round their tree-log homes, they usually plant rice or tapioca, and then, having harvested it, they pass on to make another home. The first problem, the Mass Education official pointed out, was how to make contact with people who are naturally suspicious of the unknown. The most successful means of contact discovered by these two teachers was to leave salt and textiles against the trees on the edge of clearings. When they returned they found that the Kubu had taken them and put food in their place by way of exchange. Gradually the Kubu lost their fears of outsiders and the teachers were able to establish classes amongst small groups of them. 'When they came back to the Department to report to us,' the Mass Education official said—he was a Batak from Central Sumatra—'these teachers gave us many useful suggestions for our work. They never asked for big salaries or an increase of wages; they always wanted more salt and more textiles since these were the goods which were of interest to the Kubu. Indeed, they were an introduction to the Kubu.'

Gradually as the Kubu lose their initial fear—of other Kubu as well as of the outsider—they develop a village organization and again the teachers find salt and textiles are in demand.

The dialect of the Kubu is based on the Malay language of East Sumatra and is therefore not so very different from Bahasa Indonesia which has the same origin. The two teachers discovered on several occasions that the word 'Merdeka', meaning freedom, and the slogan of the revolution, was known by the Kubu. They had heard it from guerrillas who had escaped from the Japanese during the war, or from the Dutch during the first or second military action in 1947 or 1948. The guerrillas were probably the first contact the Kubu had made with Indonesians outside their own tribe.

As we flew, mile after mile, crossing the Equator at one point, this Indonesian discussed the special problems of education amongst these earliest peoples of his country. Some of them—the Papuans in West Irian, for example—are still in the Stone

Age period. 'We want to lead them out of the Stone Age,' he said. 'Their lives are lives of fear. Devils are everywhere, in trees, in stone and wood and in rivers, in the clouds and under the earth. Their lives are one long struggle to appease these spirits. If we help them in the right way, if we can win their confidence. education will end those fears. This I am afraid applies mainly to the children. Adults, and certainly men and women over forty, have lived too long with these fears to overcome them.'

One day in West Kalimantan, I met several young Dayak teachers, one of them the leader of the Dayak national movement which he represented in Parliament. The Dayaks—they number just under half a million—are the original inhabitants of Borneo. As wave followed wave of immigrants, Chinese as well as European, the Dayaks were pushed further and further back into the interior where they now live in the upper reaches of the Kapuas River. Since the building of schools has less news value than the hunting of heads (the last of these ritualistic adventures was fifteen years ago), the Dayaks have not received any honourable mention. They are an almost entirely agricultural people; they are divided into forty-nine different tribes with different dialects and customs. Half of them still live in 'long houses'—a habit which was formed in earlier days of tribal warfare. But in the Indonesian Republic many changes are taking place. The Dayak national movement, formed three years ago with Government assistance, has now 200,000 members with membership cards and subscriptions, one rupiah a year for a man and half a rupiah for a woman. The money is spent on education; more than fifty schools have been opened under the Republic, and because trained people are so few, all but nineteen of them are run mainly by Catholic teachers. Nineteen are in the remotest parts of Dayak territory and provide education for the first time. Then the movement is encouraging the growth of co-operatives, a common language, and individual homes to take the place of the long houses.

I discovered this same emphasis on education among the Toradjas, the original inhabitants of Central Sulawesi. They too are animistic, and a great deal has been written about their religious ceremonies—and especially about their custom of burying the dead in the face of cliffs with models which hold the spirits at the entrance. But there is a new outlook now, especially amongst the younger generation. It was expressed in 1951 in the collection of enough money to send 500 students down to the nearest Middle School—300 miles away in Makassar. I met a number of them in Makassar, young men and women of about sixteen, excitedly discussing the schools they would help to build in their own villages. 'And it won't be long', one of the girls said to me, 'before we have our own Middle School.'

I asked a Dutch lecturer one day whether he thought the Republic could carry out its ambitious schemes in education. He answered, 'I don't know, but of one thing I am sure, there was never a time when so many people wanted to learn.' It was this passion for education which remains my most vivid memory of the country.

NOTES

[1] *The States of Democracy in South-east Asia*, by H. I. van Mook, p. 69.
[2] Ibid.
[3] *The Dutch East Indies*, by Amry Vandenbosch, pp. 215–16.
[4] Ibid.
[5] Ibid.
[6] Ibid.
[7] *Island India goes to School*, by E. R. Embree, Margaret Simon, and W. Bryant Mumford, p. 72.
[8] *Colonial Policy*, by A. de Kat Angelino, pp. 217–18, 1931.
[9] *Effects of Western Civilisation on Indonesian Society*, by Professor W. F. Wertheim, 1950.
[10] *Indonesian Affairs*, Vol. II, No. 5/6, Oct./Nov./Dec. 1952, p. 57. Issued by the Ministry of Information.
[11] *Indonesian Review*, Oct./Dec. 1951. 'Development of National Education in Indonesia,' p. 393.
[12] *Indonesian Affairs*, Vol. III, No. 4/5, April/May 1953. Issued by the Ministry of Information.

CULTURAL TRENDS IN THE REPUBLIC

A Common Language

IN a country which has 200 provincial languages, and peoples of widely different stages of cultural expression, a common language is essential. Most of the existing languages are related to one another, but differences in form and structure mean that the Sundanese, for example, cannot understand Javanese, or the Javanese understand Madurese, although they all live in Java. Some languages, like the Bobongkos vernacular in Sulawesi, are spoken by only a very small group; Javanese is the language of 30 millions. In the local schools provincial languages will continue to be taught but Bahasa Indonesia is now compulsory for them all.

The question arose as to what was the most suitable common language. In Dutch times, Javanese might have satisfied many Dutchmen. It was the language of more than half the people, and many Dutchmen spoke it fluently. But they still addressed the Javanese in Dutch because the Javanese language is based on class distinctions; one language in which to address the Sultan, another for friends and relations, and a third for those who were socially inferior. So the Dutch liked Javanese to speak in High Javanese, but they themselves overcame the problem of selecting the right language by speaking in Dutch. There were Dutchmen who thought that Dutch might become a common language. Thus, G. J. Nieuwenhuis, a much respected educationalist, once remarked:

'If but one million Indonesians were familiar with Dutch, then Dutch books and other Dutch products would be more eagerly sought after and highly prized in the colony.'[1]

Dutch was clearly not a probable choice as a *lingua franca*. Today it is gradually disappearing. English is now the first foreign language and Bahasa Indonesia the common language.

Since the sixteenth century the Malay language has been used in the Indonesian archipelago, mainly along the coastal area where trading communities were concentrated. When Dutch traders came first they too used Malay. Many new words were added to the language as trading contacts increased—Chinese, Hindu, Arabic, Portuguese, English, and Dutch. This is the reason why there are differences between Bahasa Indonesia based on Malay, and Malay as spoken in the Malayan peninsula. Towards the end of the Dutch regime, Malay was already taught as from the fourth form of primary schools; up to that point children knew their regional language and had also begun to learn Dutch. It was necessary for all administrative posts and in all commercial relations. For the small number of children who went to secondary schools, English was a compulsory foreign language. But to know English a child had to know Dutch intimately since all translations were from Dutch to English, and even English classics were read mainly in a Dutch translation.

With the development of nationalism, the use of Malay became more and more a matter of loyalty, and political parties began to use it for their propaganda. In 1918, the Government sponsored a publishing house which printed a few books in classical Malay as a concession to nationalist feeling. This Government publishing house, called the Balai Pustaka, was the long-delayed outcome of a Commission set up in 1908 to provide guidance in suitable reading matter in the Malay language. It started work by publishing the old 'hikayats', stories of Javanese heroes. Between 1918 and 1941, the Balai Pustaka issued about 2,000 books on old and new Malayan and Javanese literature. These were sold at a very low price, and these 300,000 copies a year did a great deal to spread Malay as a language. The Balai Pustaka had several periodicals and, perhaps most important of all, set up small public libraries in many parts of the country. It was a very important factor in spreading an interest in the Indonesian language.

In 1924 a member of the Volksraad, Djajadiningrat, made nationalist propaganda by speaking in Malay in an assembly where only the Dutch language was used. He was widely criticized and the Dutch Press campaigned against such outrageous behaviour. The All-Indonesia Youth Organization then passed a resolution in 1930 pledging support for the use of Malay, and, finally, in 1938 at a congress in Solo, it was launched as a national language by the *Pudjangga Baru* (*The New Poet*), a literary monthly started by young nationalist writers of whom the most important were Takdir Alisjahbana and the brothers Pane.

When the Japanese occupied Indonesia, they had the effect of giving Indonesians their first opportunity to use Bahasa Indonesia as the language of administration. It was a virtue born of necessity; the Japanese banned Dutch and English and then made their own language compulsory in the schools. It was never popular, if only for the reason that their script was difficult and they had far too few people who could be spared to teach it. The result was that teachers and Government officials and traders were suddenly faced with the need to learn the Indonesian language. It was now used in all official pronouncements, in official correspondence, and in all educational institutions. 'Moreover,' as Takdir Alisjahbana points out,

'because the Japanese were determined to enlist the energies of the entire Indonesian population in the war effort, they penetrated into villages in the remotest backwaters of the islands, using the Indonesian language as they went. Thus the language flourished, and imbued the people with a feeling new to most of them. As more and more of them learned to speak it freely, they became aware of a common bond. The Indonesian language became a symbol of national unity in opposition to the efforts of the Japanese ultimately to implant their own language and culture. By the time, therefore, of the Japanese surrender, the position of the Indonesian language had improved enormously both in strength and in prestige vis-a-vis not only Dutch but also the various regional languages of the archipelago, which had had no opportunity to develop during the occupation.'[2]

When the Republic was formed in August 1945, Bahasa Indonesia was at once proclaimed as the official language; this was repeated in the Inter-Indonesian Conference in July 1949; in the Round Table Conference Agreement, Article 27 states that all official documents 'shall be in the Netherlands and Indonesian languages' whilst Article 36 of the Constitution says that the language of the Republic shall be Bahasa Indonesia.

Today Bahasa Indonesia is used in all Government publications, in newspapers, in cinemas, and it is used exclusively in every school after the first three years of primary education during which period a local vernacular is taught. Already many of the world's classics are translated into Bahasa Indonesia; on any bookstall you can buy translations of such varied classics as *Hamlet, Don Quixote, Of Mice and Men*. The language itself is constantly enriched, by using abstract ideas, subtleties of expression, and technical terms. Young Indonesian writers, very conscious of its limitations, started a 'language committee' in 1942 to compose technical and other terms in Bahasa Indonesia; they were issued four years later in the form of a technical dictionary and published by Takdir Alisjahbana. The Committee still meets to discuss the broadening of the language to meet modern conditions and to express modern ideas. With Bahasa Indonesia compulsory in the schools and with the spread of public libraries which the Mass Education Department of the Ministry of Education and Culture is now sponsoring, the language will be firmly established within a generation.

The Development of Indonesian Literature

Indonesian literature is new both in its form and in its content as well as in its language. During the centuries between the Hindu-Javanese period of Madjapahit and the explosion of nationalism in the first half of the present century, literature was almost static and, with the exception of Java and Sumatra, it was mainly confined to folk-lore.

In Java, the Pandji stories were the best known literature and they are still popular today and feature in dances and drama. They are narratives of events, more or less in chronological sequence, with no central plot. They were originally meant for recitation and, as one Indonesian—T.P.C. Sutopo—describes them, 'they bring the audience "into a dream-world of heroes who were half-gods, of beautiful princesses, of gallant princes, of wars in which magic weapons were the rule".' They usually start with the birth of the ancestor of some known or mythical hero and after describing the adventures of a long line of descendants, bring hero and heroine together in a happy ending.

There were many popular stories bound up with Hindu traditions and with the lives of local heroes. Poetry was largely restricted to the Malayan quatrain known as the 'pantun', consisting of four lines, usually romantic, and reminiscent of early English ballads. Many of them, again like English ballads, were handed down from generation to generation. The first and third lines always rhyme, and the second and fourth. The first two lines try to create a frame of mind in the reader. Subjects from nature are usually chosen because they will produce harmony with the thought conveyed in the last two lines.

The following are three examples of pantuns:

> 'Many people wear bracelets,
> I'm wearing one round my ankle.
> Many people forbid "not to do"
> I'm the one who follows my heart.'

> 'A diamond fell on the grass
> lies on the grass sparkling
> Love is like dew on top of grass
> So . . . the sun shines . . . so it disappears.'

> 'When flood time comes, the sea covers the oysters
> After this happens, the ebb tide comes.
> If you follow your heart in excitement
> Then fear will banish and courage rises above.'

In Java, Sumatra, and Bali, and in parts of the other main islands, the most popular form of poetry was the epic. Subjects were usually taken from the *Ramayana* and the *Mahabharata* or they revolved round local heroes. Little of this literature is as yet known to the West, or, for that matter, outside the island to which it belongs. Sir Thomas Raffles translated the 'Brata Yudha' 'or Holy War, or rather the war of woe' from the Kawi or classical language of Java. Snouck Hurgronje translated epic poems of Atjeh. It remains to be seen whether young Indonesian writers will rediscover their earlier literature and make it known to the outside world.

Coming to more modern times, there were two main factors which combined to stimulate the literary output in the period between the two World Wars. The first was the familiarity which a young generation had acquired with Western literature, translated into Dutch and sometimes read in the language of the author. The second was the stimulus of nationalism, the desire to express their own culture, and to find a synthesis of East and West.

The first sign of this new movement in literature was a novel in Indonesian by Takdir Alisjahbana, in 1929, just a year before the Youth Movement had adopted its slogan of 'One nation, one people, and one language'. Takdir introduced social ideas into a static cultural tradition and set a standard of devotion to the ideals of nationalism. By founding a monthly review, the *Pudjangga Baru* (*The New Poet*), in 1933, he gave an impetus to the language and provided a forum for young nationalist writers. But the form and the content of Takdir Alisjahbana were Western. An official publication describing his influence states:

'He urged his people to go to the West, to welcome and to open themselves to Western culture, and to strive for its dynamic spirit, which had already brought the peoples of the West to a high state of evolution. Through the slogans "Go to the West" and "Make your spirit dynamic", a concept and a philosophy of life grew which was hundred per cent Western in character, whilst parallel to this there arose a strengthened national consciousness which desired a release from colonial pressure.'[3]

This young generation of intellectuals, mainly concentrated in Java and Sumatra, looked to the West for their inspiration. They became conscious of the long gap between the classical Hindu-Indonesian period and their own times. Sjahrir represents the cultural conflict of this generation.

'In our country', he wrote, 'there has been no spiritual or cultural life and no intellectual progress for centuries. There are the much-praised art forms, but what are these except bare rudiments from a feudal culture that cannot possibly provide a dynamic fulcrum for people of the twentieth century? What can the puppet and other simple and mystical symbols offer us in a broad and intellectual sense? They are only parallels of the out-dated allegories and wisdom of medieval Europe. Our spiritual needs are needs of the twentieth century; our problems and our views are of the twentieth century. Our inclination is no longer towards the mystical but towards reality, clarity, and objectivity.

'In substance, we can never accept the essential difference between the East and the West, because for our spiritual needs we are in general dependent on the West, not only scientifically but culturally.

'We intellectuals here are much closer to Europe or America that we are to the Borobodur or Mahabharata or to the primitive Islamic culture of Java and Sumatra. Which is our basis; the West, or the rudiments of feudal culture that are still to be found in our Eastern Society?'[4]

Not every young writer agreed with this intellectual approach of Sjahrir to the desirable trends in Indonesian culture. In the *Pudjangga Baru* group, two schools of thought existed; one, led by Takdir himself, looked to the West and believed that Indonesian writers should reflect modern thought and twentieth-century social problems. If Indonesians were to play an important part in the world, then they must adapt themselves to its changed conditions. 'Violently', Sukesi Budiardjo says,

'he challenged those Indonesians who thought that the mastery of Western techniques was sufficient and that they could then revert to their former status.'[5]

Knowledge of the West, in Takdir's view, made writers better Indonesians. He defined the duty of a writer thus: individuality in both the community and literature must be subordinate to the community; the artist must fulfil his role not only as an individual but as a leader in the country's struggle for freedom. Associated with him and, broadly speaking, sharing his views, were Mohammed Yamin who wrote in a Western style, but chose subjects of Indonesian history, and Armijn Pane whose novels portrayed social and psychological conflicts between the new and the old world.

The second school of thought in this pre-war period is represented by Sanusi Pane, a poet and dramatist who also contributed to *Pudjangga Baru.* In India, where he lived for many years, he found his inspiration in Hindu classics. Since they also were part of the pattern of Indonesian culture, he advocated a continuity in history and chose the ancient stories of the Hindu-Indonesian period as his model. Sanusi Pane wanted Indonesian writers to look to the past history of their own country. Here, not in the Western world, Indonesians would rediscover themselves. Between these two schools of thought, controversy inevitably arose; the discussion was published in a book, *Polemik Kebudajaan (Controversy on Culture).*

A third group of writers found their inspiration in Islam. Like young nationalists of that period they looked to Egypt where Islamic scholars sought to counter the scientific trends of the Western world by a reformed, modernized Islam. The best known is Hamka, the editor of the *Pedoman Rakjat (People's Guide).*

Suddenly in 1942 the cultural atmosphere changed. The Dutch had gone. The Japanese had taken their place. They did not know the language, nor, for that matter, the country. They set out to win over Indonesian intellectuals by political persuasion or by the promise of important posts in their propaganda machine. They used poets in a number of ways; when they wanted more home guards, for example, they asked poets to write heroic novels and short plays in which home guards were heroes; when they wanted more cotton they asked them to write poems on cotton.

But within a few months the Japanese, who claimed when they arrived to be liberators, behaved with such brutality that many Indonesian writers began to find ways of resisting this new power which added barbarism to what was familiar in colonialism. And even many of those who seemed to be co-operating with the Japanese propaganda machine were without any illusions as to their temporary masters. Writers and poets were shepherded into an organization called Pusat Kebudajaan

(Cultural Centre) set up by the Japanese. It gave many writers more opportunities than they had in Dutch times; they wrote a great deal during those days, but the conditions of Japanese censorship were such that very little was published. Novels were charged with political desperation; poems were introspective, sad, a call to action, nostalgic for the gentler days of peace, even though it was a Dutch peace.

Young writers who grew up during those years showed a mood that was different from that of the older writers. The generation of *Pudjangga Baru* had lived in relatively easy days of nationalist struggle. Life under the Japanese, except for those who joined Pusat Kebudajaan and became part of the propaganda machine, was tortured and uncharted. Removed from the stimulus of the Western world, uprooted from their own past traditions, with many of which they were out of sympathy, young writers adopted styles that reflected their own agitated, nervous lives. The ablest of them was a poet, Chairil Anwar, whose first verses were written in 1943, when he was twenty-one. He enriched the Indonesian language with new words and new ideas and influenced the writing of most of his contemporaries. He became the centre of 'the generation of '45' as it was called to distinguish their outlook from the pre-war writers. After the revolution he and his colleagues formed an association called Gelanggang (Arena) and their first manifesto, published in 1946, shows how deeply the years of struggle against Dutch and then Japanese colonialism had influenced their outlook:

'We are the rightful heirs to the culture of the world, and this culture we will advance according to ways of our own. We were born of the mass of the people, and the meaning of "people" to us is a group of mixed variety out of which a sound new world can be born.

'Our Indonesian-ness is not only because our skins are brown, our hair black, our cheek-bones high, but much more because of what is expressed as the true emanation of our hearts and minds. We are not going to give a definition of what constitutes Indonesian culture. When we speak of Indonesian culture, we are not thinking of polishing up the

305

products of the old culture to make them glitter and in order that they may be praised, but we are thinking of a new cultural life which is sound. Indonesian culture is determined by all the voices sounding from all parts of the world, and spoken out with our own voice, in our own language, in our own forms. We have to oppose every measure taken trying to hamper and to prevent correct and right views of values.

'Revolution means for us the selecting of the outworn values which must be thrown out. Therefore we hold that the revolution in our own country is not yet concluded. In our findings it is possible that we are not always original; what is intrinsic in reaching those findings is consideration of humanity. By our method we seek, examine, and conclude, and so we express our own character.

'Our valuation of surrounding conditions (of the community) is the valuation of people who understand the existence of mutual influences between the community and the artists.'

In the spring of 1951, two years after Chairil Anwar died (he was then only twenty-seven), his influence was still the liveliest among poets and writers of his generation. Fellow students of his in Medan (Sumatra) described his earliest writings which were handed round on scraps of paper during the Japanese occupation. In Djakarta he was still the most talked of among modern poets. His poetry reflected his own life, his individualism, his wanderlust, his sensitive comradeship with those who were fighting, now against the Japanese, now against the Dutch. He was the first to write in a modern style and gave to the new language a subtlety and an intensity not previously achieved by any other writer.

A volume of his poems translated into English and entitled *Flaming Earth* was published by friends in Pakistan a year after his death. The three poems which follow are taken from it:

To the Painter Affandi[6]

'One day when I'll have no words,
And lose my courage to enter my home,
When scared, I'll stay at the threshold.

306

It is because of the instability,
Of which all things bear the impress.
"Death will come to destroy" is my bare consciousness.

My hands will stiffen and finish the writing,
Spiritless I'll suffer, without hope, as I dreamt,
Give me then a small room in the high tower,
Where you alone will ascend.

You turn away from the noise of the world,
From its flaws, glorious from outside,
But false are its thoughts. You will worship,
Till the closed darkness goes aside.'

(January 1947)

When Death Will Come

'When death comes
No one will mourn for me, I know,
Not even you. . . .
I do not need your grief.

I am a wild animal,
Wounded, one that the herd has left.
In pain I turn challenging the wind.

With the poisoned wound I'll fly
Until the wind has cauterized the pain.

I shall bear the agony and live on
Another thousand years.'

Night Watch

'On the march, I do not know what time will bring.
Agile lads, old men with sharp eyes.
The dream of freedom and the stars of certainty
Keep me company as I guard this dead area of my beat.
I am one with those who dare to live,
I am one with those who enter the night,
The night made sweet with dreams, without dust,
On the march. I do not know what time will bring.

307

Other writers belonging to the 1945 group grew up under Japanese rule followed by underground resistance. Pramudya Ananta Toer was imprisoned by the Dutch from 1947–9 and translated Steinbeck's *Of Mice and Men* in his cell; his short stories recently published are stories of the revolution. Idrus is another popular short-story writer. His work *Tjoretan dibawah tanah (Underground Notes)* published after the revolution is an outspoken attack on the Japanese. Political subjects tend to overshadow others in contemporary Indonesian writing. An exception is a young woman teacher, Noersjamsoe, a poet and essayist. This poem, 'Only One Tint', is characteristic of her writing:

> 'A large pattern of my embroidery is done now,
> The stitches are various and the shapes differ.
> When I examined the pieces one by one,
> Clearly I saw the shining
> Of only one tint among the threads,
> The red colour of love.'

> (January 1947)

These and many other young writers are to be read in several literary magazines: *Mimbar Indonesia*, edited by Professor Supomo, H. B. Jassin and others, and the supplement *Gelanggang (Arena)* of Siasat, to which Rosian Anwar is a regular contributor.

The writers who have been mentioned belong mainly to Java and Sumatra, and the magazines are all published in Djakarta. In other parts of the country, with the exception of Bali, few writers have as yet emerged. I Goesti Njoman Pandji Tisna is a Balinese writer whose style was influenced by Tagore. His novels are all set in Bali. He writes of the Kings of Bali and into their history he weaves popular folk-tales. His approach is romantic, although he is an intensely practical man who has built a modern co-educational school in Singaradja on the proceeds of a cinema.

Unlike other fields of art Indonesian literature has not yet acquired any characteristics which differentiate it from that of other countries. To begin with, there was no real tradition; folk stories, stories based on ancient epics, and pantuns were not in themselves an inspiration for contemporary writers. The question of language presents a second problem; most present-day writers were introduced to literature through the medium of Dutch; even today when Indonesians want to discuss abstract ideas or scientific subjects they naturally use Dutch. In other words, existing literature in the Indonesian language is still extremely small. Meanwhile, during the life of the Republic, far more foreign literature has been made available in translation, whilst English is gradually taking the place of Dutch as the first foreign language. In 1948 the Balai Pustaka set up a working programme; making up arrears, introducing world literature to Indonesia, publishing the work of Indonesian writers of literature and science and children's books. How much this work has grown is reflected in figures for 1948, '49, and '50 which were 183,500, 430,800, and 603,000. Modern literature topped the list.

The world is now open to Indonesia, and any discussion with young writers reflects the same problems that exist elsewhere. The same controversy takes place on the virtues of realism and fantasy. The pattern of contemporary writing is still so largely Western that it is too early to judge what will be an essential Indonesian contribution. The number of writers is extremely small. They come almost exclusively from the sophisticated circles of Java, Sumatra, and Bali. We may expect to find new ideas, new styles of writing as people in other islands become literate and able to express themselves. And, above all, we may expect to see through Indonesian eyes the lives, the hopes, the frustrations, the achievements of men and women in the Republic as well as the picture of their past history as they themselves feel it.

Music

Unlike literature, the world of music is varied and distinctive. Its traditions are sometimes local and sometimes shared with other countries in South-east Asia. In the Christian villages of the Minahasa, an orchestra composed entirely of bamboo instruments—flutes and drums—leads processions as brass bands do in this country. Travelling through a village in the spring of 1951, I joined in one such procession to a small church hall for the wedding of a Menadonese girl to a Sangi Island bridegroom. The music was partly Indonesian, partly Western-style marches, and the ceremony ended with the singing of an Indonesian version of 'All people that on earth do dwell', to the tune of the 'Old Hundred'. These 'suling' bands as they are called are part of the village life of Sulawesi and of the Molucca Islands. Boys and men—I have never seen a woman playing in a flute band—will produce effects of considerable musical beauty which comes as a surprise to the Western ear accustomed to instruments of greater complexity and wider range. In Sula-wesi conch shells are often added to the orchestra. They produce a curious hortatory sound which is probably the reason why the Burmans use them as we use trumpets for ceremonial purposes. In Menado an orchestra composed entirely of conch shells pro-duced the melody of an Indonesian folk-song.

An orchestra which is increasingly popular, especially in Su-matra and West Java, is called the 'shake-angklung'. Indonesian and Western scales can be used to play tunes with the effect of musical rattles. The angklung, like the suling, is made from bamboo tubes, open at one end, closed at the other, with one half of the opened end cut away like a quill pen. These tubes, graduated in length, are fitted into a bamboo rack in such a way that the top (open) end can move whilst the closed end is more or less confined. A group of such racks, more like toast racks than musical instruments, will form an 'orchestra' which pro-duces surprising effects of notes and chords and tunes.

But the orchestra for which Indonesia is best known is the gamelan. In Java and in Bali most large villages or groups of small ones have their own gamelan; most of the instruments are made by local craftsmen and the orchestra, often stored in its own bamboo shelter in the centre of the village, is used for all marriages, festivals, and religious ceremonies. The orchestra often practises together, sometimes all night long; they have no written music but classical themes are known to all the players who embroider them with an infinite number of variations. They use a five-note scale and four-four rhythm. The gamelan orchestra has all kinds of combinations of gongs, metal and wood xylophones with or without sound boxes, drums, sulings (flute), and the rebab which is described as 'a bowing lute'. The instruments are divided into different groups according to their function: the flutes (sulings), and the rebab play their own melody which is independent in rhythm from the main tone; the gongs (bonang) and the metallophones with bamboo resonators over which metal rods are hanging (gender) give the leading melody in a strict rhythm; short-toned metallophones without resonators (saron) and xylophones (gambang) are accompanying instruments; a number of gongs and kettle-gongs are punctuating instruments which underline the melody by strong beats on the end tones of the parts and verses, and, lastly, drums which are used to underline the rhythm. The principle of the Balinese gamelan is similar but the music tends to be more melodic and, as the sober Javanese will point out, more 'tuneful, and easier for the Western ear'. In the largest gamelan in Bali, 'the Gamelan Gong', European harmonies are sometimes introduced into the traditional polyphony.[1]

The gamelan will undoubtedly survive in Java and in Bali, where it is the traditional music of centuries. The dances of Java and Bali are unthinkable without the gamelan. But Western music is much more popular and far more often played in the towns of both islands. And it seems extremely unlikely that the gamelan will spread to other islands where the alternative to their local orchestras is music from the West.

Thus the main trend in music is one of Westernization. The gamelan in Java and Bali is not easily changed, neither are Western melodies adaptable to it. It will remain as part of ceremonial and as accompaniment for traditional dances, but it is too early to be sure how far new compositions will be written for the gamelan in the future.

Design

No one can stroll along the remotest dirt track in Indonesia without finding pleasure in the infinite variety of design in textiles worn by men and women. The style is always the same for the women; occasionally smart ladies in the city vary the cut of the kebaya (the blouse), but the kain (sarong) is always a straight piece of material wound around the waist and pleated in folds. The slendang (a long scarf) never varies in style though it may fall gracefully over the head or bulge with the weight of a baby, a dozen fowls, bundles of wood, or bunches of bananas. In pattern and colour every woman shows skill and a sense of design, whether in symbol or floral motif. Both are traditional. I do not remember any Western pattern. But two American dress designers visited Java and Bali in 1951 making copies of Indonesian motifs which they subsequently transferred to Bikini swimsuits.

Two processes are most commonly used in materials, called 'ikat' or 'tie and dye', and batik. Ikat is said to be seven centuries old. This may well be true, for the method of weaving needs only dyes and a great deal of patience. Threads to be woven are first of all dyed; then before they are woven they are stretched on a bamboo frame. For each colour dye, those threads not to be dyed are tied off with plant fibres. The final effect is of colour blobs, as if different colour inks had been allowed to run within prescribed circles. Every part of the country seems to have its own special ikat pattern; in Sumatra the 'ship' ikats of Kroe are designed with figures of boats carrying the souls of the dead; the Dayaks in Borneo are famous for their stylized figures of men, animals, and plants; in Sumba Island stylized trees have human heads and the pattern is called 'skull trees'; in Djogjakarta the ikat slendang has a formalized circle pattern, usually in vivid red, purple, or green. The Balinese have their more elaborate style ikat slendangs, and a ceremonial occasion becomes a feast of colour unmatched anywhere in Indonesia.

The second technique adopted in textiles is called batik, a process which lends itself to an even greater variety of colour and design than ikat. Birds and flowers, natural and stylized, are the popular subjects in batik in Java, Bali, and South Sumatra. In the other islands women will now buy batiks instead of printed cottons if they can afford it. In the suburbs of Djogjakarta and in factories in Djakarta, thousands of women are employed in batik work. With their tjanting tools they outline the pattern in molten wax with which the material is covered. Then they dip the material in a cold dye solution made from natural vegetable dyes and those parts not covered with wax take the dye. The wax is removed and the same process is repeated for every colour used in the pattern. This slow individual process produces the loveliest of designs, but it is obviously an expensive process. The majority of women can usually afford only one batik; they wear it only on special occasions. The Japanese soon sensed the Indonesians' love of colour and made cotton sarongs by mass production. The bazaars in 1951 were still stacked with them, folded neatly in piles like stacks of brightly coloured paper. For thirty rupiahs you could buy a fairly good cotton sarong, whereas batik cost anything from sixty to four hundred rupiahs. The most expensive of all were woven with gold thread, as heavy and elaborate as the robes of an archbishop. A woman weaving all day long took about six months to make these special sarongs for ceremonial occasions—weddings or festivals. They may cost as much as four thousand rupiahs, and women pass them on to their daughters like a wedding veil in this country.

The skill and traditional taste in the design of batik are shown in many handcrafts; wood carving in Java, Sumatra, and, best of all, in Bali; silver work for which Djogjakarta and West Sumatra are best known; ivory work in Bali; mats made of cane or grass, baskets and bags and hats are made in cottages throughout the islands, but the most brilliantly coloured come from Sulawesi, Kalimantan, and the Moluccas. Patterns are standardized and local; silver jewellery in the bazaars of Bukit Tinggi is quite distinctive; silver cutlery and tableware from Djogjakarta is world famous; leather wayang figures, delicately cut with hand-carved ivory handles, are a familiar sight in Djogjakarta. Balinese carvings are popular in Javanese bazaars and they are exported to Singapore and the Philippines. The problem of these artistic handicrafts is how to make them on a commercial basis without reducing the craftsman's skill.

Painting

The renaissance in Indonesian painting is comparable with

that of Mexico, although it is as yet much less widely known. With the exception of Bali, which has its own individual style, Indonesian painting has developed along parallel lines with those of the West. No tradition of Indonesian painting seems to have existed in 1814 when a Dutch painter named Payne recognized the talent of young Raden Saleh, a Javanese nobleman. Payne took him as a student and then arranged for him to take advanced lessons in Europe. His princely birth gave him *entrée* to the Dutch Royal family and to Royalty in other European countries, including Queen Victoria. Whatever were the merits of his paintings, he gained fame as the first modern Indonesian painter. The Nationalist Party, Budi Utomo (the Noble Spirit), celebrated the centenary of his birth in 1914 by starting a 'Raden Saleh Fund' to help young Indonesians who showed artistic ability.

Raden Saleh was the first to break away from the anonymous work of artists whose work was based on the Hindu epics. His best known works, 'Between Life and Death' and 'Fire in the Forest', are in the National Museum at Amsterdam. He introduced Western technique and Western landscape and for a century few artists showed any originality. Suddenly a young painter, Sudjojono, came forward. He formed an association called 'Persatuan Ahli Gambar Indonesia'—generally known as 'Persagi' (Association of Indonesian Pictorial Artists). Sudjojono broke with the classical period of Hindu-Javanese art and attacked the romanticism of the Raden Saleh school.

> 'The paintings we see around us today', he wrote in 1930, 'are nothing more than a lot of landscapes; rice fields being ploughed, rice fields under water, pure and calm, or mountains painted the bluest of blues . . . Everything equally beautiful and romantic, everything equally delightful, tranquil, and peaceful.'

Sudjojono gave his services to the nationalist movement; he was a witty speaker and a clever caricaturist as well as a brilliant artist. Some of his finest paintings portraying heroes of resistance are in the home of President Sukarno, who is a great admirer of Sudjojono and intensely proud of the renaissance of

Indonesian painting. The second pioneer of modern painting is Affandi. He worked as a commercial artist in Bandung before the war and through the 'Pelukis Rajat', which he formed, had an important influence among the young painters who belonged to it. He too was opposed to the romantic and academic outlook of earlier painters, and, like Sudjojono, he encouraged independent approach and social responsibility in art.

The Japanese, albeit for their own propaganda ends, gave far more encouragement to Indonesian painters than their Dutch predecessors. By bringing all artists into an organization the Centre for Culture helped to create a communal interest which is such a marked feature of the artistic world in Djakarta today. For the first time, Sudjojono had a studio where he could teach students. A motto written up in a picture showing his studio and pupils at work read: 'Search for the characters of Indonesian unity.' Painters who were unknown in Dutch times now held exhibitions which stimulated an interest in art and an appreciation of the new trends of naturalism and impressionism.

Two months after Japan's defeat, a Congress of Indonesian painters took place in Djakarta to discuss the general principles of art in the Republic. Today a visit to the homes of such artists as the two brothers Agus and Otto Djaya, Henk Ngantung, Hendra, Mochtar Apin, O. Effendi, and Emiria Sanusa reveals the strength and individuality of Indonesian painting. Subjects are as varied as style. Some of the finest paintings are inspired by the revolutionary movement. There is a wide variety of portrait painting and most artists have painted a self-portrait. Some of the painters show a strong Western influence, usually French, but there is no one who shows any sign of Japanese influence.

Gradually painters are travelling abroad and the existence of Indonesian painting is recognized. They went first to Holland and exhibitions by Indonesian artists are now a familiar feature of Dutch cultural life. Paris has welcomed and acclaimed the painter Salim. He has lived in Provence for some years and his work is a delicate synthesis of Western and Indonesian style. Affandi was widely acclaimed in India. For two years he travelled round the country, exhibiting his own work and that of his fellow-artists. Some of his finest paintings were done in India. When his work was shown in London, critics praised it in such phrases as 'the most liberated work to come from Asia' (Michael Rothenstein) and 'more exciting and moving than any new work I have seen for a long time' (John Berger). Eric Newton compared Affandi's 'basic humanity and a basic vitality' with that of Van Gogh—a parallel which he said 'was the only clue he could find towards understanding Affandi's work'. In Paris and Rome he was equally acclaimed.

Outside Java the liveliest work is carried out in a new school of painting directed by a famous teacher, Mohamad Shafei, in Kayutaname. Exhibitions are held in the Institute of Culture in Padang Panjang, but artists in Sumatra are much less known than the group in Java. Eastwards, in Bali, a change of subject rather than of style reflects the new mood in painting. Balinese painting had remained almost static since the days of the Madjapahit period. It was exclusively religious in subject and artists were anonymous. Sometimes a painting was the work of several artists, since the community rather than the individual has long tended, and still tends, to be the rule in Balinese society. 'The Balinese artist', Miguel Covarubbias writes:

'builds up with traditional standard elements. The arrangement and the general spirit may be his own, and there may even be a certain amount of individuality, however subordinated to the local style. There are definite proportions, standard features, peculiar garments, and so forth to represent a devil, a holy man, a prince, or a peasant, and the personality of a given character is determined, not so much by physical characteristics, but rather by sartorial details . . . Balinese art is not in the class of the "great" arts like great Chinese painting—the conscious production of works of art for their own sake, with an aesthetic value apart from their function. Again, it is too refined, too developed, to fit into peasant arts; nor is it one of the primitive arts, those subject to ritual and tribal laws, which we call "primitive" because their aesthetics do not conform to ours. Their art is a highly developed, although informal Baroque folk-art that combines the peasant liveliness with the refinement of the classicism of

Hinduistic Java, but free from conservative prejudice, and with a new vitality fired by the exuberance of the demoniac spirit of the tropical primitive.'⁷

Miguel Covarubbias, a Mexican artist, lived in Bali in the nineteen-thirties. His description still holds good of the paintings exhibited in the shops of Den Pasar and other centres which tourists usually visit. But in villages reached only by walking across miles of rice-fields, Balinese painters are experimenting; they have now introduced perspective into their painting and they paint everyday subjects, the cockfight, scenes in the market, rice sawahs with peasants planting and harvesting, the natural friezes of ducks on the horizon or temple festivals. The Balinese panorama may be the same, but some of the most experimental artists today do not cover their canvas with a mural-like design, but emphasize individual figures, animals, long bamboo poles decorated with bundles of sacrificial rice straw which bend and sway outside temples on feast days.

Balinese painting is, like all Balinese art, part of everyday life. A new temple, or an old one restored, invariably shows local talent. Sometimes highly sophisticated paintings of Hindu gods adorn the temple plinth, but it is not unusual to see such incongruities as pictures of rather out-of-date aeroplanes or motor-cars in garish colours.

In the shops of Den Pasar in 1951 one could occasionally find antique calendars painted on cloth; these were used to establish the horoscopes of children and were divided into squares for each of the days of the month. The figures were Hinduistic in type; the faces and gestures remind one of paintings in the Ajanta Caves of Hyderabad. More modern calendars were painted on a kind of stiff parchment; the figures were all mythological, gods and devils and misshapen animals, erotic scenes, sadistic and sensual.

In the past twenty years Balinese painters have had the stimulus of foreign artists. In the 'thirties, the German painter Walter Spies and the Dutch painter Bonnet formed a community in Ubud, a village of great enchantment. In small houses built on the slopes of a deep ravine, local painters met artists from abroad and from other parts of Indonesia. Here, and in the nearby village of Mas, artists developed an individualism which

Covarubbias describes as having 'rescued Balinese painting from its latent state'. Today such painters as I. Sobrat and Gusti Nyoman and Ida Bagus Anom have their own styles of expression though their subjects are similar and remain part of Balinese life, landscape, and traditions.

Drama

Drama in Java and Bali means the wayang. The word itself stands for 'shadow' and the wayang is generally known as a 'shadow-play'. This form of entertainment has been popular throughout Indonesian history; some anthropologists suggest that it is part of the old ancestor-worship of the Indonesians, others that it came from India. Whatever may be the origin of the idea, Javanese and Balinese have given it their own individuality, their own interpretative translations and elaborations of the Hindu epics, the *Ramayana* and *Mahabharata*. The Javanese version will differ from the Balinese and both will often differ widely from that of India.

The most popular story dramatized in the wayang is called the Arjunavivaha, taken from the *Mahabharata*. The episode was chosen for translation into Javanese by a famous king, Airlangga (1011–49), whose own experience, it is said, resembled that of the hero of the epic, Arjuna. Arjuna, the Javanese version relates, was an ascetic whom the Lord Shiva decided to test. Seven beautiful nymphs were sent from heaven, past the moon and the stars to the spot where Arjuna was in meditation. He resisted them all. The Demon King insisted on taking one of the nymphs for his own enjoyment. She discovered his vulnerability whereupon Arjuna slew him, lived happily with the seven nymphs until he returned to earth and to his presumably long-suffering wife. The Balinese have a different version, but the symbolism is always the same; the ultimate defeat of the powers of wickedness.

Puppet plays take the place of theatre; they are performed with highly decorative figures and they are never acted by human beings except in the wayang wong and the wayang topeng. Puppet figures are elaborately made. They are cut from buffalo hide; the artist dries the hide, places his pattern on it, cuts it out, then touches it up and polishes it. The dyer then paints it and gilds it, flattens it out and adds a horn handle. Figures illustrate the conflict of good and evil forces in Hindu epics; the good invariably triumph. The 'good' forces are puppets with almond-shaped eyes and long, elegant, sensitive noses. The 'bad' forces have hideously enormous noses and large goggly eyes. When the dalang (puppeteer) arrives in a Javanese or Balinese village or performs his play at a ceremony, he collects a crowd round him as a Punch and Judy show does in an English village. He puts up his white screen, and hangs over it a lamp which burns coconut-oil, or, if he is very up-to-date, an electric lamp. He sits crosslegged under the lamp. In a long oblong box about 4 feet by 2 feet he keeps his reserve of puppets. Near the screen he has two trunks of a banana tree; in one he sticks the 'good' puppets, in the other, the 'bad'. Behind him sits the gamelan orchestra. He uses a horn gavel and an iron rattle to mark the rhythms or to emphasize his story. The gendang player who always leads the gamelan and the dalang have a subtle, intimate relationship. The dalang does not ask the conductor to play a certain tune; this would be undignified. So he introduces his theme by association of ideas. Take the tune 'Maskumambang', a word meaning gold floating on the river, but also hidden in it is the word kumbang, meaning bee. So the dalang starts talking about the one who loves honey, the gamelan conductor thinks of the word kumbang and then arrives at Maskumambang and plays the tune.

Traditionally the men used to sit in front of the screen where they could see the actual puppets, and the women sat the other side where they watched the shadows. But audiences are now mixed; all of them know the puppets as they come before the screen, and the dalang displays his skill by the variations he makes on familiar traditional themes. People recognize Hanuman the monkey god from the *Ramayana* or Arjuna, the hero of the *Mahabharata*, as unmistakably as an audience in the West would know characters from the Bible. The success of the performance depends on the skill of the story-teller—the dalang.

Wayang is so popular in Java and in Bali that an educationalist saw its potentialities in mass education. The Republic is based on Five Principles (the Pantja Sila): Belief in God, Nationalism, Humanism, Sovereignty of the People, and Social Justice. Faced with the problem of popularizing those principles to people who are 80% illiterate, Mr. Hadisuno decided to make use of wayang. He was himself a wayang master, a dancer, a musician, and a painter. In his hands, Arjuna, the favourite hero of the *Mahabharata*, became Nusantara Putra or 'Indonesia'. He played the role of a nationalist leader. The wicked figure 'Pendjadjah Muka' was the colonizer. To his traditional clothes, this expert in mass education added a lion's headdress and gave him a tousled mane designed of cartridge belts. Two more figures, with the face of Arjuna, were named Miss Merdikaningsih and Miss Merdikaningrum;[8] they represented the puppet states set up by van Mook before sovereignty was transferred. A skilful dalang can tell a good story with these new wayang figures, adapting the characters to portray national leaders familiar to any audience. He can inspire leather figures —called 'wayang koelit' (leather shadows)—with humour and irony, with comic turns which any political speaker would envy, with a sense of tragedy, and finally, end triumphantly with the birth of the Republic.

There are other forms of wayang, all of them adaptable to comedy, to tragedy, to any period of time; wayong wong, in which the actors are men wearing costumes and masks patterned on traditional figures of the puppets, representing gods and goddesses of the *Mahabharata* and the *Ramayana*; wayang krutjil, where the puppets are made of wood painted and gilded; wayang golek, the latest form of wayang, which uses three-dimensional puppets made of wood. The shadow principle is always the same, except for these wayang golek, which resemble our 'Punch and Judy' figures.

In the past few decades a new type of drama called sandiwara has evolved, along Western lines. Sandiwara usually deals with contemporary or recent historical episodes in Indonesian life, and with social problems rather than with stories from Hindu epics. At the moment such theatres are confined to the larger cities.

The Films

Some of the actors and actresses who played in sandiwara became the first stars of Indonesian films. This is a new industry, started only in the 1930's. Most small towns have cinemas today, many of them having been built during the Japanese occupation as part of their propaganda machine. In the early days of the Republic the Government set up a Film Distribution service and in Djakarta a Government-sponsored company specializes today in documentary and educational films, as well as in newsreels. The highest standard in films has been reached in documentaries of Indonesian life—the building of new towns, the making of a gamelan, new methods of rice-cultivation, furniture making, and local customs. Newsreels are usually well edited, emphasizing subjects related to the Republic, films of Indonesian delegations abroad, of visitors to Indonesia, sport and events in other Asian countries. Episodes from the history of the Republic have already been used for major films. In 1951 'Six Hours in Djogjakarta' was showing throughout the archipelago. This was a moving story of a guerrilla attack on the town in 1949. It was acted by non-professionals, some of whom had actually taken part in this incredibly brave effort to occupy the town when it was held by well-armed Dutch troops.

In Djakarta, a Board of Film Censors looks at every film produced in the country as well as at foreign films. Any open expression of sex emotion is frowned on as undignified, out of keeping with Indonesian traditions. War preparations, royalty, the private lives of film stars, all receive equally short shrift. Hollywood has a foot in the film world, whilst Chinese films are becoming increasingly popular. And the Chinese own the great majority of cinemas.

Wild Westerns are popular, historical films have prestige popularity, and in spite of the protection of morals which the film censors would like to impose, crowds fill the cinemas for typical screen romances. Premieres in Djakarta are like premieres in London or New York except that there are, as yet, no glamorous film stars to attract the public. In this, the most Westernized town of the Republic, the visitor has a choice of several luxury cinemas which would look homely in an Amsterdam square. But he will rarely see a wayang performance; the President sometimes arranges a wayang evening in the grounds of his house. He enjoys it himself and it is a popular gesture reminding Indonesians that they have their own traditional drama. Otherwise Western entertainments, the cinema, the jazz band, have captured Djakarta. 'You must go to Djogjakarta, or to Bali,' people often told me, 'if you want to hear the gamelan or see wayang.'

The Dance

In Bali and in most parts of Java, the dance is inseparable from the gamelan. It has the quality of ballet, it is stylized, and often portrays a story from one of the Hindu epics. Dancing is not communal; the audience plays the role of spectators.

Many of the dances which belong to Java were originally part of animistic ritual, symbolizing tribute to the gods of sun and moon, of earth and sky, of planting and harvest-time, of the appeasement of evil spirits which haunted the village. Other dances are based on the Pandji stories, romantic renderings of known or mythical heroes. The *Ramayana* and the *Mahabharata* in Java and Bali, as in the case of Burma, Cambodia and Siam, provide most of the stories introduced in dance form. And although, with the exception of Bali, none of these countries professes the religion of Hinduism, the characters of these Hindu epics are known intimately. In Bali this applies to a still greater extent, for Islam failed to supplant Hinduism. But, whereas in Bali dances have become an integral part of the life of every village, in Java it has mainly flourished in the Sultan's palaces. In the polygamous society of pre-war Java, Sultans could assemble in their Courts the most beautiful girls from surrounding villages and develop in them every refinement of stylized dancing. Many dances could be performed only inside the kraton, and Sultans developed their own ballet cycles danced to their own gamelans. In Djogjakarta, for example, the Sultan invariably entertained his guests to a *Ramayana* cycle; Prince Mangkoenegoro's ballet was famous for its Langendrijo cycle, based on legendary episodes of the Madjapahit Empire, and it was acted entirely by girls who also sang their own accompaniment.

The Republic has produced many changes. The present Sultan of Djogjakarta, famous for his courageous defence of the town in December 1948, is a genuine democrat. A Faculty of the university is crowded into part of his kraton whilst dances which were once performed only before his family and guests are now watched by thousands of people from the surrounding villages. The performers are no longer restricted to his friends and relatives. Prince Tedjokusumo, elegant and dignified, proudly describes his classes of 500 children who come to the kraton for dancing lessons. The rice cultivators now dance the famous Serimpi, which was once the favourite of Court life. It represents two princesses who fall in love with the same prince. The subject is one which lends itself to the elaborate stylized movement of hand and foot so characteristic of Javanese dancing. Javanese dancers who visited England in 1946 included it in their repertoire.

Apart from classical dancing there are many traditional dances performed at ceremonial feasts, weddings or funerals, rice planting or rice harvest. One popular individual dance is called the 'hobby horse'. The spirit of the horse is supposed to have entered the body of the dancer—always a man or a boy—and his movements, kicking, pawing, neighing, and frisking in the field, are played realistically and rhythmically as if the performer were horse-tranced.

The dances of Java are sombre compared with those of Bali. Balinese movement is quicker, décor is gayer, and gongs and drums dominate the gamelan orchestra. Here, the village rather than the Court has its own special dance cycle. Village dance teams are almost as popular as village football teams in this country, and onlookers as enthusiastically discuss the performance. There are at least 200 dances with local variants of many of them. Yet, although Bali has the reputation of a place where everyone dances, where every private and public festiva is accompanied by dancing, it is in fact a specialized art.

'It is a singular fact', writes Beryl de Zoete, 'that though dancing accompanies every stage of a man's life from infancy to the grave, there is no spontaneous communal dancing, and among a people of peasants practically no seasonal dancing. It may be that temple service and processions are an important substitute. Outside the temple, however, the dancer or actor—for the same word applies to both—is differentiated from others by the fact that he dances, whether he be of high caste, or low, raja or priest, gold or silver or iron smith, wood carver or fisherman or simple worker in the rice-fields; for dancing needs special training, and is not everybody's business, though nothing but inability or lack of inclination could possibly stand in the way, and the fact that he is a dancer does not interrupt his normal life in the village unless he is so famous as dancer and teacher that dancing and teaching take up all his time. The dancer in Bali is simply another of those anonymous artisans who are both the guardians of its traditions and continually renewing its cultural life.'[9]

The Legong dance, about eighty years old, is the most delicate of all Balinese dances. Two girls, rarely more than thirteen years old, perform this hour-long dance to the accompaniment of the gamelan orchestra. They are introduced by a third girl, the chondong, who dances solo and then, after passing her two fans to the legongs, retires from the stage. The story of the dance, usually a scene from ancient epics, is told by a dalang, but the audience knows it all by heart; it is the elaboration of the story in which the dalang expresses his skill. When Balinese dancers performed in London in September 1952, the Legong was the most widely praised of the programme.

Most performances include the Kebiyar, which is almost entirely danced in a sitting or squatting position, change of position being made by the knees. The mood of the Kebiyar is expressed in the hands, the arms, and the face. The dancer is almost always a man, although a young woman dressed as a man occasionally performs it. He can introduce humour and tragedy; he can be languorous or martial, now hawklike, now like a swan. The Kebiyar is a new dance, created in the 'thirties. The choreographer was Mario, and he is still talked of wherever the Kebiyar is discussed; he not only created the dance, he set a standard. Miguel Covarubbias, who was then preparing his scholarly book on Bali, used to watch Mario at the regular weekly concerts of the Belaluan gong in Den Pasar.

'Mario', he writes, 'sat cross-legged in the centre of a square formed by the instruments of the orchestra. He was dressed in a long piece of brocade wrapped around his waist like a skirt, with one end trailing on the ground, and a sash of gilt cloth bound his torso. Jasmine and tjempaka flowers were stuck in his small turban, and over his left ear he wore a trembling great hibiscus of hammered gold mounted on springs. In his right hand he held a brocade fan. He sat there motionless, in concentrated intensity, until at a signal from the drummers the orchestra struck a sudden crashing chord. Mario straightened like a startled cobra, tense and nervous, holding the fan over his head as if to shade his eyes. The opening theme was fast and furious, and Mario began to dance, waving his fan energetically, darting glances from side to side as if at an imaginary enemy. The tempo increased to a frantic climax, broken suddenly by a melancholy solo on the reyong. Mario relaxed and danced delicately, his expression softened, and his movements became languid. With half-closed eyes he swayed from right to left, his elbows almost touching the mat, fanning himself or deftly arranging the flowers on his head-dress with quivering fingers. The high keys introduced the main theme; Mario flung his train to one side and hopped on his crossed legs around the square, bobbing up and down. In a coquettish mood he paused in front of the musicians, a smile on his face and his head jerking from side to side, finally centring his attention on the leading drummer, who, captivated by the infectious rhythm, beat his drum, furiously swaying and shaking to Mario's movements. Throughout the dance there were sharp contrasts, changing moods that followed the music, alternating "strong" motives with amorous, playful ones, the dancer wriggling like a trained cobra, swaying in a way that recalled the dance of a praying mantis to fascinate its prey, or stiffening with commanding elegance.'[10]

Mario's pupil, Sampih, performed the Kebiyar in London. He was regarded as one of the best Kebiyar dancers in Bali, until he was found dead, presumably murdered, in 1953.

Of the three most popular dances in Bali, the Legong has grace and elegance, the Kebiyar an infinite variety of rhythm,

and the third, the Djanger, an excitement which infects performer and audience. Boys and girls, generally about twenty of
them in equal number, form a closed square. In the centre sits
the 'dag'—the dalang of the wayang—who stirs enthusiasm.
Then the dag goes outside the square and tells the story, usually
of Arjuna in search of the magic arrow which will destroy the
forces of evil personified by a wild boar. This is the most spectacular Balinese dance, and capable of a wide variety of interpretation of emotion. The headdress of the dancers is like a tiara
of golden flowers, and to Western eyes the ensemble has great
fascination.

In Bali and in Java, dancing is as specialized as ballet and
needs as much training. Elsewhere in Indonesia, it is more spontaneous, the movements much less intricate, and the music less
sophisticated. In the Moluccas and the Lesser Sunda Islands,
many dances resemble long-drawn-out English folk dances, in
which the slendang takes the place of a shawl. Dances with
handkerchiefs are almost identical with English folk dances. In
the Minahasa they dance the Menari, symbolizing a proposal
of marriage; when the girl shows her assent by dropping her
shawl, the dance ends. The Toradjas in Central Sulawesi
have special dances associated with their long funeral ceremonies and handkerchief dancing very similar to Morris dances.
Sumatra again has its own characteristic dancing. The Tari
Piring is performed by a group of dancers who hold in the palms
of their hands plates on which lighted candles stand; the plate
symbolizes prosperity and the candlelight stands for life. This
dance in the Menangkabau area of Sumatra was originally performed as thanksgiving to the rice goddess when the harvest was
gathered. But times change and the meanings of dances change
with them; the girls who dance the Tari Piring today, with
rhythmic circular movements of candlelight, may tell you that
they are portraying a prince assisted by his lady attendants
searching in the dark night for the engagement ring so thought-
lessly mislaid by his beautiful fiancée. In South Sumatra, in
the area which was the centre of the Hindu kingdom Srivijaya,
dancers still perform a classical piece originally intended as a
ritual for distinguished visitors. It consists of slow-moving

gestures in which girls, in heavily brocaded clothes and magnificent headdress, collect vases and boxes used in concocting
betel-nut.

One dance seems common throughout the archipelago. Any
night on his or her way home the visitor may see a crowd
gathered round two men or boys who seem at first sight to be
engaged in mortal combat. But this is not the scrapping of two
people who have quarrelled; it is the highly stylized dance
called Penchak. It is reminiscent of judo; the excitement of the
best Penchak dancers (and the Menangkabau claim theirs as
the finest) is the skill with which they slither with grace and
dexterity away from the pointed knives they hold in their hands.

In the towns, sambas and rumbas and jazz orchestras are
fashionable, but only one-sixth of the people live in towns with
more than 20,000 inhabitants. Will Western-style dancing
gradually push on one side or relegate to ceremonies the traditional dances of Indonesia? It might seem unlikely, but this has
already happened in Djakarta. Javanese dances are now performed only as a star turn in official ceremonies or in an occasional school. People dance to Western music the night through,
but the same people would regard a performance of traditional
Javanese dancing as a curiosity, possibly a bore.

Only in Bali does dancing still seem an integral part of life, a
means of self-expression, a part of the ritual of living. But Bali
is different in many respects from other islands, and the impact
of the Republic has not had the full force it has achieved in Java
and Sumatra.

The cultural problems Bali presents are different from those
in other parts of Indonesia where Islam was superimposed on
Hindusim and animism. The question that perplexes older
generations of Balinese today is whether the new, often Western,
ideas which have penetrated the cultural life of other parts of
the Republic will change that of Bali. Younger Balinese see the
question differently; how, they ask, can a synthesis be found not
only between what is valuable in Balinese society and what
might be learnt from the West but between Balinese ideas and
those that are implicit in the Pantja Sila? 'Can we retain the
qualities of Balinese culture whilst we encourage people to feel

an integrated part of the Republic?' To these questions I believe that only the Balinese themselves can find answers.

With the spread of education, these questions will be asked by the peoples of other islands; the Dayaks, who have a rich tradition of folk music and dance; the Toradjas, whose artistic feelings are expressed in ceremonial dance and wood carving; the Papuans with their sense of colour and design in wood and stone and beads. Within a generation, the consciousness of nationhood has led people to challenge the static society in which their ancestors lived for centuries. The first result of literacy is a desire for self-expression.

There is, as yet, no culture that can be called 'Indonesian'. There is a variety of cultures in different stages of development. The largest and the most influential group is in Java. The political power is there, the administrative centre is there. The temptation to Javanize other peoples might arise in the minds of enthusiastic young educationalists. One of the first needs therefore is to provide inter-Indonesian cultural relations. It is internationally valuable that in India and Britain, in France and Holland, there are great admirers of Indonesian painting. It is internally essential that people in Makassar and Pontianak should also be given the opportunity to know their distinguished compatriots. At the moment, people in East Indonesia are practically unknown to those, say, of Sumatra, and vice versa. The Ministry of Education and Culture has room for another department which would promote national unity through inter-Indonesian cultural relations.

Whilst it is too early to speak of an Indonesian culture, of one thing we may be certain: the static period of colonial rule has ended. The horizon of the village is extending to that of the Republic; the horizon of the Republic will become the world. And, after centuries of isolation, Indonesians can join in and contribute to the culture of the modern world.

NOTES

[1] 'The Indonesian Language—By-product of Nationalism', by Takdir Alisjahbana. *Pacific Affairs*, December 1949.
[2] Ibid.

Cultural Trends in the Republic

[3] *Education and Culture*, No. 4. Published by Ministry of Education and Culture.

[4] *Out of Exile*, by Sjahrir, pp. 66–7. Letter dated June 20th, 1935.

[5] 'Modern Indonesian Literature.' Lecture given by Sukesi Budiardjo, November 1950.

[6] Affandi was the leading painter in the first Exhibition of Indonesian Painting held in London (May 1952) and was acclaimed by art critics as a painter of genius.

[7] *Island of Bali*, by Miguel Covarubbias, pp. 164–5, 1937.

[8] 'Sih' means to love. 'Rum' means aura; both are used sarcastically.

[9] *Indian Dance Tradition in South-east Asia and a few aspects of Balinese Dance*, by Beryl de Zoete in programme of Javanese Dancers, London, 1946.

[10] *Island of Bali*, by Miguel Covarubbias, pp. 232–4, 1937.

CHAPTER XV

SOCIAL WELFARE, PUBLIC HEALTH
AND MEDICINE

THE modern idea of social welfare developed late in the period of Dutch administration at a time when the nationalist movement in Indonesia and the growth of Socialist thought in Holland forced it on the colonial rulers. Three main factors contributed to this change in the Dutch attitude towards Indonesia. In the first place van Deventer's appeal *A Debt of Honour* had stirred the consciences of many young Dutchmen then entering the Civil Service; his idea was that when the needs of East Indian finances had been met, the Dutch were in honour bound to use the surplus millions for more education and for the economic and social welfare of the people. Secondly, as Mr. J. S. Furnivall points out, 'the interest in native welfare was no longer, as with van Hoevell, humanitarian, or, as with many Liberals, opportunist; it was economic. It had become a paying proposition to raise the standard of living. The promotion of welfare and expansion appealed to Labour even more than to Capital.' Thirdly, Indonesians themselves began to demand that all the fruits of their labour and their fertile soil should not be harvested exclusively by the peoples of foreign lands. From 1908 onwards, they could no longer be treated as a vast reservoir of cheap labour. Government authorities responded by a paternalism which meant far more opportunities for a limited number of people, especially in Java and Madura; the development of popular credit facilities; improvements in agriculture; cooperatives and, in the same two islands, roads and a few railways. This period of rapid imperialist expansion lasted until the depression began in the early 'thirties. The more the profits from Western enterprises, the more money, it was argued, was available for social services. But the general picture of people's welfare, in Java and Madura, did not show any marked improvement, for better welfare services and higher production were counterbalanced by a rapid increase of population from 28 million in 1908 to 41 million in 1930. When the depression happened in the early 'thirties, social welfare services were the first victim.

Why, the question is often asked, did the work of so many sincere Dutchmen and Dutchwomen lead to such comparatively small results? Why, at the end of Dutch rule, were the Javanese, with whom they were most in contact, so poor, and only one in ten able to read and write? 'I do not wish . . . to underrate the quality of the work accomplished by the Dutch in a very great variety of fields,' a well-known Dutch professor says, 'nor the high-minded intentions of many who lent their co-operation in the Ethical Policy plans. But their activity was out of all proportion to the size of the economic problem in Indonesia as a whole; it was even insufficient to cope with the unfavourable effects of economic penetration, to say nothing of achieving any permanent rise in the general level of welfare.'[1] To which analysis of Dutch social welfare policy we may again add a psychological appreciation by the friendly English writer on the subject, Mr. J. S. Furnivall. His comments were confined to Java and Sumatra, where social welfare organizations were concentrated. He argued that they did nothing to satisfy national feeling, they were fundamentally paternalistic, and doomed, in the long run, to defeat their ends. In a Javanese village, he recalls, he once found himself humming a tune. Its significance at length dawned upon him. The words of the hymn were:

> 'Can a mother's tender care,
> Cease towards the child she bare?
> Yes, she may forgetful be,
> Yet will I remember Thee.'[2]

To put the problem briefly: by the time the Dutch rulers had adopted the paternalism of the twentieth century, political and economic forces had produced a nationalism which could never be satisfied by Dutch plans of social welfare, however enlightened and sincere they might have been or however far-reaching and liberal in their application. In the last decade of Dutch rule,

331

that is within living memory, their social welfare schemes were highly developed in Java, and it was on Java alone that most visitors, including research scholars, based their conclusions. What they did not understand was that under the surface of this seemingly humane, advanced administration, young men and women were beginning to prepare for self-government.

Whatever else were the results of Japanese occupation, one point is very clear; it had the effect of helping Indonesians to acquire experience and self-confidence in planning their own social welfare. At the same time, conditions were so bad that the demand for more social welfare developed and when independence finally came, that demand increased. Now, as education spreads into the remotest villages, men and especially women of all political parties and of none begin to think in terms of a welfare State.

The objective of social welfare in the Republic can be summarized as the enrichment of community life along lines compatible with Islamic and local traditions, and integrating what is valuable in their own traditions with that which is considered valuable in modern, though not necessarily Western nor Soviet, ideas. Village people are beginning to adopt a positive attitude towards social welfare. The ·effect is seen in local initiative in every area. It is often stimulated and led by men and women who were natural leaders in the days of struggle. The Republican Constitution lays down that 'The State shall provide for the needs of the poor and waifs', and that 'The family is entitled to protection by society and the State'. Just what this means when translated into deeds is still a matter of experiment, but the main lines of welfare administration have already been formulated.

The centre of all social welfare is the 'desa', which most nearly corresponds to the English village. Nine-tenths of the population lives in villages. In the Republic each village has a desa council consisting of all the inhabitants over eighteen; a representative body elected from and by the desa council. The administration includes someone in charge of clerical and information work; a social body to deal with such matters as education and health; a body for religious affairs; a person or group to look after the people's welfare and, lastly, a group responsible for dealing with problems of law and order. Where the land belongs to the village, about one-fifth of it is given to financing village administration. Many tasks are communally executed—the building of a paddy house where surplus rice is stored and from which rice loans can be obtained, a village association to organize mutual help, a village bank, a village co-operative where sugar and salt, cloth and imported goods can be bought at a reasonable rate. Local conditions naturally are varied, but this is the usual type of desa administration which has to carry out plans made at the centre.

Social welfare is under a Ministry of Social Affairs with a Minister who changes as the Government changes and a Secretary-General who is a permanent civil servant. In certain fields of social welfare the responsibility of the Ministry is more or less clearly specified; the welfare of particular categories of people who are unable to provide for themselves (demobilized soldiers, for example), the handling of prostitution, the traffic in women and children, the control of narcotics. Social questions also come within the scope of the Ministry of Public Health, the Ministry of Education and Culture, the Ministry of Justice (which is responsible for the care of juvenile delinquents, prisoners), and the Ministry of Defence (which is responsible for the social problems of demobilization). And, since social welfare in the Republic concerns a largely illiterate population, the Ministry of Information is used to publicize schemes through posters and wall newspapers, films and radio sets for collective listening in villages. Thus a complicated problem of co-ordination has to be faced which would be difficult in any society. It is infinitely greater where colonialism has so recently given way to independence. The Ministry of Social Affairs has a staff of about 2,600, of whom nearly 300 work in Djakarta. The work is new, and only a very few men and women have had any professional training for social work. This shortage of trained personnel was recognized in the earliest days of the Republic, when it was still fighting for its existence. A school for social workers was set up in Solo in 1946, and in 1950 it was extended to provide three-year courses for men and women. Most of its students have entered Government service on graduation, and some of them have been sent abroad, to Holland, England, and the United States, for further training. Gradually, cadres of trained people are building a social welfare State on an Indonesian pattern.

Building a Public Health Service

Indonesia was extremely fortunate in having as its first Minister of Health a doctor with long experience, great ability, and unquestioned integrity. Dr. Leimena, born in Amboina in 1905, graduated in the Medical Faculty in Djakarta in 1930, and nine years later he was given a special award for outstanding work. In all the political negotiations with the Dutch Government from the Renville Agreement to the Round Table Conference, he played an important, conciliatory role as a member of the Indonesian delegation and as Chairman of various committees. He was from 1948 until August 1953 Minister of Health. It is not generally recognized how much greater are the health problems which face the Republic than those with which the Dutch Government tried to cope when they were responsible. It is not only that Japanese occupation, followed by two Dutch military actions, undermined or destroyed existing facilities, but that the Republic must meet the requirements of every part of Indonesian territory. They cannot afford to concentrate on Java as the Dutch did.

Dr. Leimena's first task was to make a register of the working personnel and an inventory of equipment. He had to bring together into one central health organization the nine separate health services which had been conducted by the Central Dutch Government until the transfer of power in December 1949. In 3,000 islands, many of them very isolated, he had only 0·8 hospital beds for every 1,000 people. Comparative figures are: United States, 10·4; Great Britain, 7·1; Netherlands, 4·2; India, 0·24; Japan, 3·5. When he reckoned the number of doctors, he found that the figure was 1 doctor for 60,000 people. Comparative figures are: Britain, 1 for 1,000 people; Japan, 1 for 1,200 people; Netherlands, 1 for 1,500 people, and India, 1 for 6,300 people. Out of a total of 1,200 doctors for the whole of the country, 633 were already in Government service; 50 of them were health officers in the army, and the remainder had their own practices, almost exclusively in the bigger cities. To the doctors, the Minister of Health had under his charge 121 assistant chemists, 16 midwives with a lower High School education, 353 Dutch nursing personnel, 3,325 'mantries' (nurses, usually male, with a short training), and 221 midwives with an elementary education. But the shortage of personnel was only one part of the problem. He had to find men and women who were willing to work in remote villages where they had far less financial remuneration and less opportunities of improving their medical standing. Outside Java and the larger cities, he had to plan for a largely illiterate people who were accustomed only to the most primitive hygiene, people who trusted magical qualities of men and women whom they knew as much as they suspected the surgeon's knife and the doctor's vaccination needle. Thus the building up of a successful health service implied education in hygiene and confidence in modern medicine as well as the training of personnel and adequately stocked laboratories.

The Ministry of Health bases its work on the existing desa administration, employing local people wherever possible. In the first instance a trained man or woman visits the desa, discusses local problems with the headman. With his co-operation assured, the villagers are then called together to form a local group. They then survey existing conditions, including the number of people who are literate, methods they have of disposing of refuse, their dietary, sanitation, and the incidence of a hundred and one skin diseases. All this is so closely linked up with customs and beliefs that discussion is almost impossible unless the accepted leaders of desa life understand their value. Records are made showing the results of improved hygiene and medicine. But basic statistics on mortality or morbidity are extremely scanty and trained, competent people who can work in the villages are lamentably few. More than 90% of the whole Indonesian population live in rural areas, in about 28,000 desas. The Ministry of Health aims at one hygiene officer for every desa, and for every group of desas (depending on the size) one hygiene centre and a polyclinic. Here, pregnant mothers can have ante- and post-natal treatment, and women are trained in fundamental principles of midwifery. There is in most desas a 'dukun beranak'—an unqualified midwife. The number of qualified midwives is so small that these 'dukuns' will be called on for some time to come. Even so, the Ministry of Health argues, they can learn such elementary facts as how to sterilize scissors, and that in difficult cases expert medical attention must be obtained if possible.

This complex of curative and preventive health work in a regency is under the direction of a regency doctor, and every health worker is responsible to him. The scheme of public health is applicable in its main features to the country as a whole, but it has been concentrated so far on Java, where two-thirds of the people live, and Bandung (West Java) was selected as a model area. Among the common diseases, malaria is still classed as enemy number one; the mortality rate of a chronically endemic region is 40 per 1,000. In East Java, 50% of the people have one attack each year. Framboesia (often called yaws) is another extremely common disease affecting 15% of the people as a whole, but in special areas the incidence is 70%. In 1950, 40% of these cases were in an infectious stage, and of these infectious cases, 75% were children. Thus, three million infectious children exposed at least as many more to the danger of framboesia. Trachoma is very common in the coastal areas, especially in Java. Venereal diseases are very high, especially in the cities. The incidence of tuberculosis has increased during the war and post-war years. It is estimated that there are 70,000 lepers spread over the whole of Indonesia, and again, the highest proportion is in Java.

In facing this vast problem Dr. Leimena has had valuable assistance from the United Nations, especially from W.H.O. and U.N.I.C.E.F. In 1953, there were twelve W.H.O. personnel working on Ministry of Health programmes; they included doctors, nurses, laboratory technicians, a public health engineer, and an entomologist. Their work is still too largely concentrated on Java, although it is true that so large a proportion of Indonesians live there.

In Bandung, a Tuberculosis Programme was carried out with U.N.I.C.E.F. who supplied the BGC vaccine; more than 10,000 had been examined and X-rayed, 70,000 children and adults tested and 33,000 inoculated by the spring of 1953. In Tjilatjap, W.H.O. concentrated on malaria, studying the Anopheles mosquito which transmits it along the coastal areas of Java. A W.H.O. team has helped to train more than a hundred workers in Maternal and Child Health—they came from all parts of Indonesia to the centre in Djogjakarta. Many other schemes are already beyond the blueprint stage; the training of nurses, assistance in plague control and airport sanitation, and research into unbalanced diets which cause a number of preventable diseases.

Perhaps the most spectacular campaign for which the Ministry of Health has been responsible is that which is called the Treponematoses Control Project. Its aim is to eliminate framboesia within a few years. The disease has been a major scourge for many years. In 1914, the Dutch Health Service gave individual arsenical treatment in the limited number of polyclinics which then existed, and again in 1919 a mass injection was carried out in a few areas, but it was never systematically done and there was no serious effort made to re-examine patients. In East Java, where the incidence was at least 15%, of which 40% were in an infectious stage and of those 75% were children, an Indonesian doctor, Dr. Kodijat, planned a systematic framboesia 'control' plan which involved mass treatment. But he was never given sufficient money nor materials to put his plan into any considerable operation. When the Republic took over the health of the country, Dr. Leimena signed an agreement with the United Nations Organization to deal with framboesia on a large scale. U.N.I.C.E.F. provided supplies, transport, equipment, and technical advice, and in May 1950 the scheme was started in the villages some twenty miles from Djogjakarta. It was wonderfully successful, largely as the result of Dr. Kodijat's devoted leadership. He brought together a group of young doctors and nurses in varying stages of training. In time they expanded the campaign to cover nine areas in Java, three in Sumatra, two in Kalimantan, one in

Bali, and one in Flores, covering a total population of 8,634,432 people.

In May 1951, when 60,000 people had already been treated with penicillin injections, I spent a day with a framboesia team. We started off early one morning—our three trucks contriving a kind of tight-rope performance as they travelled along the narrow dirt-tracks across many miles of paddy fields. The party consisted of a team of nine medical workers led by Dr. Kodijat, the inspiration of the campaign, and his devoted assistant, Dr. Sardadi. Our transport, equipment, and supply of penicillin were supplied by U.N.I.C.E.F. and the W.H.O. The personnel were all Indonesians. At last we came to the village. The headman greeted us in a small bamboo hall. Men, women, and children were there with the small white cards given them a week earlier by a team of nurses who had made a thorough inspection of the population. The headman spoke for a few minutes, expressing his desire for a healthy village. The doctor followed, explaining that people could be cured with two injections of penicillin. He ended his speech with the words: 'And you will all come back for a second dose, the day after tomorrow?' 'Yes, we'll come,' they shouted.

The treatment began. One by one, people came forward as their names were called. Their identity was checked by two local officials sitting at a table under a clump of bamboo and banana trees. Then the patients queued up to have their penicillin injections; they had framboesia in all kind of stages, with scars of all sizes. The worst example was a small child whose nose and mouth were already rotting away. 117 out of 120 had answered the penicillin roll-call. We found two more just packing up in the tiny market; the third had found a family feast too great a temptation to resist even for a penicillin injection.

A year later, a re-survey was taken in this and the surrounding villages. The results were (1) the number of patients who had been cured clinically was 84·7%; (2) of this group, 15·32% framboesia cases, mostly relapses, emerged. This means a percentage of 3·14 of the total number re-examined; (3) framboesia cases found among the newborn and the migrated population was very low; in total 0·16%; (4) the bulk of framboesia found during the re-survey comprised people examined during the general campaign and found not suffering from the disease at that time, in total 10·49% of the number examined.

This and other statistical material which is being collected all the time will be invaluable in future work. The problem which faces the Government is how to cure the estimated 12 million sufferers as swiftly and as efficiently as possible and how to protect the remaining 60 million healthy people. In the summer of 1952, Dr. Leimena called together in Surabaya Inspectors of Health from all over Indonesia to discuss short- and long-term programmes to cope with this problem. The difficulties seem almost insurmountable, but the results so far have been far better than was anticipated. When the Asia Regional Conference of U.N.I.C.E.F. met in Bangkok in 1952, Dr. Leimena reported:

'In comparison with the difficulties faced by the Government, those faced by International Agencies have been small. Every credit belongs to the Government for their perseverance in overcoming obstacles in getting the yaws campaign started, and the greatest credit of all for the work that has been done belongs to the men in the field. . . . We have treated up to date nearly half a million cases. . . . We have perhaps 4% or 5% of the job done, and we are planning to expand it very fast. Our goal is to treat a million cases a year and even then it's a ten-year job.'

Thus, within a generation, the Republic hopes to eliminate this peculiarly horrible and infectious disease. The achievement is impressive, the optimism courageous.

The fact still remains that Indonesia, like other ex-colonial territories, is lamentably short of doctors and nurses and there are as yet no cadres of specialists in any field of medicine. The figure of 1,200 doctors for 78 million people, which works out at the rate of 1 doctor for nearly 100,000 people, is far more serious than it might appear at first glance. At least one-third of them practise in Djakarta and the majority of the remaining 800 (or even less) practise in the big cities, mostly as private practitioners. Their work is easier in the cities and their remuneration much greater.

Outside Java, the work of a doctor is difficult and often dreary; he has little equipment, and what there is, is usually out of date; he is short of drugs, in fact, short of almost everything which we take for granted in hospitals in the West. He has practically no trained staff and he frequently has to cover hundreds of tiny scattered desas with a population which may reach a quarter of a million. The Ministry of Health's scheme of polyclinics for every group of desas is an answer to this problem in many respects, but it is still in its infancy. There still remains the appalling shortage of doctors. Within the next ten years, Dr. Lemeina estimates Indonesia's three medical colleges will produce only fifty to two hundred doctors per year. This means that during the next ten years Indonesia will still need the services of at least three hundred doctors brought in from other countries.

The Republic has built two new Medical Faculties—in Djogakarta and in Surabaya. In Dutch times, the Medical Faculty in Djakarta was the only one which provided training. Dutch authorities assumed that the few, the very few, who wanted to do advanced medicine could have the training in Holland which was provided for Dutch students. Today, the Faculty in Djakarta has professors of surgery, gynaecology, neurology, and psychiatry, of diseases of the eye, ear, and throat, lecturers in children's diseases and in dentistry. Their research facilities are still very few, even in such fields as that of tropical medicine, and those who wish to specialize still have to take their training abroad.

In colonial times, the double system of education was reflected in the training of medical students. They could train in the Medical Faculty in Djakarta and for this they had to pass the final examinations of either the high school (H.B.S.) after five years of post-elementary school study, or the A.M.S., for which they had to graduate from a three-years' course at the 'Mulo'. Then followed two types of degree; one from the Faculty after five years of theory, two years of practical work and a thesis, which provided a qualification equal to that of a doctor in Holland; the second was 'Nederlands Indisch Arts', which was granted to graduates from the Medical School in Surabaya after seven years' theory and one and a half years' practice. This degree was considered inferior and was not the equal of the doctor's degree from Djakarta. Further, whilst the holders of both degrees were equally free to practise medicine in Indonesia, there were certain positions, such as superintendents of large Government hospitals, which were open only to the holder of the Djakarta degree. The double system was unsatisfactory and was generally regarded as an unnecessary complication.

One of the first steps taken by the Ministry of Health was the regularization of this medical degree so that it could be taken at any one of the three Medical Faculties which the Republic now possesses—in Djakarta, Djogjakarta, and Surabaya. But this was not the only problem; it proved difficult to attract young men and women to take up a profession which required seven years of study. In the medical profession, opinion was divided as to the wisdom of making a shorter course; some argued that to shorten the course might lead to a deterioration in the standards of the profession; others believed that in the present emergency a large number of less specialized doctors was the solution, since the longer course of training was not essential to treat a very considerable proportion of the most prevalent diseases.

When the Congress of Medical Practitioners met in Bandung in January 1953, they passed a resolution urging the Government to shorten the period of study from seven to five years. The Chairman suggested that this should be conditional on graduates being given facilities for following a post-graduate course of study during a three-year period of compulsory public service. The training of specialists, he said, must also be widened, and not restricted as at present to a few centres. They could be trained in local hospitals when suitable arrangements were made.

A visit to the new Medical Faculty in the Gadjah Mada University in Djogjakarta gave me a good idea of the difficulties of accommodation which must be added to those that have already been described. About 500 students were there in May 1951; many of them had chosen Djogjakarta because of its early associations with the foundation of the Republic. All classes were given in the Indonesian language. A pioneering atmosphere

341

prevailed in this unusual university compound, a Sultan's palace, which the Sultan of Djogjakarta presented to the nation in 1945.

Medical students listened to lectures in the Pendopo, where guests of state were received on ceremonial occasions in Dutch times. Elaborate chandeliers still hung from a decorated ceiling and large gilded mirrors and life-size portraits of past Sultans still decorated the walls. There was no hot-water supply and home-made zinc-annealed sterilizers were heated over blow-lamps. Attached to the Faculty, and housed in what was formerly the carriage shed, students and doctors gave free treatment in a polyclinic and hospital. In a spacious room which once stored the magnificent instruments of the Sultan's gamelan, dispensers now provided free medicine. Anatomy classes were held in the room where drinks of tea awaited guests. And so on. Everywhere buildings, outhouses, and verandas were occupied by students and the hospital and clinic were always crowded with patients. But it was neither the makeshift arrangements nor the lack of apparatus which made the most lasting impression; it was the determination of students and lecturers to make this into a first-class Medical Faculty.

Students came from all parts of the country, and when they had graduated they would have to serve the first three years in Government service—a ruling made in August 1951, as part of the Ministry's efforts to increase personnel. Afterwards they could, if they chose, become private practitioners, in which case they must avoid Djakarta, Semarang, Bandung, Malang, and Medan where too great a proportion of doctors, dentists, and midwives had already settled down.

When the enormity of problems is considered—the shortages, the aftermath of war, the lack of personnel, transport and equipment, and the illiteracy of the population—the Republic has every reason to be proud of the advance which has been made towards building up a healthy nation.

NOTES

[1] *Effects of Western Civilisation on Indonesian Society*, by Professor W. F. Wertheim, p. 3, 1950. (Paper given to I.P.R. Conference, Lucknow, 1950.)
[2] *Asiatic Review*, p. 655, 1935. Report of lecture by J. S. Furnivall.

CHAPTER XVI

POLITICAL PARTIES AND TRADE UNIONS

U NLIKE India, Burma, and Ceylon, Indonesia has not yet had a post-independence General Election. The present Parliament is still provisional, still largely appointed as all its predecessors have been since the early days of the Republic.

The basic principles of parliamentary democracy were laid down in the Constitution, largely drawn up in the last months of Japanese occupation and announced, in a preliminary form, on August 18th, 1945. The Preparatory Commission for the Independence of Indonesia (Panitia Persiapan Kemerdekaan Indonesia) took another important step that day; it elected Sukarno as President and Dr. Hatta as Vice-President. On the following day it issued a decree dividing the country into eight provinces: West Java, Central Java, East Java, Sumatra, Kalimantan (Borneo), Sulawesi (Celebes), Maluku (Moluccas), and Sunda-Ketjil (Lesser Sunda Islands). President Sukarno appointed a governor for each province from among its own people, the first step towards representative government. The next step came a few days later, by which time the Preparatory Commission had been dissolved by President Sukarno and in its place had come the Komite Nasional Indonesia Pusat (Central National Committee) which was known as K.N.I.P. This body, an embryo parliament, gave a mandate to one of its own representatives from these eight provinces to form local committees. In the revolutionary days between Japan's defeat and the arrival of Dutch troops, the local leadership was naturally provided by men and women who emerged from the resistance movement. Their work was to assist the governors in their administration, and they formed the nucleus of local government. They were usually young, enthusiastic, inexperienced in local government, but keen with the enthusiasm and devotion of resistance workers who had won their victory.

Meanwhile, in Djakarta, the first Cabinet was announced on August 31st. It consisted of well-known Nationalists and it was responsible to the President. But it did not satisfy many of the revolutionary young men and women who felt that more leaders of the resistance movement should have been included. Further, they did not agree with the presidential system whereby the Cabinet was responsible to the President. At the beginning of October a group of people organized a petition which was signed by 50 out of 150 members of the K.N.I.P. urging that it should be changed from an advisory to a legislative body to which the Cabinet would be directly responsible. This petition was handed to President Sukarno, and on October 18th Dr. Hatta on behalf of himself as Vice-President and of the President agreed to this change. In this decree (Presidential Decree No. 10 (1945)) it was also stated that K.N.I.P. would delegate its powers to a small representative committee which would be in virtually permanent session. This Working Committee was responsible to the larger body. With Sjahrir as Chairman and Amir Sjarifuddin as Vice-Chairman, the Working Committee (Badan Pekerdja) was composed mainly of men who had played an important part in the underground movement. They were Socialist in outlook, and they were determined to lay the foundations of a democratic Republic. They acquired considerable influence in these early formative days and Sjahrir's widely circulated pamphlet, *Our Struggle*, did more than anything else to mould the minds of young men and women who were so suddenly called on to shoulder the responsibilities of government. It faced courageously the psychological heritage of Japanese as well as Dutch rule. Sjahrir recognized the brutalities of resistance and war and the urgent need to direct the youth of his country into constructive channels. When times were unsettled and beliefs were as yet unformulated he put forward a political thesis of great importance; the nationalist revolution, he suggested, was only part of the democratic revolution and unless people could look beyond nationalism to the creation of a democratic society, there were serious dangers of the growth of an Indonesian type of Fascism.

'Our revolution is both a national awakening', he wrote, and a democratic revolution, made inevitable by the feudal nature of our country and society. . . . The outward form of our revolution appears nationalist, but from within, following the laws of social evolution, it is *democratic* and has a *socialist* form. . . . Having made certain of the true nature of our struggle, it is obvious that our revolution must be led by a democratic group with revolutionary ideas, and not by a nationalist clique which is for ever serving one or another fascism, whether it is Dutch colonial fascism or Japanese military fascism. . . . We must prove that the essence of our country's belief is that our people should have freedom of thought, speech, religion, writing, choice of livelihood and education and that all governing bodies should be elected by popular vote.'[1]

Sjahrir wrote *Our Struggle* whilst he was Chairman of the Working Committee. It must be remembered that when the Committee was formed in October, Dutch troops had already landed in Java and Sumatra. Conditions everywhere were not only revolutionary but they involved a war against returning Dutch troops and the British who brought them back. The Working Committee acted as a Cabinet. To avoid difficulties, it published a statement as to its position; firstly, that with the President, it would set out the broad outlines of State policy; it would not have the power to interfere with the details, this being the sole right of the President. And secondly, its role was to establish with the President the laws affecting all fields of administration. Their execution would be in the hands of the President, assisted by the Ministers and their staffs.[2]

Thus the Working Committee in some of the most decisive days of the Republic's history was not only a centre from which administration was planned but through its Chairman it became the focus of political leadership. It provided a democratic alternative at a time when a group round Tan Malaka tried to get rid of Sukarno and Hatta and to substitute themselves as dictators. The combination of Sukarno, Hatta, and Sjahrir produced a team at the top which won the confidence of the majority of people, especially in Java and, later, in Sumatra.[3]

Two important decisions taken by the Working Committee

345

on October 30th and published on November 23rd, after the President had endorsed them, related to local government and to the setting up of political parties. In the first place, it was decided to bring all spontaneously formed local K.N.I.'s under the chairmanship of local leaders appointed by the central K.N.I.P. The plan was that the local K.N.I.'s should function as provincial administration and that every one should also have a small Working Committee with a maximum of five members locally elected. Where conditions permitted, the K.N.I. was elected and was thus representative of the people. But in areas where fighting against Dutch and British troops had begun this was usually impossible, and in the islands outside Java, Madura, and Sumatra, where Dutch troops had taken over with little resistance, the plan was clearly impracticable. The second decision was to abandon the one-party system and to allow the setting up of political parties. The K.N.I.P. announcement on November 3rd, 1945, said that it

'favours the establishment of political parties, because with the existence of political parties all currents of thinking which are to be found in society are able to be canalized into a regulated force.'[4]

This was the reversal of what usually happens—the building of a parliament on the basis of political parties. In Indonesia, as Roeslan Abdulgani said in his lecture already quoted, political parties were 'parliament-made parties', and

'from then on there has existed competition between parliamentarism and the party system in their development.'[5]

Most of the leading political parties in the Republic today were born during the last two months of 1945; the Partai Nasional Indonesia (P.N.I.); the Madjelis Sjuro Muslimin Indonesia (Masjumi); the Partai Sosialis (Socialist Party) which was a merger of the Partai Sosialis Indonesia with Amir Sjarifuddin as Chairman and the Partai Rakjat (Socialist People's Party) with Sjahrir as Chairman; the Partai Komunis Indonesia (P.K.I.) and a number of religious parties, notably the Christian Party and the Catholic Party. Youth organizations came together in a loose federation, but the most important, and at times very influential, youth group was the Pesindo (Pemuda Sosialis Indonesia)—Indonesian Socialist Youth. Trade unions, women's organizations, local armed organizations grew up at this period. They were often centred round some personality rather than based on a political theory, and they undermined the strength of the Republic by their efforts to destroy the authority of K.N.I.P. The climax came when Tan Malaka and his group, by a series of wildly unscrupulous manoeuvres, tried to force the resignation of Sukarno and Hatta. The crisis which followed was only overcome by changing the nature of the Government. Henceforth, the Cabinet was responsible to K.N.I.P. and when the latter was not in session—and its meetings were infrequent—the Working Committee was to act as its deputy and the Cabinet would be responsible to it. Sukarno not only approved this move, but he asked Sjahrir to become Prime Minister. Sjahrir agreed on condition that he could choose his Cabinet. This was agreed and on November 14th, 1945, Sjahrir announced his choice; they were mainly colleagues of his in the anti-Japanese underground movement or well known for their administrative experience. This was an important moment in the life of the Republic, not only because of the fierce battles which were then being fought against Dutch and British troops, but because it extended the rule of the people. The Working Committee was enlarged from 15 to 25 members; 17 of them came from leading groups and were directly elected by K.N.I.P. and they in turn elected 8 other members, one from each province, on the basis of suggestions from governors and local K.N.I.'s. An analysis of members gives some indication of the growth of political parties: the P.N.I. had 10 members; the Socialist Party, 5 members; the Masjumi, 4 members; the Christian Party, 1 member; Young Women's Party, 1 member; non-party, 4 members.

Sjahrir was confirmed as Prime Minister in a second and then in a third Cabinet, the last one being in office from October 1946 until June 27th, 1947. During this period political parties became more consolidated, especially in Java and Sumatra. Personalities counted more than political doctrines. The immediate problem was how to get rid of the Dutch and political differences were focused on such issues as the Linggadjati Agreement. At a point when it was extremely doubtful whether the then K.N.I.P. would support the concessions which were involved, President Sukarno took matters in his own hands and issued a Decree (No. 6) increasing its numbers from 200 to 413. His action was strongly resented and only the threat of his own and Hatta's resignations secured endorsement. When this enlarged K.N.I.P. met for the first time—in February 1947—the President stated that in his opinion until the country was 'able to leave the composition of the representative bodies to the electorate, it was the task of the President himself to nominate and appoint members because of the fact that the President himself was regarded as the representative of the whole people'.[6]

This K.N.I.P. of 413 men and women elected a new Working Committee of forty-seven, seven of whom were representatives from Kalimantan, Sulawesi, Lesser Sundas, Maluku, the Chinese, the Arab, and the Indonesian-born Dutch communities.

Sjahrir's third Cabinet came to an end because of the lack of support for his far-reaching concessions to the Dutch. President Sukarno assumed full powers of government and at his request Sjarifuddin formed a Cabinet of the Masjumi, P.N.I., and the Socialist Party, plus the Partai Sarekat Islam Indonesia (P.S.I.I.), a breakaway party from the Masjumi which Sjarifuddin was able to use by promising cabinet posts to its leaders. Their concessions far exceeded those which Sjahrir had been willing to make, but when they halted at the request for a Dutch gendarmerie, war began. During the first military action, power was concentrated in the hands of the Working Committee. Sjarifuddin resigned in January 1948, when neither the Masjumi nor the P.N.I. would endorse his signing of the Renville Agreement. Once more President Sukarno assumed full powers. This time he asked Dr. Hatta, a non-party man, to form a Cabinet. It was dominated by the Masjumi and the P.N.I. and it lasted until the transfer of sovereignty. The development of political parties and parliamentary government was confused throughout this period by the policy of Dr. van Mook in setting up Federal areas where elections were held under Dutch auspices. He was usually able to find a few men who were disgruntled for personal reasons, men who were against what they considered a revolutionary policy by the Republican Government, civil servants who were opportunists, and those who belonged to the feudal aristocracy, especially in East Indonesia.

Just before the transfer of power, the K.N.I.P. held its last meeting to discuss the political course of the Round Table Conference. When the votes were cast, 226 members supported the R.T.C. Agreement, 62 members voted against it, and 31 members voted blank. The Secretary-General of the Ministry of Information points out that 'compared with the number in 1947, the number of Members of Parliament at that meeting was about 100 less. The reasons for this are still not fully known.'[7]

The next parliamentary development was a bi-cameral system, consisting of the Parliament of the Republic of the United States of Indonesia and the Senate. The Parliament consisted of members from the now defunct K.N.I.P. and of the Federal areas. The Senate consisted of representatives from the member States. It was an impossible arrangement as we have already seen in the discussion on the Unitary State.

Finally, when the Unitary State was formed on August 17th, 1950, Parliament assumed its present form. It is still an appointed body. Of the total 236 members, 148 had already served in the House of Representatives of the R.U.S.I., 46 of them were members of the original K.N.I.P., and 13 of them were members of the Working Committee. President Sukarno asked Mohammed Natsir to form the first Cabinet. By so doing, he acknowledged the fact that the Masjumi Party, which Natsir led, was the largest in the country. When the Natsir Government fell in March 1951, the next Prime Minister, Dr. Sukiman, was head of the Masjumi's Legislative Council. In February 1952, Dr. Sukiman resigned following an ill-judged, unpopular agreement which his Foreign Secretary had secretly made with the American Ambassador on the subject of financial assistance. In a country where personalities still count more than political parties, political bargaining becomes a kind of substitute for a General Election. This is what happened in the spring of 1952.

The Masjumi leaders were under a cloud, in view of the unhappy affair of Foreign Minister Subardjo's agreement with Ambassador Merle Cochran. They were also divided amongst themselves. The P.N.I. was in a strong position to hold out against the Masjumi demands for certain key posts in any new Coalition Government, not least of all because it took a very clear line against American military aid and the continued presence of the Dutch in such organizations as their Military Mission. It was therefore a P.N.I. man—Dr. Wilopo—who was able to form a Cabinet whilst the Masjumi had to be satisfied with the Vice-Premiership, the Ministries of Interior, Religious Affairs, and Agriculture respectively. The United Muslim Party held the Ministry of Social Affairs. For the remainder of the Cabinet, non-party men—the Sultan of Djogja and Dr. Bahder Djohan—held the posts of Defence and Education Ministers respectively. The Catholic and Christian Parties were both represented. Two Socialists held posts as individuals—Dr. Sumitro as Minister of Finance and Lukman Wiriadinata as Minister of Justice. But they were in the Cabinet as individuals with the consent of the Socialist Party whose policy it was—and is—not to join any Government until it has been elected by the people.

Thus the basic problem of any Cabinet was whether the P.N.I. and the Masjumi were prepared to act as a coalition. After the Natsir Government fell in March 1951, this co-operation became more and more difficult; there was, of course, the fact that the Masjumi had a religious basis and the P.N.I. was a secular party though the vast majority of its members were Muslims, but there existed many personal cross-currents and conflicts, born in earlier times in the history of the nationalist movement, sometimes political, more often personal. In this struggle for power between these two major parties, the P.N.I. with its Nationalist basis appealed to the left wing, usually Marxist parties, and added to its strength both centrally and locally by increasing co-operation with the Communist-controlled Trade Union Federation (S.O.B.S.I.), and with the Communist Party (the P.K.I.). The Socialist Party and the P.N.I. had a great deal in common as far as ideology and

programme were concerned. But the wounds of earlier attacks by
the P.N.I. on Sjahrir remained open and Sjahrir himself often
displayed an intellectual arrogance. These personal considerations prevented the two parties from finding any basis for co-
operation.

Finally, in June 1953, the uneasy coalition of Masjumi and
P.N.I. came to an end and the Wilopo Cabinet resigned. For
the next two months one formateur after another tried to find
some basis on which another coalition of these two main parties
could be resumed. They failed. The result was a Cabinet
dominated by the P.N.I. which took the four portfolios of Prime
Minister, Foreign Affairs, Finance, and Economic Affairs.
There were three portfolios given to Islamic organizations: the
Nahdatul Ulama, which had broken a year before from the
Masjumi in which it represented the right wing, had a Vice-
Prime Minister, and Ministers for Religious and Social Affairs
respectively; the Moslem Political Federation Party (P.S.I.I.)
had the portfolios of Communications and of Public Welfare.
The remaining posts were held by extreme Nationalist parties
(the Greater Indonesian Federation held those of a Vice-
Prime Minister, Home Affairs, Public Works, and the Progressive Faction held Defence), and by left-wing or pro-Communist
parties (Education portfolio went to a well-known left-wing
non-party man); Information and Health were taken by the
People's Federation Party nominees, Labour by the Partai
Buruh (Labour Party), and Agriculture by that of the Peasants'
Association. The Communists did not join the Cabinet as a
party, but they had their spokesmen there and—a very important addition—the Communist-led All Indonesian Federation
of Trade Unions (S.O.B.S.I.) at once expressed its support.
Thus, whilst the majority of members of the present Cabinet
are not Communists, the Communist Party has achieved a position in which its manoeuvring genius can find plenty of scope.
Indeed, as between the P.N.I. and the P.K.I. it is now a question of who uses whom. The P.N.I. will probably not hesitate
to use the P.K.I. as an ally against the Masjumi; the P.K.I.,
anxious to avoid any type of religious State, will find many allies
in the P.N.I. But these two parties will be rivals for the support

of many smaller political parties which cannot be identified with a religiously based party like the Masjumi. As for other religious parties—the Christian and the Catholic—they are both divided as to whether or not they support the present Cabinet.

Thus there is as yet no political equilibrium in the Republic, nor can there be unless and until the issue is taken out of the personal political jigsaw of Djakarta and put to the people. Every one of the thirteen Cabinets has been committed to holding the first General Election. It is now generally recognized that such an election is essential. For if Cabinets can come and go as the result of individual decisions or personal clashes, the whole idea of parliamentary government is undermined, and the machinery of government and military administration suffer. Further, since political life is so much concentrated in Djakarta, the seat of government, those fissiparous tendencies, always just below the surface in a c untry geographically constructed like Indonesia, begin to assume dange ous proportions.

Before the present Cabinet took office, steps were taken with a view to holding the first General Election in 1953. Local elections held in the Minahasa (June 1951), in Djogjakarta (July 1951), and in Makassar (August–September 1951), provided useful experience on which to base elections for the whole of the country. Then, on April 1st, 1953, an Electoral Law was enacted by the Provisional Parliament, signed by the President, and promulgated by the Minister of Justice. Basic points of the Electoral Law are these: (1) all citizens of eighteen and over, and married people of younger age, have the right to vote irrespective of their sex, property, status, or residence; (2) the electors elect directly the members of the Constituent Assembly and the Parliament; (3) the voting will be by secret ballot; (4) the electoral system used is to be a proportional electoral system; the country is divided into 16 constituencies (3 for Java, 1 for Djakarta Metropolitan area, 3 for Sumatra, 3 for Kaliman-tan, 2 for Sulawesi, 1 for Maluku, 2 for Lesser Sunda Islands, and 1 for West Irian); and (5) provision is made for independents to stand as candidates as well as for political party nominees. The basis of voting is that for every 150,000 people one delegate should be elected for the Constituent Assembly and for every 300,000 people, one delegate should be elected for the uni-cameral Parliament.

As soon as the Electoral Law was passed, the provincial governors were instructed to nominate candidates for the electoral committees. Nine men and women, mainly Members of Parliament, were named as the Central Electoral Committee and civil servants were sent to the provinces to report and advise on electoral procedure and preparations. At this point the Wilopo Government fell. The P.N.I. Government which succeeded it, like all its predecessors, was committed to the holding of a General Election, and on April 16, 1955, it was announced that elections for Parliament and the Constituent Assembly would be held on September 29th and December 15th, 1955, respectively. Time schedules were given except for some areas.

In any country the Government in power tends to have initial advantages when the time comes for a General Election. This is specially true in Indonesia which has achieved less political equilibrium than the other newly independent Asian countries. By the beginning of 1955 the main political parties had already shown their trump cards. The P.N.I. scored a high mark by having as one of the visitors at their annual Conference no less a man than President Sukarno. The P.K.I. with the approval of the Central Electoral Committee and the Minister of Justice has evolved the shrewd vote-catching emblem of 'P.K.I. and Non-Party' which enables them to bring under their umbrella a large number of uncommitted candidates with vaguely Marxist views. Just how well this policy works is indicated in their first published list of non-party people who will stand as candidates on the P.K.I. ticket; they include two well-known painters, a University lecturer, several administrative people attached to provincial governors' offices and to the West Irian Bureau, youth leaders, trade union officials and one man whose publicized qualification is 'member of the Indonesian football team'. Some of these candidates could undoubtedly contribute to the welfare of the country, but the political result is that the P.K.I. becomes a puppet master. The Masjumi and the Socialist Party are seemingly concentrating on attack in their first election canter. The present Government, they complain, has failed to deal with the problem of security whilst the country's economy and the standard of living of the people have sharply declined. They say, with some justification, that corruption has increased, although since the Election campaign may be said to have started, the Minister of Economic Affairs resigned following criticism of his Department's licence abuses. And they point to the fact that whilst Ali Sastroamidjojo's Government does not actually depend on the P.K.I. for its majority, the P.N.I. is effectively the P.K.I.'s 'lengthening piece'. This is certainly much too simple an analysis of the P.N.I., an evaluation which is influenced by many personalities. The General Election will not settle any of these problems; in the words of Natsir's weekly *Hikmah*, 'it will not be a magic Open Sesame to rapid prosperity, but will give a real picture of political strengths, and, by bringing about greater stability, purify and strengthen democracy'.

Indonesia faces problems almost as great as those which India so successfully overcame; difficulties of communications, by sea and land; the need of trained officials; the lack of records; the task of printing voting sheets in local languages as well as Bahasa Indonesia; the use of symbols which are intelligible to those who can neither read nor write—still the majority; the observance of a secret ballot; the guarantee as far as possible from local pressure either by the mosque, by the landlord, or moneyed employers. The problem of insecurity, mainly in Amboina, West Java and South Sulawesi, is one which India did not face. But in Burma, where a General Election was held, lasting over a period of several months, as the Indonesian Elections may well do, the Government was faced with a rebellion by Communists and by Karens as formidable as those which face the Government in Djakarta. Indonesians who followed the elections in these two newly independent countries felt that here was a challenge to themselves. Machinery may be imperfect and the people may be less politically conscious in Indonesia than they were in India and Burma. But a General Election, apart from giving authority to a representative Parliament, is in itself a tremendously important education in democracy.

The main parties which will go to the poll are the Masjumi, the P.N.I., the Socialist Party, and the Communist Party. What will be their programmes, how far they will gather into their fold some of the satellite parties, will only begin to emerge as the target date of the election is discussed.

The Masjumi

The Masjumi, the largest political party, is scarcely a party in the Western sense of that word; it is based on Islam and its beginnings were in the mosques rather than in the committee room. Since at least 90% of Indonesians are professing Muslims, visiting the mosque at least on Fridays, the Masjumi reflects their everyday lives, and, only secondarily, a political doctrine and an election programme. This is its strongest organizational advantage, although it is its weakest dialectical basis. Indeed, until party political life means more than it does at the present time, the Masjumi can still carry on without any clearly thought-out political programme.

A parallel with the Indian National Congress might suggest itself, but it would be misleading; the Indian National Congress though predominantly Hindu, because the majority of Indians were Hindus, was not based on Hinduism; secondly, the Congress developed as the country-wide organization for independence, whereas the Masjumi, although it had a nationalistic basis, did not reflect a struggle against colonial rule. The Masjumi was formed during the days of Japanese occupation; it brought under one banner the variety of organizations which had a common Islamic basis, the Mohammadiah, formed in the 'twenties, the Nahdatul Ulama, [8] and the Partai Sarekat Islam Indonesia. On November 7th, 1945, three months after the proclamation of independence, the Masjumi was acknowledged the only political Islamic organization. All Muslim religious leaders in Java, Sumatra, and Madura were members, and most larger landowners and business men, whilst the heads of villages, often Hadjis, who had made the pilgrimage to Mecca, were included in its ranks. It was loosely organized, since its cadres coincided with those of the country's religious formations. Its programme as accepted in the spring of 1946 when the country was still in the throes of post-war political struggle reflects the more progressive thought amongst that section of its members who were, roughly speaking, religious Socialists.

The Masjumi became an integral part of the national life at the end of 1946 when it established the Indonesian Association of Islamic Peasants. Through this organization, money was channelled which was paid as zakat (a voluntary contribution to the community); 5% of the crop from irrigated land; 10% of the crop from non-irrigated land; $2\frac{1}{2}$% of money saved during the year; 2% of reserve capital; 2% of a merchant's trade capital; one of every forty head of cattle. Village boards made the assessment and money which was collected in this way was used to help poor and landless peasants; loans were made at a much cheaper rate than the Chinese moneylender had always imposed, and buying and selling co-operatives were introduced. So important was the organization in Central and East Java that by the middle of 1948 most of the area under Republican control was covered by it. A parallel organization, similarly under the Masjumi, the Indonesian Islamic Commerce Organization (Sarekat Dagang Islam Indonesia), collected zakat from merchants and its success was such that it formed a Bank to advance credit and help people to start business.

This type of organization, developed during the country's post-war struggle for independence, suggested a social welfare State in which the Masjumi provided most of the administrative framework. The views held by the majority of the Masjumi's Executive Council can be summarized thus:

'1. Complete independence of Indonesia.

'2. Following of and emphasis upon the principles of social justice and democracy found in Islam.

'3. A mixed economy should be followed—co-operative, socialistic, and capitalistic.

'4. Emphasis should be on the co-operative sector with the State advancing credit to develop this.

'5. As the Government acquires sufficient capital and administrative personnel, it should gradually nationalize transport, communications, mining, oil-production, large plantations, and any large-scale industry so long as such nationalization is to the country's best interests.

'6. Small-scale economic enterprise on an individual basis—so long as it is not uncontrolled—is socially healthy, in particular because it develops individual initiative and responsibility.

'7. Foreign capital is welcome so long as it is non-political and so controlled that the Indonesian worker is protected and excessive profits are not taken out of the country.

'8. In non-nationalized economic enterprises the Government should ensure that owners of the capital do not take excessive profits and that the workers share in the profits.

'9. Absolute neutrality in the "Cold War"; alignment with neither U.S.S.R. nor U.S.A.'

This outline of Masjumi principles is substantially the same in 1955. Independence is now an accomplished fact. Two Masjumi Governments, led by Natsir and Sukiman respectively, have been put to the test. Two wings of the party are now easily distinguishable. At the conference in August 1952, the left wing gained control of the Executive Council and Natsir was appointed Chairman. The programme which was adopted stressed that the Republic should be based on Islamic teachings guaranteeing the freedom and security of all citizens. Government structure should be in the form of a Presidential system, with the President as chief executive responsible to a People's Assembly which should consist of a Parliament representing the people and a Senate representing administrative regions. Full and equal political, social, and economic rights must be given to women. Rapid industrialization was called for to enable Indonesia to be independent of the need to import industrial goods and to provide avenues of employment. Foreign capital was welcomed. Nationalization of essential industries was advocated, the order of priority being the circulation bank, essential communications, public welfare enterprises, and mines. Workers should receive 'social wages' in addition to ordinary wage payments to assure a reasonable living standard for a family of man, wife, and two children. On international affairs, the programme stated that any kind of foreign domination was contrary to Islamic principles. Indonesian foreign policy should be aimed at the maintenance of world peace and the cultivation of friendly relations with all countries but particularly with those countries believing in God and democracy. Foreign aid could be accepted but only on condition that it did not involve any military or political commitments or place restrictions on Indonesian sovereignty. West Irian must be transferred to the Republic. Indonesia should actively participate in the United Nations.

This programme, combined with the election of Natsir as Chairman, was regarded by the right wing as a move towards a form of Socialism. The extreme right-wing section, the Nahda-tul Ulama, withdrew from the Masjumi and made an alliance with the Partai Sarekat Islam Indonesia (P.S.I.I.) and the Partai Islam to form an All Indonesia Muslim League which aims at 'materializing happiness for the people and the State in accord with the teachings of Islam'. This group now has a sizeable parliamentary faction working for a specifically Islamic State. The Partai Sarekat Islam Indonesia (P.S.I.I.) consists of the older generation of the Masjumi, men who fundamentally oppose Socialism and Communism on religious grounds. They split with the Masjumi partly because of bitter opposition to any negotiations with the Dutch, partly because of the close association of some of the leaders of Sjahrir's group, and—a vital point in Indonesian politics—because a separate party provided several of its leaders with claims to Cabinet posts. The importance of this new All Indonesian Muslim League remains to be seen, but it is likely to canalize right-wing Islamic opinion.

More extreme than this League is the Darul Islam (the Islamic State) which is not a political party but which stands logically with the Masjumi and the P.S.I.I. Darul Islam bears a relationship to the Masjumi which is in some ways similar to that of the Hindu Mahassaba to the Indian National Congress. It is fanatical in policy and terroristic in practice. Whilst the Masjumi officially would dissociate itself from Darul Islam, the Masjumi's half-hearted suppression of the movement is partly based on support for its ideas amongst the more extreme

Muslims, particularly those who are opposed to any Western influence. There is, for example, only a very thin dividing line between the Masjumi and Darul Islam in ideas which are held by many Achinese; they believe not only in a theocratic State based on Islam, but in an Islamic world. To them the Arab world is the advance guard; in the first stages, this may involve support for the Anglo-American world against that of the Communist countries, since their victory would mean control of strategic bases from which to make a further conquest. The difference between this extreme view and Darul Islam is one of tactics rather than of ideas.

Darul Islam is confined mainly to Java. It arose in Central and East-central Java and in the west, around Preanger, where extreme Islamic views prevailed. The leader, Kartosuwirjo, had his own Islamic school in West Java, organized conferences in March 1948 for the avowed purpose of mobilizing local units against the Dutch; this defence organization, consisting of Mohammedan Hizbullah units of the Masjumi, adopted the name Darul Islam and very early in its career decided to form an autonomous State: the Negara Darul Islam. It was run on Islamic lines as completely as the Border Regions of China were run along Communist lines in the period before the Communists won control over the whole of that country. The Darul Islam State in West Java had its own army, its Islamic schools, and its own system of taxation. At first it was loyal to the Republic and it formed a hard core of resistance to the Dutch at a time when Republican leaders were still carrying on negotiations under the auspices of the United Nations Committee. But after the second military action, when Republican resistance was well organized and the days of compromise were clearly over, the local leaders of Darul Islam degenerated into a local terrorist organization bent on maintaining its own separate existence. So far had its original leadership lost control, that local leaders combined with Dutch troops to disrupt the Republic; in certain villages they co-operated with the Dutch renegade Westerling, forcing the Republic to take steps to suppress them. In the first instance, Mohammed Natsir, Chairman of the Political Council of the Masjumi, attempted to meet disloyalty by political

359

warfare, by a Masjumi-sponsored campaign of pamphlets and speeches aimed at contrasting the religious ideas of Islam with the distorted, terroristic activities of Darul Islam. His plan had some measure of success; it drew away many people who had originally been attracted to Darul Islam with sincerely held, if fanatical, views of an Islamic State. But the terrorists remained, and remain until now, when they are a threat to the stability of the Republic in West Java and may find support in other parts of the country where there is frustration and agrarian unrest.

Parties based on Nationalism

Since Nationalism is a more dynamic political concept than Islam, and since the politically minded youth are often only incidentally Muslims, the Partai Nasional Indonesia (Indonesian National Party)—generally known as the P.N.I.—had the initial advantage of a strong political appeal. It was the largest political party in the early days of the Republic. Both President Sukarno and Dr. Hatta supported a P.N.I. Government for a few weeks following the Proclamation of Independence. Most of its present leaders came into prominence at that time, and hold their positions by virtue of this association.

The P.N.I. has always had a much more closely-knit if smaller organization than the Masjumi and a far more closely coordinated policy. Until the transfer of power, the Nationalist basis of the P.N.I. enabled it to put forward Nationalistic slogans which attracted many on the left who were not primarily concerned with Islamic ideas, and those who were not attracted by the Marxism of Social Democracy or of Communism. It was always opposed to any compromise with the Dutch, and its leaders, unlike Sjahrir of the Socialist Party, did not assume the possibilities of agreement through peaceful negotiations. Thus it was strongly opposed first of all to the Linggadjati Agreement and then to that of Renville.

The P.N.I. drew its members from the middle classes who were not attracted by the Masjumi nor by Marxism, the small proportion of business men, and many men who had served in the lower ranks of bureaucracy in Dutch times. The leaders however came from the ranks of those Nationalists who belonged

to the earlier P.N.I. Dr. Gani, who was its Chairman in 1946;
Dr. Ali Sastroamidjojo, one-time Minister of Education, then
Ambassador in Washington and now Prime Minister; and
Sujono Hadinoto, Chairman in 1948. This group of able,
experienced men, well-known for their earlier part in the
Nationalist struggle, has enabled the P.N.I. to play an important role in successive Governments. Thus, whilst the Party, as
such, has far less following in the country than the Masjumi,
whilst it does not reach into every village and lacks the advantages of the Masjumi in its rule through the mosques, the P.N.I.
is second only to the Masjumi in numbers. The leaders of the two
parties have maintained a bitter rivalry throughout for power
in successive Governments. Like the Masjumi, it has a left wing,
which is near to the Socialist Party. But it always put Nationalism first. Sujono Hadinoto, when he was Chairman, formulated
its goal as a Socialistic society which he maintained could not
be won until 'national freedom and a sovereign national State'
were attained. Now that that national struggle is over, the
objective of a Socialist society would not be admitted by most
P.N.I. leaders today. The Socialists combined in their Nationalism the ideas of national independence and a Socialist State of
society: the two were always consciously integrated. This was
not so in the case of the P.N.I. Yet during the past two or three
years the left wing of the P.N.I. has had a great deal of influence
in formulating its policy. At its sixth National Congress in
Surabaya in December 1952, a policy statement was unanimously accepted which may emerge as an Indonesian adaptation of Marxist principles. The political conception embodied
in this statement was 'defined as "Marhaenism" (or "prole-
tarianism") which sets the objective of achieving a form of
socialism "conforming to the established tradition of mutual
assistance (gotong rojong)" '. The P.N.I. call this socio-
nationalism, and they envisage a Socialist society based on the
peasantry, who are the most important, the workers, the youth,
and the women. They reject the Marxist doctrine of class
struggle in the conditions of Indonesia, and believe that a
Socialist society will be finally established not after a transitional period of capitalism, as the Marxists do, but in a direct

transition from a feudal-communal society to a Socialist society. The trend of thinking is fairly clear, although there is as yet no specific programme laid down by the P.N.I. It may not be acceptable either to the Communists or to the Socialists, but it has an economic idea as its basis, not, as in the case of the Masjumi, a religious concept. At its seventh and largest Congress in Bandung in December 1954, the P.N.I. delegates, representing, it was said, 7,000,000 registered members, reaffirmed this policy of Marhaenism, and the P.N.I. as the political party through which radical and revolutionary changes in Indonesian society could be achieved. But the main Resolution related to international affairs rather than to any practical working out of Marhaenist policy. Here it was on easier grounds. Always uncompromisingly committed to non-involvement in the 'cold war', the Resolution went on to support the five principles of co-existence. It also suggested that the abolition of the Indonesian-Dutch Union should be followed by the abolition or the replacement of all Round Table Conference agreements affecting financial and economic fields. Extremely important as these questions of economic involvement with Holland undoubtedly are in the economy of Indonesia, the P.N.I., like other political parties, uses it as an alibi for a sounder economic policy of its own.

Just as the Masjumi has its satellite parties, based on a more extreme Islam, so too the P.N.I. has the potential allegiance of a number of smaller parties, based on Nationalism. The largest one—Partai Persatuan Indonesia Raja (Greater Indonesia Federation)—has nineteen seats in the present Parliament. It was formed in December 1948 by members of the P.N.I. who did not support its fierce opposition to Dr. Hatta's concessions to the Dutch. It was joined by civil servants, many of whom had spent most of their lives in Dutch administration. Largely confined to Java, the leaders came mainly from Javanese aristocratic circles, and their paternalistic attitude towards the masses prevented them from attracting younger and more progressive members. But it has always included extremely able men in its ranks who have played an important part in the life of the Republic, not so much because of their political views but because of their special experience. The Chairman, Mr. Wong-sonegoro, is a good example. In Dutch times he held juridical posts in the Sultanate of Solo and was Regent of Sragen. In Republican days he was Home Affairs Minister in Hatta's Cabinet, after acting as Governor of Central Java. In the critical days which followed the downfall of the Wilopo Cabinet, he, with Presidential assistance, was the only man who could act as a successful formateur. In Dr. Ali Sastroamidjojo's Cabinet, which resulted, he was the Vice-Premier. In November 1954, when the Cabinet was re-shuffled, he still supported the present government, even though it meant a split in the P.I.R. At this moment it was highly significant of the balancing position which the P.I.R. holds in the government, that the Ministry of Economic Affairs was given to a P.I.R. man, Professor Rooseno. It was the failure of this Ministry, and the widespread criticism of Mr. Iskak, its Minister, which led to the crisis. Professor Rooseno's background is typical of that of most of the P.I.R. leaders; professionally an architect (he worked as a young man with President Sukarno in Bandung), he served as a civil servant in Dutch times. When the Republic was proclaimed he played his part in the intellectual life of the country; he was one of the founders of Gadjah Mada University and afterwards lectured there and in Bandung on architecture and engineering. He then became Minister of Public Works in Dr. Ali Sastroamidjojo's first Cabinet before he was transferred to the Ministry of Economic Affairs.

Thus, the P.I.R. plays a much more important role in the government today than it has ever played before. And foreign observers who, obsessed by the bogy of Communism, tend to overlook this point when they hastily suggest that Dr. Ali Sastroamidjojo's government only exists by virtue of the votes which the P.K.I. can command in Parliament. In the country, it is doubtful where the P.I.R., now the second largest nationalist party in Parliament, stands. In its leadership, the Wongsonegoro group, which advocated support for the present government, was able to command a majority (17 out of 19 votes), but in the country, its members are seemingly critical and may become part of the opposition.

Secondly, the Partai Indonesia Raya (Parindra) with six seats in Parliament. This was formed in 1935 in Solo by Mr. Suroso for the purpose of improving Indonesian conditions through co-operation with the Dutch administration. Later, in 1941, its policy was still co-operation, and 'Indonesia Merdeka', which was its objective, did not imply separation from the Netherlands. At its Ninth Congress in Djakarta in August 1952, Mr. Suroso, the Chairman, and now Minister of Social Affairs, said that the programme of Parindra was still based on faith in the Almighty, on the objective of a Socialist society, and on opposition to all forms of capitalism and imperialism. Whilst foreign capital was needed to develop Indonesia's wealth, he believed, it must be so restricted as not to stifle the growth of national capital. He suggested a dualist economy, combining private enterprise and planned economy; a free 'liberal economy based solely on private enterprise could only develop into a capitalist pattern'. On foreign policy, he strongly opposed any participation in a Pacific Pact, since this would be in conflict with an independent foreign policy.

Parties based on Marxism

Unlike the Masjumi and the P.N.I. with a known potential group of smaller satellite parties which may move in such a direction as to secure the victory of either in a General Election, the Socialist Party stands alone. Although it is a Marxist Party it is divided on fundamental differences of tactics as well as theory from the Communist Party, the P.K.I. Further, it has no allegiance to Moscow. In the early days of the Republic, two Socialist groups, one led by Sjahrir, the other by Amir Sjarifuddin, combined to form the Partai Sosialis Indonesia (P.S.I. as it is generally called). From its earliest days a division existed in the Party based on personal loyalty as well as on political doctrine. Sjahrir, intellectual, aloof from the masses, and Sjarifuddin, brilliant and warm-hearted, disagreed on such fundamental matters as an alignment with the Soviet Union and revolutionary activities based on class struggle. Sjarifuddin, Sjahrir told him at the end of 1947, would have to decide whether he was first a Nationalist or first a Communist. When the split occurred in February 1948, Sjahrir's group formed the Indonesian Socialist Party, and Sjarifuddin took his followers some months later into the Communist Party. With them he took a leading part in the Madiun rebellion. He was shot at the end of 1948 for his part in this ill-timed, disloyal, and disastrous affair.

The Indonesian Socialist Party was weakened by Sjarifuddin's disaffection, and to this day it has never found amongst its leaders anyone with his appeal to the masses. On the other hand, it was stronger because it was united. In Sjahrir it had a leader of integrity, a man who had consistently supported the Nationalist Movement in underground work during Japanese occupation; his brilliant advocacy of Indonesia's cause before the United Nations gave him the standing of a world statesman; his writings reflected a clear, philosophic mind, constructive and courageous. All these are qualities which are invaluable in a Socialist Party and it is undoubtedly true that Sjahrir attracted into its ranks a large number of young idealists, students, intellectuals, civil servants, and professional people. In the days of national struggle he was as important to the country amongst those ranks as President Sukarno was in his peculiarly dramatic challenge to the masses. But whilst President Sukarno still holds his position as President of the Republic and retains his popularity amongst the people, Sjahrir has increasingly isolated himself, refusing to sanction the co-operation of his Party in successive Governments. Individual members have become Ministers but the Party in Parliament plays the role of a constructive opposition. For some time, young though he was, he played the role of elder statesman; Ministers consulted him and his word counted in the making of Cabinets as well as of policies. But as Ministers gained experience, Sjahrir retreated into the background. He developed the Crippsian moral arrogance without the Crippsian austerity. He had little contact with the masses.

It was probably a question of personalities rather than policies which kept the Socialist Party out of the three Cabinets of the Republic. Had Sjahrir been in the Government, he could have rallied round himself and his Party left-wing members of the

Masjumi and the P.N.I. as well as those of other smaller parties. Either as the Government or as the Opposition, the Socialist Party could have played an important role, giving a cohesion to Indonesian political life which it lacks at the moment. But Sjahrir has adopted a policy of the sidelines rather than of the centre of the stage, believing that his special contribution to Indonesia is that of training the nucleus of an efficient Socialist Party. Round the Party in Djakarta he has collected some of the ablest young people in the country; men and women who have the idealistic approach of the Independent Labour Party in England in the 'twenties. Outside Java, the Party has branches, especially in Sumatra, in Kalimantan, and Sulawesi. As a rule, the members consist of professional people, civil servants and teachers, writers and journalists, and sometimes trade union officials. For some years they have organized training schools, generally of three months' duration, where Socialism was studied in its theory and in application to the conditions of Indonesia. When the Party held its first conference in Bandung (February 1952), it adopted a statement analysing the position of Socialism in Asia. Placing the emphasis as Sjahrir himself has always done on the psychological basis of Socialism, the statement compared the rise of Socialism in Asia with that in Europe. Asian society in general did not experience 'the revolution for the emancipation of the individual nor the struggle of liberalism against feudalism' which characterized Western Socialism; until the twentieth century, 'it was a walled-in and incarcerated society'. Whereas in the Western world Socialism developed parallel with the movement for individual freedom, in Burma, India, and Indonesia the impact of Western imperialism was to slow down social progress; the alliance of Western imperialism and Asian feudalism had a common aim in maintaining primitive agrarian and feudal conditions. Therefore the Socialist movement developed as an attack on the alliance of foreign colonialism and its own feudalism.

'Socialism', it continued, 'is democracy in its most perfect form. It regards the "spirit and mentality of Cominformism" as completely contrary to the Socialism based on democracy as we see it . . . "distinct from the Fascist or Cominformist totalitarian systems, it is convinced that Socialism can only be implemented if the people as a whole fully and actively participated in its implementation". The party's economic aims were stated as "security for each inhabitant to abolish unemployment, to increase prosperity, to expand production, and to attain a more equal distribution of income and wealth—to increase the level of production by the abolition of unsuitable methods of production because of their outdated, irrational, and inefficient character and to improve the technique of production in all fields with the rational utilization of the different natural resources which are still unexploited in Indonesia".'

The statement bears the imprint of Sjahrir's analytical mind. But political analysis is sterile unless it is applied to existing conditions. In Indonesia, as in India, the majority of the electorate are still illiterate and they are still lacking the strong social sense to which Socialism makes its appeal. A Socialist Party must depend for its electoral success on peasants and workers, and although Sjahrir himself has more than once expressed the 'dangers when the intelligentsia [are] alienated from the common people', his politically trained cadres do not yet reach them. This is the problem of the Socialist Party between now and a General Election. Failure to recognize this problem in the Indian Socialist Party deprived it of its role as a constructive Opposition and ultimately as the alternative to Congress.

The Communist Party (*Partai Kommunis Indonesia*)

The Communist Party, the P.K.I., follows the pattern of any other Communist Party in a colonial country. Revolutionary ideas were introduced by Westerners into the Nationalist movement; a split occurred between the moderates and extremists, primarily on the methods by which colonial rule could be overthrown; the extremist section found its inspiration and leadership in the Russian Revolution and formed a Communist Party in 1920, which became a branch of the Comintern some months later. Its members worked on two fronts: in the nationalist movement and among the workers. At that time, the nationalist movement, Sarekat Islam, as we have already seen in the chapter 'Islam, Marxism, and Nationalism', was firmly in the hands of such devout Muslims as Hadji Agus Salim and Tjokroaminoto. They argued convincingly that Islam and Communism were incompatible, and the Communists were unable to capture the movement. But they had greater success among the workers who instinctively responded to an economic appeal, and the then Communist leaders, Semaun, Alimin, Musso, and Tan Malaka, were all actively engaged in agitation in the early 'twenties, and the first federation of twenty-two trade unions was virtually a Communist organization. Semaun, the first President of the P.K.I., organized labour unions in Semarang and, following an incitement to the railway workers to strike in 1923, he was exiled. He later formed the Union of Indies Seamen in Amsterdam, and acted as a liaison between the Comintern, the P.K.I., and the Perhimpoenan Indonesia in Holland. Alimin, who is Chairman of the P.K.I. today, worked among the Union of Civil Servants and the Longshoremen and Seamen's Union; he escaped in 1925 from the country, but kept up his revolutionary contacts from Malaya. Musso was an executive member of the P.K.I. and an active strike leader until he was exiled after the failure of strikes in 1925. He returned in 1948 and was mainly responsible for the Madiun rebellion, as a result of which he was captured and shot. Tan Malaka, after a political training in Moscow, was one of the most active Communists in the 'twenties. He too was exiled for organizing strike action.

The early 'twenties saw a rapid increase in strike action and in membership of the trade unions. The Communists were unable to capture control of Sarekat Islam, but in the struggle between them for leadership of the workers, they were powerful enough in 1920 to form the first federation of twenty-two trade unions. In 1924, both Alimin and Semaun attended the Congress in Canton organized by the Red International of Labour Unions. On their return, in accordance with the Communist line laid down in Canton, they intensified their activities in the unions and two years later were responsible for the general uprising. It met with much less response than the Communists expected, with the exception of Banten and the west coast of Sumatra. The Dutch suppressed it with extreme ruthlessness, outlawed most of the Communist leaders, and suppressed the Party. It did not function again as a legal body until November 1945, but its members, depleted by thousands who were exiled to the malarial swamps of Boven Digul, continued to work in the trade unions.

Communists in Indonesia, as in every other colonial country where a general uprising had been organized following the Canton Congress, were divided on the issue of the correctness of its timing. Alimin and Musso were both in favour of it. Tan Malaka led the opposition which believed it premature, and his following in Sumatra was large enough for Alimin to blame him for its failure. Tan Malaka had expressed views in the Fourth Comintern Congress in Leningrad in 1922 which were then regarded as a deviation. With the knowledge of Sarekat Islam's appeal to the masses, and the failure of Communists to get control of it, he had argued that Islam in Indonesia must be regarded as an expression of nationalist struggle, and that Communists must adapt their policy accordingly. When he broke with the P.K.I. after the failure of the general uprising he joined up with the so-called Trotskyist Communist Party formed a year later in Bangkok. Alimin, Musso, and Semaun all remained loyal to the Comintern, and all of them spent periods in Moscow.

This pre-war dissension was immediately reflected in the early days of the Republic. Many Communists, released in 1942, had worked underground during Japanese times. Others had been sent to Australia and worked there among the trade unions, specially the dock workers. Two Communist Parties at once came into being: one, led by Alimin, the other by Tan Malaka. Tan Malaka's party was disbanded following an attempt to kidnap Sjahrir and to organize a coup against the Republic. Many of his followers were imprisoned for life, and Tan Malaka was killed in circumstances which are a mystery.

The P.K.I. at first linked itself with the Socialist Party and the smaller Labour Party whilst building its own cadres. Those were days when the Republic was struggling for its existence, when no left-wing party could afford to be outside the ranks of resistance to Dutch rule. The P.K.I. aimed at capturing the leadership of this struggle through the People's Democratic Front which gained many adherents in 1948, especially in Java. In February and March 1948, several Indonesian Communists had attended conferences in Calcutta at which the Communist line was formulated. In the World Federation of Trade Unions and the International Youth Congress, from this time onward, the P.K.I. (following the Cominform programme) began to advocate the repudiation of all agreements with the Dutch (including the Renville Agreement which they had supported at the time); the nationalization of all foreign properties without compensation; alignment with the Soviet Union; the defeat of Anglo-American imperialism; opposition to the Marshall Plan. It was not a convincing programme at a time when the country was still partly occupied by Dutch forces, when van Mook was making some headway in building up his Federal areas, and when economic blockade was sapping the strength of the Republic. Some of the older Communist leaders were far from enthusiastic about this change of policy; Nationalism was to them as powerful a force as Communism. But younger members who returned from World Congresses in Prague (August 1947) and Calcutta (February and March 1948) infused with the new party line of active revolution and with developments in Eastern Europe including non-co-operation with the Marshall Plan, won the day in Indonesia.

Their return coincided with the breakdown of negotiations between Hatta and the Dutch, the long inactivity of the United Nations Committee, van Mook's Federalizing plan, and a series of concessions by Hatta's Government. The People's Democratic Front, through which the P.K.I. worked, inevitably made a strong appeal. Events moved quickly in the summer of 1948 when Musso arrived from Moscow, bringing with him his 'Gottwald Plan' as he called it. Musso, exiled in 1926, had spent most of his time in Moscow. He arrived on August 12th, travelling under the assumed name of Suparto, with Suripno, a brilliant young Communist who had been recalled by Dr. Hatta to explain an agreement he had made on his own accord in

Prague for the exchange of Consuls with the Soviet Union. Just as in 1924 Alimin had returned from the International of Red Labour Unions to advocate a general uprising against the Dutch, so in 1948 Musso returned to organize an uprising against the Republic.

Musso at once took over the Party leadership. 'There are grounds for believing', Mr. Kahin writes, 'that the Communists anticipated that their plan

'would provoke an American-sanctioned Dutch attack against the Republic either during or after their seizure of power. Indonesia would then become a chaos of guerrilla warfare. In the course of the warfare the P.K.I. felt certain that it would emerge in control of the guerrilla movement and ultimately, following their expected expulsion of the Dutch, in control of Indonesia.'[9]

Musso was scarcely known to the younger members of the P.K.I., but he spoke with the authority of Moscow. On August 20th, 1948, he put forward his policy to the P.K.I. meeting in Djogjakarta. The first step was an invitation to the Masjumi and the P.N.I. to form a 'National Front', a move which gained time and drew attention to the Republican Government's fruitless efforts to defeat the Dutch. Their refusal, which was expected, led to a denunciation of Hatta's co-operation with 'imperialist powers', of the Republic's 'reformist' tendencies, and their Western orientation. Sukarno and Hatta were 'tools of America'. The next step was the Madiun coup on September 14th. The rebel forces were estimated at three to four thousand well-armed men. The P.K.I. had concentrated on this area for some time and had its own 'Red Army School'. A rebel administration was set up in Madiun and broadcast appeals were made to people to support their 'National Front Government', to do away with the National Bourgeoisie and so on. Prime Minister Hatta at once received offers of support to put down the rebellion from the Dutch. His reply was immediate: he needed no help. An Emergency Bill empowering the President to take measures 'outside the law and standing regulations' was passed and the rebellion was soon put down. The

371

Republican army was not affected, and indeed, as soon as the units in Madiun declared their loyalty to the Republican Government, danger of civil war was over. By the end of September, Republican troops had reoccupied Madiun. Some thousands of prisoners were taken and a certain number of Communist guerrillas escaped to the hills. The leaders of the rebellion were imprisoned and, later, as Dutch troops entered Djogjakarta in December, they were shot—Musso, Sjarifuddin, Suripno, Maruto Darusman, and Harjono.

This unsuccessful rebellion not only lost the P.K.I. its ablest leaders, it lost them a great deal of support which as a party they have not yet regained. For although it may be true, as some Communists allege, that the rebellion was premature, that it was provoked by Dutch agents, the fundamental issue was quite clear; the P.K.I. acts on instructions from the Cominform, its allegiance is not to Indonesian Nationalism but to world Communism.

The P.K.I. was not suppressed in spite of its disloyalty. Dr. Hatta's Government was strengthened by his prompt action, and morale in Djogjakarta measurably improved. But the Madiun rebellion was quickly overshadowed by the second military action in December 1948, and many Communists joined the guerrillas to fight for the Republic. By the time sovereignty was transferred in December 1949, events outside Indonesia contributed towards the prestige of Communism. The Chinese Communists had extended their control from the small areas round Yenan (where Alimin had once lived with Mao Tse-tung) to the whole of China, with the exception of Formosa; American policy in the Far East had gone a long way to substantiate the earlier attacks of P.K.I. leaders; Dutch colonialism was still controlling West Irian.

Today, the P.K.I. has fifteen members in Parliament, where it loses no opportunity of attacking 'Anglo-American imperialistic plans for war', the re-arming of Japan, the A.N.Z.U.S. Agreement (described as the first step towards a Pacific N.A.T.O.), the continuation of Dutch control in West Irian, the large number of Dutch still employed in administration, the Dutch Military Mission, and Dutch stranglehold of Indonesian economy and trade. The P.K.I. works through a number of peace and cultural organizations, and advocates a National Front. One of its ablest spokesmen, D. N. Aidit of the Central Committee, speaking in Palembang in July 1952, reflected the influence of Chinese Communism on the Indonesian Party. Advocating a National Front, he added that the P.K.I. was quite prepared to work together with the national industrialists who were already convinced that an imperialist economy would not benefit them.

In the political field, the P.K.I. has undoubtedly increased its influence in the past two years. But its main strength rests in its control of the largest federation of trade unions—S.O.B.S.I. In a General Election this is where its following will be determined. Whilst the leaders of S.O.B.S.I. are almost exclusively Communists, this does not apply in the provincial branches; nor does it follow that the masses are Communists. In the General Election, whenever it is held, the P.K.I. with its potential mass support will challenge the Masjumi, just as it challenged Sarekat Islam in the 'twenties. Conditions are different, political consciousness has developed through national struggle, but the fundamental issue is the same; Communism, with its materialist dynamic, challenges the deeply rooted power of Islam.

Partai Murba

The second Communist Party, founded by Tan Malaka, has a certain personal following especially in West Sumatra, which was his home. Tan Malaka himself was released from prison at the time of the Madiun rebellion, and supported the Hatta Government in suppressing it; indeed, the Siliwangi Division which was used against the Madiun rebels included many of Tan Malaka's followers. He founded the Partai Murba at the end of 1948, and it at once attracted many young Communists who were also nationalists. But its membership is still insignificant. Nevertheless, the idea of Communism which has its allegiance to Indonesia rather than to Moscow makes an appeal, and the Partai Murba has certainly attracted a number of able young men and women. Younger political workers for whom the Republic is moving much too slowly are attracted to the

Partai Murba. They put forward a programme which includes the confiscation and exploitation of foreign enterprises, the nationalization and collectivization of plantations, mining, industry, transport, and finance. But, like the Partai Sosialis Indonesia, they seem to have few contacts amongst the workers, and their influence in the Trade Union Movement is weak.

To sum up: political parties have not yet found their equilibrium. The largest party, the Masjumi, still has the great advantage of an organization which, with the exception of Bali and the Christian areas (Minahasa, Amboina, and the Batak lands of Central Sumatra), brings it into the daily lives of people through the mosque. The P.N.I. can still find Nationalism a strong appeal and adds to it their social welfare State idea. The Socialist Party, idealistic, international in outlook, with cadres of young and able members, does not yet reach to the masses. The P.K.I. through its control of the largest Trade Union Federation (S.O.B.S.I.) and a number of 'front line' organizations, can exploit nationalism and social revolution but it does not yet reach the peasants for whom the mosque remains their guide. There remain satellite groups of the Masjumi, the P.N.I. and the P.K.I., plus the Christian and Catholic Parties whose support will certainly be actively canvassed before the General Election. Thus many moves are possible on the political chessboard before the Republic achieves stability. The most probable development before the country goes to the poll is the formation of *blocs* comprising parties with a certain ideology in common. For there is a growing belief that the present system of sixteen political parties is unworkable.

Trade Unions

The wide disparity between the standards of ruler and ruled was at the root of nationalism, a part of the conscious revolt of politically minded people against foreign capitalism. The trade union idea developed as an integral part of the Nationalist Movement. In the same year—in 1908—that Budi Utomo was formed by men with a moral approach to nationalism, the first Indonesian trade union was formed among the workers of trolley and railway companies in Java. Its objectives were the improvement of working conditions, pensions, and medical aid. Three years later the batik traders in Java combined in self-protection against Chinese exploitation to form a society called 'Sarekat Dagang Islam' (Islamic Traders' Association). In the riots they organized to improve the economic conditions of workers in the batik mills, they were the forerunners of strike action. By 1917 workers from the sugar estates and railway workers were well enough organized to make themselves felt in Sarekat Islam, the focus of Nationalist feeling. At the Djakarta Conference that year, they introduced Marxist slogans, and attacked foreign capitalism. Two years later, trade unions were an important factor which the Dutch could not afford to overlook since they constituted a threat to their supply of cheap indigenous labour. Twenty-two trade unions now had a membership of 77,000 workers; Pawnshop Workers' Union, Industrial Workers' Union, Union of Rail and Tramway Workers, Union of Sugar Employees, all of them in the Trade Union Alliance.

The trade unions themselves were weakened by internal struggle. Communist members regarded its control, as they do today, as part of their own political advancement. Muslim nationalists, who were working for their country's independence in Sarekat Islam, did not envisage a change in the structure of Indonesian society; they were nationalists pure and simple. The Communists, led by Semaun, founder of the Union of Railways and Tramways Personnel, saw in nationalism a weapon of Marxism. At first they co-operated with non-Communist unions in the United Movement of Workers, but in 1921 they withdrew from the union, taking with them fourteen out of the total of twenty-two. With their headquarters in Semarang, they set up a new organization which was the driving force behind the strike of Government pawnshop workers in the following year; 79 out of 360 pawnshops responded to their call for strike action.

Strikes became a serious threat to Dutch economy in the following years; trolley workers, Government employees, stevedores, teachers—all organized strikes and in so doing developed their national consciousness. In 1925 the Dutch Government passed a law making strike action illegal. In the uprising organized by the Communists in 1926-7, trade unions were weakened when thousands of people, including many trade union members, were arrested and sent to the malarial swamps of New Guinea (West Irian). The period of revolutionary trade unionism was robbed of its dynamic leadership. Efforts were made to establish another central organization in 1929; the leaders, Sunarjo and Marsudi, were arrested and banished to join earlier victims in New Guinea on the grounds that their organization—the Indonesian Trade Union—joined the League Against Imperialism. The next effort was made in East Sumatra, among the workers of the plantations; the leader, Dr. Kusuma Sumantri, was arrested on the grounds that he was disturbing the peace and he was banished to the Moluccas. In the 'thirties, Sarekat Islam succeeded in forming a central trade union for Government employees and Dr. Sutomo formed a similar body for private employees which organized a campaign against wage decreases in West Java. But trade unionism was extremely weak in the last years of colonial rule and during the years of Japanese occupation it was altogether forbidden.

As soon as the Republic was founded in 1945, trade unions became a legal expression of struggle for better working conditions. The Indonesian Workers' Organization, set up in Djakarta in November 1945, had as its first task the taking over of industrial and administrative jobs from the Japanese. A year later, a central body was formed in Djogjakarta called the Central Organization of Indonesian Labour (Sentral Organisasi Buruh Seloeroe Indonesia, generally abbreviated to S.O.B.S.I). Its principles were stated as the defence of the workers against unfair exploitation by foreign capitalism, the furtherance of political and economic democracy based on social justice, and the establishment of relations with labour movements in other countries. It was represented in the Central National Committee and was an important source of strength to the left wing. By 1947, in spite of the difficulties through which the Republic had passed, it had a total membership of approximately 1,200,000. Of the total, according to figures published by the Ministry of Social Affairs, 1,000,000 were employed on the rubber, quinine, tea, coffee, and tobacco estates; 25,000 were teachers; 30,000 were on sugar plantations, and of the remainder the most important were oil workers, 16,000; forestry, 18,000; railways, 10,000; and mines, 10,000. S.O.B.S.I. is organized along similar lines to the Trades Union Congress with a General Assembly representing each union. Policy-making is mainly controlled by the central administration; the parallel with the T.U.C. is close, but with this fundamental difference, that S.O.B.S.I. has always reflected the political activities and programme of the P.K.I.

S.O.B.S.I. became affiliated to the World Federation of Trade Unions in 1947, and it has consistently adopted a Communist policy; in 1948 it played an important political role in rallying opinion against the Hatta Government then engaged in fruitless talks with van Mook. In the Madiun rebellion, S.O.B.S.I. leaders were among the main organizers. But whilst the leadership consisted of Communists, the rank and file of its members were not. Had they been, the Madiun rebellion would have had far greater success and seriously undermined the Republic. The loyalty of its members was put to the test three months later when Dutch troops occupied Djogjakarta in their second military action. Many of them joined the guerrilla movement; they played a major part in organized resistance and to them was entrusted the destruction of factories, estates and stores, and sabotage behind the Dutch lines.

When the fight was over, and power was finally transferred to the Republic in December 1949, S.O.B.S.I. emerged as the main body representing organized labour and practically every trade union was included in its ranks. Its leaders were mainly Communists although the majority of its members belonged, and probably still belong, to other parties or to none. But Communist control of the main Federation of Trade Unions is an important aspect, politically as well as economically, internally as well as externally, in the life of the Republic. It must be seen against the background of the Round Table Conference Agreement which left Dutch interests in virtual control of a considerable part of Indonesian economy; financial agreements, plantations, communications, such important industries as oil and mining were still mainly in Dutch hands. This meant in effect that whilst the Republic had won political independence, its economy was still linked with that of its former colonial ruler, and workers were still employed on enterprises and on thousands of acres of plantations for foreign masters. With this in mind, the Republican delegation at The Hague had demanded and obtained certain provisions which would impose safeguards for Indonesian workers on the foreigner. Article 12, for example, stated that housing and other social welfare arrangements should be improved on estates, and that 'within the earliest possible period' eligible Indonesians should be included in 'the direction (and management) and staffs of the enterprises' and that they should co-operate 'in establishing training courses with the objective that after a reasonable period the predominant part of the leading personnel of the staff of the enterprises will consist of Indonesian nationals'. Later, the Constitution of the Republic stated that everyone had a right to just working conditions and a living wage, and Article 21 stated: 'The right to demonstrate and to strike is recognized and shall be stipulated by law.' Thus, for the first time, trade unions were recognized as the legitimate safeguard of workers' rights. S.O.B.S.I. still represented the majority of workers.

The first real test of trade union strength took place, as might have been expected, on the estates; they were foreign-owned, and in many of them housing conditions were disgraceful, wages were low, working conditions were notoriously bad. In August 1950, the largest union in S.O.B.S.I.—the Plantation Workers' Trade Union, usually known as S.A.R.B.U.P.R.I., called out its 700,000 workers on the estates in Java, Madura, and Sumatra, after several months of fruitless negotiations with Dutch owners. S.A.R.B.U.P.R.I. demanded that privately owned plantations should pay wages at the same level as those paid on Government-owned plantations; they claimed a minimum wage of 3.50 rupiahs per day together with improved social security measures. The Estate Owners' Association (Algemeene Landbouw Syndicaat), which controlled about 900 plantations, had been paying 1.20 rupiahs per days to men workers and 80 cents to women. When they offered to increase this amount to

2.20 rupiahs, S.A.R.B.U.P.R.I. rejected it and called out its members. At this point the Minister of Labour said that whilst he would do everything to end the strike, he considered the demands of the workers were perfectly reasonable. Some plantation owners in Central and West Java at once agreed to meet the strikers' demands and in these cases work was at once resumed. After the Minister's mediation, the Plantation Owners' Association proposed, and S.A.R.B.U.P.R.I. accepted, a minimum wage rate of 3 rupiahs a day of seven working hours, with payment of 2 rupiahs for Sundays, on which no work was done; they also agreed to pay half wages for the period during which the strike had lasted—from August 20th till September 15th. This was the first victory for the Indonesian trade unions.

Following the successful strike on foreign-owned plantations, workers in other fields had resort to strike action. Conditions in the first winter of full Republican control were extremely severe; the loss of factories resulting from Dutch military action, dislocation due to the transfer of authority, the lack of goodwill on the part of a section of Dutch business men unwilling to accept defeat, and the extreme shortage of trained Indonesian personnel—all these factors contributed to unsettled conditions. In January 1951 there were forty strikes; the majority of them were in Java, in Standard Vacuum, British-American Tobacco, in S.O.C.O.N.Y., the Goodyear Rubber Factory, in the furniture and textile industries, and among the harbour workers; in Sumatra the plantation workers; in Kalimantan workers of the Dutch oil company, B.P.M. Most of these enterprises were in part or wholly controlled by foreign interests, mainly Dutch or Dutch-American. Strikes were easily organized, sometimes before the good offices of the Ministry of Labour were used. They had a political as well as an industrial side. In fact, they reflected the growing opposition of the P.K.I. to the Government, to its close association with Holland, and its seeming willingness to depart from a policy of neutrality in foreign affairs. But whilst this opposition was led by the P.K.I., industrial and agrarian unrest were at least as important.

The Republican Government met problems arising from this increasing number of strikes by issuing an ordinance regulating the settlement of labour disputes. It stated that 'he who strikes, or who orders, suggests, invites, enforces, or provokes a strike or lockout in a vital enterprise, service, or body, is liable to be taken into custody for a period up to one year, or to be fined a sum not exceeding 10,000 rupiahs'. Further, it laid down that 'disputes between workers/officials and employers/management in a vital enterprise, service, or body shall be reported by the representatives of the workers concerned, or by the representatives of the employers/management to the Committee for Settlement'. The Committee, whose decisions were binding upon both workers and employers, was composed of the Minister for Labour, as Chairman, and the members were the Ministers for Traffic, for Trade and Industry, for Finance, and for Public Works respectively. Outside of vital enterprises which were mainly those belonging to the State, either partly or wholly, this ordinance of February 13th, 1951, stated that disputes should be reported to an office to be established in every provincial capital or in every municipality, the members to consist of representatives of the Ministries involved in the committee already listed.

This was a desperate ordinance, cancelling, although the Government emphasized its temporary nature, the right to strike which is the basic right of trade unionism. It had immediate results in those areas where political pressure was weak; in East Sumatra, S.A.R.B.U.P.R.I., under Socialist, not Communist, control, at once referred its dispute with the plantation owners to the local Committee; in Bandung, textile workers went back to work; in Borneo, oil-workers who had intended striking announced their decision to take advantage of the local Committee. Meanwhile the Government was criticized for its ordinance; the P.K.I. and S.O.B.S.I. leaders both condemned it as being undemocratic, the P.K.I. adding that it was proof of American intervention.

The ordinance was in fact a very unpopular measure, and when a new Cabinet was formed in April 1951, the Minister of Labour almost immediately announced that the Government was considering lifting the ban on strikes. The basic cause of labour disputes, he added, was the demand for higher wages.

Trade unions must be efficiently organized and he appealed to them to act jointly with other groups of the population. In September 1951 the ordinance was removed and a new Emergency Act came into operation for the settlement of labour disputes. This did not deprive workers of the right to strike but it was aimed at reducing the possibilities of strike action. Two procedures for settlement between employers and workers were provided, mediation and arbitration. When a week's negotiations have yielded no results, the case is referred to the Minister of Labour. Both management and workers are free to submit any case for settlement, and the recommendations, either made by officials of the Labour Ministry or by an arbitrator, are considered as binding on parties to the dispute.

This new Labour Ordinance had the effect of reducing the number of strikes in 1952 and 1953. A considerable number of disputes, concerning such issues as the payment of bonuses for the Lebaran days (the biggest Muslim festival of the year, and celebrated on as large a scale as Christmas), have been settled by the intervention of the Ministry of Labour. But it is no solution to the wider problems of low wages, poor housing conditions and social provisions, especially on many foreign-owned plantations. The Government naturally aims at canalizing workers' discontent through the Ministry of Labour; this would give them greater control of the workers and presumably undermine the political influence which Communists can still mobilize through S.O.B.S.I., and the militant trade unions, especially in industries still under Dutch control. The Congress of Oil Workers, held in Djakarta at the beginning of 1952, is a good example. The purpose of the Congress was to create one large union out of the existing seven unions representing 60,000 workers. The resolutions passed stated that S.O.B.S.I. is recognized as the 'only Indonesian central trade union actively fighting imperialism'; that the W.F.T.U. is recognized as the 'only actively anti-imperialist trade union federation'; that the struggle against imperialism and its supporters must be intensified; that the united struggle for peace must be energized by the formation of a 'broad anti-imperialist front nationally and internationally'; and that a struggle must now be waged 'for setting

381

up of an Indonesian People's Democratic State'. All delegates present signed an appeal for a Five-Power Peace Pact.

This programme, reflecting Cominform policy, was challenged at the S.O.B.S.I. Conference in Djakarta in October 1952, but it was not substantially altered, and it remains the same today. Non-S.O.B.S.I. members who were present as observers won support for their proposals to cut out such terms as 'Socialist', 'People's Democracy', and 'class struggle' from the S.O.B.S.I. programme. S.O.B.S.I., they stated, must not operate as though it were a political party. But decisions were taken to create an All-Indonesian Workers' Front and a national reconstruction front, whilst congratulatory messages were sent to the Asian Peace Conference in Peking and to the W.F.T.U.

There is no doubt that S.O.B.S.I. is the most dynamic force in Indonesian trade unionism. It has a membership of about 1,000,000 workers distributed among thirty-five unions representing almost every section of workers. The second largest Federation is K.B.S.I. (All-Indonesian Trade Union Congress) founded in Bandung in May 1953 by the amalgamation of several other groups of unions. Whereas S.O.B.S.I. stands for nationalization of essential industries and services, K.B.S.I. states that it is democratic, non-party, and aims at social justice. Their membership is stated to be nearly 900,000. And, thirdly, there is a federation called S.O.B.R.I., to which the Islamic trade unions are affiliated.

Thus there is a certain parallel between the main lines of political and trade-union development. So long as foreign economic domination lasts, and Dutch business concerns and Chinese traders still play the dominant role in their respective spheres, the Communist leaders of S.O.B.S.I. can undoubtedly win mass support for their anti-imperialist line. Marxist slogans will continue to make their appeal to men and women who expected the victory of nationalism to bring rapid changes in their own lives. But outside the more advanced, more politically minded areas of Java and Sumatra, in the vast under-populated lands of Kalimantan and Sulawesi and the islands to the east of them, trade unionism has scarcely penetrated. Almost every family depends on agriculture and the peasant remains the unknown but important factor.

NOTES

[1] *Our Struggle*, by Sjahrir. Translated and published with the title *Indonesia's Fight* by Perhimpoenan Indonesia, London.

[2] The chapter 'Internal Politics of Revolution' in *Nationalism and Revolution in Indonesia* by George Kahin describes this early period of the Republic in detail, with full documentation.

[3] The Revolution in Sumatra developed separately and violently at first, with the result that it was not incorporated into the Republican administration until the middle of 1946.

For a detailed account of the Sumatra Social Revolution, see Chapter VI, 'Internal Politics of Revolution', in *Nationalism and Revolution in Indonesia*, by George Kahin.

[4] 'Parties and Parliament.' Address delivered by the Secretary-General of the Ministry of Information, Roeslan Abdulgani, at the staff training course on November 1st, 1952, and reprinted in the Ministry's publication, *Indonesian Affairs*, Vol. II, No. 5/6, Oct./Nov./Dec. 1952, p. 10.

[5] Ibid., p. 11.

[6] Quoted by George Kahin in *Nationalism and Revolution*, p. 202. The chapter deals in extensively documented details with the Republic's internal politics during this period.

[7] 'Parties and Parliament', by Roeslan Abdulgani. *Indonesian Affairs*, Vol. II, No. 5/6, Oct./Nov./Dec. 1952, p. 11. Issued by the Ministry of Information.

[8] This, the right wing of the Masjumi, broke away in April 1952.

[9] *Some Aspects of Indonesian Affairs and Nationalism*, by George Kahin, 1950.

CHAPTER XVII

BUILDING A NEW ECONOMY

N o colonial Power has developed an economy as closely dependent on its colonial territories as the Dutch did in the case of Indonesia. Indeed Holland as a great trading country in the world's markets owes her position primarily to the riches of her former colony which in pre-war days accounted for 90% of the world's total of quinine; 86% of pepper; 75% of kapok; 37% of rubber; 28% of coconut-palm products; 19% of tea; 17% of tin; 3% of sugar; 4% of coffee, and 3% of oil. It was the riches of Indonesia which made Holland a world Power. Indonesia directly or indirectly provided an income to one in every seven Dutchmen. Through Dutch eyes Indonesia was 'tropical Holland', a grand investment paying high, regular dividends.

Indonesians of course see the picture with a different focus. Whatever were the economic and social benefits of Dutch rule —and for a small section of the population they were many— they watched the riches of their soil developed to suit the economy of the colonial Power; profits were spent in the enrichment of the foreigner; exports and imports were determined by the needs of 10 million people in solid, comfortable Dutch homes; transport by land, by river, and by sea was planned to suit the convenience of foreign traders, foreign tourists, and foreign communities.

Whilst it would be impossible to strike any balance sheet of Dutch rule in terms of guilders, it can be said that an annual sum of £28 million in direct gains and £16 million in indirect flowed into the Dutch treasury.[1] But the criticism of Dutch rule, of British or French colonialism, is directed far more to the psychological effects than to the financial balance sheet. Many Dutch economists have recognized the problems imposed by the economic dualism of Indonesian society. The aims of the

Western ruler were dictated by the needs of his own community whilst those of Indonesian rulers were based on long-established traditions formed in a period when money economy was far less important than social obligations, voluntarily accepted or imposed. Once this money economy was established, every consideration of production and of trade was based on the needs of Dutchmen living alongside their canals, not on the Indonesians living in their desas or their tribal communities. In the development of Indonesian economy, Chinese immigrants were used by the Dutch to reinforce their policy. In early days, the Company leased lands to them as well as to other people and farmed out the collection of taxes and tolls; in the 'culture' period, Chinese became middlemen so that 'all that the natives sold to Europeans they sold through Chinese, and all that the natives bought from Europeans they bought through Chinese',[2] and they controlled all the opium shops, pawnshops, and gambling houses where local earnings often found their way. At the end of the last century, thousands of Chinese coolies were imported to work on the plantations of Sumatra and the tin mines of Bangka and Billiton, and during the present century, when the number of Chinese has increased from 537,000 (1900) to 1·9 million (1947), their interests have widened and their influence in industry, trade, and commerce increased. Three times as numerous as the Europeans in Java, and thirteen times more outside it, the Chinese are a closely knit community with few social ties either with the Europeans or with the Indonesians. They challenge smaller Dutch concerns on the one hand, and, on the other, they have experience in trade and a money economy which is superior to that of the rural population. For years, Chinese traders have travelled into the interior of Kalimantan and Sumatra, buying up such produce as kampong rubber (latex collected from a small number of trees as opposed to the plantation rubber), tobacco, coffee, kapok, rice, and tapioca. They not only pay a low price, but the peasants are often paid beforehand and then have to borrow money so that Chinese traders become moneylenders as well. They take goods to sell in Chinese bazaars. They sell batiks to the village women made by Indonesian women in Chinese-owned batik factories.

o

In Dutch times, they were the trade intermediaries. In the Republic, they often have a greater advantage over the Indonesian who was never encouraged to take part in trade nor given any position of responsibility. This raises many difficult problems, especially in remoter districts where peasants are often at the mercy of the Chinese middleman for the sale of their produce, and in many industries—batik is a good example—where Chinese have established a near monopoly.

In pre-war times, only a very small proportion of Indonesians were engaged in commerce or in finance, and an even smaller proportion had positions of importance in the vast administrative system of Dutch trade. The Indonesian was a producer of raw materials, a rice-cultivator, a rubber-tapper, a tin-miner, or worker in plantations of sugar and coconut-palm, of tea and coffee, of quinine and kapok. His wages depended on movements in world trade, on fluctuations controlled, if at all, only by the bourses of Amsterdam and Rotterdam. Whether or not he could buy cheap goods, cloth for his family, a bicycle or a tawdry mirror, depended on decisions taken by Chinese traders and Dutch business men who controlled the balance of exports and imports. This applied primarily to the densely populated island of Java, to the more developed coastal areas of Sumatra, and to Kalimantan. In other islands, with the exception of certain coastal towns and a few areas such as the Minahasa, village economy underwent only very superficial changes throughout the period of Dutch rule. Many Dutchmen argue that this is greatly to their credit; they point to the disruption of village life in Burma, for example, and pride themselves on their recognition of local adat. The Indonesian nationalist interprets this worship of adat as a peculiar form of Western hypocrisy; the maintenance of village economy, he argues, perpetuated the Dutch idea of the Dutchman as a skilful business man and industrialist, while the Indonesian, uncomplaining and embedded in his own social traditions, continued to extract the riches of his soil by methods his ancestors used centuries ago. To this argument Dutch apologists reply that the Indonesian lacks business qualities, that he is suspicious of investing his small capital; he dislikes mass production, his standards of work are uneven, and his style confined to his traditions; he does not naturally plan ahead or adapt himself to Western planning; he works to satisfy his immediate requirements, either of the family or of the village, and not with a view to amassing capital, however small it may be. The Indonesian nationalist will retort that colonial rule provides neither the incentive to improve technique and increase production nor the opportunity to integrate what is valuable from the technical West into rural Indonesian society. It was not in Dutch interests, not even in the interests of the small Indonesian aristocracy which was attracted to Dutch society, that methods should change, that the people living in malaria-infected jungle should desire, let alone demand, a healthy life and up-to-date agricultural equipment. The thesis can be carried a step further; the economy of Holland depended for its success on maintaining Indonesia as a source of raw materials, which were provided by cheap, often indented, labour; on the discouragement of industrial development; on maintaining, as far as it was practicable in a competitive world, a monopoly of her trade. If a slump occurred in Holland, as it did in the early 'thirties, then the rubber-tapper in Sumatra or the tin-miner in Banka and Billiton was the first to suffer its results. If a boom occurred, as it did in the 'twenties, the same rubber-tapper or tin-miner undoubtedly had a share in it, however disproportionate, but he was in no position to control the proportion, nor to determine the flow of imports into his village on which he could spend his increased earnings.

The interests of Dutch concerns involved a dual economy in the colonial period. There was the modern money economy, mostly in the hands of foreigners, in which all modern techniques in banking, transport, and so on were applied. Side by side with that system there was the village economy which was hardly touched by modern methods until about 1880. The village was a self-sufficient unit of production and consumption. When Western economy began to need the raw materials for its factories and markets for its manufactured goods, the Dutch passed the so-called Agrarian Law opening up parts of Indonesia to the foreigner so that he could obtain long leases over big areas of rich soil. At this point the West penetrated into the village economy of the country. Cheap labour was needed for the estates; it was found in the surrounding villages. Money came into the villages and people began to use it for imported goods and then to pay taxes. They welcomed the opportunity for additional work and in time their need for credit outgrew the possibility of attracting money from outside. Credit institutions merely led to usury or practices like the 'idjon' (selling the crop while it is still on the field—idjo means 'green'), and share-cropping undermined and often poisoned the existing village economy.

At the end of an analysis of the structure of Netherlands Indian economy in which he discussed the main characteristics of colonial society, the economic contact between colonial groups and the role of colonial capital, a distinguished Dutch Professor of Tropical Economics in the University of Leiden comes to this conclusion:

'It is certain ... that, while Western influence on the native community is far-reaching and many-sided, the degree to which natives take part in Western economic life is one-sided and circumscribed, so that there is no reasonable proportion. It is also sure that, where it is a matter of employment, this native participation in Western processes is limited to jobs of secondary importance. And, finally, it is certain that Western economic influence in the colony is focused in money traffic, that the demands of this money traffic unsettle the Oriental community to a very marked degree, that the Government encourages colonial money traffic and hence is largely responsible for the way in which the latter reacts upon Eastern society.'[3]

The dual economy led to the disruption of an existing rural pattern of society. And because the colonial Power benefited from monopolies, the new money economy was vulnerable to world conditions over which the people had no control.

When political power was transferred to Indonesia in December 1949, her economy had been subjected to two major crises: the Japanese had used plantations ruthlessly, by not replanting trees, cutting down tea bushes etc. and enforcing the migration of labour, and they had geared Indonesian economy to the requirements of their war machine. Then came the Dutch military action and blockade. The scorched-earth tactics of Indonesian guerrilla armies complete the picture. Political sovereignty was not reflected in the economic arrangements which were made at the Round Table Conference at The Hague in 1949. It was as if a new engine had been fitted into an old car with Queen Juliana moving across from the driver's seat and President Sukarno taking the wheel. The brakes and the gears remained the same. It remained to be seen whether the driver could alter not only the speed of the car but, more important still, its direction.

Although the Dutch gave way on the fundamental issue of the transfer of sovereignty (except in the case of West Irian), the financial and economic concessions which they won at the Round Table Conference ensured for themselves a certain continuity in their control of or influence in Indonesian economy, and imposed on the new Republic a variety of burdensome obligations. The Republic assumed responsibility for debts amounting to at least £200 million; it was tied to Holland on such matters as the exchange rates of currency. It had to take over for two years officials in Dutch administration. Many of them resigned immediately, whilst the divided loyalty of those who remained became a constant source of trouble and frustration. It agreed to recognize the rights, concessions, and licences for the operation of Dutch business enterprises and to restore rightful claimants to the actual exercise of their rights subject to certain conditions. It undertook to extend or renew to existing and new enterprises and estates the rights, concessions, and licences required for their continued operation on a sound business basis and to guarantee the lawful owners of such enterprises the continuity required for normal long-term business operation 'except in those cases which are in contravention of the public interest including the general economic policy of the Republic'. It guaranteed to observe the principles of non-discrimination as between foreigners of all nations and to recognize the special interests of the Netherlands in Indonesia without prejudice to the right of the Republic to make regulations necessary for the protection of national interests or economically weak groups.

The Dutch, guilder-minded to the last days of their political power, reluctantly yielded control to people whom their policy had deprived of administrative and commercial experience. To many young Indonesians this hard-bargaining was evidence that Dutch colonial psychology persisted; they felt that they had been cheated, and their incentive to work was undermined. The structure of Indonesian economy still remained with its unbalance, based on the production of agrarian raw materials mainly for export. Foreign and inter-island transport, so essential for an island nation, remained in Dutch hands. When every point is taken into consideration, Dutch experience and efficiency, their vast investments, their intensive development of Java and parts of Sumatra, their commitments based on their ex-colony, their wartime sacrifices, the fact remains that the conditions imposed by the Round Table Conference, and accepted under international pressure by the Republic, seriously compromised Indonesian economy in the first years of its existence and will continue so to do for some time to come.

The Republican administration, in short, inherited a colonial economy with its basic weaknesses and its inconsistencies. Whilst it is true that too much responsibility must not be attributed to the Round Table Conference Agreement, it is extremely important that the psychological effects are not underestimated. A newly independent country had become responsible for, though it did not own, vast enterprises mainly in Java, representing Dutch investments of about £500 million in plantations, tin mines, oil wells, shipping transport, and public utilities. Few were in 'running order' since Japanese occupation and two Dutch military actions had destroyed or dislocated large areas of production. Secondly, the Republican administration became responsible for, though it did not control, the widespread trade on which the lives of millions of Indonesian peasants depended for the sale of their produce and the purchase of essential consumer goods. This trade was mainly in the hands of industrious Chinese, who, unlike the Dutch, were not confined to Java and the larger towns of other islands, but who doggedly combed the riverine villages of Kalimantan and the remote mountain villages of Sumatra. Thirdly, those who were in charge of administration were faced with the difficult task of integrating into a working machine Indonesians who as yet had not acquired managerial skill, and Dutchmen whose efficiency was often undermined by resentment, sometimes by disloyalty. Fourthly, a series of strikes, almost exclusively on foreign-owned plantations, led to a considerable degree of instability. In some cases, workers, discontented by the terms of the Round Table Conference Agreement, refused to hand over plantations to their previous Dutch owners; in others, advantage was taken of the unpopular transfer to indulge in large-scale thefts which had a disastrous psychological effect on the morale of both sides. To this industrial confusion yet another difficulty must be added. Fighting continued for some time between K.N.I.L. troops under Dutch control left in Indonesia and guerrillas, who were against the R.T.C. Agreement, and gangsters who refused to return home. The accumulative effect of these problems was a sharp drop in production in the early days of Republican administration which has not yet returned to the pre-war levels.

The Government was committed to a long-term policy of building a balanced economy. Its short-term policy reflected some of the characteristics of the colonial unbalance which it inherited. The only alternative was what the able economist Dr. Sumitro calls a policy of 'consistent deflation', with drastic reductions in salaries, higher taxation, greatly reduced imports, followed by mass unemployment, decreasing production, and the disruption of social stability on a large scale. For the first two years, until the world market price of raw materials fell, a boom in rubber and tin provided a temporary balance of payments, especially in the dollar areas. But this temporary advantage was not reflected in a rise of the standard of living nor an increase in production. The boom provided the biggest profits to foreign enterprises since the peak period of 1926. Further, the increased demand for Indonesia's raw materials was neutralized by the fact that the economy of industrial countries was now geared to the needs of war with the result that the Republic could not buy consumer goods, nor capital goods urgently needed for reconstruction and development. The structure of national income, Dr. Sumitro said, 'remained weak and limited as before. It was temporarily disguised under the veil of the Korea boom.' The problem of Indonesia was not primarily finance and money, but 'production and hard work'. This meant developing the skill of the village people, providing them with the technical means of modern life, and introducing new and more diverse products.

The aim of the Government, as expressed in Article 38 of the Constitution, is to build a national economy on a co-operative basis. 'Colonial capitalism as power in the form of an economic organization still has a strong position', Dr. Hatta told the nation on Co-operative Day.

> 'We can only break this power down by establishing a people's economic system on a co-operative basis. . . . Indonesia is rich, but the people are poor. The co-operative system in economic fields is the only means by which a poor people can attain welfare.'

Dr. Sumitro (Minister of Commerce and Industry in the Natsir Cabinet, Minister of Finance in the Wilopo Cabinet and now Professor in the University of Indonesia) has devoted a great deal of his drive and ability to the building up of co-operatives. He regards them as self-help for the people themselves and as the only way of meeting the problems of Dutch and Chinese Control over external and inter-island trade. His Ministry's plans, made at the beginning of 1951, now show tangible results; by the end of December 1953 the number of people's co-operatives was 8,223 (there were 5,770 in 1951); and the total membership was 1,392,345 (the 1951 figure was 1,000,324). Further, by the end of July 1952, 5,900 people (including 158 women) had attended training courses and of that number 4,750 passed their tests and returned to their villages in all parts of Indonesia to become the backbone of the co-operative movement. Parallel with the growth of village co-operatives, the Ministry of Trade and Commerce has helped to transform village credit banks into village credit co-operatives with the aim of soon creating an autonomous central co-operative credit bank.

In Java, where the density of population and a constant

under-employment makes some degree of industrialization an urgent need, the Ministry of Economic Affairs has made cottage industry co-operatives the basis of village economy. Cottage industries—weaving, pottery, leather work, carving, silver work —are a very marked feature of village life and, if developed along efficient lines, they can become an important industrial potential. The Government decided that assistance could best be given by superimposing upon groups of co-operatives a 'Central' Production Plant which would help them to become self-contained and economic enterprises. The 'Central Production Unit' purchases raw materials and sells it to the production unit on a non-profit basis; it prepares and processes raw material; it gives technical guidance on improved methods and processes, and provides mechanical finishing of products to a standard quality. This scheme has been financed partly by the Government and partly by the T.C.A. Grant Aid Programme, which has contributed $200,000 for hand tools and $500,000 for machinery and equipment. The United Nations Technical Assistance Administration have supplied two small industry experts and twelve specialist experts to give technical guidance through training and development institutes of industry, chemistry, testing materials, leather, textiles, ceramics, and batik.

The 'Centrals' scheme has now functioned long enough to provide some idea of the effectiveness of its work. Take, for example, the improvements in pottery. The Institute of Ceramics in Bandung designed a new kind of kiln and a new type of potter's wheel. Village people were soon convinced that these were far more efficient; whereas their old methods with open-type circular kilns meant many rejects—sometimes 15%—because the firing was uneven, they can now produce better quality goods and better designs comparable in quality and cheaper in price than imported pottery. How much this can mean in the economy of the country is illustrated in the import statistics for 1951 which showed a figure of 25 million rupiahs for the import of tea sets etc. Similarly, in the case of textiles; the Textile Institute in Bandung has designed a small hand-operated loom and worked out plans for standardizing dyeing yarn and finishing and dyeing cloth for sarongs. Previously

o*

individual units did this work in small quantities, which was uneconomic. Throughout this section of village industry in Java the 'Centrals' idea has taken hold of the villages; there are now twenty-one 'Centrals' covering a variety of village industries; the making of small wooden and metal tools; the designing and development of parasols; improvements in leather work and the introduction of new designs.

At the present time the 'Centrals' are managed by a Board of Directors consisting of local people and a representative of the Department of Industry. They are operated as a private limited company with the Government holding the controlling interest. The suggestion is that when all initial loans are repaid to the Government, the Department will withdraw their control and local Boards of Directors will be entirely responsible.

This cottage industrialization is clearly most important in over-populated Java with its large measure of under-employment and seasonal fluctuations. But the idea is one which is applicable to other parts of the country and the Government will be wise to extend the schemes now operating in Java. It is difficult for people in the industrialized Western world to appreciate how much this cottage industrialization means in building a balanced economy. Men, women, and children have a natural talent for all kinds of handwork; their weaving looms, pottery wheels and carving tools are usually old-fashioned in design and uneconomic in the amount of labour they demand; they sell their work to middlemen, mainly Chinese, at prices which do not allow the accumulation of any capital. With the few rupiahs they receive for exquisitely designed jewellery or hand-woven materials, they purchase cheap, tawdry, mass-produced oddments from the factories of Japan and Hongkong. The 'Centrals' scheme cuts through this vicious circle, by making it possible for consumer goods in certain fields to be economically produced without the exploitation of labour which has characterized Japanese village industries. The 'Centrals' assist by developing local talent, by cutting down foreign imports. In due course they should help to raise the standard of living of village people who constitute 90% of the total population.

Whilst the Republic has made great progress in the development of Co-operatives and Centrals, it has so far failed to tackle the problem on which its future largely depends, transmigration, a matter of life or death for Indonesia. Unlike most other countries with a large population, she has abundance of rich, uncultivated land. Thousands of acres of jungle in Sumatra and Sulawesi lie untouched. In South Kalimantan vast swamps could produce enough rice to make up Indonesia's total annual deficit of 650,000 tons, and enough fish to feed the whole country. Transmigration is the key to Java's overcrowding which is increased every year at the rate of 600,000; it is the key to a desperate shortage of foodstuffs and it is essential for a balanced economy. To solve this problem, it is admitted that 20 million people must be moved. This means that every day, 2,000 people have to be settled outside Java; in the past two years the Government has moved 20,000, and some of them have returned home. Dutch administration failed to solve the problem. The Republic cannot afford to fail. What is needed is a Government Department which can collect and co-ordinate the activities of a variety of personnel. Representatives from Kalimantan, Sumatra, and other under-populated areas should be asked to prepare their own estimates of the number and type of immigrants they can absorb. Representatives from the Ministry of Communications must plan transport and organize the building of small vessels for inter-island traffic since the country is still almost entirely dependent on Dutch shipping. Representatives from the Ministries of Information and Education must publicize the advantages of transmigration. Representatives from the trade unions must co-operate in the multitude of labour problems that are involved and women's organizations make their contribution to social welfare. The State Planning Bureau of Dr. Ali Sastroamidjojo's Government stated in February 1954 that transmigration 'ranks second in the priority list' (food was ranked first). 'Any kind of development on Java', it continued, 'is impeded by the population pressure which reduces the income per head, leaving no opportunity for an expanded market to absorb industrial products. This lack of market limits the possibilities for industrial expansion only to

395

import-replacing industries.' Yet although the urgency of trans-migration is officially admitted, and 180 million rupiahs were allocated for transmigration schemes in 1954 as against 67 million in 1953, large-scale plans still remain chiefly on paper and the end of the year survey showed how much transmigration was still lagging behind schedule.

Assuming the success of such plans, Indonesia still remains fundamentally an agricultural country, producing, however, raw materials which will have a world demand in any foreseeable future. Her industrial development depends on the relation of her exports and imports, since practically all technical equipment must be purchased abroad. Unlike India, there is no established trading class; there are no Indonesian Birlas. Originally, the Government tried to overcome this problem by providing financial facilities in certain reserved trades to about 250 importers. Money was allocated for import licences in textiles, weaving yarn, and sundry goods. But this experiment did not prove a success. 'To impose upon the economic system an artificial class of Government-created and subsidized Indonesian capitalists might do something to help national pride,' but, as Sjahrir said—and his view is shared by many others—'it does nothing practical to solve the basic economic problems. What the "benteng" experiment has done is to encourage corruption, not production.'[4] The present tendency is to develop foreign trade along lines of State trading. Step by step the Government has freed its hands to become an independent trading nation. In August 1951, the Java Bank was taken over from the Dutch whose main banking concern it had been for 125 years. This was followed by the setting up of a Stock Exchange in Djakarta supervised by the Stock Exchange Association with a predominantly Indonesian membership. In finance, as in other departments, the lack of trained staff is still a serious handicap. The result is that foreign members—almost exclusively Dutch—are only gradually being replaced. Since 1950, only twenty-six specially selected Indonesian candidates have been considered fit to take responsible positions.

When the Finance Minister reviewed the operations of the

Java Bank on the 125th anniversary of its foundation, he announced that on December 31st, 1952,

'there were 218 importing firms on the books, 130 of these being Indonesian concerns, 14 Chinese, 31 Dutch, and 16 owned by proprietors of other nationalities.'[5]

The Bank had opened credits amounting to 108 million rupiahs. Half of this total was for Indonesian firms, 9 million rupiahs for Chinese concerns, 43 million rupiahs for Dutch firms and 9 million rupiahs for firms belonging to other nationals.

Parallel with the Java Bank, a Directorate of Foreign Economic Relations set up by the Ministry of Trade and Industry deals with an increasing number of bilateral agreements. These are important for two reasons: they break the Dutch monopoly, giving Indonesian trade a chance to find its own level, and to depend on normal economic requirements rather than on the necessities of a colonial Power; and they facilitate a much wider range of imports which in turn means a diversification of small industries.

The European Office of the Central Purchasing Agency, itself a new organization, issued statistics which indicate the present trends in Indonesian trade with Europe.

	Value of Orders placed 1952	Value of Orders placed Jan.–June 1953	Value of Orders being negotiated July 1st, 1953
Dutch guilders ..	19,006,731·98	13,204,705·13	33,276,182.35
British pounds ..	20,202.10.4½	45,706.0.7	132,240.53
German marks	434,826·54	256,973·33	325,255·75
U.S. dollars ..	12,103·22	1,242·70	10,477·69
Belgian francs ..	2,647,607·20	60,425·00	571,925·00
Swiss francs ..	26,137·00	475·00	1,751,295·00
Danish kroner ..	1,640·37	—	1,660·00
French francs ..	23,327,765·00	—	33,866·50
Swedish kroner	25,440·00	866,723·26	889,653·26
Number of orders	818	213	200 [6]

Since these figures were made available several factors have encouraged the extension of Indonesian trading; the Chinese

People's Republic has now emerged as a trading nation; Japan has increasingly shown a desire to be free from some of the economic entanglements with the United States and to regain her pre-war position in South-east Asia; and, thirdly, Communist policy has developed a trade offensive the results of which are only now beginning to be calculable. In the second half of 1954, Indonesia signed an agreement (in July) with Czecho-Slovakia by which she will export rubber (the Czechs will pay 10% above the price current on the London market for Indonesian rubber), tin, copra, coffee, etc., and will export machinery, motor cars and motor cycles, ceramics and textiles. A Trade Agreement with Rumania, signed in August, covered similar products. The Poles have a permanent trade representative in Djakarta handling the trade agreed on in the treaty of 1953 which was renewed in July last year. With East Germany there is a barter agreement. A trade delegation to the Soviet Union suggested that credits might be forthcoming and that the U.S.S.R. could be an important market for such materials as rubber, tin, oil and copra. The Trade Agreement signed with the Chinese People's Republic on September 1st provides for the exchange of goods to the value of £6 million; cotton goods, silk, and machinery are Chinese imports, and the Indonesians will export rubber, tin, copra, etc.

During the past year, new Trade Agreements have also been signed between Norway and Indonesia, the total value of which is 47,245,000 florins. The Norwegians will provide paper and agricultural equipment and Indonesia, coffee, rubber, tin, etc. An agreement with France brought up to date an earlier one and added a new arrangement providing credits up to 12,000 million francs in respect of capital goods ordered by Indonesia in the current trade year. A Trade Mission has visited Latin-American countries. Its leader expressed the view that Argentine, Chile and Mexico, which until now had obtained rubber through the New York market, now wished to make *direct* purchases from Indonesia, provided that quantity and quality could be guaranteed. Similarly, there was a considerable market for Indonesian tea which in the past had always been imported via Holland. A trade delegation consisting of senior officials of the Ministries of Economic Affairs, Foreign Affairs and the Bank of Indonesia is planned to visit the Middle East and a Trade Agreement has now been signed with Egypt. Here again, in Dutch times, Indonesian tea held a strong position in the Egyptian market, as did other produce such as spices, coffee, hides and skins. But they were imported via Holland. The Republic aims at direct trade. In short, Indonesia has emerged as a trading nation on her own behalf. Holland's trading monopoly has finally been broken and in the future Dutch trade will be determined more and more by normal economic requirements rather than by the necessities imposed by colonialism.

Indonesians, like other countries with the unbalanced economy imposed by colonial rule, are faced with alternative types and sources of capital investment. One is the normal industrial investment now in foreign hands, but conceivably in Indonesian hands at a later stage of development. Such capital is subject to heavy risks, and, at the present time, to the difficulties of insecurity in certain parts of the country. The rate of interest is high and the foreigners are considerable, even main, beneficiaries. This type of private capital investment is not only considered as inadvisable, it is not likely to be forthcoming; the current earnings on capital invested in the United States manufacturing industry average between 15 and 20%, and an even higher rate would therefore be necessary to attract it into less developed countries.

The second type of foreign capital investment is one which can be directed towards those new industries on which alone the country can make any considerable progress: non-profit-making development of utilities, roads, harbours, communications, irrigation schemes, electric power projects, all of them under Government control and therefore holding a Government guarantee.

The difficulties which arise from the admission of foreign capital are exacerbated by political considerations. At the present time, and in any foreseeable future, the United States is the most important source of exportable capital. The sum of 3·1 million rupiahs which America has made available through T.C.A. for the year 1952–1953 is a humiliating sum. Indeed, it is much less than the amount of money Indonesia would make on her own account if the United States did not take advantage of her position to control the world price of rubber and other raw materials. (A fall of 1 cent per lb. in the price of rubber costs Indonesia $300 million per year.) In view of this prevailing suspicion of American policy, the Government has now offset the embarrassment of economic dependence on the dollar by joining the Colombo Plan. The total capital which is envisaged in carrying it out is relatively small, but, as Sudjatmoko writes, 'whilst the functioning of the Colombo Plan depends to a considerable extent on United States support, the significance and importance of the Plan lies beyond these limits'. The countries responsible for the Colombo Plan are regarded as seriously wanting to encourage economic progress and not merely to increase the pre-Republican flow of raw materials to the industrial nations of the West. Asian nations for the first time are planning the allocation of resources on priorities which they themselves fix.

One problem that is raised when the subject of capital investments is discussed is whether the Republic in any near future is likely to adopt a policy of nationalization. Again, there are those, usually on the political left, who advocate nationalization over a wider or narrower field according to the political complexion. The main fields where nationalization has been put forward with some vigour by the Communist-controlled Trade Union Federation, S.O.B.S.I., is oil, tin, and plantations, the three fields where most Dutch as well as other foreign capital has been invested. At the moment this is mainly propaganda. The Government would seem to be against any substantial measures of nationalization; the shortage of trained personnel is one reason against it and the second reason lies in the generally accepted need for foreign capital. But the issue is one which will be determined ultimately more by political than by purely economic considerations.

But capital investment is not the only problem; the need for 'human investment' presses on every scheme which the Government plans. In many cases, as a Group of Experts appointed by the Secretary-General of the United Nations points out, 'investment in people would lead to a greater increase of the flow of goods and services than would follow upon any comparable investment in material capital. This is most obvious in two spheres, the sphere of public health and the sphere of education.'[7]

In the second category, the same experts give priority to agricultural extension services, suggesting that

'an increase of 50% in two decades or less would be possible even without any substantial increase in capital or any substantial reorganization of the agricultural system, if farmers were taught modern techniques—mainly the use of fertilizers and of seed control.'[8]

Whilst there are still many question marks as to the future of Indonesian economy, the general outline is already fairly clearly defined. Certain elements of the colonial structure remain. Although key positions in the economic life of the country are still in Dutch and Chinese hands, the Republic has already laid some of the foundations of an economy which combines co-operative, socialist, and capitalist enterprise. With the exception of the Communists, most political parties, trade unions, and other organizations support the general principles embodied in this kind of mixed economy, and there is undoubtedly widespread enthusiasm for the co-operative system. The Government is thoroughly committed to an extension of the co-operative movement, and, since there is practically no vested interest in capitalism among the present generation of Indonesian leaders and few, if any, wealthy 'party bosses', the future role of co-operatives in Indonesian economy may be of great, and possibly decisive, importance.

The social forces which were released by nationalism and its final victory provided an impetus to socialist, not to capitalist, planning. Whilst complete socialization is not widely considered as an immediately practicable policy, there is general acceptance of the Government as responsible for the economic life and development of the country. Government officials, and not representatives of any financial or commercial group, purchase the railway's engines from Vienna which will replace old stock on the railways in Java, bulldozers from America to build new roads in Sumatra, and irrigation machinery from West Germany to drain the swamps of Kalimantan. The training of a generation of technicians is organized by the Government. In short, State planning and co-operatives are gradually taking the place of Dutch colonial monopoly in the economic structure of Indonesian society.

NOTES

[1] Calculation made by Arthur S. Keller in *Netherlands India as a Paying Proposition*. Published by Far Eastern Survey, New York, January 17th, 1940.

[2] *The Chinese in South-east Asia*, by Victor Purcell, pp. 501–2. Issued under joint auspices of the Royal Institute of International Affairs and Institute of Pacific Relations. Oxford University Press, 1950.

[3] *The Structure of Netherlands Indian Economy*, by J. H. Boeke, pp. 192–3. Published by I.P.R., New York, 1942.

[4] *Manchester Guardian*, March 3rd, 1953.

[5] *Indonesian Information*, Vol. IV, No. 2, February 5th, 1953. Published by Ministry of Information.

[6] Ibid., No. 12, November 16th, 1953. Issued by Ministry of Information.

[7] *Measures for the Economic Development of Underdeveloped Countries*, p. 52. United Nations, 1951.

[8] Ibid.

CHAPTER XVIII

MEETING THE WORLD

INDONESIANS meet the world today, neither as colonial showpieces nor as decorative, though subsidiary, motifs in the pattern of benevolent paternalism, but as citizens of an independent country. Indonesian Ambassadors have equal status with Dutch Ambassadors in thirty-eight countries; their representatives have an equal share in the work of the United Nations and in international conferences on technical, industrial, social, and educational problems; Indonesian students travel everywhere in search of the best and the most suitable training; Indonesian Trade Missions roam the whole world, free to make beneficial agreements now that the products of their 3,000 islands are no longer concentrated on the enrichment of Holland. The Indonesian horizon has been extended with bewildering speed. The Dutch are gradually accustoming themselves to the fact that Holland is no longer an Empire but a small European nation which may reasonably hope to maintain some ancient trading interests in the Far East.

The Republic joined the world community with a diary in which there were no engagements. True, she started her adventure with the troublesome chaperonage of the Netherlands-Indonesian Union, but this did not determine her association with other Powers, nor influence her decisions on matters of foreign policy. This influence could not survive once the Dutch joined N.A.T.O. By becoming a strategic and an economic outpost on President Eisenhower's world map of the American century, they became committed in the 'cold war'. This made the Netherlands Indonesian Statute suspect and unworkable since it stated that the two countries would co-operate in their foreign relations and that neither would make a treaty with a third party without consultation with the other. As Holland aligned herself more closely with America, Indonesian Governments became increasingly committed to 'positive neutrality'. The Union Statute had long become a dead letter when a protocol for its abolition was formally signed at The Hague on August 10th, 1954. Every Republican Government was committed to its dissolution, every political party demanded it. Many Dutchmen also regarded it as a meaningless symbol, and were more relieved than embarrassed when Ali Sastroamidjojo's Government showed more toughness than its predecessors and put an end to it.

The artificial ties imposed by a colonial relationship might have given way, as they did in the case of Britain and her former Asian possessions, to the healthy friendliness with powers which believe in co-existence. Two military actions plus the fact that the Dutch have to this day refused to consider ways and means of transferring West Irian to the Republic go a long way towards explaining why this did not happen in the case of Indonesia and Holland. Indeed, in her foreign relations, Indonesia has moved further and further away from Holland. By the time the Republic could formulate a foreign policy, her two most important neighbours—Burma and India—were already committed to neutrality. It was argued that in the event of a war—and until the tension eased in 1954 after the Geneva Conference, a war was regarded as probable—these three countries could remain neutral. Further, if from this centre—this area of peace as Nehru calls it—the perimeter of anti-war forces could be extended to other Asian and Arab nations, a third world war might be averted. This common measure of agreement was expressed in Treaties of Friendship with India and with Burma in the spring of 1953. A similar Treaty was signed with Pakistan and came into effect in May 1953. Religious associations have always drawn Egypt and Indonesia together; as the leading Arab country and the first to recognize the Republic in its earliest days, the Egyptians have enjoyed a warm reception in the Republic. In December 1952 it recognized King Farouk as 'King of Egypt and the Sudan'. General Neguib's Government had a far warmer welcome, and the Indonesians officially suggested that the Egyptian Prime

Minister should be invited to the Conference in Colombo. When the Asian Prime Ministers met, Dr. Ali Sastroamidjojo persuaded his colleagues to support his idea of an Afro-Asian Conference. As ex-colonial countries they were all anxious to support the African struggle against colonialism and the Indonesian Prime Minister was asked to take preliminary steps for such a conference. Dr. Ali Sastroamidjojo has on more than one occasion expressed his view that the centre of international affairs has now passed from Europe to Asia; that the balance of power in the world is shifting to Asia and that Indonesia's desire for peace 'would be best satisfied if the present shifts led to the serving of the interests of Asia and the abandonment of the outdated policy of subjugating Asian wishes to those of other continents'. This idea was uppermost in the minds of the Prime Ministers of Indonesia, India, Burma, Pakistan and Ceylon when they met in Bogor at the end of 1954. The result of their discussions was a joint invitation to twenty-five 'sovereign' States to attend an Afro-Asian Conference in Indonesia at the end of April 1955. These States extend from the Gold Coast to Japan; all the Arab States are included—unhappily at the expense of excluding Israel; the Central African Federation, Libya, Egypt, the Sudan, Gold Coast, Ethiopia and Liberia were invited as the independent parts of Africa. Iran, North and South Vietnam, and more significantly, the Chinese People's Republic.

Indonesia's emphasis on co-operation with African nations is only partly due to the community of religious interests with Muslim countries such as Egypt and Tunisia. So long outside the main stream of world affairs, Indonesians are still sensitive to the fact, which is indisputable, that most people know them and their country only through Dutch eyes. They may increase their prestige by carving for themselves a special niche in the history of post-war nationalism. At the same time, whilst other Asian leaders may feel that problems such as the future of Indo-China and Peking's membership of U.N. must be given priority, none of them doubts the value of African nations being free to play an increasing role in the world.

It is difficult to understand why Indonesia, like India and Burma, paid so little attention to the colonial war in Indo-China. Indonesians might reasonably have been expected to give their blessing, if not their specific approbation, to President Ho Chi Minh. But their concern to remain neutral in the 'cold war' proved stronger than their desire to give support to a colonial struggle and in 1950 when the issue was debated in Parliament simultaneously with the question of recognizing the Chinese People's Republic, the members were non-committal on the Vietnamese issue—an attitude that was made easier by the fact that the Vietnamese Republic had not recognized that of Indonesia. At the same time no one supported Bao Dai and a compromise motion, introduced by Mohammed Natsir, urging caution and the need for more information, was only carried by a margin of eleven (49 to 38). A few months later, Natsir himself was Prime Minister and referred to this equivocal policy:

> 'As regards the question about the Government's standpoint vis-a-vis the Ho Chi Minh Government, the Government's reply is the same as that of the Hatta Government, that is, that recognition should be given to the whole people —should it be united by democratic procedure—rather than to a part of the people.'[1]

Successive Governments in Djakarta did not modify this policy one way or the other until the spring of 1953, when two 'unofficial' observers were sent to establish the facts of the war, then extended to Laos and Cambodia. When the Sastroamidjojo Government took office in August 1953, no reference was made to Indo-China in official statements of foreign policy. At the end of the year, it was left to the Minister of Labour, Professor Abidin, to state officially that the Government 'which is committed to support the freedom struggle of all peoples against colonialism, is wholeheartedly behind the efforts of the Indo-Chinese to attain their independence'. This belated recognition of the Vietnamese cause was made at a ceremony marking International Solidarity Day and was accompanied by a statement from the Committee demanding an immediate end to the war, a speedy armistice, and a peaceful solution. Later, when Nehru had announced to the world his suggestions for a cease-fire in Vietnam, the Indonesian Government followed suit, and from then onwards joined with the Colombo Powers in all its proceedings to bring an end to the war.

Unlike the Vietnamese war, the Korean war became overnight an issue for the United Nations, and Indonesia, which became its sixtieth member in September 1950, could not remain inactive. Events in Korea played a negligible role in Indonesian affairs, but at Lake Success decisions had to be made. On the main issue of the war, there was no doubt as to Indonesian neutrality. Immediately the war started, the Government stated that they had no ties with North or with South Korea. 'North Korea is under Russian protection and the South Korean representative is sponsored by the United States,' their first statement ran. 'This so-called civil war is the first and foremost matter concerning the two Powers in the "cold war", namely the Russians on one side and America and Britain on the other.' A month later the Government denied facilities to warships taking part in the Korean operations and Indonesian citizens were barred from volunteering for service in Korea on penalty of losing their citizenship.

At Lake Success, Indonesian policy was vacillating, and on occasions unashamedly opportunist. Her delegation was usually led by Mr. L. N. Palar, who had put his country's case so ably in the days when it was fighting for its existence. He now co-sponsored a resolution to set up a three-person cease-fire group and a second one for a seven-nation group to consider a peaceful solution. On the vital issue of crossing the 38th parallel, Indonesian support was given both in Peking and at Lake Success to the series of proposals made by India. But when these failed and the crucial resolution naming the People's Republic of China as an 'aggressor' was moved in the Assembly in February 1951, Indonesia abstained. Only India and Burma, apart from the Soviet *bloc*, registered their opposition. When the Additional Measures Committee, set up as a result of the 'aggressor' resolution, proposed an embargo on the shipment of war material to China, Indonesia again abstained. By this time—

May 1951—Indonesia was enjoying 'the Korea boom' in rubber and tin, and there were serious misgivings as to the wisdom of the embargo resolution. They were partially resolved by taking advantage of the doubt as to whether or not rubber was a strategic commodity within the meaning of the resolution.

The Korean war has played a very small part in the affairs of Indonesia. There was little public interest. It was only casually followed in the press, ministerial statements accorded it scarcely more than a passing reference. At Lake Success expediency determined instructions which were given to the delegate. In the final conference at Geneva, Indonesia, like most other Asian Powers, was not invited to take part. All in all, the war in Korea has been more important to the economy than the foreign policy of Indonesia; in the former it created a vital, though artificial boom in the demand for her raw materials, in the latter it was a side issue.

Economic considerations played a similarly important role in Indonesian policy towards a Japanese Peace Treaty. When America and Britain sent invitations in September 1951 asking fifty-five nations to take part in discussions on a Japanese Peace Treaty, the Sukiman Government vacillated. Whereas India, Burma, and Yugoslavia turned down this invitation, the Indonesians took the line of least resistance and gave permission to a delegation to attend the Conference in San Francisco as observers. The then Foreign Minister, Dr. Subardjo, tended to pursue a pro-Japanese line and this made him an easy victim to American pressure. The result was that the Japanese Peace Treaty was signed at San Francisco by the Indonesian delegate. When Dr. Subardjo returned to Djakarta, he gave the following explanation of his decision:

'My entire delegation after sizing up the situation in and around the Conference decided to advise the Government to sign the treaty. This advice was given as a consequence of the results we obtained in regard to our claims concerning war reparations and the question of fishing rights. These claims will form the subject of a bilateral treaty with Japan and its basic principles have been agreed to by the Japanese delegation.'

But this decision received a great deal of criticism in the Indonesian Press, and even *Merdeka,* which was considered as Dr. Subardjo's mouthpiece, had to reinforce its support by saying that 'he was wise to sign the Treaty in order not to be branded as carrying out a policy in line with the Soviet *bloc*'.[2] The officially blessed magazine *Indonesian Review* provided another explanation:

'If Indonesia had followed in the steps of India, that is, decided to conclude a separate peace treaty, the sphere of good will would certainly be absent and Indonesia would certainly not be able to count on any support from the United States.'[3]

To put the matter bluntly: the Foreign Minister, supported by some of his colleagues in the Masjumi Party to which he was a recent convert, were trimming their sails to catch American dollars. As events were soon to prove, this departure from neutrality into the orbit of American influence did not reflect the majority of responsible opinion. Outside Communist circles which were inevitably committed to the Soviet *bloc*, although this was not always honestly admitted, people felt that the growing subservience of the Foreign Ministry to the American Ambassador in Djakarta undermined their standing in such countries as India and Burma, and weakened their position *vis-à-vis* the Chinese People's Republic as well as their large Chinese community. The result was that Indonesia's signature to the Japanese Peace Treaty was never ratified by Parliament. In 1955, no separate treaty has yet been signed with Japan, and no settlement has yet been made on the controversial subject of reparations. The incident undoubtedly had the effect of lowering Indonesian prestige in India and Burma where the idea gained strength that Indonesia was an uncertain partner in international affairs, even on the issue of a Japanese Peace Treaty where a common front might have been assumed. If her policy on this matter were doubtful, how far could she be trusted on the wider, more controversial subjects involved in a South-east Asian area of neutrality?

This uncertainty was reinforced soon after the San Francisco Conference. On January 5th, 1952, Foreign Minister Subardjo secretly signed an M.S.A. Agreement with the American Ambassador, Mr. Merle Cochran. Article 511-B of that agreement included certain military clauses. This signature therefore implied military commitments to the United States and was unquestionably a departure from the Government's policy of neutrality. When the matter was brought before the Cabinet on February 8th many of his colleagues attacked Dr. Subardjo, not only on grounds of policy, but because he had gone behind their backs in secret meetings with the American Ambassador. His reply was that international usage gave him the prerogative to make this agreement on his own initiative and that in any case the Prime Minister had been informed; a statement that Dr. Sukiman would neither admit nor deny. Dr. Subardjo's own party, the Masjumi, announced that it could not accept responsibility for the signing of the M.S.A. Agreement but would leave Parliament to decide the fate of the Cabinet. The P.N.I. rejected the agreement and demanded the resignation of the Government. On February 21st, after a crisis in which personalities played almost as large a part as policy, the Foreign Minister resigned, and two days later the Prime Minister and his Cabinet followed before Parliament could be called together. To add to the confusion an official broadcast made the bewildering remark that the 'resignation of the Cabinet should not be construed as meaning that the State would shirk its obligations arising from an agreement with a foreign country' and that they were fully aware that Dr. Subardjo's signature to the Mutual Security Aid Agreement 'had made a commitment'. This was indeed cold comfort for the American Ambassador, for whom the statement was presumably intended. For one point had emerged clearly, namely that no military commitment with the United States, even if only by implication as in the case of the M.S.A. Agreement would be endorsed by the Indonesian Parliament. This was not a matter of party. It was fundamentally a question of national pride. By their willingness to consider such a commitment, the Masjumi leaders compromised themselves as well as their party, and in the Government which was formed after several weeks of political bargaining, both the Prime Minister and the Foreign Minister belonged to the P.N.I.

When a new agreement was signed with America to take the place of Dr. Subardjo's secret agreement, it had no military clauses. The Wilopo Government, which held office from April 1952 until June 1953, was by no means amenable to American pressure, and when Mr. Merle Cochran resigned as Ambassador in February 1953, many editorial writers commented on his failure to draw Indonesia into the American sphere of influence. Economic considerations served to underline this marked drift in foreign policy. The 'Korea boom' was over and American interests in the tin and rubber markets of the world held a dagger at the throat of the raw material producers of Indonesia. A drop of a few cents in the price of rubber represented more than the whole amount which was provided by Technical Assistance Funds. The Anglo-American agreement to prohibit the shipment of strategic materials to China and other Communist countries was regarded as a victory for American diplomacy and a potential threat to South-east Asian countries so dependent on the export of rubber, tin, and other raw materials. The daily paper, *Indonesia Raya*, an independent paper not attached to any political party, wrote at this time:

'Do the United States and the United Kingdom regard the South-east Asian countries as children they can use as tools to do as they wish? They have brought down the prices of our raw materials, they have tried to forbid the South-east Asian countries to trade with their opponents, and now they are trying to persuade us to close our ports to ships transporting goods to their opponents' countries. What have they given us in exchange for all this?

'Low prices for our raw materials, and high prices for their industrial output and all kinds of other products. Indonesia should show the attitude she has adopted to such an appeal, which in any case, would not be in the interests of the Asian peoples but would only serve America's interests.'

The Wilopo Government—and any other conceivable Indonesian Government would have had to make the same decision—had to consider where its economic interests could be best furthered. Financial aid, technical assistance, and capital goods were, and remain, necessary for industrial expansion. The fact that United Nations aid was increasingly coloured by the requirements of America's 'cold war' policy led Indonesia, as it did other South-east Asian countries, to be careful of becoming dependent on this source of assistance. The Colombo Plan was free from such entanglements, and in December 1952, the Cabinet decided to take part in its activities. This Plan, a Cabinet spokesman said at the time, would open the door to possibilities of technical and economic aid from countries other than the United States, without binding Indonesia militarily or politically, and it would deepen relations with India and Pakistan.

Parallel with its activities as one of the Colombo Powers, the Wilopo Government strengthened its ties with Communist countries through trade agreements with Poland, Hungary, Czechoslovakia, and Eastern Germany. These were supplemented by the exchange of Cultural Missions, and by direct contacts with people instead of the secondhand relationships which existed in the days of Dutch rule. When the Wilopo Government fell in June 1953, on questions of internal, not foreign affairs, the pattern of Indonesian policy was already outlined. Differences between political parties were far more of emphasis than of disagreement, and the new Foreign Minister, Sunario, at his first Press conference said that he did not intend to effect any radical changes in the foreign policy of his country. But on several issues the present Government has acted decisively where its predecessors fumbled. At long last, for instance, Indonesia and the Soviet Union have exchanged Ambassadors. All parties were committed to this policy in previous Governments, but the delaying tactics of the Masjumi had prevented its implementation. Similarly, all Governments were committed to the dissolution of the Netherlands-Indonesian Union. The Government of Dr. Ali Sastroamidjojo achieved it on August 10th, 1954. They were all committed to the transfer of West Irian to Indonesian sovereignty. It was raised in the United Nations in 1954 and the focus of international interest on the issue may prove a step towards solution. In short, the present Government has carried out a more active policy than that of its predecessors. After the failure of American dollar diplomacy to draw the Republic into its economic and strategic orbit, the course of

Indonesian foreign policy was set. There is today no group in the country which could win any measure of support for commitments, outside those of the United Nations, which remotely implied economic or military dependence on the United States. The balance of power, as seen from Indonesia, has shifted from Europe to Asia; the Geneva Conference with China's emergence as a decisive influence in world affairs, and the leading role which India has played in one situation after another, provide plenty of evidence for the realism of this analysis. As long as the policy of co-existence is followed by Communist Powers, Communist and non-Communist have a common policy. The fact that Communist propaganda is more demonstrative should not be allowed to obscure the issue; if Indonesian Communists had been as formidable as part of the American and Dutch Press would have us believe, the present emphasis on neutrality with Colombo Powers would long ago have given way to exclusive co-operation with Moscow and Peking.

The Communists and their supporters naturally give priority to the Chinese People's Republic and the Soviet Union in all considerations of foreign, as indeed of domestic policy. And in that order. The history of China and Indonesia has often been interwoven, and nearly 2 million Chinese living in the Republic feel a loyalty to China, whatever Government may be in power.[4] The success of Communism in China has naturally given a considerable fillip to Chinese Communists living in Indonesia. But no political party could have adopted any other line than that of recognizing the Government of Mao Tse-tung. Again, the present Government has acted where predecessors only passed resolutions. Parliament decided to recognize Mao Tse-tung in June 1950, but it was left to Ali Sastroamidjojo's Cabinet to fix the exchange of Ambassadors in April 1953.

The official policy of the Government includes all the items which figure in Communist propaganda. When the World Peace Conference held a meeting in Djakarta last January, its resolutions were only more dramatically worded versions of Government objectives. But the Government—and in this it undoubtedly reflects the majority of public opinion—makes a wider interpretation of positive neutrality. The emphasis is placed on co-operation with India, Burma, and Ceylon as fellow Colombo Powers endeavouring to build an area of peace in South-east Asia, and special references are made to Pakistan with which Indonesia has close religious ties. In evaluating the foreign policy of Indonesia, people often overlook the fact that she is overwhelmingly a Muslim country and that to satisfy the majority of his people Dr. Ali Sastroamidjojo must think as carefully of other Muslim countries as the Communists have to consider those which have Communist Governments. The idea of an Afro-Asian Conference, sponsored by Indonesia, was in line with his policy. It introduced a number of Muslim countries in Africa to the independent Powers of South-east Asia. And it appealed to the anti-colonial sentiment which still dominates every political party.

The outstanding event at the Afro-Asian Conference was Prime Minister Chou En-lai's offer to have direct talks with the Americans on the subject of Formosa. But for the Muslim world, which accounted for about half of the countries represented at Bandung, the possible reorientation of Egypt's policy towards neutralism has far-reaching significance. The smaller powers of North Africa are closely associated with Egypt, whilst other Muslim nations already committed in varying degrees to strategic and financial dependence on the West may gradually loosen their ties and move towards the area of neutralism.

Many different points of view were expressed by the delegates in Bandung, but on the colonial issue they spoke with a similar voice. They all supported the rights of the people of Algeria, Morocco and Tunisia and nationalist leaders from those countries were able to put their case to an audience representing about half the peoples of the world. Thus Dr. Ali Sastroamidjojo's objects in proposing the Afro-Asian Conference were remarkably well fulfilled.

In an overall picture of world affairs since Indonesia became an independent Republic, it can perhaps be said that her special contribution has been this effort to extend the area of neutrality to countries still fighting against colonialism. Sometimes vacillating, sometimes purely opportunistic, Indonesians are now meeting the world with a clearly cut policy which has the general approval of all political parties and of an increasingly vocal public opinion.

NOTES

[1] Declaration read at the opening of Parliament on September 21st, 1950. Published in *Indonesian Review*, Vol. I, No. 1, p. 63.

[2] *Indonesian Information*, Vol. 2, No. 18, October 4th, 1951, p. 1. Published by the Indonesian Embassy, London.

[3] 'Indonesia at the San Francisco Conference,' *Indonesian Review*, Vol. 1, No. 5, October–December 1951, p. 375.

[4] On December 24th, 1954, Radio Peking announced that an agreement had been reached with Indonesia on the problem of Chinese dual citizenship. On April 22nd, 1955, during his visit to the Bandung Conference, Prime Minister Chou En-lai and Foreign Minister Sunario signed a treaty which laid down a period of two years during which choice of nationality may be made by the Chinese living in Indonesia. Those who have not made their choice at the expiry of the two-year period are automatically to be given the nationality of the father. Chou En-lai expressed the hope that those who made their choice of nationality under this treaty would abide firmly by its provisions and called upon them, whether they chose Indonesian or Chinese citizenship, to work jointly together to further friendship between the two countries.

CHAPTER XIX

AFTER NATIONALISM?

A STORY is told of Confucius that when he was once asked to say what were the three things vital to a ruler, his reply was: 'Sufficiency of food, sufficiency of military power, and sufficiency of popular faith in the ruler.' When he was asked what he would omit if only two things were possible, he replied: 'Omit military power.' And if only one were possible? 'Let the people lose their food,' he answered, 'but keep their faith.' Many years later, Mrs. Vijaya Lakshmi Pandit, addressing the students of Gadjah Mada University in her capacity as President of the United Nations, expressed a similar idea. 'Europe', she said, 'has become great because she possessed men and women who wholeheartedly served their country and who did not particularly seek to gain their own profits. Asia's greatness collapsed because she did not possess people of that calibre. We should face this bitter fact and say to ourselves: this will not happen to Asia any more. Whatever will happen we, people of Asia, will serve ideals which are higher than our own greed, i.e. ideals which will first of all involve society, then our country and finally the world.'

Many Indonesians would admit that not all the ideals they cherished whilst fighting for their independence in guerrilla warfare have been achieved in the Republic. Young men and women, who spent the most impressionable years of adolescence in resisting first the Japanese and then the Dutch, now talk nostalgically of the 'Djogja days' when the country was united. They knew with passionate conviction what they were fighting against; the constructive problems of independence had not yet made their massive impact. When they did, Indonesians were, as a whole, less equipped to meet them than were their newly independent colleagues in South-east Asia. In some areas under

416

British rule, several generations had matured in the certainty that their independence was only a matter of time. No nationally conscious man or woman in India or Burma or Ceylon doubted that one day the British Government would have to fulfil its commitments and the powerful wing of the Labour movement, which was against all forms of colonialism, worked closely with the Asian nationalist organizations. And although Government after Government in Whitehall found ways and means of postponing the fulfilment of their pledges, they none the less met the demands of their Asian citizens for training in every branch of administration. This did not happen in the case of Indonesia. The Dutch thought of it as 'the ageless Indies', and above all, 'our Indies', whilst the most fervent nationalist leader in pre-war days did not seriously expect to see an independent Republic in his own lifetime. In pre-war days, Indonesians were presented as happy children. Today many Dutchmen still adopt a heavy father attitude. This is deeply resented by Indonesians, especially as they become aware of the narrow horizon which restricts the outlook as well as the influence of what was once their ruling power. Whereas Britain's stature grew in the minds of Asians whom she ruled before the war, that of Holland has diminished for the peoples of Indonesia.

To these contrasts between British and Dutch colonial rule, and to the relative unpreparedness of Indonesian Nationalists to take power, we must add the wide divergences of philosophical tradition and background. There is both in Hindu and in Buddhist philosophy an asceticism which lends itself to self-sacrifice and self-discipline, to the devotion of one's life to an ideal. Gandhi was a natural figure in that climate of other-worldliness. It is impossible to imagine him as a leader of Indonesian nationalism. The idea of renunciation is not part of Islamic thought, and it has never developed as a social force in the Indonesian nationalist movement. This has had far-reaching results, not so much in the period of struggle when a common enemy may be sufficient driving force to produce a common effort, but in the period of power when personalities have played such an excessive role in Republican life.

Religion is here only reinforcing geography. The wide

separation of thousands of islands, with their widely divergent development, retarded the growth of a cohesive nationalist movement and a leadership which provided a common inspiration. President Sukarno's slogan 'From Sabang to Merauke' (that is, the Indonesian equivalent of 'from Land's End to John o' Groats') is a new concept in Indonesian history. It still has a much wider significance in Java than in any other part of the Republic.

These are all factors which must be reckoned with in an evaluation of the Republic. They are easily underestimated for the world still tends to look at Indonesia through Dutch eyes, success or failure is more often than not judged according to other standards in South-east Asia which are not applicable, and events in Java are allowed to obscure the realities of life elsewhere in these 3,000 islands. At the same time, it is true that the Indonesian pattern is more elusive than that of India, for example, or of Burma. There is an undercurrent of uncertainty, a suggestion of instability. This goes deeper than the fact that Indonesia has not yet held its first General Election, although the failure of any Government to implement its pledge to do so is one of the contributory causes of the present instability.

The victory of nationalism meant the end of colonial rule, but it did not mean a social revolt. It inspired the desire for social change in the minds of thousands of young men and women, and it led to a greater degree of social and political consciousness among the masses. They belonged to all political parties and to none. Nationalism was and still is such a powerful driving force in Indonesian political life that with the exception of the two extremes, the Nahdatul Ulama and the P.K.I. (the Communist Party), political parties have no sharply defined features; the first party is based on an extremist form of Islam, the second is theoretically extremist, but constantly shifts its course to meet the prevailing winds of public opinion always with its main direction plotted in Moscow and Peking. Thus political parties overlap. They have a right wing and a left wing and on their peripheries there are outstanding political figures whose position is determined far more by personal considerations, often personal feuds and jealousies, than by any fundamental differences in political philosophy. A General Election does not solve these problems, but political life is healthier if people have the chance of expressing their choice as to who should rule them and the rulers themselves have a greater sense of duty if they are directly responsible to the electorate.

There is no doubt that the long delay in holding the first General Election in Indonesia has helped to increase party intrigues, given a false emphasis to personalities at the centre, and led to indifference and scepticism among people outside Java or led them to carry on with their own affairs without too much attention to Djakarta. Externally, it has had the effect of stimulating people's doubts as to the stability of the Republic, doubts which have been strengthened by Dutch propaganda and activity. Although traditions and post-war conditions in India, Burma, and Ceylon are different from those in the Republic, it is nevertheless true that General Elections in these countries proved an effective mobilization of popular energy, an incentive to responsible rule at the centre and in the provinces, a demonstration to the world of political maturity. With this in mind, many people ask the very relevant question why a General Election has been so often postponed in Indonesia, why, indeed, the Government only now asks for the mandate of the people. The excuse of difficult communications is not enough; India had to cope with as great a problem in an area stretching from Himachal Pradesh to Cape Comorin. Internal rebellions cause many difficulties, but Burma had a Communist and a Karen rebellion on her hands in 1951 when she held her first General Election, extending it over several months. Again, the problem of illiteracy. This applies to every country in Asia. The unhappy fact in Indonesia is that party manoeuvres and personalities still play too large a part in political life, especially in Djakarta. And the conflict between Islam and Marxism for control of the nationalist movement remains unresolved.

The significance of the present Government is that for the first time, political leaders who subscribe to what might be loosely termed a Marxist view of society are now in key positions, where they can play a decisive role in domestic and in foreign policy. In all previous Governments, the Masjumi either held or could control a majority of Cabinet posts. This party, which is still the largest in the country, is not represented in the Government formed in July 1953. It is still the best organized party, since the mosque remains the centre of religious and of social life throughout the country, except in the Minahasa, the Moluccas, and Central Sumatra which are Christian and in Bali which is Hindu. But it does not represent any dynamic of social change, and its outstanding leaders seem to be more and more on the defensive, standing for a static pattern of society which does not meet the economic or the cultural needs of the people. During the past year it has had to meet the propaganda of the Communists, dishonest though it often was, linking together the Masjumi and the disruptive tactics of Darul Islam. While it is true that early Masjumi Governments failed to tackle this problem, it is quite untrue to suggest that progressive and able men like Natsir and Rum have anything in common with this fanatical wing of Islam. The Masjumi's advantage in having the ready-made organization of the mosques at its disposal may become less important, for the parties in the Government, above all the P.N.I., have made full use of their position in appointing their nominees to key posts in provincial administration. For the first time in its history the P.N.I. has the chance of building up a nation-wide party able to challenge the Masjumi. There are signs that the Socialists may draw nearer to the Masjumi, a development which is not as curious as it may seem at first sight. The extremists of the Masjumi—the Nahdatul Ulama—broke away from the party and are in the present Government. The left wing, which includes Natsir and Rum, has a great deal in common with the Socialists, and in their joint opposition to the P.N.I. and to the P.K.I. they might find some electoral basis of alliance. There remain a number of smaller parties which have members in the present Cabinet, and the Communists. Among the smaller parties, there are those like the P.I.R. which are on the whole anti-Communist and conservative, others like the Partai Buruh which are Communist but not linked with Moscow, and the B.T.I. (Peasants' Association) and the S.K.I. (People's Federation Party) which are Communist in orientation.

The problem facing any aspirants for political power is how to win over the uncommitted as well as how to convert the hostile and the apathetic. The Communists concentrated their activities in the Trade Union Movement until several factors had the effect of widening the area of their appeal, the first internal, the second based on external developments. Whilst the P.K.I. is not officially represented in Dr. Ali Sastroamidjojo's Cabinet, there are enough Ministers with what might be called a general Marxist approach to influence policy in a Communist direction. The P.K.I., which gives a general support to the Government, acts as a kind of pressure group, both through its political organization and through the largest Federation of Trade Unions—S.O.B.S.I., whose policy it largely dictates. The external factor, which has undoubtedly helped the P.K.I. more than any other party, is the emergence of Communist China as a world power. The P.K.I. is much closer to Peking than to Moscow; its members study Mao Tse-tung more closely than Lenin.

Communist propaganda magazines, leaflets, and books written for every section of the community, well prepared and cleverly illustrated, can be seen on bookshops and on street markets from Sumatra to Kalimantan; they come from China or from Hong Kong, and only in a much smaller number from Moscow. Chinese propaganda broadcasts from Peking in Chinese and in Indonesian languages have had an influence which it would be hard to estimate, but that they have played a powerful part in the lives of the two million Chinese as well as among Indonesians, there can be no doubt. The emphasis is on Communist achievements, on peace; it is against Western ideas and above all it is anti-imperialist. This association of imperialism and the Western world, especially with America, is easily understood by the least politically conscious peasant. It appeals to him as one who was only yesterday a colonial subject; it appeals because the peasant everywhere wants peace; it appeals because America's post-war policy has alienated the majority of Asian peoples, suggesting a new form of imperialistic ambition. In short, the Chinese Revolution is a major instrument in the growth of Marxist ideas; the peasant still goes to the mosque on Fridays, the Hadji may still be the village headman, but glowing accounts of life in China appeal to women and men in the rice-fields, to workers on plantations still partly owned by the Dutch, and to those who recognize the need for more rapid industrialization or modernization (the two are not the same) in various sectors of the country's economy.

The P.K.I. has naturally made the most of these advantageous conditions, and its first pre-election move has led to a good deal of controversy. In the list of Names and Emblems for the General Election, the P.K.I. has renamed itself the 'Indonesian Communist Party and Independents', a strategic recognition of the fact that its real strength depends on bringing non-Communists under a Communist umbrella. It is still too early to estimate their chances of success. But there is no doubt that Marxist ideas have won many adherents and that Marxism is a challenge to Islam as a dynamic force in Indonesian society. It makes its appeal to a far wider area of popular feeling than the P.K.I. and any political party to achieve power will have to accept the general concepts of Marxist philosophy.

The non-Marxists will unquestionably resist active social changes; the secularists may hope to preserve traditions with a feudal background; the extreme Muslims may hope to deepen the hold of Islam on Indonesian society. But these are rearguard actions rather than a front-line attack. The mosque is likely to remain the centre of social and religious organization for the majority of Indonesians, and Islamic Law and customs colour the pattern of their society. But the desire for change, and the growth of self-confidence that comes from responsibility, will force the pace of progress. People want a better standard of living; they demand improved labour conditions; they need security, and believe that if the Government dealt with this question more energetically, conditions of security would be possible; they want the technical 'know-how' which made the West, and, later, Japan, rich and powerful. They are not interested in ideologies but in results. It matters less to many Indonesians that China is a Communist nation than that it is now a world power, laying the foundations of an industrial country. Thus, whilst the Communist Party, as such, has had only a limited appeal, it can scarcely be doubted that no political party could hope to win any considerable support by a policy based on anti-Communism; the bogy in the Indonesian mind resides in Amsterdam and Washington rather than in Moscow and Peking.

Whatever Government is in power in Indonesia, these tendencies will remain. The extreme wing of the Masjumi wants an Islamic State with an emphasis on close relations with Islamic countries. The Communists, however opportunist tactics might obscure it, want a Communist State which becomes integrated with other Communist countries. But between these two extremes, the majority of people are concerned with a Government which will settle some of the outstanding problems, fulfil pledges in the domestic field, and build closer relations, not only with the Communist world, but above all with India, Burma, Pakistan, and the Middle East.

What then are the problems which urgently call for a solution? Although this may not be immediately obvious, the first one is how to decentralize the present administration. In the conditions that existed at the time of the transfer of power, a Unitary State was essential for building a central authority over widely flung and extremely different types of people. 'Unity in Diversity' on the Republic's coat of arms was the expression of this need. But the problem now is how to maintain diversity in unity. The growth of this problem is a sign of progress, evidence of the cultural and political awareness of people in islands outside Java. As long as the Dayaks in Kalimantan were kept in their long-houses, the Toradjas of Sulawesi, the Kubu of Sumatra, and the isolated men and women were left in ignorance, Java could maintain its central position and Javanese could monopolize most of the administrative positions at home and abroad. Those days are over. A girl from Timor studying midwifery in England; Toradjas travelling to Makassar for higher education; Menangkabauers holding important posts in Embassies abroad; Achinese studying Mass Education in Los Angeles, and Balinese studying social problems in India—these are all signs that this problem is gradually being solved. Too gradually, and only under pressure.

The demand for regional autonomy, and with it the increasing share of the provinces in local as well as in central administration, is one which would be made of any Government. It has been most emphatically voiced until now in Sumatra, Bali, and Atjeh. In the middle of 1953, Mohamad Shafei, a Member of Parliament, and one of the country's most distinguished educationalists, raised the question of local autonomy in a parliamentary debate. If people were to remain loyal to the central Government, he suggested, then some kind of federal administration must replace the present over-centralized rule in Djakarta. From Bali a similar request took a different form. Why, asked Balinese leaders, was their religion (Hinduism) not recognized and represented in the Ministry of Religious Affairs and in provincial services? The reply was that for a religion to be recognized it was necessary to designate both a 'Holy Book' and a Founder. The Balinese held a conference at the end of 1952 to comply with these demands, but so far the Government has not recognized Balinese Hinduism. In the case of the Achinese, who are as firmly attached to Islam as the Balinese are to Hinduism and far more dogmatic, the Government in Djakarta too long delayed demands for increased self-government. It was always improbable that the Achinese, with their tradition of independence and their aptitude for rebellion, would remain satisfied with their status as part of the province of North Sumatra. At last, on September 20th, 1953, Tengku Daud Buereuth (a religious leader who was Governor of Atjeh when it was a separate province) led an armed revolt and declared that henceforth Atjeh was part of the 'Indonesian Islamic State' proclaimed by the fanatical Darul Islam leader, Kartosuwirjo, in 1949. The result was a local war in which more than a thousand Achinese were killed. After this unnecessary waste of lives, the Government in Djakarta gave a belated promise to review the plan for regional autonomy and to go ahead with economic developments in Atjeh.

The much publicized problem of internal security is in part the result of over-centralization. For as long as there are disgruntled people who feel that the bottleneck of Djakarta slows down provincial plans, there is plenty of soil which is fertile for trouble-makers. In the early days of the Republic, Dutch army officers, remaining in the country by virtue of the Round Table Conference, were able to find supporters among the dissatisfied people of Moluccas and the Minahasa. In Makassar they found allies among the feudal lords of South Sulawesi.

But there are other causes which account for local rebellions which still threaten the security of the Republic. The most dangerous lies in the Darul Islam organization which aims at a theocratic State. In West Java, where it is strongest, a disciplined army of 5,000 well-armed men has fought the Government forces for more than four years with disastrous results for the country's economy. Confined in the beginning of the revolt to West Java, it now seems to be linked with rebellious forces in Atjeh and in South Sulawesi. No Government has yet seriously faced this problem. The problem of insecurity remains dangerous in these limited areas. Its importance has, however, been greatly exaggerated by hostile contributors in the Dutch, American and, sometimes, in the British Press.

A problem to which far too little attention has been devoted is that of transmigration. More than 40% of the population live in the islands of Java and Madura. The area of cultivable land in these areas is insufficient for the peasants, whilst industry remains as yet too undeveloped to absorb enough of them. A usual estimate is that Java is overpopulated to the extent of 20 million people. The Central Transmigration Board has prepared many blueprints, and the present Government allocated 180 million rupiahs in 1954, compared with 67 million in 1953, to deal with this problem. Even so, the number of people involved is only 90,000, comprising about 18,000 families; 10,000 of them are planned for South Sumatra, another 3,200 for Central Sumatra, 3,800 for Kalimantan, and 1,000 for Eastern Indonesia. If these plans materialize, then the pressure of population in Java will be reduced, and less developed areas can become economic and social assets to the whole country.

Transmigration is only one of the problems which face Indonesia's economy. The second is based on the extent of foreign control. Take the case of big estates, an important item in a country where 64 to 70% live on agriculture and associated undertakings. Figures which were issued in July 1954 by the Central Agricultural Department show that of the big estates in Java and Sumatra which employ 561,000 and 239,000 workers respectively, no less than 96% of them are foreign owned. The third difficulty lies in the fact that so large a proportion of middlemen are Chinese, whose main consideration is not necessarily the progress of Indonesians. The fourth is the result of restrictions on trade and on finance involved in the Round Table Conference Agreement. If the Republic had far more trained people than she has today these difficulties would still exist and would still cripple her economy. On the other hand, their existence underlines the need for more carefully considered short-term and long-term plans than any that have so far emerged from the present Government.

The Republic needs a far more closely co-ordinated financial and economic policy. A great deal of uncertainty exists about such important issues as foreign exchange and foreign capital investments; about the rules which determine import and export licences; about the scope and area of industrialization which is vital to raise the standard of living and to accumulate national capital; about the role of co-operatives in the national economy, and about the division of nationalized and private industry. Have the Indonesians themselves yet made up their own minds either on their internal economy or on the question of foreign capital? Have they faced the price they must pay for foreign capital?

The Republic needs an efficient, stable, and incorruptible Civil Service. This is not only a question of numbers. There is a shortage of trained people, but there is also a marked tendency in Indonesia, as there is in India, for young men and women to choose relatively easy positions in the Civil Service. The amenities of city life and the possible opportunities for travel abroad are often inducements to leave village life, which is isolated and backward. Unlike the Chinese, neither the Indonesians nor the Indians have yet succeeded in inspiring a great many young men and women to make the village the centre of their pioneering enthusiasm.

An efficient Civil Service needs stability. The frequent

changes of government have resulted in changes of personnel
and programme so that few Ministries have had the time or the
continuity for planning. There is, in addition, an extremely
dangerous tendency to make political affiliations the criterion.
This and the existence of corruption in some of the Ministries
have led to a good deal of foreign criticism. At the same time
the comparison that is too often and too easily made with the
period of Dutch rule is mistaken, for the basis of the Republic is
fundamentally different. Many of the present difficulties are
the growing pains of a nation which is only now discovering
itself.

This process of self-discovery in Indonesia, as in other
countries recently freed from colonial rule, is complex and
difficult. The older generation, after many years of struggle, has
achieved a certain measure of stability, in some cases, of power
and relative wealth. They are often too busy, sometimes too
complacent, to ask themselves how the victory of nationalism
can become the prelude to social change. They are apt to repeat
the old political slogans and fall back on the shortcomings of
their ex-colonial rulers instead of facing the problems which
arise from their own lack of experience or personal rivalry.
Will the younger generation which is growing up in an independent country, with a wider horizon and knowledge of the
modern world, face the challenge of building a new society
based on Indonesian traditions? Some may be tempted by the
material advancement of the more technically developed
countries and others may see short cuts in following the line of
Peking and Moscow. But for the majority of Indonesians with a
different background and with different economic and social
problems, they must find their own solution.

The achievements of the Republic have been made in the
democratic way, and there is every reason to believe that this is
the path which the vast majority of Indonesians choose. But the
democratic method is still on trial in Indonesia, as it is throughout South-east Asia where people are able to make their choice.
At home, a young democratic Republic, Indonesia is in the first
place the closest colleague of India, Pakistan, and Burma; the
horizon is now widened to include the People's Republic of

China. And beyond the borders of Asia, she looks to the unresolved colonial struggles of Africa, believing that in the continued existence of colonialism lies the greatest threat to peaceful
coexistence.

BIBLIOGRAPHY

MAIN WORKS OF REFERENCE

ANGELINO, Dr. de Kat: *Colonial Policy.* The Hague. 1931.

BALL, W. Macmahon: *Nationalism and Communism in East Asia.* Melbourne University Press and I.P.R. 1952.

BOEKE, Dr. J. H.: *The Structure of Netherlands Indian Economy.* I.P.R. 1942.
The Evolution of the Netherlands Indies Economy. I.P.R. 1946.

BOUSQUET, G. H., Professor: *A French View of the Netherlands Indies.* I.P.R. 1940. Oxford University Press. 1940.

BROEK, Jan O. M.: *Eocnomic Development of the Netherlands Indies.* I.P.R. 1942

CHAUDREY, I.: *The Indonesian Struggle.* Ferozons (Lahore). 1950.

DUBOIS, Cora: *Social Forces in Southeast Asia.* Minneapolis. 1949.

FURNIVALL, J. S.: *Netherlands India.* Cambridge University Press. 1939.

HAAR, B. Ter: *Adat Law in Indonesia.* Translated from Dutch. I.P.R. and Southeast Asia Institute. 1948.

Islands and Peoples of the Indies. Smithsonian Institution, Washington. 1943.

JACOBY, Erich H.: *Agrarian Unrest in Southeast Asia.* New York. 1949.

KAHIN, George Mc.T.: *Nationalism and Revolution in Indonesia.* Cornell University Press. 1952.

KENNEDY, Raymond: *Bibliography of Indonesian Peoples and Cultures.* Yale University Press. 1945.

de KLERCK, E. S.: *History of the Netherlands East Indies.* W. L. & J. Brusse, N.U. Rotterdam. 1938.

MADAN, B. K. (Editor): *Economic Problems of Underdeveloped Countries in Asia.* Indian Council of World Affairs and Oxford University Press.

VAN MOOK, H. J.: *The Stakes of Democracy in South-East Asia.* New York. 1950.

RAFFLES, Lady: *Memoir of the Life and Public Services of Sir Thomas Raffles.* John Murray. 1830.

RAFFLES, Sir Thomas Stamford: *The History of Java.* 2 vols. Black, Parburn and Allen and John Murray. 1817.

SJAHRIR, Soetan: *Out of Exile.* John Day & Co. 1949.

THAYER, Philip W. (Editor): *Southeast Asia in the Coming World.* Johns Hopkins Press. 1953.

TREVELYAN, G. M.: *British History in the Nineteenth Century*. (1782–1901.) Longmans, Green & Co. 1922.

VANDENBOSCH, Amry: *The Dutch East Indies*. University of California Press. Third ed. 1942.

VENKATASUBBIAH, H.: *Asia in the Modern World*. Asian Relations Conference and Indian Council of World Affairs. New Delhi. 1947.

VLEKKE, Bernard H. M.: *Nusantara*. Harvard University Press, 1943.

WERTHEIM, W. F.: *Effects of Western Civilisation on Indonesian Society*, I.P.R. 1950.

SOURCES

(Those quoted are marked with an asterisk)

Chapter I

DEKKER, N. A. Douwes. *Tanah Air Kita*. A book on the country and people of Indonesia. W. Van Hoeve. The Hague and Bandung. 1950.

*_The World Encompassed by Sir Francis Drake_, compiled by Francis Fletcher. 1628. Reprinted by the Hakluyt Society. 1854.

Chapter II

BASTIN, John: *Raffles' Ideas on the Land Rent System in Java and the Mackenzie Land Tenure Commission*. Nijhoff's. The Hague. 1954. *Raffles and the British Policy in the Indian Archipelago, 1811–16*. Reprint from Malayan Branch Royal Asiatic Society Journal. May 1954.

BATTEN, C. G.: *Daendels-Raffles*. London. 1894.

BOULGER, Demetrius C.: *The Life of Sir Stamford Raffles*. London. 1897.

CRAWFURD, John: *History of the Indian Archipelago*. Edinburgh. 1820.

KATTENBERG, Paul R.: *A central Javanese village in 1950*. Data Paper. Southeast Asia Programme, Cornell University. 1951.

*MOOR, J. H.: *Notes on the Indian Archipelago and the adjacent countries*. Singapore. 1837.

*SUBANDRIO, Dr. Hurustiati: *Javanese Peasant Life*. Thesis submitted for Academic Post-Graduate Diploma in Anthropology. University of London. 1951.

WURTZBURG, C. E.: *Raffles of the Eastern Isles*. Hodder & Stoughton. 1954.

Bibliography

Chapter III

HURGRONJE, Professor Snouck: *The Achenese*. 2 vols. Holland. 1893–4.
*INTERNATIONAL LABOUR OFFICE. *Proceedings of the I.L.O. Conference*. 1929.
MARSDEN, William: *History of Sumatra*. London. 1811.

Chapter IV

*THE ROYAL DUTCH PETROLEUM COMPANY: *Diamond Jubilee Book, 1890 to 1950*. The Hague. 1950.

Chapter V

*ADAM, Leonard: *Primitive Art*. Penguin Books. 1940. Enlarged Edition. 1949.
Report of the Committee on New Guinea (Irian), 1950. Part II. Secretariat of the Netherlands-Indonesian Union. 1950.
RAY, Nihar-Ranjan: *Dutch Activities in the East*. Calcutta. 1945.
*TAULU, H. M. Segjarah: *Perang Tondano*. Menado. 1937.

Chapter VI

BAUM, Vicki: *A Tale from Bali*. Geoffrey Bles. 1937. Reprinted. 1942.
COAST, John: *Dancing out of Bali*. Faber and Faber. 1954
*COVARUBBIAS, Miguel: *The Island of Bali*. Cassell and Company. 1937.
de ZOETE, Beryl and SPIES, Walter: *Dance and Drama in Bali*. Faber & Faber. 1938.

Chapter VII

A Manual of Netherlands India. H.M.S.O. 1920.
Asian Relations, being the Report of the Proceedings and Documentation of the First Asian Relations Conference. New Delhi. March–April 1947. New Delhi. 1948.
COEDÈS, Professor George: *Histoire ancienne des états hindouisés d'extrème-orient*. Paris, 1947.
KROM, N. J.: *Hindoe-Javaansche Geschiedenis*. The Hague. 1926.
*van NAERSEN, F. H.: *Cultural Contacts and Social Conflicts in Indonesia*. 1946
*PANIKKAR, K. M.: *Asia and Western Dominance*. Allen & Unwin. 1952.
STUTTERHEIM, W. F.: *Oost-Javaansche Kunst*. Java. 1917.
*TAKAKASU, J.: *A Record of the Buddhist Religion as Practised in India and the Malayan Archipelago*. Oxford. 1896.

Chapter VIII

*BERG, Professor C. C.: Article on 'Indonesia' in *Whither Islam?* (Edited by H. A. R. Gibb.) 1932.

431

EMERSON, Rupert, MILLS, Lennox A. and THOMPSON, Virginia: *Government and Nationalism in Southeast Asia.* I.P.R. New York. 1942.

INDONESIAN MINISTRY OF INFORMATION: *Lukisan revolusi rakjat indonesia, 1945–1949.* Djakarta. 1950.

*KARTINI, Raden Adjeng: *Letters of a Javanese Princess.* Duckworth. 1921.

Offizielles Protokoll des Congresses gegen Koloniale Unterdruckung und Imperialismus. Brussels. 1927.

THOMPSON, Virginia and ADLOFF, Michael: *The Left Wing in Southeast Asia.* I.P.R. and Williams Sloane Associates. New York. 1950.

*VEENSTRA, J. H.: *Diogenes in der Tropen.* Amsterdam. 1946.

Chapter IX

ELSBREE, Willard H.: *Japan's Role in Southeast Asian Nationalist Movements, 1940–45.* I.P.R. and Harvard University Press. 1954.

*GANDASUBRATA, S. M.: *An account of the Japanese Occupation of Bandjumas Residency, Java, March 1942 to August 1945.* Data Paper No. 10. Dept. of Far Eastern Studies. Cornell University. 1953.

JONES, F. C.: *Japan's New Order in East Asia. Its rise and fall, 1937–45.* Oxford University Press. (Royal Institute of International Affairs.)

van MOOK, Dr. H. J.: *The Netherlands Indies and Japan.* Allen and Unwin. 1944.

PIEKAAR, A. J. Dr.: '*Atjeh en de oorlog met Japan.*' Gravenhage-Bandung. 1949.

Chapter X

*GERBRANDY, Professor P. S.: *Indonesia.* Hutchinson. 1950.

Report to the Combined Chiefs of Staff. By the Supreme Allied Commander, Southeast Asia. 1943–1946. H.M.S.O.

WEHL, David: *The Birth of Indonesia.* Allen & Unwin. 1948.

WESTERLING, Raymond ('Turk'): *Challenge to Terror.* W. Kimber. 1952.

*WOLF, Charles Jnr.: *The Indonesian Story.* I.P.R. and John Day Company. 1949.

Chapter XI

*Official Reports of the United Nations.

FINKELSTEIN, Lawrence S.: *Indonesia's record in the United Nations.* Carnegie Endowment for International Peace. International Conciliation.

Chapter XII

*VANDENBOSCH, Amry: Chapter on 'Indonesia' in *The New World of Southeast Asia.* 1949.

Bibliography

Verslag vande Commissie tot Bestudeering van Staatsrechtelejke Hervormingen. Batavia. 1941.

Chapter XIII

DJAJADININGRAT, R. L.: *From Illiteracy to University*. New York. 1944.
*EMBREE, E. R., SIMOND, Margaret, MUMFORD, W. B.: *Island India goes to School*. University of Chicago Press. 1954.
FURNIVALL, J. S.: *Educational Progress in South-East Asia*. I.P.R. New York. 1943.

Chapter XIV

*ALISJAHBANA, Takdir: *The Indonesian Language. By-product of Nationalism*. Pacific Affairs. December 1949.
*ANWAR, Chairil: *The Flaming Earth*. Edited, with introduction by Ahmed Ali. Karachi. Friends of the Indonesian People Society. 1949.
*BUDIARDJO, Sukesi: *Modern Indonesian Literature*. Lecture, November 1905. Indonesian Embassy, London.
*COVARUBBIAS, Miguel: *The Island of Bali*. Cassell & Company. 1937.
*de ZOETE, Beryl: *Indian Dance Tradition in South East Asia and a few aspects of Balinese Dance*. Programme of Javanese Dancers. London. 1946.

Chapter XV

THOMPSON, Virginia and ADLOFF, Richard: *The Left Wing in Southeast Asia*. I.P.R. and William Sloane Associates. New York. 1950.
THOMPSON, Virginia: *Labor Problems in Southeast Asia*. I.P.R. and Yale University Press. 1947

Chapter XVI

*FURNIVALL, J. S.: *Progress and Welfare in Southeast Asia*. I.P.R. 1941.
*LEIMENA, Dr. J.: *The Upbuilding of Public Health in Indonesia*. Djakarta. 1952.

Chapter XVII

Colombo Plan for Co-operative Economic Development in South and South-East Asia. London. 1950.
ECONOMIC COMMISSION FOR ASIA AND THE FAR EAST. *Economic Survey of Asia and the Far East*. United Nations. Annual Report.
HOPKINS, Harry: *New World Arising*. Chapter, 'Indonesia: The Island Bridge'. Hamish Hamilton. 1952.
*KELLER, Arthur S.: 'Netherlands India as a paying proposition,' *Far Eastern Survey*. New York. January 17th, 1940.

MENDE, Tibor: *South-east Asia between Two Worlds*. Turnstile Press. 1955. (Chapter on Indonesia.)
*PURCELL, Victor: *The Chinese in South East Asia*. Oxford University Press. 1951.
MITCHELL, K. L.: *Industrialisation of the Western Pacific*. I.P.R. 1942.
SITSEN, P. W. H.: *Industrial Development of the Netherlands Indies*. New York, 1944.
*SUDJATMOKO: 'Indonesia and Foreign Aid.' Article in *Siasat*.

PERIODICALS

Asiatic Review. Journal of the Royal Asiatic Society (Quarterly).
Bijdragen tot de Taal-, Land-, en Volkenkunde van Nederlandsch-Indie. (Contributions to the knowledge of the Language, Country and People of the Netherlands Indies.) Published by the Koninklijk Instituut voor Taal- Land- en Volkenkunde. The Hague. (Quarterly.)
Data Papers. South East Asia Programme. Department of Far Eastern Studies. Cornell University, U.S.A.
Far Eastern Survey. American Institute of Pacific Relations. (Fortnightly.)
Far Eastern Quarterly. Far Eastern Association. New York.
Indonesie. Published by Van Hoeven, The Hague and Bandung. (Quarterly.)
Journal of the Malay Branch of the Royal Asiatic Society. (Annual.)
Orientatie. Published by Nix & Co. Bi-monthly. Bandung.
Pacific Affairs. Published by the Institute of Pacific Relations. (Quarterly).
Reports and other publications by the Instituut voor de Tropen, Amsterdam.
Verhandelingen en Mededelingen van de Koninklijke Academie van Wetenschappen, Afdeling Letteren. Amsterdam.

Articles of special interest on contemporary events and on Indonesian history often appear in newspapers and magazines. Of the ten dailies now appearing in Djakarta the most important are *Merdeka* (non-party); *Abadi* (Masjumi); *Indonesia Raja* (independent); *Pedoman* (Socialist); *Pemandangan* and *Mimbar Indonesia*. The *Times of Indonesia* is in English. The cultural and social articles in *Siasat* (fortnightly) and *Pudjangga Baru* (monthly) are building up an Indonesian historiography freed from the colonial attitude which characterized so much of Dutch writing.

Bibliography

OFFICIAL PUBLICATIONS

Economic Review of Indonesia. Ministry of Commerce, Industry and Agriculture.

Education and Culture. Ministry of Education and Culture. (5 issues only.)

Indonesia, Country, People, Transition and future. Ministry of Information.

Indonesian Affairs. Ministry of Information.

Indonesian Information. Information Dept., Indonesian Embassy, London.

Indonesian News. Information Dept., Indonesian Embassy, London.

Netherlands News. Netherlands Embassy, London.

Pudaya. Ministry of Education.

INDEX

437

Index

439

Index

Regrets Brigadier Mallaby's death, 213; Welcomed in Djogjakarta, 257; Underground links with Hatta and Sjahrir, 180–1

SUKIMAN, Dr., Leader, Right-wing Masjumi, 357; M.S.A. Agreement, 410; Prime Minister, 1951–52, 349

SUKKABUMI, 286

SULAWESI (Celebes), 70–108; Japanese occupation, 188–9; Makassar, 86–92; Minahasa, 79–83; Moluccas, 93–9; Resistance, 9; Toradjas, 83–5; West Irian, 99–108

SUMATRA, 37–64; Atjeh, 49–56; Cultural centre, 315; Dance, 326; Emergency Government in, 251–2; Hindu influence, 132–4; Islam, 134–5; Japanese administration, 187; Medan, 40–9; Pacification, 9; Padang and Benkulen, 56–64; Palembang, 37–40; Penal Sanction, 44

SUMBAWA, 124–5

SUMITRO, Dr., Develops Co-operatives, 392; Minister of Commerce and Industry, 392; Minister of Finance, 350, 392; Views on economic structure, 391

SUNARIO, 160, 412

SUPOMO, Professor, Presidential speech to University of Indonesia, 287–8

SURABAYA, Battle of, 214; Brigadier Mallaby's death, 212–4; British landings, 212; Faculty of Dental Surgery, 287; Health Congress, 339; Medical Faculty, 340–1; P.N.I. Congress, 1952, 361; Strikes in 1926, 157; Strategic site, 32

SURAKARTA, 29, 312

SURIPNO, Executed, 372; Madiun Rebellion, 245–6, 371–2; Recalled from Prague, 245; Signs agreement with Soviet Consul, 245; Takes Musso to Indonesia, 246, 370

SUROSO, Mr., 364

SUSILO, Dr., 188

SUSUHUNAN, 19, 20

SUTOMO, Dr., 165, 376

TABANAN, 252

TABANG, 218

TAHA, Sultan, 39

TAMAN SISWA SCHOOLS, Foundation of, 144; Growth of, 144; In the Republic, 282–3; Ki Hadjar Dewantoro, 144; Mohammad Said, 283; Nationalist Movement, 158

TAMRIN, Moh. Husni, 155

TAN MALAKA, Attacks K.N.I.P., 347; Attempts coup, 369; Comintern representative, 157; Exiled, 368

TARAKAN, 175, 193

TERAUCHI, General, C. in C. Japanese forces, 194, 196; Lord Mountbatten's instructions to, 205

TERNATE, 94, 96; Administration, 96; Sir Francis Drake's visit, 5; Sultan of, 94

TER POORTEN, General, 175, 176

TIKU, Puang, 84

TIMOR, 124–5

TISNA, I., Goesti Pandji co-educational school, 121; Novelist, 308

TJAKRANINGRAT, Mr., 242

TJOKROAMINOTO, 153, 368

TOER, Pramudya Ananta, 308

TONDANO, Battle of, 81–2; Dutch Treaty, 80; Pacified, 82

TORADJA LANDS, Governor-General Heutz' expedition, 84; Poso, 83; Puang Tiku's revolt, 84; Sadang, 83; Sigi, 83

TORADJAS, Customs, 84; New schools, 85, 295–6

TRADE UNIONS, 374–82; *see also* under K.B.S.I., P.E.R.B.U.P.R.I., S.O.B.S.I., S.A.R.B.U.P.R.I.

TRANSMIGRATION BOARD, 425

TREATY OF 1824, 8, 52

TREATY OF SUMATRA, 1871, 52

TREATY WITH CHINESE PEOPLE'S REPUBLIC, 415

TSIANG, Dr., 238

TYADDHIL, Christiana Marta, 95, 96

UDIN, Sultan Hasan, 88

U.N.I.C.E.F., Framboesia project, 337; In Djogjakarta area, 338–9; Dr. Leimena's report, 339; Tuberculosis project, 337

UNION OF INDONESIAN WOMEN, 159

UNION STATUTE, 403, 404

UNITARY STATE, 265–76

UNITED NATIONS COMMISSION FOR INDONESIA, 249, 250, 253, 255

VANDENBOSCH, Professor Amry, Analysis of administration, 154, 271–2

VISMAN COMMITTEE, Publication of Report (1941), 166; Suggested reforms, 273

VLEKKE, Dr. B., 148, 152

443